Southern Literary Studies
LOUIS D. RUBIN, JR., EDITOR

The Achievement of Robert Penn Warren

The Achievement of
Robert Penn Warren

JAMES H. JUSTUS

Louisiana State University Press
Baton Rouge and London

Designer: Joanna Hill
Typeface: Linotype Garamond
Composition: Service Typesetters
Printer: Thomson-Shore, Inc.
Binder: John Dekker and Sons, Inc.

LIBRARY OF CONGRESS CATALOGING IN PUBLICATION DATA

Justus, James H.
    The achievement of Robert Penn Warren.

    (Southern literary studies)
    Includes bibliographical references and index.
    1. Warren, Robert Penn, 1905–   —Criticism and
    interpretation. I. Title. II. Series.
PS3545.A748Z73   813'.52   81–3714
ISBN 0–8071–0875–8   AACR2
ISBN 0–8071–0899–5 (pbk.)

        Grateful acknowledgment is made to Random House, Inc., for permission
    to quote from the copyrighted works of Robert Penn Warren. Excerpts from
    All the King's Men by Robert Penn Warren are reprinted by permission of
    Harcourt Brace Jovanovich, Inc., copyright 1946, 1974 by Robert Penn
    Warren. Excerpts from Robert Penn Warren, *Selected Poems, 1923–1943*,
    are reprinted by permission of the William Morris Agency.

Winner of the Jules F. Landry Award for 1981

To my mother
Elizabeth Huff Justus
and to the memory of my father
Howard Newman Justus (1885–1976)

Contents

Preface and Acknowledgments

I would like to think that my views of Robert Penn Warren are fully original, but of course they are not. My observations about both the themes and aesthetic effects of his works reflect efforts of many perceptive critics. For almost as long as I have been reading Warren —more than thirty years—I have also been reading criticism about Warren. Although I have found much that strikes me as muddled, pedestrian, or wrongheaded, much more of this commentary, even earlier than Leonard Casper's pioneering book in 1960, attests to the intelligence and tact of critical enterprise at its best. Although only the most obvious of my debts are acknowledged in the notes, this book would not have taken the shape it has without those discriminating critics whose perceptions have been gradually absorbed into the mainstream of Warren commentary. The temptation for everyone who has written on Warren is to analyze those themes and moral situations that, because they recur so frequently and obsessively, constitute the massive centrality of an entire corpus. For example, it is questionable that Warren's single most perdurable theme—self-knowledge—can yield new critical discoveries, but it soon becomes clear to every reader that to avoid it is to distort Warren's work at its very source. Fidelity to these writings in all genres requires a succumbing to that temptation. Nevertheless I have tried to emphasize the *ways* by which we become aware of such themes and situations, the technical accomplishment of their rendering that alone justifies our thinking of Warren as a literary artist. He is not primarily a moralist or a cultural gadfly, but a man of letters whose distinguished career compares favorably with that of two other twentieth-century American artists of multiple gifts, Edmund Wilson and Allen Tate.

Although this study has been neither conceived out of the pressures of a formal thesis nor executed according to a strict methodology, I have written about Warren from a premise that should here be stated explicitly: the belief that his work derives in large measure from the cultural circumstances of place and time in his career. It is shaped by his being both a border southerner and a transregional intellectual; the values of the country and small town, including the tangled benefits of social cohesion and Christian assumptions about the nature of man, are often seen in conflict with the values of a life governed by art and the academy. While my readings stem from a deep respect for the texts as they exist, I have attempted not only to show Warren's continuities with a southern literary tradition but also to place his work within a larger context, notably the various streams of American writing of the nineteenth and early twentieth centuries.

In addition to those specific debts to other critics of Warren noted in appropriate places in this study, I am grateful for the general encouragement, advice, and example over many years of Richard Beale Davis, Robert Daniel, Robert B. Heilman, Arnold Stein, Louis D. Rubin, Jr., and the late James Hall. I am happy to acknowledge the incisive criticism of my colleagues at Indiana University, Terence Martin and Wallace E. Williams, who generously read and commented on the manuscript; their efforts—along with those of my superb editor, Martha L. Hall—have reduced if not eliminated stylistic infelicities and prevented worse errors than those that may yet remain. Much of this book was written during two sabbatical leaves of absence, for which I thank the president and Board of Trustees of Indiana University.

Earlier versions of Part One appeared originally as "The Mariner and Robert Penn Warren" in *Texas Studies in Literature and Language*, VIII (Spring, 1966) and "Warren and the Doctrine of Complicity" in *Four Quarters*, XXI (May, 1972). I wish to thank the University of Texas Press and La Salle College for permission to reprint in revised form this material printed first in their journals. Three segments in Part Four appeared originally as essays. Substantially unchanged is "On the Politics of the Self-Created: *At Heaven's Gate*," which first appeared in *Sewanee Review*, LXXXII (Spring, 1974). "All the Burdens of *All the King's Men*" was written for *The Forties: Fiction, Poetry, Drama*, ed. Warren French (Everett/Edwards, 1969), and an earlier version of "*The Cave*: Ceremonies of Effort" appeared in *Modern Language Quarterly*, XXVI (September, 1965); both of these essays are now considerably revised. My thanks go to these editors and publishers.

Abbreviations

In the interests of both stylistic pacing and the limitations of space I have noted directly in the text page references only for extended quotations from Warren's work—usually those consisting of a sentence or more. Secondary references and additional commentary can be found in the notes gathered at the end of the text. Abbreviations of Warren's works are as follows:

I. New York: Random House or its affiliates

NR	*Night Rider* (1939)
AHG	*At Heaven's Gate* (1943)
WET	*World Enough and Time: A Romantic Novel* (1950)
BD	*Brother to Dragons: A Tale in Verse and Voices* (1953; rev., 1979)
BA	*Band of Angels* (1955)
S	*Segregation: The Inner Conflict in the South* (1956)
SE	*Selected Essays* (1958)
C	*The Cave* (1959)
LCW	*The Legacy of the Civil War: Meditations on the Centennial* (1961)
W	*Wilderness: A Tale of the Civil War* (1961)
F	*Flood: A Romance of Our Time* (1964)
WSN	*Who Speaks for the Negro?* (1965)
HM	*Selected Poems of Herman Melville: A Reader's Edition* (1970)
TD	*Homage to Theodore Dreiser, On the Centennial of His Birth* (1971)
MM	*Meet Me in the Green Glen* (1971)
SP	*Selected Poems: 1923–1975* (1976)
PCT	*A Place to Come To* (1977)

II. Others

JB	*John Brown: The Making of a Martyr* (New York: Payson & Clarke, 1929)

ITMS   *I'll Take My Stand: The South and the Agrarian Tradition*
        (Baton Rouge: Louisiana State University Press, 1977)
AKM   *All the King's Men* (New York: Harcourt, Brace, 1946)
JGW   *John Greenleaf Whittier's Poetry: An Appraisal and a
        Selection* (Minneapolis: University of Minnesota Press,
        1971)
DP   *Democracy and Poetry* (Cambridge: Harvard University
        Press, 1975)
Talking   *Robert Penn Warren Talking: Interviews 1950–1978*, ed.
        Floyd C. Watkins and John T. Hiers (New York:
        Random House, 1980)

The Achievement of Robert Penn Warren

Introduction

I can show you what is left.
                    —*World Enough and Time* (1950)

Oh, nothing is lost, ever lost! at last you understood.
                    —"Original Sin: A Short Story" (1944)

Any reader who progresses systematically through Robert Penn Warren's canon—or even the reader who has mastered one or two books in addition to *All the King's Men*—is struck by how compulsive and interrelated are those images, situations, and rhetorical stances that coalesce as dominant themes. The painful struggle for self-knowledge; the seductive pull of idealism and abstraction, concurrent with the kind of resignation that threatens to sink into irony and cynicism as idealism falters; the need for melodrama, violence, and psychological suffering to counter the discovery of social disorder and personal inauthenticity: these are the major fictive and poetic themes that Warren articulates in every major work, including his first, *John Brown: The Making of a Martyr* (1929).

The aesthetic patterns of all these themes, however, derive from an antecedent vision, a moral persuasion that is sometimes masked in rhetorical garrulousness, which sometimes glimmers only fitfully because of an inadequate explicitness to sustain it. Put simply, that vision is an orthodox Christianity chastened and challenged by the secular faiths peculiar to the twentieth century: naturalism (deriving from late nineteenth-century skepticism) and existentialism. The mutuality of an artist's general vision and his specific artifacts is a commonplace—forms of art follow forms of belief. But it is the signal mark of our century that the artist's "belief" is not, perhaps cannot be, coherent and self-sufficient, that it is nourished at the same source with its enemies: contradiction, detraction, counterpoint—second thoughts, nays, and *yet*. W. H. Auden once named two "absolute presuppositions" that every poet holds: that a historical world of unique events and persons exists, and that it is both fallen and redeemable. From these presuppositions the poet then must proceed to order and harmonize incompatible or resistant feelings to make his poems.[1] Warren, no less than Flannery O'Connor, is committed to the received orthodox view of man and the world: both fallen, both standing in urgent need of redemption. But unlike his younger contemporary, Warren rests uneasily in the theological formulas available within a rigorous and comprehensive system.

The right to define oneself, says Warren, is one of our legacies of Christianity, and though in his own work that difficult process is enacted in secular contexts and transpositions, the massive orthodoxy lying behind this recurring quest is always evident. Even the terms of Warren's enactments are theological: "The story of every soul is the story of its self-definition for good or evil, salvation or damnation."[2] Yet his "orthodoxy" shows a tenacious resistance to religious answers preformed and institutionalized and an equally tenacious grappling with the complacent despair of accommodated man. This resistance and grappling account for the extraordinary dynamics of Warren's particular vision. Unlike O'Connor, when Warren draws large and startling figures for those with bad eyesight or when he shouts to the hard-of-hearing, the figures and the message are complicated by distortion and echo. Indeed, the area of Warren's greatest strength is invariably in the struggle to reconcile rather than in reconciliation itself, and in the better novels and poems it is a vital process that dramatizes harsh failures and piecemeal solutions.

Of all the critics who have perceived the complexities of this writer's moral vision, George Core has phrased it most succinctly: "Warren's real subject, it is clear, is the dramatization of the soul in conflict with itself, its darkest impulses in constant bloodletting with its most humane instincts."[3] This dialectical movement constitutes alike the drama of most of the major fictive protagonists and the personal quests undertaken in much of the poetry beginning with *Brother to Dragons* (1953).

In the earlier poems Warren's personae, locked in their foresight of the extinction of the self, sink into complacency. Velleity, that lowest level of will, characterizes the recessive marine lovers of "Bearded Oaks" and "Picnic Remembered." In other poems the personae respond to naturalistic certainty by resorting to more strenuous substitutes for the exercise of will to achieve self-knowledge: sexual passion, public service, war. Inner compulsions often find enactment in public ceremonies of violence. In the earlier fiction the price of egotism—at once the cause and consequence of ignorance, pride, and the evil act—is precisely that human area to which Warren directs our attention. The spiritual drifter Jack Burden and the romantic monomaniac Jeremiah Beaumont equally leave behind them a trail of active evil even as they search for their way out of the dark wood. The course of salvation in Warren's works is never very straight. The goal of every protagonist and the need of many malaise-ridden speakers in the poems are the same: an adequate selfhood, a breaking out of the debilitating sense of incompleteness and fragmentation. The price for that integration of self is not the loss of certain spiritual certitudes, but their hopeful and sometimes desperate testing. The struggle requires realistic appraisals of one's powers and possibilities in a world not yet redeemed.

If the stress on one set of terms—dark impulses—owes much to the Hawthornesque tradition, another—humane instincts—derives from the Emersonian; but only the most simplistic reading of those two citizens of Concord denies the sometimes delicate teetering between the terms in the work of both writers. Although man's innate depravity can never be shunned or taken lightly, his latent potential for redemption cannot be forgotten. I find no evidence in any of his writing that Warren would even wish to contradict one of Emerson's definitions of man:

> Man is not order of nature, sack and sack, belly and members, link in a chain, nor any ignominious baggage; but a stupendous antagonism, a dragging together of the poles of the Universe. He betrays his relation to what is below him,—thick-skulled, small-brained, fishy, quadrumanous, quadruped ill-disguised, hardly escaped into biped,—and has paid for the new powers by loss of some of the old ones. But the lightning which explodes and fashions planets, maker of planets and suns, is in him. On one side elemental order, sandstone and granite, rock-ledges, peat-bog, forest, sea and shore; and on the other part thought, the spirit which composes and decomposes nature,—here they are, side by side, god and devil, mind and matter, kind and conspirator, belt and spasm, riding peacefully together in the eye and brain of every man.[4]

Perhaps those darker impulses and humane instincts do not ride very peacefully together in most of Warren's characters, but their very rage and agony are testimony to the human need for reconciliation, recovery, reclamation.

The ceremony of linking hands, the recognition of continuities, the joy in the surprising discovery that love is possible in a fallen world are never easy processes in Warren's work. Because Emerson's "quad-

rumanous" side of man is not transformed into spirit and thought by
mere assertion, a despair of the beastly burns through the most energetic wills, issuing in betrayal and violence. Tender-minded earlier
readers, using such terms as "revolting," "unpleasant," and "sex-
centered," were unable or unwilling to accept the naturalistic bluntness
with which Warren dramatized the dialectic between "darkest impulses"
and "humane instincts." Even John Crowe Ransom, while recognizing
the "tragic sense" apparent in the best poetry, was put off by the domi-
nance of naturalism in "The Ballad of Billie Potts" and the first two
novels.[5]

Some readers of Warren still regard the pull of naturalism as an
occasional and basically early impulse that after "The Ballad of Billie
Potts" and *At Heaven's Gate* is gradually replaced by a beneficent
humanism, or at least a grim faith in man's capacity for love. Such
is not entirely the case. Although recurrent images of death and the
use of Jungian-like shadow selves, closely associated with Warren's
naturalistic orientation, are more dominant in the early work than in
the later—as are the expressions of Eliotic despair and Poundian disgust over a broken world—only the most facile formulations of a
naturalistic vision are purged with the writing of "Mexico Is a Foreign
Country: Five Studies in Naturalism," the sequence that appeared first
in *Selected Poems*: *1923–1943*.[6] In a fundamental way, naturalism
for Warren is not merely as real as original sin; it is virtually the secular counterpart of original sin. Just as his belief in that doctrine was
not purged with the writing of "Original Sin: A Short Story," so belief in its corollary has never been purged. Warren is too much the
secular poet to believe that intimations about man's fragile and uncertain meaning can be dissolved in the certain acid of God's grace.
Nevertheless, the orthodox doctrine of man common to western Christianity, the doctrine uncompromised by the more cheerful modes of
latter-day arminians, pelagians, and social gospellers, is stronger in
Warren than in any of his contemporaries, not excluding the textured
religiosity of the later Eliot. Warren has not written his own *Four
Quartets* and, I think, is unlikely ever to do so. The emergent vision
that made possible the two kinds of poetry in Eliot that "Ash Wednes-
day" demarks and defines has not been possible for Warren; and the
reason may well lie in the closeness, the mutually corroborating nature,
of both his naturalistic and his Christian view of man.

At bottom the separation is less radical than it might seem. The
religious geography of a part of Warren's South—the Protestant fun-
damentalism of the hill country—has had a profound and lasting effect

on his work, not merely in the narrative creations like Ashby Wyndham, Billie Potts, Jeff York, or Old Gillum, but also in the pervasive mood and attitude of the more personal speakers in the lyrics. The hounding persistence of guilt traced throughout *Eleven Poems* is transposed into sophisticated intellectual struggles of man with his own darker impulses in Warren's earliest poem to be preserved ("To a Face in a Crowd") and in lyric after lyric in the volumes since the 1950s. "What poetry most significantly celebrates," said Warren in 1975, "is the capacity of man to face the deep, dark inwardness of his nature and his fate."[7] The simpler but no less articulate narrative poems using colloquial speakers repeat the same inescapable conclusions about man's nature and his fate, if not the anguished dialectical stages leading to them.

Old Gillum's message to the townspeople is simple, assertive, and pronounced with a resignation derived from an uncompromising ethic of primitive biblicalness:

> I'll name you what's true fer folks, ever-one.
> Human-man ain't much more'n a big blood blister.
> All red and proud-swole, but one good squeeze and he's gone.
>
> (SP, 239)

The direct homily recalls Ashby Wyndham's dour definition of man ("a hog hollerness"), and the sentiment behind it is the same for countless figures in both the prose and poetry. God's justice is the given; what is so often missing in Warren is any *sure* sense of a balancing mercy or the joy that should result from the promise of that mercy. Warren's troubled characters may be in Italy, Mexico, Kentucky, or Harvard Yard, but they occupy the same geography of the soul.

These speakers are constantly in danger of succumbing to acedia, the name medieval churchmen gave to the deepest despair and which, consciously or otherwise, locates its source at the cross itself, in the Son's typal cry that the Father has turned away His face. That temporary lapse—since typologically Jesus is the Second Adam as well as the Son of God—is more often than not extended into a permanent state for the children of Adam, what Ashby Wyndham calls collectively "the pore human man." Once convinced that God has turned away His face, other Wyndhams in Warren's work fall into spiritual lethargy, depressions so profound that murder and suicide are the inevitable outs; of their more sophisticated counterparts a few, such as the speaker in "The Mango," with metaphorical pot-valiance assert man's innocence and God's sin; others intellectually take the next step, denying God or meaning in the world but striving to wrest meaning out of it anyway.

Conceptually and practically, no giant step separates Warren's selective naturalism and his brand of orthodox Christianity. As they function in the attitudes of speakers, they are virtually synonymous.

For this reason it is a mistake to see the strain of naturalism merely as an early phase in Warren's career. In some of the early poems it is an attitudinizing and mannered element, but its attraction continues into the more mature work. The unspecified terrors, guilts, and anxieties are the product of a mind temperamentally Christian and intellectually skeptical—and ill at ease in either commitment.[8] The aesthetic strengths in that unease are not hard to name: a dramatic sense of opposing polarities, a series of balanced tensions forever testing the terms of each belief, a nervous tentativeness in any reconciliation. As Cleanth Brooks has reminded us, the strengths of such themes in literature depend not upon generalizations to be affirmed but situations to be explored.[9] Warren is at his weakest, his art is the frailest, when the affirmation is disproportionate to the exploration—when polarities mesh or reconciliations are asserted without much more to justify them than a leap of faith or a desperate willingness to believe.

The leaps into full reconciliation, however, are remarkably few in number. Even at his most hopeful, when his "liberal" strain is most explicit, as in his explorations of race relations in *Segregation* and *Who Speaks for the Negro?* and his evaluations of national character in *The Legacy of the Civil War* and *Democracy and Poetry*, Warren is wary of the tendency to see ourselves in the light of our wishes and desires and dreams. The blood and irony that Ellen Glasgow once declared as desperate correctives to the genteel southerners' view of themselves are the correctives that Warren implicitly exercises in his varied analyses of national as well as regional life. Unlike many of his contemporaries, however, Warren has never been a nagger on the durable Waste Land issue, though he has occasionally sketched some of the same desiccated moral landscapes and figures stupefied by despair. His naturalistic orientation, bolstered by the confirming doctrines of Christian orthodoxy, would, we might expect, insure a body of work that in its totality projects a gloomy picture of man in his ill-made society. But the quality of American life, its basic middle-class values, and its apparent helplessness in the face of political and economic exploiters do not figure, except in his forays into sociology, as major subjects in his most durable work. Such subjects are rather assumed, functioning as understood conditions of social disarray or as operative metaphors of spiritual drift and suicide.

Warren's inclination has always been toward the symbolic heightening of society for essentially moral fables, and that tendency has meant no *U.S.A.*, no *Epic of the Wheat*, no *Trilogy of Desire*. We might go one step further. The nature of American life is, at least on one level, irrelevant to Warren's central concerns. It is there; it is what we have. Even if it is a burning house, as James Baldwin characterized it to Warren, it is our burning house. What can finally make community— "all one flesh at last"—into something superior to a melting-pot homogeneity is human choice. James Farmer's definition of *integration*— "maximum opportunity" for choice—finds its response in Warren's "agony of will"—the human imperative to act in a world that apparently resists human shaping.

If many of Warren's poems and novels seem obsessively concerned with the "arithmetic of losses," what is the gain? As in "Billie Potts," "Original Sin," *All the King's Men*, and *World Enough and Time*, the gain appears to lie somewhere between the belief that *nothing is lost* and a chastened respect for *what is left*. The first suggests a temporal and spatial transcendence, an assertion of psychic, even genetic, continuity: fathers and grandfathers, Philip of Spain and Anse Gillum, adolescent boxcar showoff and *gobbo*, the European South and the American Southeast, Mississippi catfish and Mediterranean gullet, Kentucky owl and Italian civetta. The second suggests the more limited human knack for making do—seeing hope in the slenderest green thread, cultivating the pride peculiar to survivors, forcing imaginative reenactments of moments from the past, cherishing the depleted peace after raucous defeats. In each case the gains are more often potential than realized, and even when realized are unspectacular advances. Knowing the past, the road taken, holds no guarantees of a fulfilled future, but its knowledge at least intensifies the present moment, the life lived now.

ONE

Repudiations and Reconciliations
A Cycle of Themes

Listen—it is always
The dearest that betrays.

—Brother to Dragons (1979)

Does he think I am his son? I cannot
be sure. Nor can I feel that it matters,
for each of us is the son of a million fathers.

—All the King's Men (1946)

I. Fathers and Sons

In "Gull's Cry" and "The Child Next Door," two of the poems in *Promises* (1956), the speaker is momentarily angered by what he sees as either a raw, undifferentiated nature (a gull presides over "the irrelevant anguish of air") or a nature that incorporates into its scheme imperfection and "malfeasance" as casually as it does instinct and intelligence. For one who takes seriously his philosophical discriminations and moral responsibilities, the vacant beauty and meaningless blessing represented by a defective child are affronts to cosmic order and to the human urge to contribute in some modest way to that order. But the speaker recovers, returns with a stiff smile the mechanical *ciao* from this "monstrous other," and thinks: "*This is the world*." Imaginatively, all being in the dusty Italian yard he suddenly sees linked in a creation that must of necessity comprise the "filth of fate": defective child, father, mother, lovers, goat, goose, gander, beetle. Despite the naturalistic way the world is joined, he can celebrate the continuities of life in a vision of communal "heart-joy."

Human discomfort in the face of imperfection is characteristically troublesome to the speakers and protagonists in Warren's work. When ideal constructions of reality fail to be confirmed by actual experience or are unceremoniously shattered by the malice or chance of the world, they may seek physical solace; more frequently, however, their response shows a psychological need to locate causes for the disjunction and to punish those persons or forces responsible. In "The Mango on the Mango Tree," one of the Studies in Naturalism (1944), the speaker is convinced that "monstrous, primal guilt" is God's and innocence is man's: both mango and man are linked as victims of God's injustice. The imaginative transcendence of a fallen world that we see in the two poems of *Promises* is not yet available to the speaker in "The Mango on the Mango Tree," who, unable to admit his own pride, is unable to bring himself to say, "*forgive*."

Attribution of one's loss of innocence is not usually so metaphysical, however. A temperamental sullenness, a quirky malaise, a soul sickness that erupts in vindictive acts of violence: these symptoms of the disappointed idealist usually occur first in more tangible contexts. Characteristically, a Warren protagonist learns at first hand the nature of the human condition when, for one reason or another, he rejects the father.

In *A Place to Come To*, Jed Tewksbury suffers the indignity of a roistering father whose indiscriminate vitality disturbs the staid moralisms and conventional pieties of the community. Like the sons of old Tolliver (*Flood*), old Budge (*Meet Me in the Green Glen*), and old Harrick (*The Cave*), Jed must come to terms with a personal affront based on social embarrassment. The particular circumstances of his father's death force the son into schoolyard confrontations, but the tears and blood of a nine-year-old are exorcised by the mature son through ritual storytelling in which the son becomes the father by means of gestures, countrified dialect, and reenactment of the death. To titillate his little audience Jed performs an act which is meant to assuage and replace grief. It is, however, an expedient, self-conscious imitation of stereotype (of the tall-tale hero) and cliché (of the southern idiom hardened by television and movie repetition); the performance, because it is also a betrayal of his origins, brings not assuagement but self-hate along with the shock and the applause.

In some instances the father's flashy sexuality and blustering self-assertion are only the most blatant excuses for the son's rejection. The embarrassment of a seemingly chaotic vitality unmodified by the communal restraints within which the tamer and more cultivated son wants to live may also be complicated by jealousy and resentment of that primitive state. More commonly, the father's frailties are less spectacular; the son sees only failure in its modest manifestations—patience, inefficiency, awkwardness. Thus, the rejection comes from a perception of inadequacies: the father does not measure up to the high and extravagant ideal image carried in the son's head.

Accommodating himself to a successful financial and social life under Bogan Murdock's aegis, Jerry Calhoun fantasizes his father's down-at-heels farm into "the old Calhoun place," an urbanite's hideaway from which have been banished all signs of human imperfection—that is, his Uncle Lew, Aunt Ursula, and his bumbling father. Only a countervision of confession, when he can admit to his father "I wanted you dead," can dispel both former contempt for his real father and chagrin at his misplaced faith in the bogus father. While young Jeremiah Beaumont defends his father before old Marcher (his maternal grandfather who wants him to change his name in return for the estate), he admits that the quarrel with the old man stemmed not from a love for his father but from his pride. Beaumont determines to die neither in "worldly failure and sick hope" like his father nor "bitterly in the midst of wealth and great place" like his grandfather. "I came to see," he writes, "that both were bound to the grossness of nature and the vanity of the world" (WET, 26). Before his life is over, Beaumont will know himself to be bound by both.

Amantha Starr and Hamish Bond in *Band of Angels* are linked in their festering resentment of the parent, who is blamed for their unhappiness and uncertain identity. It takes most of her adult life for Amantha to understand and forgive her sinful father; Bond goes to his death unreconciled to the pride of his mother. Rau-Ru, in turn, rejects Bond, who has nourished him out of a violence both internal and external. Tobias Sears, the heady Yankee idealist, rejects the accommodation with the world that he sees staining the youthful principles of his father, a friend of Emerson. A phrase from Housman that becomes part of the epigraph to *Band of Angels*—"the wrong my father did"—suggests the self-indulgent, immature grievance in which many of Warren's protagonists find recourse. Sons come to repeat the sins of their fathers, since both sons and fathers are subject to the same weaknesses; what a few seekers of self-knowledge come to find is that both sons and fathers are also subject to the same virtues, or at least the same possibilities of virtue.

The revolt against the father and the subsequent and often excruciating struggle to come to terms with him constitute a basic drama enacted on many levels and with varying degrees of intensity. A primary level is the personal, in which the private identity, in order to assert its integrity, must reject the very source of its own generation. Another level is the generic, the natural tendency of the species to establish generational independence, which necessarily means a breaking away from a governing authority received and sanctioned by biological and social convention. At higher levels, the rejection of the father is a drama of political and mythic dimensions in which the father functions as a particular nation, god, or generalized truth.

Warren's paradigmatic drama is often enacted on multiple levels. Amantha Starr's story in *Band of Angels*, for example, takes on more than ordinary interest because this story of an unexceptional woman "betrayed" by the biological father intersects both with a struggle for identity that becomes national and a challenge to the past that is mythicized as the tenacious and demanding father. In "Natural History" what begins as a generational conflict on the generic level, abstracted from dream, takes on the resonances of the mythic before the poem ends. The "naked old father" dancing in the rain and the mother counting like money "her golden memories of love" cause clocks all over the continent to be stopped and all flights out of Kennedy airport to be canceled. They are dangerous acts:

> As much as I hate to, I must summon the police.
> For their own good, as well as that of society, they must be put under
>   surveillance.   (SP, 22)

The song of the father "tells how at last he understands," and the speaker here, as in countless other poems, is self-tortured because he fails to understand what the father understands; from his perspective that stage must come only with death: "They must learn to stay in their graves. That is what graves / are for." Beyond the son's break in identification with the father, a natural stage in the psychological growth of the child, the speaker's sentiments assert symbolically that the claims of the past are invalid, that the burdens of the past—its failures, its accommodations, even its glories—must be forgotten in order to live in and by the present moment.

In *Band of Angels*, "Natural History," and dozens of other works both major and minor, such acts are momentous in the emotional lives of Warren's characters. That chilly decisiveness has its harsh penalties, however, and the protagonist comes to learn that a rage to construct himself anew means alienation from others—not merely the father— and dissociation of the self. The bewildering pain of a floating identity unanchored to others drives him to another rage: to assert the primacy of a communal selfhood without which his own self is amorphous. "We're all one flesh at last," a common rubric in Warren's work, is the synecdochic recognition of the common frailty of man caught in webs of deceit, delusion, ignorance, and a murderous innocence that believes that the abstract ideal or the governing idea must be translated into act at whatever cost. Acknowledgment of universal imperfection, then, leads the protagonist back to the father, at once the most actual and the most symbolic summation of community. The typical resolution is for the protagonist to see things as they are, to recognize that the world moves at its own pace and with its own purpose, that chaos and confusion are man's lot, and that father and son alike are caught up equally in the commonality suggested by the phrase, "the frail integument of flesh."

Coming to terms with the father is most clearly depicted in Warren's narratives, beginning as a subordinate but powerful emotional force in *Night Rider*. Perse Munn's blundering progress toward commitment and violence is marked by an ambivalent relationship with a series of paternal types: Captain Todd, Mr. Christian, Doctor MacDonald, Professor Ball, and Senator Tolliver. (The genesis of this novel, the novelette "Prime Leaf," is directly and simplistically focused on the conflict of father and son.) But beginning with *At Heaven's Gate* the narratives obsessively depict the child's slow growth toward maturity, a state of self-knowledge that requires recognition of the father's sins and compromises, which is to say his humanity. The fall into that knowledge is the *felix culpa* without which no regeneration is possible. Jerry Calhoun and Sue Murdock (*At Heaven's Gate*), Jack Burden (*All the King's Men*), Jeremiah Beaumont (*World Enough and Time*), Amantha Starr (*Band of Angels*), Isaac Sumpter (*The Cave*), Brad Tolliver (*Flood*), and Jed Tewksbury (*A Place to Come To*) are protagonists whose stories are shaped by this difficult process, but most of the fictions they dominate contain many subordinate characters whose dilemmas echo those of the central characters.

But if the near-mythic pattern of the son's rebellion against the father is most obvious in the fiction, it also emerges in the poetry, including some of the earliest poems Warren has chosen to preserve and in a few that were soon discarded in later collections. One of the latter is "Genealogy" (from *Thirty-Six Poems*), in which an autobiographical context is more explicitly established than in most of Warren's poems before *Promises*. Grandfather Gabriel is caught at the historical moment of the birth of his son and the death of his wife, a kind of ironic balancing that a tender-minded young poet might have sentimentalized into a grander, more cosmic observation; instead it becomes the occasion for some fashionable assertiveness: "Your grandson," says Warren, "keeps a broken house."

> There's a stitch in his side no plasters heal,
> A crack in the firmament, maggots in the meal;
> There's a mole in the garden, fennel by the gate,
> In the heart a curse of hell-black hate
> For that other young guy who croaked too late.[1]

This is of course another kind of sentimentality, the poetizing sensibility of a prodigy, a grownup version of the boy in "Revelation" who, in speaking harshly to his mother, imagines all history and all creation—time and space—reverberating from his single act of pride. Here in saying *I wish I were dead* the young man of derivative despair extends his disappointment into a slightly more serious realm, in which he regrets that the *father* had not died. This affected stance is not expunged, though the poem in which it is most melodramatically struck is; but in more mature poems the tendency toward Wertherian and Byronic sentiments is worked into structures firm enough to absorb them, even to fight against them.

What is more interesting among the early poems such as "History" and "The Ballad of Billie Potts," is the way in which Warren transposes the nakedly personal into mythic and folkloristic structures. In these poems the image of the father is projected out of emotional ambivalence into something considerably more complex. "History" in fact asserts the awe of the son for his forefathers, especially for their energy, perseverance, and foresight. Like westering pioneers they push on, coming "bad ways" with dry watercourses in "bad country of no tree" to reach the envisioned place:

> A world
> Of ripeness blent, and green,
> The fruited earth,
>
> . . . .
> It is a land of corn and kine . . . .   (SP, 295)

If the awe of the voice is mingled with a criticism of these forefathers' single-mindedness to "possess" and "abide" despite the native inhabitants and beasts already there, that flaw is poignantly neutralized by their prophecy:

> In our new land
> Our seed shall prosper, and
> In those unsifted times
> Our sons shall cultivate
> Peculiar crimes,
> Having not love, nor hate,
> Nor memory.   (SP, 295)

"History" is one of Warren's most effective and affecting poems. Though it still retains some flavor of Eliot (notably "The Journey of the Magi"), the basically natural speech rhythms are compressed into short lines which simultaneously prevent the flowering of colloquial laxness which mars much of "Billie Potts" and force a stern dignity on to the total poem. The cadences are threaded into a grander fabric of familial and national history that is also human history. Already the dilemma of fathers and sons is suggestive of the burden of history, the larger-scale theme with which Warren increasingly concerns himself.

That larger dimension in "Billie Potts" is mythic, with its archetypal story of crime and punishment that is completed by reconciliation between father and son. Further, its regional setting, the Kentucky area between the Cumberland and Tennessee rivers, suggests the greater "land between the rivers," the biblical Mesopotamia.[2] Shreds of the Eden story, not as generative myth but as metaphorical parallels, are to be found in both "History" and "Billie Potts." And because of Warren's fascination with the nature of innocence, the contrary will of man, expulsion, the agonizing journey that is the inward search for the "true self," and the difficult reconciliation between the fallen-away children and the Father, these metaphorical parallels announce themselves in many combinations in other narrative lines. The literal "land between the rivers" is depicted as a place already fallen, rank with fetid bottomlands, sloughs, tangled canebreaks, gutted red hills—a landscape that "steams and simmers." This geography is to figure again in *World Enough and Time*. The west that Jeremiah Beaumont had once envisioned as the speculative lands that would make him wealthy is the very place, beyond the Cumberland to the swampy backwaters of the Ohio, to which he and Rachel are transported from their jail cell. Here among the mudflats and canebreaks of the decadent empire of the Grand Boz, Jeremiah sees himself coming "to lie in secret in the pathless woods and dark entrails of America." And his is a journey that begins specifically with the plot to murder Colonel Fort, a surrogate father. Little Billie must return to his father, "the old man / Who is evil and ignorant and old" for a sacramental death; Beaumont begins his return journey to expiate the murder of a man whose only errors were those inescapable ones of the flesh.

"Billie Potts," with its contrapuntal structure of alternating ballad and gloss, is both local and general. Little Billie is the "wanderer," forgetting name and deed in the innocence of west; but, as the more learned gloss insists, "you" are also the wanderer, "Weary of innocence and the husks of Time," and, like Billie,

> You come, back to the homeland of no-Time,
> To ask forgiveness and the patrimony of your crime;
>
> And kneel in the untutored night as to demand
> What gift—oh, father, father—from that dissevering hand?
>
> (SP, 281)

Just as Warren returns to western Kentucky for the setting of *Brother to Dragons*, so he returns to the same intertwining themes: the struggle to understand the evil penchant that is man's lot involves a coming to terms with the father who has already made his peace with human imperfection. In this conjuration of ghosts, the most notable is Thomas Jefferson, who, as he first speaks, reveals his bitter disillusionment that man's bright promise of perfectibility has been dealt a shattering blow with his nephew's brutal stroke of the meat-ax against a slave. But Jefferson's agonizing progress toward some kind of moral renewal is conducted by R.P.W., whose function is not limited to his being a "commentator on the action" or even the "chief advocate of reconciliation in the poem."[3] R.P.W. is in fact a chief actor in this drama, and his reconciliation is just as crucial as that of Jefferson; his voice, his character, his dilemma are a further personalizing of the device of the parenthetical gloss in "Billie Potts," and the purpose is the same in both works: to join the local and the general, to serve as confirming demonstration that the real issue is, as Warren puts it in his prefatory note, "a human constant."

Structurally the "no place" and "any time" of the drama are anchored firmly to actual times and places, specifically July, 1946, and December, 1951, when Warren and his aging father visit Rocky Hill, near Smithland in Livingston County, Kentucky. These passages have been termed "digressions" functionally akin to the interpolated story so favored by Warren in his early fiction.[4] It is true that R.P.W.'s "conversion" frames what is for Warren the main action of the poem, Jefferson's conversion, but for the reader the spiritual experience of R.P.W. is as significant as R.P.W.'s manipulation of Jefferson. And insofar as that experience precedes and necessarily conditions the rehabilitation of Jefferson, R.P.W.'s role is the more important of the two.

The victory at the end of *Brother to Dragons* is aesthetically earned by the interdependence of R.P.W. and Jefferson. If the founding father of the republic must accept the evil of man in order to believe in the fullness and reality of man, R.P.W. must accept not human evil (of whose reality he is already complacently convinced) but the unheroic, the ordinary, the failure-prone deeds of men who must adjust to compromise. That is the bitter "percoon" of his father that he accepts, the metaphorical medicine which makes him realize that the failure to achieve grandly, to win all battles material and spiritual, is a human failure that must be shared by all sons as well as by all fathers.

But the frame of *Brother to Dragons* does not contain the last word on the subject. The Gabriel poems in *Promises* contain "Founding Fathers, Nineteenth-Century Style, Southeast U.S.A.," in which portraits of both the famous and the nameless are searched for comforting words for their descendants. But their thin voices have "nothing to tell us for our complexity of choices, / But beg us only one word to justify their own life-cost." The poem ends with a chastened plea for understanding. Let us, Warren says,

> try to forgive them their defects, even their greatness,
> For we are their children in the light of humanness, and under
> the shadow of God's closing hand.   (SP, 243)

In *You, Emperors, and Others*, the dying father's face in "Arrogant Law" is studied for some secret wisdom, but it is a "strange face" which seems to "withdraw / Into more arrogant dispensation . . . ." And "Mortmain" is Warren's poignant elegy to the death in 1955 of his father, whose dying gesture seems symbolic but the meaning of which remains uncommunicated. That the reconciliation dramatized in *Brother to Dragons* might have been only a rhetorical victory haunts the volumes of poetry after that great work in 1953. Subsequent poems betray a nagging dissatisfaction with the father's reconciliations and an obsessive yearning to understand that dissatisfaction.

Finally, with "Reading Late at Night, Thermometer Falling," Warren announces his final attempt:

> So, sir, I,
> Who certainly could never have addressed you on a matter
> As important as this when you were not dead, now
> Address you on it for the last time, even though
> Not being, after all my previous and sometimes desperate efforts,
> Sure what a son can ever say to a father, even
> A dead one.   (SP, 70)

The process is familiar: the Warren speaker in the present recalls an almost static scene, precisely detailed, in which his father reads in a "colding house," and the evocation of that scene generates other scenes that reinforce the thematic burden of the first. Although what his father reads cannot be seen—it is history, law, or a Greek reader—the speaker associates the moment with the idea of dreams unfulfilled, a state that to him is unbearable but which is a satisfactory one to his father, who has "Lived / Into that purity of being that may / Be had past all ambition and the frivolous hope . . . ." The speaker returns to a still earlier moment, when he had found an old photograph of his father as a young man looking authoritatively from

> eyes
> Lifted into space.
> And into the future
> Which
> Had not been the future.

His father's dreams of being distinguished as a jurist or a poet dissipate in the immediate and pressing realities of supporting a growing family. The "foolishness" of ambition is sacrificed for "obligations." What is left, however, even in the diminution of compromises, is the image of a man of fortitude who never sacrifices his belief that truth is important; his remembered statement—" 'It is terrible for a man to live and not know' "—becomes a legacy for the son, whose signature it becomes in work after work.

The past in "Reading Late at Night" is the "Eater of dreams, secrets, and random data"; the present "is another country" which must come to terms with that great ravishment; but the speaker cannot be wholly content with that realization. He knows that "Indecipherable passion and compulsion"—that itch to do more, see more, be more that lurks in the human psyche—can, because they are untranslatable, manifest themselves as "Self-indulgence, habit, tic of the mind, or / The picking of a scab." The potential self unserenely accommodated to contingency and time, as the speaker knows, can be a source of gnawing discomfort in the soul, or it can erupt sporadically in bouts of petulance, pettiness, self-pity, quirks of behavior, even violence. What Warren finds in the case of his father are the conditions that so typically nourish those dissatisfactions in his fictional characters; it is to Warren's credit that he refuses to distort that record to make it square with the patterns with which he and we are now so familiar. Although his shaping of his father's image possesses a rawboned integrity which the shaper cannot help but admire, it is an admiration laced with a vaguely puzzled querulousness. But if in 1953, with his father alive, Warren can be reconciled to his father's reconciliations, he can ultimately go farther in his own reconciliations after his father's death:

> And I,
> In spite of my own ignorance and failures,
> Have forgiven you all your virtues.
>
> Even your valor.   (SP, 71)

Jack Burden can remark that "the truth always kills the father"— that is, the recognition of the shared imperfection of man symbolically and, in Burden's case literally, destroys the father—but that the truth is necessary, that "all knowledge that is worth anything is maybe paid for by blood." It is, of course, a secular echo of a theological principle that only through the shedding of blood is there remission of sin. But another truth dominates the texture of Warren's work: that for all our acknowledgment that "we're all one flesh at last," we are also irremediably alone; indeed, the drive toward communion takes on more urgency in the face of that bleak discovery. R.P.W. links these joint truths near the conclusion of *Brother to Dragons*:

> I have . . . shared the most common
> Human experience, which makes all mankind one,
> For isolation is the common lot,
> And paradoxically, it is only by
> That isolation that we know how to name
> The human bond and thus define the self.   (BD, 205–206)

Warren has admitted that the question of fathers recurs in much of his work, but, significantly for the broader implications of that work, he points out that the son's dilemma with the father as he is and as the son would like him to be is as much an aesthetic device as it is a theme in its own right. Finding the perfect father, he says, is the urge to fuse the two halves of the world, the fact and idea—a formulation which ambitiously reflects Warren's grand reading of American psychological as well as literary history: the dialectic between the "Emersonian and the Hawthornian."[5]

As an aesthetic device, however, this formulation also suggests another level in his own work, the cultural, on which the revolt against the father is waged. Like most twentieth-century intellectuals, Warren is painfully conscious of how massively central to the American cultural tradition Emerson really is—painfully, because Emerson is the father of both the finest and the shabbiest of children: Walt Whitman and William James, and also Andrew Carnegie and Mary Baker Eddy. Warren's temperamental distaste for Emerson has never been passive or casual; it intrudes itself early and late as a recurring worry which can neither be forgotten nor resolved. Finding the perfect father in a literary tradition is, as Warren suggests, no simple matter, partly because the son is always so extravagant in his demands. His own later career attests to the complexity. However more congenial Hawthorne is to his sensibility and vision than Emerson, Warren's characteristic skepticism, his visceral insistence upon the reality of evil, dissolves frequently in images of light and sunshine and in explicit assertions of joy and hope. It is a movement, in fact, observable in some of Hawthorne. Further, Warren's compositional habit of leaping nervously from the sensuous image to the aphoristic generalization and abstraction is one shared by both Emerson *and* Hawthorne.

Nevertheless, like much of the writings of the Southern Renascence, Warren's work in several genres reveals an implicit and sometimes outright criticism of those qualities and predispositions in America that have been associated with Emerson: the extravagant belief in the "infinitude of the private person," from which stems, in often vulgarized fashion, an entire interrelated cluster of attitudes: inevitable progress (and the corollary idea that history is "bunk"), the power of man to shape himself as he will, and a trust in the transcendent power of the ideal to change actual circumstances. Emerson as Warren's *bête noire* shows up early and simplistically in the biography that is very much a young man's book, *John Brown: The Making of a Martyr*.

While neither Emerson nor Thoreau gave John Brown money, Warren reminds us that in 1859, when the old man was hanged, "they gave back to the world his own definition of himself" (JB, 245). If his death made the gallows as hallowed as the cross, that was precisely the value at which Brown wished to have himself assessed. The "extraordinary innocence" of Emerson, writes Warren, is exhibited in the fact that "he spent his life trying to find something in man or nature which could correspond to the fine ideas and the big word. In John Brown, Emerson thought that he had found his man" (JB, 245).[6]

In 1929 Warren could easily associate Emerson and the Transcendentalists with the historical moment which saw the decline and defeat of the South: a rabid, self-righteous, and hypocritical exercise of power in the name of an expedient higher law. When John Brown meets Franklin B. Sanborn, a friend of Emerson who is to become a loyal believer in old Brown, Warren allows himself a sketch written more in self-indulgent sarcasm than in irony. Sanborn,

> just out of Harvard, was a very young man, who had given up schoolteaching in order to follow God's will and work for the Massachusetts State Kansas Committee. He was an excessively earnest young man, confident of himself, and confident that he knew God's will; beyond this he possessed to a considerable degree that tight especial brand of New England romanticism which manifested itself in stealing Guinea niggers, making money, wrestling with conscience, hunting witches, building tea-clippers, talking about Transcendentalism, or being an Abolitionist. (JB, 226–27)

The authorial hostility evinced in Warren's portrait of Sanborn recurs in a much later sketch, which is simultaneously softened and heightened by the use of situations and idioms borrowed from the frontier humorists. In *Wilderness*, Warren allows his battlefield confidence man, who has been both a minister and a doctor before operating a "perambulatory embalming establishment," to quote Emerson on self-reliance:

"I have tried many things, it is true, and usually with no mean success. The sage of Concord says that the proper American tries many
things, storekeeping, farming, schoolteaching and so on. And though
my roster of occupations is different, I offer myself as that Emersonian American. I am a man of parts and —"

"Yeah, and if you'd kept 'em in your pants they wouldn't of got
you out of the preaching business," the nondescript man said.

"I freely acknowledge a certain proneness to temptation contingent
upon a robust constitution and attractive personality. But I left the
ministry of my own free will, sir. Patriotic motives, gentlemen." He
turned to the group. "You see, there is a great need for embalmers
with our troops. Even in winter, with exposure and disease, business
is not slack. I mean, there is a grave need. Ha-ha."

He paused, looked at the unsmiling faces and said: "Wit is the
salt of human life. But the dog saltest not his meat."   (W, 146–47)

The deflationary technique here is wide ranging: the appeal of and to
Emerson among the fradulent and the shabby, the suggested further
irony that such people may well *be* Emersonian Americans, the amusing
parallels between Emerson and this Emersonian (giving up the ministry, being a man of parts though the whole world say nay), and the
crass imitation of the Emersonian adage. The whole episode is a set
piece in the manner of a Mark Twain burlesque.

But the Emersonian streak in Warren is not all burlesque. The party
of hope invades the Warrenesque protagonist with some regularity. The
Man of Idea marches frequently through the pages of the fiction, sometimes as strangely attenuated "reflector" characters (Sugg Lancaster of
World Enough and Time, Tobias Sears of *Band of Angels*), sometimes
as fleshed-out emblematic characters (Adam Stanton of *All the King's
Men*), and sometimes as sympathetic seekers testing their commitments
in the mire of actuality (Adam Rosenzweig of *Wilderness*). Over the
years the hostility is transposed into more workable and useful attitudes—a nagging irritability, a puzzlement just ambivalent enough to
produce Emersonian characters and dilemmas. For all his pol-wise
cynicism, Jack Burden struggles against ideal images of both the self
and the world with the fervor of a distraught idealist philosopher; Jeremiah Beaumont could be described as an amateur Kentucky Platonist
who spends a career "trying to find something in man or nature which
could correspond to the fine ideas and the big word"; and even later
figures, such as Brad Tolliver and Jed Tewksbury, are caught up in
debilitating efforts to force correspondences between the actual world
and the ideal images of it carried in their heads.

If, as Warren claims, he has an almost "pathological flinch from Emersonianism, from Thoreauism, from these oversimplifications . . . of the grinding problems of life and of personality,"[7] it is a curiously creative flinch, since he has never ceased to be fascinated with this character type; such figures in fact are recurring versions of the Emersonian American that contribute to the complex moral dramas characteristically enacted in Warren's fiction. He both presides over and is the chief participator in the strenuous effort to yoke actuality to the ideal. And that effort itself, in both its foolishly misdirected and harshly regenerative aspects, is the constitutive drama that unfolds in work after work. That he should have written a suite of poems called "Homage to Emerson" attests to Warren's unresolved relationship to the most seminal literary father in American literature.

II. Mariners

In the early fiction and some of the poetry Warren's intertwined themes of alienation, the rejection and acceptance of the father, self-knowledge, regeneration, and the presumptive good of community all find their most effective expression through the means of a single device: the interpolated storyteller. This technique for widening and deepening thematic implications through the use of alternative points of view is related to Warren's fascination with *The Rime of the Ancient Mariner*. Among the several insights in "A Poem of Pure Imagination" is Warren's reminder of the affective structure and layered points of view of that great romantic work. The primary narrative situation in Coleridge's poem is the overlay and constant impingement of two storytellers: the Mariner and the omniscient poet whose emotional alliance is with the Wedding Guest. What the Mariner tells his auditor is the substance of what the poet tells us, and in the telling he is forced to adopt the vision of the Mariner both to make moral sense of the experience and to retain the aesthetic power to galvanize quiescent and complacent souls to attention. That double concern is precisely Warren's.

Morally, the burden of man's salvation requires adequate verbalizing: resolution of guilt and responsibility requires confession (Coleridge's Mariner must explain, cajole, and persuade others of both his sin and his salvation). Aesthetically, that verbalizing assumes formal, appropriate, even ritualistic shapes (Coleridge's Mariner can begin his return journey only after he composes a poem of blessing). A similar figure in the early works of Warren invariably proclaims his guilt for past acts; his storytelling is a *memoir justificatif,* a compulsive recitation in idioms often alien to the protagonist who hears it.

In such novels as *Night Rider* and *Band of Angels*, Warren's Mariner can more often define his crime and punishment than he can his repentance and reconciliation. In some instances even part of his punishment, the self-flagellating need to tell someone about it, suffers from lack of focus; he is unable to see his true role in his own act, and often the very recital of his story is halting, convoluted, imprecise. Warren's Mariners morally relive the ceremony of confession and aesthetically reenact the process of the artist. They do not always succeed in transforming themselves into artifacts, examples of the "little myth of man's capacity for making life meaningful."[8] Some fall short of redemption, but many reach at least a point in their spiritual development where they can accept the high cost of knowledge. Since that acceptance, however, demands a strenuous self-examination, most of Warren's fictional Mariners pay dearly for their final peace.

Warren's first Mariner is Willie Proudfit of *Night Rider* (1939). The act of speaking about his past complicity in crime on the western plains is also a personal reminder that he is still a human creature in constant need of grace. Proudfit verbalizes in order to "name [that] passel of things" he is now ashamed of, to identify them, to be certain that his past definition of them still remains true. Proudfit recounts his buffalo-skinning days in terms of a crime against nature; he emphasizes the hot rifle barrel, the crumpling of the shot animal, the sympathetic gathering of the rest of the herd around the fallen member, and, finally, his own estimate of man's irrational impulse to kill the animals: "A man lays thar, the sun a-bearen down, and keeps on a-pullen on the trigger. He ain't lak his-self. Naw, he ain't. Lak he wasn't no man, nor nuthen" (NR, 408). By implication Proudfit also now accepts the shared guilt of scalping an Indian, even though that act had been committed by a partner. Proudfit tells how he begins his expiation by living with the Indians, sharing their rituals and accepting their remedies for fever. Only when he has a vision of green grass, houses in a valley, a "white church with a bell" hanging near a spring, does he end his exile of penance to begin his journey back to Kentucky. That homecoming, when he falls "face down to the water" near his old home, becomes his final gesture, and Warren sees it as a self-ennobling and necessary act.

This story has only a subliminal effect on Perse Munn, the protagonist of *Night Rider*, whose vision is too limited to see that Proudfit's past parallels his own present. But when Munn finally decides to sacrifice the protection offered by Proudfit—to leave the sparse land for Monclair estate to kill Senator Tolliver—the journey becomes an ironic reversal of Proudfit's journey from the plains to Kentucky. Munn the lawyer at last is a Mariner who has not yet learned what his crime is and who never fully understands the terms of his punishment. In contrast to Proudfit, who begins the process of regeneration after the buffalo hunts, Munn degenerates rapidly after the symbolic shooting of a dove. The difference lies in the quality of the impulse toward self-definition. Munn's is always contradictory and hazy; near the end, when he could make the most of Proudfit's successful impulse, he hardly hears the words.

A similar structuring of the Mariner theme is evident in the second novel, *At Heaven's Gate* (1943). The important figure here is Ashby Wyndham, whose handwritten "Statement" alternates with chapters dealing with Sue Murdock and Jerry Calhoun. Although his Statement should serve as a kind of purgation for Wyndham, it does not: it is merely another trial, part of his larger punishment. Unlike Proudfit, who finds peace, Wyndham finds only more pain. His theme is "the pore human man," whose dilemma is that he "wants to know, but it is his weakness." Wyndham even acquires an albatross in the form of a mule, which he drives into a gatepost and kills during one of his drunken rampages; symbolically, it images forth his guilt for striking his brother Jacob in anger. This latter act causes Jacob to sell the family farm: he turns over the scanty proceeds to Ashby, and each brother, permanently estranged from the other, sets out alone in the world.

Leaving the farm of his ancestors takes Ashby into another sin—to Massey Mountain, where he joins a timber crew stripping the mountain of its trees. His tree-chopping duplicates the earlier mule-killing; both are crimes against nature. And when he strikes a heckling unionist, Ashby repeats his earlier crime against his brother: "I ought never lifted up my hand agin him in no way. If I had helt my hand, may be nuthin would happened" (AHG, 193). Disasters multiply. He is fired and his child dies. While walking in anguish at night he hears the voice of his dead child admonishing him to "walk in the world" and tell of his sin against his brother. This moment of illumination confirms Ashby's Mariner role. From this moment on, his expiation is "telling" the Word: "I stood in the street and I told folks how it was. How the Lord had laid it on me to tell folks. I told them my wickedness and how the wicked man will come down low. I met folks in the big road and I told them" (AHG, 233).

But even while enacting his ritual of homely commination Ashby despairs as he gradually sees himself being enveloped in spiritual pride: "A man can be proud and high in the Lord lak he can in pore human pride and it is a sin. It is a worse sin" (AHG, 262). (Here the alternating chapters stop, the plots mesh, and Ashby sits in his cell, convinced that God—in all justness—has turned away His face.) Although Ashby never achieves his regeneration, his adamant compulsion toward expiation has at least one positive effect: his role stimulates the public confession of Private Porsum, his cousin who is involved in Bogan Murdock's corrupt financial schemes.

Like Munn of *Night Rider*, Jerry Calhoun is inflicted with a Mariner impulse but denied the concomitant gift for words that can give release, and therefore meaning, to that impulse. Unlike Murdock's other ex-hero, Porsum, Jerry does not have a "silver tongue" to soothe the mobs; instead he becomes an echo of Murdock in his confidential, cliché-studded rhetoric, the central function of which is to persuade business associates of Murdock's honesty. Porsum manages to repudiate his lackey role because he can still define himself; Jerry crumples passively, without the will to resist or admit defeat, because he never successfully defines himself. Only after being rescued by Duckfoot Blake and returned to the care of his father is Jerry able to begin the careful definition of self that had so long eluded him.

If in the first two novels a subordinate figure plays the role of chief Mariner, and the protagonist becomes the secondary, almost speechless Mariner, in *All the King's Men* (1946) the Mariner figure dominates both structure and texture. Jack Burden's entire story is an I-narration, a reliving and relieving of a burden, the protagonist's impulse toward self-definition. His easy cynicism; his almost automatic rejection of family, tradition, and the past; his cautious but loyal acceptance of Willie Stark; his profession ("Student of History" and newspaperman); and a talent which makes the maximum use of words—all these give him obvious advantages over Perse Munn and Jerry Calhoun. Whereas the earlier protagonists had only the impulse to tell their stories, Jack Burden has both the impulse and the talent.[9]

His task, for all that, is no easier. His very gift involves him in a compulsion toward completeness, a need to investigate all motives, to speculate if not to conclude on actions. He is not haunted; he is merely nagged by his failure to achieve a fuller self-definition. His mental and moral bent encourages him to verbalize without fear of definitiveness; his philosophical stance moves from Idealism to a scientistic naturalism before coming even to a tentative rest. After his trip west he can say, with a touch of dogmatism, that he had learned "two very great truths. First, that you cannot lose what you have never had. Second, that you are never guilty of a crime which you did not commit" (AKM, 330). He finds, however, in the thrust of events—the mutual destruction of Adam Stanton and Willie Stark—that these "very great truths" are not true, at least for him. And when the time comes to change his mind, his words also change. The verbalizing of his final position, while just as thorough, just as freewheeling, is less dogmatic and smug. In short, he is not paralyzed by an inability to "tell" at any stage of his development. This ambivalent gift is a refinement of the central tactic used by the Mariner to release his burden and to reclaim his place in nature; the "telling" is important in itself.

The yardstick by which Jack Burden measures his growing moral position is the diary of Cass Mastern, itself (like Ashby Wyndham's Statement) a "telling" of guilt and punishment which lies always in the background waiting for Burden's maturity. His first attempt to understand Mastern (when he is a doctoral candidate) ends in failure. The project is still waiting at the end of the novel when Burden, who has completed his own telling, can now edit the document. In the end he must accept his own involvement in sending Anne Stanton to Stark's bed and in causing the death of his two friends, whose lives were perhaps doomed but who themselves "lived in the agony of will." Responsibility for past events leads Burden to find the Scholarly Attorney ("for each of us is the son of a million fathers"). He can see no easy reconciliation in his future: the magnanimous act may come, but "a long time from now."

As with Jack Burden's story, *World Enough and Time* (1950) is the long, anguished telling of a Mariner figure. It is a more ambitious presentation than Burden's because of Warren's more complex manipulation of perspective. A nameless but not-quite-effaced narrator (another student of history) slips into the background, as Jack Burden was not to do, to permit full play to *his* Cass Mastern. The historian-narrator's editing of Jeremiah Beaumont's journal and the assembling of related reports about Beaumont are sometimes accurate, sometimes not. But for all his flaws, the narrator's energies are devoted not primarily to his own self-knowledge, as was true of Burden's concern with Cass Mastern, but to the unfolding of his subject's terrible progress toward self-knowledge.

If it is true that in this work Warren is exploring one modern version of the old Romance genre, then Jeremiah Beaumont becomes a version of the most sophisticated hero of the Romance: the knight in search of the Grail. Despite the antireligious postures of both Beaumont and Rachel and despite the substitution of the Ruined Maid for the Virgin, the intensity and ardor of Beaumont's rather wormy courtly love are religious. Throughout his life Beaumont's underlying motive, as well as his determining pattern of action, is a personal search for his own identity, not the disinterested search for justice that he affirms so loudly and so often that even his historian accepts it. Self, rather than

Justice, is his Grail, though its winning proves just as arduous. Beaumont, the serious man of idea who pursues his dream of self to its logical conclusion, upholds an idealism that is itself flawed; he cannot bear the thought of corrupting compromise. He is an intellectual version of Ashby Wyndham; spiritual pride, because of its conventional hierarchical status as the sin of sins, carries with it a proportionate risk and punishment.

In the motionless stupor of a backwoods swamp, with sufficient time and enough of an independent world, the lovers reorient their relationship. It is appropriate that Rachel, who throughout their fitful lives serves as her husband's excuse for his acts, should be the agent who permits him his long-sought-for knowledge. She indicts Beaumont with using her for his own dark needs, and, as she lies dying by her own hand, also forgives him. Only at this moment does he come to the point where he can define his sin (and therefore his elusive self): "It is unpardonable. It is the crime of self, the crime of life. The crime is I" (WET, 505). And in his last desperate days he seeks another act to restore a balance that had been scarcely there anyway, the symbolic moment when he can "shake the hangman's hand" and call him brother.

Beaumont writes his journal with a tenacious need to justify himself, as if his definition lay in justification. Because he is complex, and because his motives are buried beneath layers of surrogate needs, the explanations are involved and tortuous. His style is courtly, learned, a trifle quaint. His rhetoric, which reflects his technique of doing, surrounds, surmounts, and underpins both the motive and the act so that the sheer enveloping defines both in their ideal existence and, in that process, the self Beaumont hopefully seeks.

As he gradually sheds all tokens of his former self, his civilizing symbols, he retains his manuscript. Even when doing nothing more than wenching with a syphilitic or drinking with louts in the miasmic swamp, Beaumont is compelled to note these facts. Even when his exposed rationalizations grow thinner, he must still scramble for spare leaves of paper on which to record them. In short, his compulsion to "tell" falls short only of his primary compulsion to act. And when he undertakes to return to Frankfort for his punishment, the well-wrapped parcel of manuscript is the most important item he carries. After his unceremonious death, when he is cheated of the dignity of the gallows, the confession remains important for Wilkie Barron, the erstwhile friend, who preserves it despite the fact that its existence, if made public, would ruin him.

Beaumont suffers sin, punishment, expiation, and hovers about the brink of reconciliation. And if the desire to shake the hangman's hand is somehow equal to that act, perhaps the last phase of the Mariner process is completed in Beaumont. But for this protagonist, more than for any other of Warren's Mariners, the telling itself becomes the major instrument in the final, successful definition, the purgation of self to locate self.

Warren's final use of the formal interpolated story in *Band of Angels* (1955) is also the first time the Mariner figure bears a totally functional relationship to the protagonist and to the organic structure of the novel, which is one long recitation of Amantha Starr, a Kentucky planter's daughter by one of his slaves who is seized and sold as chattel at her father's death. The Mariner figure is Hamish Bond, the man who buys Amantha. The statement that triggers the story of Bond's life is his remark, "You don't even know who I am" and, a moment later, "Maybe I don't even know who I am" (BA, 176). The name is important for them both, because the formation of the name or merely the shaping of the mask is accepted as a necessary step in self-definition. Amantha passionately insists on knowing Bond's real name, a curious request that gradually grows to desperation. When he finally tells her, his story follows.

Bond's crime, slave-trading, like the initiating acts of Willie Proudfit and Ashby Wyndham, is a crime against nature. Unlike most of the other interpolated confessions, Bond's comes at a point in the cycle when his punishment is not yet over and his repentance only nebulously grasped. He can still say, "I did wrong," but his governing position is still the easy appeal to a deterministic argument: "We're just what we are." Characteristically, Bond's story suggests little to Amantha except how she has been hurt by his ambiguous profession. She confesses that she stops listening to him even in the process of the telling and describes how she forges her self-pity into a weapon: "[E]ven in that disorientation, some excitement of power had suddenly grown in me" (BA, 201).

It is a familiar feeling with Amantha. As her relations with Bond grow stronger, she perfects her technique for using him, for assigning to herself the role of punisher of Bond—not for Bond's own crimes, which certainly require punishment, but because he had unconsciously complicated Amantha's desperate search for self-knowledge. It is Amantha's defining trait that she can use her triviality of mind as an instrument of power over the male at the same time that she must depend upon it as an instrument for solving her more pressing problems.

As for her own story, the reader plays the role of unenthusiastic Wedding Guest not because her *story* is a mediocre one (rather, it proclaims its historical and philosophical magnitude even while its central concern is an individual protagonist), but because *she* is mediocre. Unlike Jack Burden's story, hers far outweighs her intellectual and forensic equipment to tell it. Instead of holding us by a glittering eye, she fascinates us because she is so remarkably tiresome when she plays the vain and hurt young lady, a type who can barely discriminate between being snubbed at a ball and being raped by a slave. Much as she communicates her anxieties, ambivalences, self-justifications, and confessions, rarely are there moments when the reader feels that Amantha knows and understands what has happened to her even while she tells all. She gives the impression of an inept raconteur, short on art but long on ego, who expects the audience to share the labor. But if we are patient, the irritations are mitigated. Her story—every scrap and shred of it, every fragmented musing on it—falls into shape from the weight of its own pieces almost in spite of her storytelling technique or the quality of her mind. It is not accidental that what finally helps to define and answer her primary question ("Oh, who am I?") is not Amantha's overexercised sensibilities or her ability as a Wedding Guest to learn from Bond's story, but merely time itself. Spiritually, she is an old woman when she achieves her reconciliation.

From *Night Rider,* where the Mariner figure speaks from the context of his recent peace, and *At Heaven's Gate,* where he speaks out in the anguish of his perpetual punishment, Warren turns from untutored folk types whose messages are heard impatiently, or not at all, to Mariner figures who are both learned and sensitive, sophisticated sufferers whose tortured fluency sometimes obscures a desire to learn the secrets of the self. If Cass Mastern's diary in *All the King's Men* comes from a man whose guilt and punishment become a model of the severe, almost orthodox conscience, the journal of Jeremiah Beaumont in *World Enough and Time* is a convoluted confession in which self-deception is so radical that it constantly baffles and misleads a shadowy historian who is trying to learn from it. The least of the functions of these nineteenth-century figures, including Hamish Bond of *Band of Angels,* is to remind twentieth-century man that moral experience is forever edged with difficulty and that there is no such thing as a "simpler time."

After *Band of Angels,* Warren never returns to the long interpolated tale as a formal device or to the Mariner figure as a foil or reflector for his protagonists. Inset narrative segments with their own integrity are still very much a part of the overall texture in the later fiction, and the protagonists, still spiritual seekers, occasionally discover wisdom figures whose experience has fitted them for the world without diminishing their moral force. But Warren's attraction for that explicit narrative vehicle and the Mariner figure whose role parallels the common dilemma of the protagonists ends in 1955.

The shift in interest represented by that watershed year can be traced in several ways. Warren's aesthetic development is at once toward the freer, open, and more personal expression typified by *Promises* (1957), his single greatest volume of poems, and toward fiction whose formal shapes tend toward the emblematic. *The Cave* (1959) has no real protagonist and no authoritative point of view; themes and patterns of action, familiar from earlier novels, fall to several characters, each of which is allowed independent ethical positions and devices for "telling." A spatial area—the cave itself—becomes not only the unifying structural element but also the orienting thematic focus. *Wilderness* (1961) uses the geographical setting of the Civil War Battle of the Wilderness as both literal place and metaphorical state. Both *Flood* (1964) and *Meet Me in the Green Glen* (1971) are stories of the buried life rendered through talismanic place—a small town in one, an agricultural valley in the other—soon to be flooded by waters created by dams. The emblematic locus in *A Place to Come To* (1977) is literally a town in northern Alabama and metaphorically the final spiritual plane of a tattered sensibility. This later fiction, while it still reflects the solidly rendered circumstantiality of the actual world, is marked most obviously by bold, if not always successful, manipulations of caricature and stereotype, artifice and rhetoric, of episodes that are more ceremonial and ritualistic than realistic, and of the author's own voice as authority.

The personal voice is anticipated for the first time in *Brother to Dragons* (1953) in which R.P.W., "The writer of this poem," plays Mariner to his own Wedding Guest. Like the protagonists prior to this work and most of them after, R.P.W. shows no diminution of the agonized, compulsive quest. The telling of guilt in this narrative poem is not an episode in an action but the action itself, the major vehicle as well as the major theme. It becomes a kind of chorale whose theme is carried by parallel, competing, and counterpointing Mariners.

The created worlds of Warren's fiction, as commentators never tire of repeating, have always been scenes of melodrama and violence; what is interesting, however, is that the two most brutal accounts of human evil in Warren's long career are both poems, as if the circumstantial actuality of Zola and Hardy which Warren emulates so often in fiction cannot adequately comprise either the moral or aesthetic significance of such deeds. "The Ballad of Billie Potts" inverts the crime of parricide enmeshed in a sequence of casual murders for greed. *Brother to Dragons* recounts a ritualistic murder and fratricide. Both are based, significantly, on old tales and historical facts, as if the most horrendous melodrama occurs independent of artistic invention. The latter story interested Warren because the crime of Charles Lewis' sons on the frontier in Kentucky was never alluded to by their uncle, Thomas Jefferson, the republic's greatest exponent of man's natural virtue. But if in the course of the poem the founding father must come to terms with human evil, R.P.W., who prides himself on having never been much deceived that way, must struggle with the possibility of human virtue. Jefferson's anguish is that his nephews' acts attest not to isolated perversion or momentary madness but that they find sympathetic echo in the very nature of things:

> the terrible texture in which
> One episode of anguish evokes all anguish
> And sets nerves screaming, and the white tendrils curl,
> In black peripheries beyond the last stars.   (BD, 132)

R.P.W. must try to formulate "an adequate definition" of the "glory of the human effort" despite not only pervasive evil but also naturalistic evidences of human frailty, failure, filth, and flesh. And in his recreations, the presence of his father is both goad and pacifier. The old man, nearing his peaceful eighties,

> has filled the tract of Time
> With rectitude and natural sympathy,
> Past hope, ambition, and despair's delectable anodyne,   (BD, 27)

and the son, who is past none of these urgencies, must work out that "most happy and difficult conclusion: / To be reconciled to the father's own reconciliation." *Reconciliation*, as I suggested earlier, is an important word throughout *Brother to Dragons*. Before the anguish is over, Jefferson and R.P.W., coil and countercoil, are brought together in chastened union. Despite vanity and error, Jefferson can still pledge his faith in sweet reason, but

> if there is to be reason, we must
> Create the possibility
> Of reason, and we can create it only
> From the circumstances of our most evil despair.   (BD, 194–95)

Despite cynicism and his own despair, R.P.W. must acknowledge the tonic uses of the knowledge of man's failures. If for Jefferson that knowledge is "the bitter bread" which he now eats in joy, for R.P.W. it is his father's memory of taking his father's spring tonic of bitter percoon, which though it would "wry your tongue" would also thin the blood: "My father said how winter thicked boys' blood / And made 'em fit for devilment, and mean" (BD, 205). It is the ritualistic expunging of natural human devilment, which though it cannot be denied, is to be resisted by man's own means.

The achievement of an acceptable equilibrium is hard-won because, for Jefferson, it means admitting the stain of vanity, the complicity of the innocent in the guilty act; and, for R.P.W., the inevitable search for virtue "despite all naturalistic considerations" that deny virtue. To accept the darker impulses that have shaped the very history of America—impulses that are something more radical than "encroachment of shadow" upon the sunny exploits of pioneers—is not to foreclose the claims of either glory or the human achievements of more modest, even anonymous, dimensions. "I have made new acquaintance with the nature of joy," R.P.W. can finally say, and though it can sometimes seem to mean nothing more than "Appetitive spur," *joy* becomes more and more frequent in Warren's diction. Two years later, in *Band of Angels,* Amantha Starr becomes the first fictional seeker whose anguished search for self-knowledge leads finally to a full reconciliation "in joy."

If, as Warren believes, the Ancient Mariner of Coleridge's poem can begin his return journey after he composes a poem of blessing, R.P.W. exorcises the sobering ghosts of Rocky Hill through his vision of the Ohio River below the house:

> And I thought how men had moved on that broad flood,
> The good, the bad, the strong, the weak, all men
> The drawn, the driven, the fortunate, the feckless,
> All men, a flood upon the flood. . . . (BD, 209–10)

Man's responsibility for every other man is possible because of the burden shared by all: his simultaneous aspiration for glory and his proneness to sin. Even if we have only "stumbled into the act of virtue," its fulfillment lies "in the degree of recognition / of the common lot of our kind." With that recognition, R.P.W., like Jack Burden before him, is "prepared / To go into the world of action and liability."

III. The Goodly Company

The best-known example of Warren's doctrine of human re-latedness is usually thought to be Jack Burden's gloss on the story of Cass Mastern, who in his personal anguish learned "that the world is all of one piece," like an enormous spiderweb: if your "happy foot or your gay wing" brushes it ever so lightly at any point, "the drowsy spider feels the tingle," springs to life to inject death; and "what happens always happens and there is the spider, bearded black and with his great faceted eyes glittering like mirrors in the sun, or like God's eye, and the fangs dripping" (AKM, 200). It is a justly famous passage; and it is sometimes cited as the final stage in Burden's difficult progress from the "brass-bound Idealism" of the Great Sleep and the scientistic determinism of the Great Twitch—his entry into the world of values represented by his nineteenth-century kinsman. Its presumable lesson is the antidote to Burden's natural habit of seeing the world as "an accumulation of items, odds and ends of things like the broken and misused and dust-shrouded things in a garret." But Burden's dour suggestion of a spider-God is not necessarily the opposing vision to a discontinuous world of discrete items.

What Cass Mastern learns is moral responsibility, a stage that Burden reaches only after disasters have fallen about him in unforeseen profusion, and his account of Cass Mastern—his "first journey into the enchantments of the past," as he archly puts it—is the substance of Chapter Four in his memoir of ten chapters. And precisely because his is a religious sensibility, Cass Mastern does not project an image of God-entrapped man. Indeed, the spiderweb passage in both substance and rhetoric is characteristically Burdenesque: the stress on fate, a naturalistic interpretation of punishment as a state beyond mere justice, couched in viscerally flamboyant images. The quiet suffering of a Cass Mastern lies in wait for Jack Burden, but the moment is not yet, and the spiderweb passage attests to the wise-guy cynicism with which he is plagued for most of his young adulthood. If there is a sense of interrelatedness in the passage, it is in the Calvinistic implication of man's helplessness in the face of divine judgment—the Hawthornesque side of Warren's concern, the brotherhood of man as a brotherhood of evil that we find depicted in "Young Goodman Brown" or "The Minister's Black Veil." But another face of that relatedness can be seen in "Wakefield" and "Ethan Brand": the injunction to participate in the common stream, not to be cut off from the "magnetic chain of humanity."

Jack Burden's moral postures are, in part, derived from the character, attitudes, and idioms of Duckfoot Blake, the cynical friend of Jerry Calhoun in *At Heaven's Gate*, and they will recur with disquieting frequency in later novels and poems—and as the distinguishing mark of protagonists in *Flood* and *A Place to Come To*. For such characters even moments of special insight are edged with heavy irony, self-deprecation, and wry cautiousness. Intellectually and emotionally capable of repeating Burden's spiderweb passage, most of these characters are in fact given space for similar utterances. But even this type, who usually undergoes a secular harrowing of social, sexual, or philosophical import, achieves a vision of human relatedness that can claim at least the possibility of joy.

If the great central fact of *The Rime of the Ancient Mariner* centers on "the broken tabu, the torments of guilt and punishment, the joy of reconciliation" (SE, 271), it is also the great central fact of much of Warren's work. The broken tabu often turns on the denial, out of pride or excessive ambition, of the familial pieties and responsibilities—the social seal of man's bond to other humans. The torments of guilt and punishment are visited on those who ignore, deny, or pervert that bond, a searing experience which for many protagonists extends throughout most of their lifetimes. The joy of reconciliation completes the cycle when through love the erring character is reunited in brotherhood so that he can, in Coleridge's words, again walk with a goodly company. The story of Jack Burden, the paradigm of this pattern, has been called the "secular adaptation of the spiritual autobiography," a formula which in its modern version begins with Defoe as "rebellion-punishment-repentance-deliverance."[10] The somewhat extravagant vision of a spider-God is a metaphorical abstraction that occurs during, not at the end of, Burden's travail. A more concretely imagined occurrence in *All the King's Men* opens the way for the regeneration of its narrator—to a final deliverance that promises spiritual peace and, potentially, joy.

When Burden discovers Tiny Duffy's role in the murder of Willie

Stark, he reports that the confrontation between him and the Boss's henchman served as a kind of purgation: "I had kicked Duffy around and my head was big as a balloon with grandeur. Then," he adds, "something happened and the yellow taste was in the back of my mouth."

> I suddenly asked myself why Duffy had been so sure I would work for him . . . and suddenly I knew that I had tried to make Duffy into a scapegoat for me and to set myself off from Duffy, and my million-dollar meal of heroism backfired that yellow taste into my gullet and I felt caught and tangled and mired and stuck like an ox in a bog and a cat in flypaper . . . . It was as though I were caught in a . . . monstrous conspiracy whose meaning I could not fathom. It was as though the scene through which I had just lived had been a monstrous and comic miming for ends I could not conceive and for an audience I could not see but which I knew was leering from the shadow. It was as though in the midst of the scene Tiny Duffy had slowly and like a brother winked at me with his oyster eye and I had known he knew the nightmare truth, which was that we were twins bound together more intimately and disastrously than the poor freaks of the midway who are bound by the common stitch of flesh and gristle and the seepage of blood. We were bound together forever and I could never hate him without hating myself or love myself without loving him. (AKM, 442)

Burden's visceral recoil from Duffy's "wink" is his single most illuminating moment. As bright boy among the king's men, he knows that the conspiratorial gesture, though only imagined, affirms a general commonality: *We're all in this together.* For Duffy the survivor, the wink is instinctive, unintellectualized, and scarcely formulable: *We're still here, and things can still go our way.* It is for Burden a shattering, disgusting shock of recognition, a sudden eruption of what he has heretofore kept firmly below his working consciousness—the realization that the canniness of a low-country patrician and the cunning of an up-country redneck are one, and that for all his stratagems and feints, Jack Burden is spiritually as well as physically tied to the Mason City crowd. It is a necessary moment for him in his uneasy progress to moral maturity.

If for most of his life Burden resembles that hardheaded ancestor Gilbert Mastern, with his vision of narrowly conceived connections with and responsibilities to other men, the bracing verification of his brotherhood with Tiny Duffy humbles him to the point where he can accept Cass Mastern's doctrine of responsibility and comprehensive human re-

latedness. The key to that doctrine is that the best of men are linked
irrevocably to the worst. It is not difficult for Burden to cherish his links
with Judge Irwin; it is sometimes harder for him to adjust to Willie
Stark and practically impossible for him to see his association with Tiny
Duffy or Gummy Larsen as anything more than an accident in time, a
temporary quirk of history.

All the King's Men concerns the moral education of its narrator, and
it is Warren's first extended fictional statement on the idea of complicity that lies at the core of that work. In *World Enough and Time*,
Beaumont correctly argues that the betrayal of one man in the human
community must be equated to the betrayal of all men, but in the vast
tissue of betrayal that knits so many relationships in this novel, Beaumont sees himself untainted. In refusing to acknowledge complicity
with the fallen world about him, he, like Jack Burden, shrinks from
the spiritual fact that he is yoked with the very people he despises.
Complicity, then, is the earned vision of those who have struggled
toward self-knowledge—that theme that runs through Warren's work
like an obsessive, never-to-be-resolved theme. Perse Munn and Jerry
Calhoun, who lack the will to pursue the significance of their hazy, ill-
defined selves, immerse their lives in a common "good" only to find
depletion and death. *Community* can be a deceptive surrogate, and
corrupting, when the self has not first faced up to its own complex
nature. In this sense, Jack Burden and Jeremiah Beaumont break
through the barrier of the ill-defined self, the crucial flaw that mars
the spiritual integrity of so many characters and personae in Warren.

In "Original Sin: A Short Story," one of Warren's best early poems,
the solemnity of his obsessive theme is in part domesticated and particularized by such metaphors of familiarity as an old hound, a hobo, a
child-like relative, a mother, and an old horse; but the lesson the
speaker learns is the same thing that similar speakers in other poems
come to understand: the unity of the self. That recognition means, in
turn, an accommodation of man's bestiality. The necessity to slake what
Warren calls the "implacable thirst of self" (in "The Ballad of Billie
Potts") often means confronting a shadow self as an image far more
sinister than that of the old hound snuffling at the door. Billie Potts's
"long return" to his fate, for example, is pegged to the natural compulsions of bee, eel, goose, and salmon; man, in this poem, is brother to
fin and pinion, just as later he is seen as "brother to dragons and companion to owls." Lilburn Lewis, though conceived as a real and depressingly tangible person, functions also (through symbols and mythic
attributes) as the very embodiment of the unacknowledged secret self

of Jefferson, the "coiling darkness" that must be embraced. *Brother to Dragons* is studded with recurring beast imagery as symbolic reminders of man's monstrousness for both Jefferson and R.P.W.

The recognition of one's full and often objectionable individuality is requisite to selfhood, and only the most determinedly naturalistic situations show the failure to strike beyond. If Job's image of himself as brother to dragons, in that biblical allusion that is the source of Warren's title, suggests the monstrousness with which the self must contend, it also implies the burden of kinship. The placing of one's self in a communal context is not merely a therapeutic prescription; it is a spiritual imperative. Yoked to the imagistic strain of monstrousness, then, is the dramatic one of mutual relationship. In *Brother to Dragons* brothers are important, literally and metaphorically, for they serve as an index to community and thus represent, potentially at least, the sanative stage in the curing of soul sickness. Lilburn-Isham, Lucy-Jefferson, Laetitia-Brother: the sibling relationships, specifically and tangibly rendered, extend outward, encompassing all varieties of literal kinship to form a gloss on the metaphorical abstraction *brotherhood*. But more: from the implicit identification in the title (dragons and owls) to the explicit ones in the text (catfish, snake), the bestial core of man must not be deflected by making symbolic mysteries from what is merely natural. If the varied faces of nature can only be "mirror to the human heart's steadfast and central illumination," those of man are more appropriate emblems for the human enterprise; Jefferson must take the bloody hand of his bestial nephew for, as Lucy tells him,"his face is only a mirror of your possibilities."

The need for community on the purely literal level is evidenced negatively by the geographical isolation of the Lewis house and family, a fact that thrusts itself all the way across the century to a curious R.P.W., who senses the chill of the site. The geographical isolation, "the shadow of the forest," is merely a setting to highlight a larger alienation, a darker shadow, "the imitigable ferocity of self" in the "insurmountable arctic of the human alienation." Almost all of the characters stand in this darker shadow. Charles Lewis flees to the "wild land" out of desperation over his intolerable emptiness. Lucy suffers in the transplanting from the cultivated Albermarle to the raw frontier. The suicide Meriwether fails to accomplish his uncle's commission to "redeem the wild world far to the Western Shore." Lilburn's chief communal activity is jug-passing with his younger brother, and Isham the parricide ironically meets his end in the Battle of New Orleans in a war of fraternal conflict.

The premise behind Warren's doctrine of complicity is the central conviction that none is without guilt. Lucy in her pride fails to comfort George, the luckless slave. Laetitia wills Lilburn's perverted attack. Isham, Aunt Cat, even George all use and are used by others. Psychologically, the interrelated characters act out valid patterns of attraction and repulsion; theologically, they reenact the mythic ceremonies by which man the created alternately ignores and entreats the creator. What is merely a visceral shock of recognition for Jack Burden is elevated to a virtual theory of behavior in R.P.W., whose notion of complicity asserts the mutuality of victim and victimizer:

> How the rabbit runs to the stone hurled by the boy's hand,
> And the stone's parabola and the rabbit's irrational
> Skitter fulfill each other, and that fulfillment is a chord
> Of music, enormous, to blacken the sky,
> And the hen in the dark hen house offers her throat
> To the delicate stitch of the weasel's tooth and to the lip's
> Insidious suction . . . .   (BD, 138)

If Lilburn needs the black George on the chopping block, George indicates his need for Lilburn when he curls himself correctly on the block to receive the ax. When rebuked by Jefferson for what seems a perverse insight, R.P.W. turns the screw still further and speculates on a paradoxical reversal of roles:

> But just suppose it true, what then? The victim
> Becomes the essential accomplice, *provocateur*—
> No, more, is the principal—the real victim
> Is he whose hand was elected to give the stroke,
> But is innocent.   (BD, 139)[11]

R.P.W.'s turn of the screw ends up as the dead-end theory of divine malevolence, in which man's will can do nothing but proclaim innocence. But none is innocent. In perfect consequence, the mutuality of victim and victimizer in the meat house is later repeated in the betrayal of those who love Liburn most, Aunt Cat and his dog, a betrayal which is also Lilburn's "deepest will."[12]

This is the dark side to complicity, of course, or what would be dark if man were unable to strike through his despair when it becomes too easefully acclimated to "the way things are." The way in which Jack Burden's incomplete manuscript and the Mastern papers follow him from one rooming house to another, from apartment to apartment, from year to year, is suggestive of the deterministic patterns which lace most of Warren's work. Blind and "groping Godward" through "crevice, cranny, chink," the force is sometimes related to irresistible grace; but most often it is merely the agent for that grace, the agent which compels one's recognition of his own darker self. That the world is all of a piece is the lesson that comes so late and so destructively to Burden; put another way, it means that man becomes wholly man only after coming to terms with that dark nightmare self that consciousness prefers to ignore.[13] Not ignoring his own dark zones prepares the way for man's disinterested exercise of charity, which, when freely extended in the world, can bring "blessedness," "hope," or "joy."

The source of this secular equivalent of salvation, which recurs with considerable frequency in much of the later work, is, again, Warren's essay on "The Rime of the Ancient Mariner," which dates from the same period during which Warren was writing *All the King's Men*: "The Mariner shoots the bird; suffers various pains, the greatest of which is loneliness and spiritual anguish; upon recognizing the beauty of the foul sea snakes, experiences a gush of love for them and is able to pray; is returned miraculously to his home port, where he discovers the joy of human communion in God . . . . We arrive at the notion of a universal charity, . . . the sense of the 'One Life' in which all creation participates" (SE, 222). That sense of the "One Life" comes to the Mariner, Warren stresses, only after he has submitted himself to "the great discipline of sympathy"; his return voyage from the stark polar regions begins once he has composed a "poem" of blessing and, though scarred, he is allowed to walk again "with a goodly company."

So also ends *All the King's Men*, as a sadder and wiser Burden picks up the pieces of his life, determined to walk through the scenes of old defeats into "the awful responsibility of Time." Amantha Starr of *Band of Angels,* after thirty years of hedging, participates in the ritualistic restoration of Old Slop, the black garbage man, and accepts fully that "commonality of weakness and rejection" in the midst of strange headstones in a little Kansas cemetery. With quite different tonal effects, many of the poems in *Promises* and volumes after it celebrate "joy," "heart-joy," "blessedness," and "beauty." With a kind of astonished humility, the intellectual and mature speaker consistently discovers lessons, however puzzling and oblique, that seem to bear on his own search for blessedness. The significant rubric (from "Ballad of a Sweet Dream of Peace") is "we're all one Flesh, at last." The ambiguous emotions of the speaker in one poem, directed toward a loved one, sum up the spirit of chastened and qualified hope:

> For I who bless can bless you only
> For the fact our histories

Can have no common bond except the lonely
Fact of humanness we share
As now, in place and fate disparate, we breathe the same dark
                                              pulsing air.
Where you lie now, far or near,
Sleep, my dear.[14]

If one mode common to the characteristic Warren protagonist is the anguished search for the defining marks of his own uniqueness and the erection of boundaries to preserve and perpetuate those proud differences, another mode is the equally anguished drive to submerge that uniqueness, to temper individuality with community. Warren's work is filled with instances in which the individual, realizing the limiting and often negating effects of his unique self, strives to join, by tearing down those isolating boundaries. Amantha Starr stoops to kiss the scar on Hamish Bond's leg, and Sue Murdock of *At Heaven's Gate* kisses the befouled face of her lover's old aunt; Willie Proudfit of *Night Rider* gives up buffalo-killing, and Percy Munn discovers that he cannot kill his alter ego. These are defining gestures of varying importance, but they all stamp the gesturers not as radical selves but as fragmented individuals responding to the need for community. Jack Burden proceeds from a mechanistic view of people and things in their atomistic dispersion (like objects in an attic, discrete, functionless) to Cass Mastern's vision of infinite and mutual responsibility. In their more ponderous ways, this is also the final vision of Adam Rosenzweig (*Wilderness*), Bradwell Tolliver (*Flood*), and Jed Tewksbury (*A Place to Come To*).

The doctrine of complicity is not, as Warren would doubtless admit, an original proposition. In varying ways it has been a ground theme in orthodox western Christianity at least since Augustine (and in more exacerbated forms in the various heresies which Augustine had to combat). Further, lifting it up as a doctrinal necessity is abstract; using it functionally as a part of man's experience in the here and now is particular. Though sometimes inclined to the very abstractness he has spoken against, Warren more often than not encloses that doctrine in the specific images of man's involvement in his world. Nowhere in the canon is the joining of the abstraction and the specific human context more successfully realized than in *Brother to Dragons*, perhaps his most impressive book. There the full implications of complicity, its hopeful as well as chilling aspects, are laid out in terms of measurable human consequences.

If in its darker premises, the rabbit and the stone, the hen and the

weasel, George and Lilburn meet in conspiring fulfillment, there is also a brighter promise in such complicity. R.P.W., no less than Jefferson, knows the betraying weakness in every man's face—the "bleared,
the puffed, the lank, the lean"—and, like Jefferson too, he believes in
"virtue." Past "all appetite and alibi," he believes in that "green, crank
nightmare of the dear green world." Under his querulous, sometimes
petulant promptings, R.P.W. brings Jefferson, stage by stage, into
realizing that only through acknowledgment of our common darkness
can there be the "incandescence of the heart's great flare." In the doctrine of complicity—akin to what Warren sees in Coleridge's great
poem—are both anguish and truth: "All is redeemed, / in knowledge."
And that aspect of complicity works for R.P.W., too. Early on, he
figuratively blesses his own foul sea snakes—the brute-faced Mississippi
catfish ("one with God") and, later, the Black Snake, *Elaphe obsoleta
obsoleta* ("the swollen head hung / Haloed and high in light"). Most
important, however, he can now bless man: the bluster of Laetitia's
brother, the common decency of Mr. Boyle, the conspiring innocence
of Isham, the compromises of his own aged father. Finally, honor as
well as outrage must be explained "by our most murderous / complic-
ities, and our sad virtue, too."

Human complicity, like other themes, images, and emphases, links
Warren firmly to a continuing tradition in American thought and art.
If in its darker manifestations it carries resonances of Hawthorne, Melville, and Henry James, its sense of psychic union and daylight health
recalls Emerson, Whitman, and William James. Most of the twentieth-
century southern writers, we are often told, share a "conservative
imagination,"[15] which I take to mean the kind of imagination that
distrusts those programs for humane social progress that take too little
account of man's intractable perversity. It recognizes and affirms the
reality of a black veil on every face, an ineluctable skepticism about
human motives, an urge toward the psychological exploitation of others
for private needs. For this sensibility original sin and total depravity are
not the soul's mumps and measles but part of the genetic composition
of man. Its literary modes are frequently the sermon, the parable, the
confession, the allegory, the melodrama, the apologue. Its area of operation is nightmare: a present infected by pollution from the past. Its
manner is often homiletic, satiric, and pedagogic. Its tone in extremis
may be that of black humor or invective. Its sin is acedia. Distinguishing marks such as these are visible aplenty in Warren's work, just as they
are in his nineteenth-century American predecessors of the conservative stamp.

But this is not the whole story. Describing Warren's works in only these terms is finally inadequate either as moral or literary criticism— just as they are reductive in our reading of those classic writers. And even if it is only a matter of convenient emphases which allow us to write literary history at all, something of an opposing imagination—the liberal?—can be seen in Warren. That is, the tradition that holds the simple, separate person as its self-sufficient goal, that respects the crushing of barriers to release man in all his fullness. It sees every man a god in ruins, it celebrates egotistic panache and elevates the will, it holds out the commendable egalitarian hope that every man's moral lot can be better than it is by an athletic assertion of love and joy. Its modes are likely to be the lecture, the lyric, the public letter, the disquisition, the tract, the pep talk, the case history. Its manner is homiletic, pedagogic, and prophetic. Its tone in extremis may be *J'accuse*. Its operating area is not nightmare but daydream: a present defined by an infinitely open future. Its sin is pride.

American literary figures do not march briskly into such neatly opposing camps despite the ordering sensibilities of those scribes who write their histories. Hawthorne goes to live at Brook Farm and looks on his few months there as the most romantic time of his life; Emerson, for all his good wishes and financial aid, refuses to live there and wickedly dubs Ripley's enterprise as "the age of reason in a patty-pan." These Concord friends are often seen as epitomizing the relative tendencies of the conservative and liberal romantic imaginations which, between them, inform the two wings of our tradition. At the core is the notion of man: his nature, his possibilities, his abilities to shape the space which for better or worse he occupies. The coiling darkness is a recurrent image in Warren's work—and takes its place in a pattern which includes the minotaur, the snake, and stagnant water; but, as I have been at pains to suggest, no single work is without the piercing alternative: the image of the green world, light, the bond. The working out of an intellectual and emotional dialectic suggested by these images is in the strongest works accomplished by a firm anchoring to dramatic situations and the circumstantiality of the actual world; but even in the weaker works, where drama is replaced by rhetoric and assertion, the final notes tend to celebrate—and the terms of the celebration are joy, surprise, and delight.

TWO

Making Peace with Mercutio
Warren the Poet

NOTE: It may be that the poet should have made early peace with Mercutio, and appealed to his better nature. For Mercutio seems to be glad to cooperate with a poet. But he must be invited; otherwise, he is apt to show a streak of merry vindictiveness about the finished product . . . and Mercutio, who is an ally of reason and who himself is given to mocking laughter, is a good friend for a poem to have.

—"Pure and Impure Poetry" (1942)

If poetry does anything for us, it reconciles, by its symbolical reading of experience (for by its very nature it is in itself a myth of the unity of being), the self-divisive internecine malices which arise at the superficial level on which we conduct most of our living.

—"A Poem of Pure Imagination" (1945–1946)

IV. Dreams and Conjurations: 1923-1953

John Crowe Ransom in 1950 remarked that the writing of "some of the choicest verse of our time" was the accomplishment for which he most honored Robert Penn Warren, the one, he added, "which I would most like to see him extending."[1] The "extending" of Warren's poetic talent was to come in that very decade with *Promises* and *You, Emperors, and Others* and the experimental verse narrative *Brother to Dragons*. While it may be an exaggeration to speak of the poetry of these years as a technical breakthrough, it is surely an "extension" of that poetry of tight compression and freighted diction characteristic of Warren for the first two decades of his career—and it is certainly an extension that is un-Ransomian.

The publishing history tells at least part of the story. As a late arrival among the Fugitives, Warren devoted his major energies and his developing craft to the making of poems. By the time of *Thirty-Six Poems* (1935), he had consolidated his early practices in idiom, syntax, voice, and prosody. A sense of coherence is apparent in *Eleven Poems on the Same Theme* (1942); and the winnowing process behind *Selected Poems: 1923–1943* (1944) suggests his own sense of achievement in his favorite genre. Then, breaking a silence of nearly a decade, *Brother to Dragons* (1953) initiates an impressive second phase, one that includes the greatest single volume of his career, *Promises: Poems 1954–1956* (1957), and *You, Emperors, and Others: Poems 1957–1960* (1960). A smaller hiatus of six years separates that second phase and the next, which is marked by a second *Selected Poems* in 1966. Since that time published volumes have appeared almost biannually, and rarely a year goes by without separate publication of poems in periodicals.

But these stages of poetic output are only partially indicative of Warren's actual practice. In his own mind, the poet sees only one break: "something happened about '45," as he puts it in one interview. Prior to that time, he says, poetry was his *"central* interest," and even when he was in the midst of writing novels "came the notion that somehow they might be poems."[2] What happened in the mid–1940s was primarily Warren's realization that the short lyrics, which had been the mainstay of his productivity since the Nashville days, were no longer adequate as the vehicle for what he wanted to say.

Two lines of force that converged on the Nashville Fugitives in the early 1920s were the revival of the seventeenth-century metaphysical poets and the more immediate, and fairly inescapable, impact of the great modernists, especially Pound and Eliot. In each case Warren had a mentor. For the first Ransom provided him the enthusiasm and the example; for the second, the more adventurous Allen Tate was the important mediator. In absorbing these distinct modes and attitudes, Warren practiced his craft, writing poetry of both kinds but steadily gaining his own voice in the imitative process; and significantly, he managed to find his distinctive voice by locating and extending for his own uses the formal and tonal possibilities of narrative.

The metaphysical recovery among the Fugitives was part of a larger revival, which included Eliot's fascination with the seventeenth-century poets who had historically been eclipsed by Milton and H. J. C. Grierson's influential edition of the poetry of Donne in 1912. All of the Fugitives were in one way or another touched by the phenomenon, but it was the oldest and the youngest—Ransom and Warren—who honored the object of this revival with the most meaningful earnest of the 1920s: imitation.

It has occasionally been observed that Warren managed better than any other of his southern contemporaries, perhaps including Ransom, to write the kind of poetry that most of them admired and wrote about. The formal precision of such poems as "Bearded Oaks" and "Love's Parable" no doubt accounts for their popularity two or so decades ago: they illustrate perfectly the well-made poem, a conscious artifact whose careful intricacies of manner wedded to portentous matter invite New Critical analysis. With its "dull astronomers," "wastrel bankrupt," "the estate of man," "beshrewed," and especially its opening stanza beginning "As kingdoms after civil broil, / Long faction-bit and sore unmanned," "Love's Parable" is perhaps as close an imitation of Donne as any non–seventeenth-century poem. And despite a basic conceit suggestive of Donne ("Twin atolls on a shelf of shade"), "Bearded Oaks" is an impeccable updating of Marvell, with its compressed quatrains, sonorousness, gracefully phrased logic, slight syntactical inversions, and delicate adjustment of vowels to suggest an emotion consonant with the situation:

> So, waiting, we in the grass now lie
> Beneath the languorous head of light:
> The grasses, kelp-like, satisfy
> The nameless motions of the air   (SP, 308)

From Ransom, Warren learned very early not only the technical resources of strict forms but also the exciting modulations possible in poetic conventions, especially in forms in which dramatic situation takes precedence over purely lyrical evocation. From Tate, Warren observed how the dissociated modern sensibility, exploited so forcefully by Eliot and Pound, could be accommodated to the southern temperament, already known to an exasperated nation for its ragged paradoxes, its touchy sense of "difference," and its aesthetic responses to the fragmentation of ideals. The impact of both these poetic traditions, the seventeenth century and the early twentieth, has yet to be appreciated fully in the work of the Fugitives, especially in that occasional poem which curiously and simultaneously forces the spirit of each into a single structure, thereby informing themes not noticeably amenable to either mode.[3]

But the moment of intense imitation was short-lived in the careers of Tate, Warren, and Donald Davidson. Their metaphysical mode, as exercised by Warren especially, caught much of the original wit, languor, and precision but little of its swift vitality—and one is tempted to say that in *The Fugitive* there are already too many subterranean ledges and emblematic gardens. Except perhaps for Ransom, this most direct appropriation of the metaphysical mode was clearly a beginning, not an end for the Nashville group. For Tate, Eliot's example, with a poetry juxtaposing intellection and naturalistic observation, was paramount. For Ransom, the cultivation of ironic whimsy within a framework of archaic diction and mock-genteel values became a distinctive signature, even in the later years of patient and devastating revision. Davidson's metaphysical efforts were always exercises, which gave way to Georgian imitations. In a curious way, perhaps because he was younger than most of his fellow Fugitives, Warren's increasing mastery involved something of all these other tendencies. The son's body in "Letter of a Mother" is described as

> a subtile engine, propped
> In the sutured head beneath the coronal seam,

> Whose illegal prodigality of dream
> In shaking the escheat heart is quick estopped.[4]

The mannered archaisms in the early poems are gradually supplanted by explicit, sometimes colloquial, articulations of a sensibility schooled in modernist attitudes. The Eliotic penchant for sudden shifts in registers is a congenial, if not always successful, device for the learning Warren. In "The Return: An Elegy," the learned terms (*antique concitation, gracious catafalque, matinal exhalation*) jostle self-consciously with realistically observed details of nature, especially in the first half of the poem; the latter half breaks through the smart juxtapositions into an associative train of things seen and events remembered, all comfortably distinctive. "What grief has the mind distilled?" may sound like a prosy Eliot, but most of the derivative lines at the end of the poem manage to struggle into an individual idiom:

> the old fox is dead
> what is said is said
> heaven rest the hoary head
> what have I said!
> . . . I have only said what the wind said
> honor thy father and mother in the days of thy youth
> for time uncoils like the cottonmouth . . . .   (SP, 318)

"The Return" is a poem of fits and starts, whose fine moments are too often overshadowed by posturings. The brilliant passage,

> turn backward turn backward O time in your flight
> and make me a child again just for tonight
> good lord he's wet the bed come bring a light . . .   (SP, 318)

is an affective conjunction of sentimental song and childhood trauma in a mature mind resisting both sentimentality and dependency, but it is also contextually obtrusive in its strengths and aggressively flashy in its effects.

The example of Eliot and Pound was important for Warren because both poets, though they also began as inheritors and imitators, developed a strong sense of the necessary voice that could be heard above the derivative. While *The Waste Land* and *Hugh Selwyn Mauberley* may lack a single, indisputable, coherent voice, their creators demonstrated the potential for unity within the dispersal technique of doing the police in different voices. These great exemplars, however, could finally offer Warren little in the refining of the most important aspect of his talent: the building up or building from situational cores primarily narrative. The exploitation of juxtaposed voices in Warren eventuates in a poem like "Pondy Woods": "Nigger, regard the circumstance of breath: / *Non omnis moriar*, the poet saith" (SP, 323). But the characteristic fact of the poem is its adumbrated narrative: a Negro waits in hiding for the inevitable posse coming with shotguns and no charity because of his "Saturday spree at the Blue Goose Saloon." Arguably, even that most characteristic of Warren's early poems, "Bearded Oaks," is not solely lyric; its peculiar force, like that of similar poems in the metaphysical mode ("Picnic Remembered," "Love's Parable," "Monologue at Midnight," "The Garden") derives from the felt urgencies of narrative situations, situations condensed to scenes in which meditation replaces action. By its very nature, the purely meditative lyric is too static to admit the exercise of a temperament such as Warren's, given as it is to the interplay of excess, the dramatic clash of opposites conceived and drawn in large outline.

Because of this tendency Warren's metaphysical poems, for all their technical proficiency, their near-perfect manipulation of sense and wit, are less accurate intimations of the best work than such early poems as "Kentucky Mountain Farm" and "Mexico Is a Foreign Country." Both are sequences, a form which becomes more and more important to Warren in part because they are hospitable to the diverse explorations of narrative. Even "Eidolon" and "Revelation" are finally more interesting poems than "Bearded Oaks" and "The Garden" because both are generated by childhood incidents—conceived as emotionally and intellectually significant moments in things that happened. For a young boy lying awake listening to the baying of the hounds, an ordinary Kentucky hunt assumes unordinary portentousness through linguistic extremes: "plunging, the rangers / Of dark remotelier belled their unhoused angers." A boy's harsh words to his mother engender consequences announced and trumpeted by domestic flowers and wild animals, a domestic act that finds its extravagant historical parallels in Augustine's Rome and Duncan's Scotland—"splendid antipodal agitation." Although in idiom and diction both poems betray their links to Warren's metaphysical manner, both significantly reach out from it, essaying another mode which exploits the textures of local effects and materials.

Along with "The Ballad of Billie Potts," the finest example of Warren's skill in transcending the purely imitative, either metaphysical or modernist, is "Original Sin: A Short Story." What these very different poems importantly share is the felt need to join the conventionally lyric impulse with story: the impersonal voice, caged in ceremonial irony, playing against the strikingly private voice that threatens to break apart the restrained order and tact. The relaxed, imperfect pentameter lines of "Original Sin" project an idiom that curiously blends the sophisticated and the homely. Although that blend was to become in succeeding poems almost a stylistic tic, this early poem retains the disciplined metaphorical progression and thematic elaboration of Warren's metaphysical lyrics while loosening them with the flexibility of the spoken voice; the internal debate of a divided self is rendered by rhetorical contrasts: "Never met you in the lyric arsenical meadows" alongside "You thought you had lost it when you left Omaha. . . ." Moreover, this poem is the first to give explicit voice to a theme which is to recur often: "Oh, nothing is lost, ever lost! at last you understood."

What the speaker of this poem understands is what similar speakers in other poems come to understand: the unitary nature of nature. The conviction coming so late and with such destructiveness to Jack Burden —that the world is all of a piece—centrally involves man's view of himself, which includes a secret as well as a conscious self; and the possibility for spiritual health lies squarely in recognizing and coming to terms with the dark, nightmare self which the consciousness would prefer to ignore. In "Original Sin" Warren gives psychological validity to that abstract necessity, drawn from a full array of philosophical positions and theological doctrines, by commonplace images which accrete rather than develop. Gone is the rhythmical or metrical tightness of his metaphysical poems, but this poem is similarly structured (the proposition in a series of five-line stanzas economically bound by only two end rhymes each). Its local texture, what Ransom once called the "tissue of irrelevancy," is compounded of unlikely images which threaten the logical self-sufficiency of its argument. That is, the abstract solemnity of the poem's statement is domesticated and made concrete by such familiar images as an old hound, a hobo, a childlike relative, a mother, an old horse; and the irresistible force of the secret self is suggested not by verbs of power but by humbler ones—*stumbles, whimpers, scarcely mewed, wander*—and by static sentences—*it stood so imbecile, With empty hands, it stood with lips askew.* Insofar as Ransom's theory of texture means the competing detail that unpredictably complicates the logic of intention, "Original Sin" is a good poem made to Ransom's order. But it is the most signal example among the early poems that points to the possibility of development and continued risk-taking in Warren's mature work.

Generally, Warren's poetic instinct in his first two volumes is quick, precise, and modish. The poems show a craftsman completely content to be swayed by others' examples, the traditions and conventions most admired by those poets he admired; but they also show a craftsman who, in the midst of his Ransom and Eliot, Dickinson, Shakespeare, and Donne, is slowly learning how to reinvigorate models out of his own needs and with his own voice. Technical competence is evident in such indifferently realized poems as "Eidolon" and such self-consciously cryptic ones as "Ransom." The latter is comprised of four five-line stanzas that conspicuously fail to advance; a kind of verbal "running in place" underscores the substantive point of the poem through blunt reiteration in its *abcbc* rhyme scheme (e.g., *air-air, unlaced, laced*) and sight rhymes (*will-wool, spilled-spelled*). In the similarly made "Eidolon" only the last two lines in each stanza rhyme, a functional device which gives Warren the enormous flexibility of blank verse as well as the satisfying aural resolution of an orthodox couplet. But Warren's achievement in these early volumes is not in their technical effects per se but, rather, in the way these effects, even those most obviously derivative, enrich and promote the poet's slowly building themes. The training of the eye, jaundiced by a naturalistic universe, to see further and more deeply into nature and man is the most dominant accomplishment; but that training is followed by other important insights: the agony of the mind to make sense of history in the satisfactory definition of the present; the struggle of the heart to find joy, the self-transcending gift which earns man his right to participate in "the One Life."

Warren's sources in mood, subject, and diction, in other words, become more comfortably adjusted to an emerging distinctive voice. Tetrameter and pentameter lines, often turgid syntax, diction that cheerfully combines the archaic and the naturalistically colloquial, situations involving esoteric perspectives: all are preserved from the earlier experiments, tinkered with, and refined into poems like "Revelation," "Kentucky Mountain Farm," "Crime," and "Monologue at Midnight." In "History," Warren brilliantly manipulates the short line and irregular end rhymes into an expression of purposiveness even in a present world sadly bereft of the vitality of its past. The materialistic rewards of the American Dream no longer satisfy; though the garden of the new world is now despoiled, man's hope for his fulfillment lies in a struggle more metaphysical than that sought by the grandsires, the responsibility to seek meaning in one's own complex nature rather than in the "languor" of the too-easily received myth:

> We are the blade,
> But not the hand

By which the blade is swayed.
Time falls, but has no end.
Descend! (SP, 296)

This poem is a considerable advancement in both technique and substance over "Genealogy," a more personal, earlier poem whose spirit
of nihilism is almost a curse on the grandfather who bore the father and
therefore, in turn, the self. The despair of simply being born is unduly
strident in "Genealogy"; the dominant note in "History" is humility.
Though the heroic vigor of the pioneer ancestors who brave the mountain passes to possess the "delicate landscape," the "fruited earth" of
material ease, is not available to depleted descendants, the speaker still
takes strength from the recollected image of the fathers in his resolution
to search for meaning in the brief years of his own span.

Although the decision in "History" to "essay / The rugged ritual"
cannot be called optimistic, it does suggest that an internal landscape is
the more difficult to possess. The artful evasions documented in "Ransom" and "Love's Subterfuge" are pointedly inadequate even as they
are being formulated. Stoicism and sexual passion may temporarily ease
the pain of public butcheries and private treacheries, but they cannot
kill the shadow self who constantly yearns for reintegration with the
conscious self. "Terror" is a corruscating attack on a society liberated
from the burdens of individual evil. The public enemies visited upon
the world cannot finally be freed from the "you" who, "guiltless, sink
/ To rest in lobbies . . . ." Unlike most of the public poems which
W. H. Auden and Stephen Spender produced so prodigiously as the
world lurched into World War II, this poem emphasizes the fact that
objectifying evil in public figures such as Franco or Hitler is too simple;
there are always the "passionate emptiness and tidal / Lusts" that allow
some who fought alongside each other in Spain to fight against each
other a short time later in Finland, "for their obsession knows / Only
the immaculate itch, not human friends or foes." The final engagement
must be on an internal battlefield. Only that realization can bring forth
an "adequate definition of terror." The speaker's friend, Harry L., is
cited as a case in which inner compulsions find enactment in public
ceremonies of violence: qualities which otherwise would be sad and
cheap become "heroics" supported by armament and mechanical con-
traptions. "Terror" is a kind of communal elegy for personal tragedies
accentuated or perverted by war, and its seven tightly controlled, rhymed
stanzas march severely to stately iambic pentameter lines; the diction
is grave but unflamboyant; the allusions call up situations from Shake-

speare and the Bible. The splendor and corruption of princes are up-dated grimly and ironically by modern princes whose madness is im-measurably aided by science: the bomb-sight, the airplane, the radio, and the more sinister exploits of Alexis Carrel—not as discoverer of a meth-od for suturing blood vessels (a modest contribution to the preserving of life) but as experimenter who attempted to keep a chicken heart alive indefinitely "in a test tube, where it monstrously grew, and slept" (a misguided promise of physical immortality). The frailties, distortions, and "passionate emptiness" of men are exacerbated rather than solved by war. "Solution, perhaps, is public," Warren comments in a related poem, "despair personal."

It is not surprising that Warren wrote so few poems using the sub-ject of war in our time; its very nature—noisy, insistent—distracts from the human point that it would invariably serve to illustrate in his kind of poetry. Even in *Eleven Poems* it is clear that both radical "solution" and radical "despair" must be stripped of obvious, institutionalized significance patently cherished by a society behaving as if evil were merely social. Just as a secret self lurks in surprising places to beseech recognition—clutching a favorite childhood toy, snuffling at the door—so its reunion with the conscious self may occur at domestically im-probable times—in a doctor's office, in a hawk's path, in the grief of a mad killer. With "The Ballad of Billie Potts," the domestication of the public event and the ceremonializing of the private come together as a seal, both confirming Warren's early practice in writing a distinctive poetry and announcing the directions which that poetry would take in its several developments.

The primary texture of Warren's early verse is highly cerebral, with an idiom of clotted intensities, dignity, and portentousness; but there are also instances of a tentative loosening, a countering of verbal density by an "unpoetic" idiom dropped, sometimes casually, to jar the con-sistency of this primary texture.[5] The spokesman for the buzzards in "Pondy Woods," for example, begins his hectoring of the black mur-derer in the colloquial ruralisms of a southern sheriff before he lapses into the improbable locutions of a Vanderbilt pedant. Apropos *The Rime of the Ancient Mariner*, Warren reminds us that there is "no reason to assume that a minor poetic form, in this case the ballad, would not be found worthy of serious development and serious freight-ing" (SE, 285). "The Ballad of Billie Potts" becomes a benchmark in Warren's poetic development: his first extended use of both of folk idiom and a "minor poetic form" for the purpose of serious art.

Although critics continue to be divided on the matter of its success,

"Billie Potts" undoubtedly is Warren's first significant effort to join
high and low styles in a single important poem. Perhaps *join* is not
quite accurate, since a clear contrast between the two styles is self-
consciously asserted:

> Big Billie was sharp at swap and trade
> And could smell the nest where the egg was laid.
> He could read and cipher and they called him squire,
> And he added up his money while he sat by the fire . . .

(SP, 272–73)

as against

> At dawn riding into the curtain of unwhispering green,
> Away from the vigils and voices into the green
> World, land of the innocent bough, land of the leaf.
> Think of your face green in the submarine light of the leaf.

(SP, 274)

In order to avoid a philosophical commentary that is only a pretentious
intrusion upon the simplicities of the narrative, Warren incorporates his
variant of Coleridge's prose gloss into his ballad as a major structural
element. Of the 472 lines of the poem, just slightly fewer than half are
authorial asides in Warren's densely wrought and morally charged manner of the mid-1930s.[6] The two styles are separated and juxtaposed
rather than merged, and the decisiveness of that contrast is reinforced
by the parentheses enclosing the segments of the high style. If there is
no verbal meshing of the two levels, however, their effects on each other
and on the reading experience of the whole poem are rhetorically complex. The effect of the high style is not simply to generalize from a
specific historical-legendary story but to turn that generalization back into application that is immediate and even more intimately specific than
the narrative itself: these segments are really asides to "you." (That ambiguous second-person pronoun, directed to the poet himself, to the
individual reader, and to the corporate reader, will in the years after
"Billie Potts" become a virtual signature of Warren's poetry.) Paradoxically, the narrative, though relatively bare, is so stripped, so economical, that its effects are more baldly archetypal than most regional
stories tend to be—and the archetypal motifs tend to transform the
poem into generalization quite as decisively as the counterpointed commentary.

Although the idiom of one style clashes visibly and aurally with the
other, the psychological resonance is similar in both. The ballad sug-

WARREN THE POET   59

gests cautionary tales equating fate and character or showing evil as its own reward in illustrative incidents with revealing local turns: disguise which dooms rather than protects, the plea of "father, stay thy hand" which is unuttered or uttered too late, the victimizer victimized, the birthmark confirming origin and identity and therefore patrimony. The authorial parentheses tend to knit up those motifs into a single patterned referent: modern man ("you"), liberated from the trammels of fate and freed to realize his character out of Time's auspices, may be saved from his delusion of unanchored liberty by his "dream," the unwilled re-enactment of the Billie Potts story.

Warren's apprentice verse (that which we know) and the poetry through his first *Selected Poems* are weakest precisely in proportion to their diminished narrative situations. Even when the result is muddled by clashing details and diverse styles, Warren is most distinctively his own poet in such poems as "The Return," "Pondy Woods," the Kentucky Mountain Farm sequence, and "Billie Potts." These are poems that adequately attest to the rich resources of the land and circumstances of the poet's childhood; more important, they provide narrative occasions for experimentation with irregular measures and idiomatic dialogue, and their deceptively open forms exert a subtle loose-reined control. The flowering of Warren's gifts in the 1950s can be seen in such early poems as these. This is not to say that Warren has no purely lyric gift; it is to say that he is most comfortable and most engaging when the lyric impulse is pegged to precisely imagined narrative situations.

The composition of *Brother to Dragons* was crucial. In retrospect it becomes a bridge from the early settled lyric to the kind of exploratory lyric characteristic of Warren's mature poems. Common to both kinds of lyricism is the persistent impulse to tell a story. The penchant for enveloping "pure" lyric outbursts in situational contexts is a dominant mark of Warren's poetry, the element of continuity from *Selected Poems* (1944) to *Selected Poems* (1976) that unites the volatile differences between, say, "Love's Parable" and "Chain Saw at Dawn in Vermont in Time of Drouth."

Within a short time in the 1940s, when he was "soaking" himself in early Kentuckiana—"subhistorical materials, like letters and journals and things like that"—Warren discovered the generative stories that would eventually result in two major works: *World Enough and Time* and *Brother to Dragons*.[7] The facts in the case of Jereboam O.

Beauchamp became the novel; those in the case of Jefferson's nephews, the Lewis brothers of Livingston County, became the "Tale in Verse and Voices." In their varied ways these books preserve the feel of the world reflected in these historical documents, especially the moral impact of the wilderness upon the more sophisticated émigré or settler of quality. Both transform an inherent penchant for melodrama into ethical dilemmas placed firmly in social, religious, and political contexts; and though both build upon vivid vignettes of frontier life, they betray nothing of the suffocating historiography represented by Bolton Lovehart's local color efforts in "The Circus in the Attic." Indeed, for all their particularity, the Beauchamp and Lewis stories seemed to invite Warren's extrapolation of them as microcosmic instances of not merely the national character but the very nature of man.

Despite the violence of the central episode in *Brother to Dragons*— the dismemberment of a slave—Warren's real interest has little relation to Senecan excesses.[8] The fact that such a startling act apparently passed unrecorded in Jefferson's papers reinforced what Warren saw as the philosophical and moral implications of the story. Of far greater concern to Warren than the melodrama of the historical story was the aesthetic problem of finding a form appropriate to its meaning. As Warren has remarked, meaning does not always come simultaneously with a form: "I've started many things in one form," he says, "and shifted to another—quite often, in fact" (*Talking*, 258). The first step of the "fumbling" process was taken when he cast the Lewis materials as a novel. He found, however, that the very circumstantiality of the case tended to "kill off the main line" of the evolving narrative. When Warren next tried to use the materials as a play, he found that "the machinery got too much in the way." Although he finally gave up the notion of casting it as a stage play, he preserved its central dramatic image, the collision of diverse sensibilities "under the unresolved urgency of their earthly experience." Seeing it as a "rehearsal" of unresolved lives, including that of the writer's, he put "the writer character in so he could participate in this process, the notion being that we are all unresolved in a way, the dead and the living."[9]

With *Brother to Dragons*, Warren for the first time exploits the faint dissatisfaction with conventional genres and techniques that lies behind his device of the two voices in "Billie Potts" and the Ashby Wyndham "Statement" in *At Heaven's Gate* by scrapping generic restraints and by transcending customary authorial controls and self-imposed limits. A kind of verbal cantata, this narrative-poem-drama boldly establishes its authority through the use of "the writer character," a device that lends emotional immediacy to a stark but time-encrusted event. To emphasize Warren's concern with the mystery of the secret self, its laborious definition, and the cost necessary for its acknowledgment by the conscious self, the tale focuses upon the brutal ax murder of a slave by Thomas Jefferson's nephew and the devastating spiritual effect of that episode on Jefferson. In form it is a kind of seance conducted by an ordering consciousness who calls up an array of historical and quasi-historical spirits to discuss "the nature of the human heart."

Aesthetically the use of "the writer character" was as generative a discovery as that of the original Lewis materials. "R.P.W." provided an orienting point around which the central participants could be arranged in their ghostly drama, but it also allowed Warren the freedom to reenact a more circumstantial drama in the frame—the two automobile trips with his father that became both a literal and a metaphysical journey. The use of himself, both as a persona and as a fully developed character, is one aspect of *Brother to Dragons* that justifies the frequent observation that it marks a watershed in Warren's career, that it is the enabling work that allowed the later poetry to develop in a more open and confessional manner.[10] R.P.W. is more than a raw self-portrait, however, and Warren's discovery of what he could do with this figure opens the way to an aesthetic resolution before it shows him the way to personal acts of reclamation and recovery. In this sense R.P.W. parallels precisely Warren's happy discovery of Jack Burden as a functional part of the Willie Stark story.

As the medium who calls up these spirits, R.P.W. is no disinterested conjurer. The spirits once called up, through his dialectical parryings he attempts to guide them into his own control. Like the authorial glosser who closes the story of Jeremiah Beaumont, he is aggressively modern, a man too schooled in the naturalistic to be put off by visions of man's glory, a man too familiar with "progress" in twentieth-century Kentucky to sentimentalize its civic failures of another era:

> Smithland had nothing, canebrake and gray clay,
> And hoot owls aren't a poultry highly prized,
> And even now no locomotive scares those owls.
> A hundred years behind schedule right now.... (BD, 17)

But like most of Warren's cynics, R.P.W. is subject to nostalgia, the emotional pull of heroic defeat, and an image of frontier life that is simultaneously vital and unmanning. With his mixture of flippancy and concern, literal-mindedness and compassion, R.P.W. is an activist Jack Burden who by taunts and concessions manages to transform Jefferson into a Jeremiah Beaumont. Devil's advocate, *agent provocateur*, modern ironist, he strives mightily for reconciliation between Lilburn and Jefferson because part of his purpose is his own self-definition, which means the acceptance of the Lilburn in his own heart.

The willingness to become self-involved in the issues of his work—to give R.P.W. a redemption parallel to Jefferson's—makes a difference in the form as well as in the theme of the work. As a character capable of being manipulated like Jefferson, Laetita, Lilburn, or Lucy, Warren's R.P.W. is a powerful and direct means for italicizing the unending struggle to understand the self and the place of that self in the world: "we are all unresolved in a way."

The long gestation and the formal experimentation are typically Warrenesque. If the novel and the play seemed wrong as vehicles for the Lewis materials, the poem was hardly more promising. But, remembering his method in "Billie Potts," Warren tried casting his story as a literary ballad—a few lines from which show up in the completed work. Even this tack seemed wrong. As R.P.W. says,

> The form
> Was not adequate: the facile imitation
> Of a folk simplicity is only
> That the action is always and perfectly self-contained . . . .

What Warren seems to have forgotten, of course, is that even with "Billie Potts" he was not content with the folk simplicity of a ballad, that its action was *not* self-contained, but required a gloss in sophisticated counterpoint verse. But had R.P.W. listened to the anti-aesthetic Jefferson ("There is no form to hold / Reality and its insufferable intransigence"), *Brother to Dragons* would never have been written at all.[11]

In its liberal use of homely idioms the work still carries overtones of the ballad as Warren uses it. More important, however, its philosophical passages, hedged about by qualifications, expansions, second thoughts, and paradoxes, resemble both the "poetry of statement," which Warren has found congenial, and the "meditation," which appears in the novels as rhetorical set pieces and as the form itself in *The Legacy of the Civil War. Brother to Dragons* takes its place at the very head of book-length narratives, a form not much admired today but one that a generation ago exerted a certain influence on poets of various temperaments, including E. A. Robinson and Robert Frost. Even the brief rage for "concert readings" of already established works—

Don Juan in Hell (from Shaw's *Man and Superman*) and Stephen Vincent Benét's *John Brown's Body*—may have suggested to Warren a freedom and flexibility not possible in realistic dramaturgy: the concatenation of speaking voices richly diverse in tone and substance, a setting which readily transcends its specificity, a time which is not bound by a continuum but which simultaneously permits past and present to intersect, and an issue crucial enough to justify the heated exchange of views in a colloquium.[12]

An accurate description of *Brother to Dragons* is that which the poet himself used to describe "Billie Potts"—a "bridge piece," a "jumping-off place"—when he began writing poems after a ten-year silence (*Talking*, 230). The term *bridge piece* suggests not only access from one point to another but also a solidification and accrual of attitudes, images, modes, and aesthetic devices—continuities as well as transitions. If it points the way that the future work would take, *Brother to Dragons* is also a formal and thematic culmination. Recurrent figures show up in sometimes exacerbated ways: the man faced with his own inexplicable nature; the betrayer and the betrayed fulfilling the mysterious compulsions for completeness in each other; the cynical observer-narrator whose own urgencies for order and meaning erupt within and parallel to those of others. The strong narrative core and the naturalistic bias are also important carryovers from earlier work. And like many of the early poems, *Brother to Dragons* insists upon the fact that commitment to truth and a concern for one's own psychic health alike require a humbling acknowledgment of personal evil. Unlike the dour conclusion of "Billie Potts," however, *Brother to Dragons* ends on a note of reconciliation with that common evil, and if it is not a triumphant affirmation, Warren at least gives significant play to potential resolution. The note of joy at the end anticipates the frequent use of personal details in the later poetry in which the unmasked "I" is hardly even a persona.

Whatever its generically impure origins, this "Tale in Verse and Voices" is a triumph of form. The skill with which Warren incorporated the varied impulses and urgencies of his own poetic practice and a melange of competing modes into a structure without clear antecedent models attests to the poet's resourceful balancing of the original and the traditional. The gravity of the subject is announced by invocations and apostrophes and rendered in basic unrhymed iambic pentameter, a pattern that is nevertheless lightened by frequent metrical irregularities characteristic of his poetry from the time Warren first read

Dante in 1938. The rhetorical possibilities of another Dantesque device —the occasional stylistic shifts from elevated to colloquial—strengthened Warren in a tendency that he had already exhibited. The personalities of Aunt Cat, Lucy, Jefferson, and Laetitia are intricately differentiated. Especially persuasive are the speeches of Lucy, whose love, though flawed, redeems her as well as her overly intellectual brother; and Laetitia, whose destructive innocence works as a weapon against both herself and her husband. A good bit of social history is crammed into a few speeches of Laetitia's brother, a commonplace frontier blusterer whose concern for the honor of his family name is almost as important as his image at the local tavern; and in Charles Lewis' haunting pursuit of his "reality" in Kentucky, where he finds only the *landscape of shadow and the shore of night.*" Warren assigns only a single speech to Lilburn (broken by exclamations from Jefferson and Lucy), for though he seems to be the central focus of the action, he functions largely as the troubled emblematic ghost of pre-Elizabethan plays— to set the seal as vivid token of a horrendous deed.

Thematically, *Brother to Dragons* posits the same urgent dilemmas and difficult resolutions that recur so frequently in previous work. For all their differences, Warren's very first "protagonist"—mad John Brown—is ineradicably linked to benevolent Thomas Jefferson through a stubborn belief in personal righteousness. Jefferson is not mad and can therefore draw back from ideological pitfalls; but like John Brown (and Perse Munn, Slim Sarrett, Adam Stanton, and Jeremiah Beaumont), Jefferson is a Man of Idea. If Warren gives his Jefferson the pride to err massively, he also gives him the sensitivity and intellect which allow him to confess to those errors and to adopt a more chastened notion of men. Like many another Warren protagonist, Jefferson must earn his difficult wisdom.

It is finally Lucy, mother of the murderer, who makes the most impressive gestures toward reclamation of the heart. It is she, of all the figures in this ghostly drama, who insists that "the human curse is simply to love and sometimes to love well, / But never well enough." R.P.W. admits, "I know your name means light," then promptly forgets it for his more appetitive thrusts with Jefferson. If Lucy's love is not the answer that satisfies her brother or R.P.W., it nevertheless serves as the necessary basis for compassion. The mother's early speeches revolve around the nature of failure. Lucy regrets not having provided a sufficiency of love in the lonely house on the frontier, a flaw that permits Aunt Cat to share the mother's love for Lilburn. Finally, unable to bind George's wounds when the slave has been mistreated by her son, Lucy recognizes her division of sympathies and blames herself for dying. It is a betrayal of George, Lilburn, herself, and "all the world's sweet need." Her death is an "instant of verification" that even love is "infected with failure" and that her own "dark fear of the dark, and the dark land" is but a version of "the darkness growing in the heart."

Such a verification is corroborated when Meriwether Lewis appears and charges his great kinsman with complicity in the "great lie that men are capable / Of the brotherhood of justice." His very presence is a rebuke to Jefferson, the mentor who in Warren's scheme represents the philosophical failure of the Enlightenment, with its assiduous cultivation of those dominant visionary impulses of the late eighteenth century. For Meriwether, weakness invites disillusion. Being "unbuckled and unbraced," he is not fitted to face the evil of men as he has been fitted to face the chaos of nature. In reinforcing the spiritual implications of Lilburn's crime, the accusatory Meriwether serves as the poet's agent not for transforming values (Warren is not suggesting the cultivation of counterutopian or destructive impulses) but for reminding us that single-minded visions of either good or evil are denials of the human which make man vulnerable to the forces always submerged below the consciousness. "The sweet reasonableness of the Enlightenment," says Kenneth Keniston, "is the backdrop for De Sade's most demonic of all envisioned republics. When the devil is denied, he manifests himself nonetheless—in some ways the more because his existence is no longer recognized and thus cannot be combatted."[13]

Meriwether's death, one caused by the "vanity of virtue," is finally charged to Jefferson, who has too eagerly preached the easy, the untried, the overly hopeful message. The Jeffersonian error, then, is not only a parallel to Lilburn's gruesome crime; it is also a farther-reaching, more chilling, more credal error. Lilburn's crime issues from the vague impulses of an undefined self; his uncle's from ideological vanity, the satisfaction that a self has already been defined—from and by the light of reason. But even when Jefferson can admit that he has been "unprepared for the nature of the world, / And unprepared . . . for my own nature," he is not yet prepared to countermand his harsh rejection of the "sentimental butcher." The philosopher-statesman who has declared that man must "cling more sternly to the rational hope" lapses into a myopic, sarcastic emotionalism as he berates his sister for "female fondness."

His total rejection of Lilburn brings Lucy to a level of perception which R.P.W., even at his most sincere, cannot reach until the very end of the poem:

> in your rejection you repeat the crime.
> Over and over, and more monstrous still,
> For what poor Lilburn did in exaltation of madness
> You do in vanity—yes, Meriwether is right.   (BD, 189)

Warren ratifies the intractable link between the Man of the Enlightenment and the Child of Darkness by having the wood of the tulip tree, for Jefferson the symbol of innocence, promise, and redemption, serve as the chopping block on which Lilburn murders the slave. Lucy charges Jefferson with fearing that what he had always denied was indeed possible: "And as George was to Lilburn, so Lilburn is to you . . . ." It is Lucy who prescribes the necessary handshake:

> For whatever hope we have is not by repudiation,
> And whatever health we have is not by denial,
> But in confronting the terror of our condition.   (BD, 192)

What is left—that recognition—is all "that's worth the having." Her argument is simple: man must strive and achieve not in defiance but within the terms of the human condition. A dream will be more noble if it encompasses the Lilburns of the world because it will be "more difficult and cold / In the face of the old cost of the human redemption."

Lucy's light, the understanding of the heart, is not the same as her brother's. Reason, that bright shaft of daylight that Jefferson reveres, is not the agent for banishing man's seemingly irrational terror; rather, the fear of his own darkness must be met by a descent into that darkness. Thus, Jefferson's acknowledgment of his own darkness echoes the lament of Job (from which Warren derives his title) that after an "upright and perfect" life he has been forced to recognize his common creaturehood as "brother to dragons and companion to owls" (Job 30: 29). As I noted earlier, those reminders are reinforced throughout Warren's poem by recurring beast imagery, and though it is associated with the monstrous inner self lying at the core of every man, its varied manifestations, as Victor Strandberg has observed, depend upon each speaker's perspective. Whether as minotaur or simply "that Thing," it rises on occasion like the snake before R.P.W., "taller / Than any man," clamoring for recognition.

And if Job's lament lies behind Jefferson's humbled position, Lucretius' admonition that the terrors of darkness must be banished not by sunlight but by "the aspect and law of nature" lies behind R.P.W.'s rehabilitation. In the segment from *De Rerum Natura* that Warren uses as an epigraph, Lucretius reminds us that the promptings of nature must be read not as superstitious premonitions but as images consonant with human nature. The catfish and the snake and Meriwether's "great bear": these natural denizens, R.P.W. makes clear, must not be freighted with emblematic meaning beyond the human need for investing them with meaning. Although his apostrophizing of the Ohio River is done in the spirit of the Ancient Mariner, R.P.W. refuses to make of it more than it is:

> But even as I experienced this mood,
> I knew that though the great river might be
> Image, it could not be confirmation,
> For even the grandeur of Nature may not be
> Our confirmation. It is Image only. (BD, 210–11)

That is, nature is true to her neutral surface, reflecting perhaps but never commanding human states of mind; and the fact that water, stone, balsam, and owl can only be "mirror" to the heart's illumination is for R.P.W. a lesson both moral and aesthetic. Because of his favored place in the hierarchy of creation, man the maker must constantly guard against presumption in helping to shape nature for his own uses.

Acknowledging the primacy of the heart's "central illumination," however, is possible for R.P.W., as it is for Jefferson, only because of Lucy Lewis. For all her maternal weakness and her own sense of failure, Lucy is able to see Lilburn and others more clearly than her brother and more compassionately than R.P.W. If both Jefferson and the narrator end their colloquy by acknowledging a communal stain, it is largely because of Lucy's achievement in casting the understanding light that her name signifies. For R.P.W. the lesson is clear. The drama he causes to be reenacted is as much an imaginative re-creation of possible history as is Quentin and Shreve's reconstruction of the Sutpen story in *Absalom, Absalom!*, and it reminds both us and R.P.W. that the resuscitation of ghosts is not for the ghosts' benefits but for those who preside over their calling up.

Brother to Dragons owes its distinctive power to Warren's commitment to poetry as, in his own phrase, a "*central* interest," to his compulsion toward storytelling as a good in itself as well as a kind of communal rite for uniting disparate sensibilities, and to his fascination for dialectic, for the working out of moral issues in terms of dramatized personalities or types. Once this major poem was completed—it required nearly six years—Warren was reinvigorated with "a whole new sense of poetry," as if *Brother to Dragons* showed him a way of completing again the shorter poems that had eluded him so long. "The narrative sense," he reports, "began to enter" the lyric poems "as a germ" in the verse that was to become *Promises.* The entire enterprise, he declares, provided a "new sense of *release*" by which he "felt freer" than he had ever felt before.[14]

V. Visions and Speculations: 1957-1980

"We are condemned to some hope," Jefferson says, and both the verb and the restricted object are grammatical clues to the substance of Warren's later poetry, which urgently address the matter of "how shall a man live?" If "the world is real," then the clear-eyed facing of it is a primary though sometimes reluctant necessity. The early verse documents the struggle of the various speakers to meet that necessity. Many of them readily assent to the seeming meaninglessness of the world, its governance, and man's experience in it; but few are able to progress much beyond the qualified admission that meaning is possible and that moments of joy, irrational though they may be, are to be richly cherished. In certain of the early poems ("Terror," "Crime," "Pursuit," "Ransom") the reluctance to face the self, even to admit the self as part of the world that is "real," shows up in techniques of evasion: immersion in bouts of travel, admiration of technology, or single-minded lust for sex or violence. In the later poems, however, the speculation and admission are transformed into the more urgent need:

> To know what postulate of joy men have tried
> To live by, in sunlight and moonlight, until they died.   (SP, 161)

The shift in emphasis does not mean a final breakthrough in wisdom. In a centrally important poem from *Promises* stratagems are still compensatory maneuvers:

> Some will take up religion, some discover the virtue of money.
> Some will find liberal causes the mask for psychic disturbance.
> Some will expiate ego with excessive kindness to servants,
> And some make a cult of honor, though having quite little, if any.
> (SP, 249)

What the shift indicates is a determination to minimize the need for such stratagems, a realization that being doomed to despair according to a purely naturalistic logic ignores a corollary, man's continued and stubborn state of being "condemned to some hope."

In much of *Promises* and in some of the following volumes the new
note is human exuberance, though the outbursts of "joy," "heart-joy,"
"delight," or "beauty" are still often qualified; but even with qualifica-
tion, we note fewer occasions in which the earlier self-pitying lapses into naturalistic bitterness. Learning to accept imperfection is the difficult
task for the later speakers, just as it was for Jefferson and R.P.W.,
imperfection bodied forth in a harsh world of departed glory, defective children, and angelic children who seem not to notice the flaws
in man and nature.

In "The Flower" the child accepts a tattered blossom in a "thinned
out" time of year with the same enthusiasm with which she accepted
the perfect flower at the height of the growing season a few months
earlier, singing "as though human need / Were not for perfection."
Similarly, the angelic sister of "The Child Next Door" smiles as if her
defective sibling is a part of her "benediction." The one-year-old child
and the angelic sister alike are both immature observers of man and
nature and are therefore something less than "human"; but, with a
kind of astonished humility characteristic of *Promises*, the intellectual
and mature narrator finds lessons, however puzzling, to be applied to
his own search for blessedness.

This renewed determination to find a way to live affects even those
poems which have always recurred in Warren's poetry—his historical
re-creations, the sometimes anguished reassessments of the Father in
both a literal and metaphorical sense, and the obsessive iteration of what
Warren calls in "Colder Fire" "this collocation / Of memories." Instead of the smart cynicism of "Genealogy," we get (from *Promises*)
"Founding Fathers, Nineteenth-Century Style, Southeast U.S.A." and
(from *You, Emperors, and Others*) the "Mortmain" sequence. "Founding Fathers" is a kind of summary mood and sentiment for Warren at
this stage, with its mixed feelings of quiet respect and muted despair
appropriate for "our own time's sad declension," the juxtaposed styles,
the obvious awe for both cranky heroism and commonplace vices, the
conflation of personal and regional history, the succession of precisely
defined details, and the prayerlike resolution emerging from one modern man's meditation on them:

> So let us bend ear to them in this hour of lateness,
> And what they are trying to say, try to understand,
> And try to forgive them their defects, even their greatness,
> For we are their children in the light of humanness, and under
>   the shadow of God's closing hand.   (SP, 243)

Implicit in this "answer" to the equally implicit question of how shall a man live is the link of human continuity—not the crude bestowing of copybook wisdom from the fathers or its sophisticated rejection by the sons. Though the last line is suggestively poised somewhere between Christian faith and deterministic resignation (does this hand of power close to protect or crush, and is its shadow beneficent or malevolent?), human kinship receives the emphasis, one that is repeated in poems with such different tonal effects as the seriocomic vision in "Ballad of a Sweet Dream of Peace" ("all Time is a dream, and we're all one Flesh, at last") and the ambiguous emotions of a lover directed to a nameless other in "Lullaby: Exercise in Human Charity and Self-Knowledge."

The first poem of "Mortmain" is specifically on the death of the father: the speaker arrives at the father's side to receive an ambiguous blessing. Although the father is unconscious, the son interprets the raised hand in light of his own need; as it drops,

> All things—all joy and the hope that strove,
> The failed exam, the admired endeavor,
> Prizes and prinkings, and the truth that strove,
> And back of the Capitol, boyhood's first whore—
> Were snatched from me, and I could not move,
> Naked in that black blast of his love. (SP, 203)

Warren rarely simplifies this precarious relationship with the past. Need is greater than knowledge: "Oh, let me understand what is that sound, / Like wind, that fills the enormous dark of my head," says the speaker in "Fox-Fire: 1956." Lessons can rarely be known in any prudential way, and though we "do not know / How cause flows backward from effect / To bless the past occasions" ("In the Turpitude of Time: N.D."), the need to know only spurs the drive to try to understand the nature of love and the secret of the serene dead, the nature of sacrifice and the degree of indifference. Even a kind of explicit answer, when it comes in the first poem in the Gabriel section of *Promises* ("What Was the Promise That Smiled From the Maples at Evening?") is enigmatic. The invoked scene is also a "vision," this time into the graves of the poet's mother and father, where their bones shine forth "in a phosphorus of glory agleam . . . ." But: "Earth was earth," and the glow dies. From the scene of woods and fields "which had once been the heart's familiar" come voices: the mother speaks simply, " 'Child' "; and the father confirms that implicit assertion of continuity with " 'We died only that every promise might be fulfilled.' "

This quiet, intensely realized poem collapses with the concluding three lines, not only because the resolution is so explicit in the manner of hand-me-down wisdom literature, but also because the thrust and detail of the poem are not configured even like a poetry of statement.

In the overall structure of *Promises*, this poem nevertheless establishes the speaker as a vital and responsible link in the generational chain, and this definition is reinforced later in the superb three-poem sequence, "Infant Boy at Mid-Century." A triumph of clarity, intelligence, and unshowy technical skill, this sequence, with absolute firmness of voice that is simultaneously modest and assertive, releases that most difficult of poetic emotions: sincerity. It is a poetry of statement at its strongest. Although it holds as backdrop the precarious existence of honor, courage, and truth, these abstract virtues never loom larger than the subject at hand—the chastened passing on of attitudes from generation to generation, wisdom not bequeathed as guidance that will automatically be absorbed in the boy's bones but, again, as reminder of imperfection waiting to trap the unwary's "need for perfection." The Eisenhower Years are perhaps too easily invoked as an unheroic age into which the infant is ushered, though chronological coincidence makes its own valid claims as poetic materials. The tone is one of tender gravity. In both theme and mood it continues the meditative vision of "What Was the Promise," stripped of that earlier poem's *memento mori* trappings.

Despite the actual foreign setting of *Promises*, the volume contains more poems about the poet's Kentucky childhood and about America generally than are found in previous volumes. Figures from the past are compulsively remembered—often in ambiguous contexts—called up in realistic terms which only exacerbate the tentative sureties of the speaker; sometimes they remain ghostly disembodiments of those from the speaker's past who may lurk in the inner dark "to spy on and count you," neither rejoicing nor grieving. Such are their limited uses for present anxieties. But such encounters, as in "Dark Woods," "Country Burying," and others, are yet considered to be the "heart's necessity." To remember may be painful, as the speaker admits in "The Hazel Leaf," but to "forget may, too, be pain."

Indeed, the most interesting poems in *Promises* (and in most of the later volumes) record the driving rage to comprehend the significance of remembered scenes, people, episodes. If some are quietly assured, as if meaning were self-evident, in others of these personal poems of continuity, the poet's visionary moments, reconstructed out of his "collocation / Of memories," strain urgently toward a meaning *almost* grasped, in incidents which most strongly resist giving up their paradoxes, which are least susceptible of ready meaning. In one, schoolchildren, secure in their "accustomed landscape," are confronted with the sudden eruption of irrationality when a poor hill farmer slaughters his family with an ice pick. Although bewildering as an event, it evokes a domestic nightmare whose literal recurrence is suggested by its headline-like title: "School Lesson Based on Word of Tragic Death of Entire Gillum Family." A communal "we" relates the episode from the limited perspective of childhood; the trivial, unknown detail—which shoe was Brother putting on that morning when he was killed?—is worried into a major preoccupation: "That was something, it seemed, you just had to know." The question becomes a kind of shorthand for the question that would come to be asked by the adult—why?—and prove no less elusive. Though he never finds out, the speaker continues

> Studying the arithmetic of losses,
>   To be prepared when the next one,
> By fire, flood, foe, cancer, thrombosis,
>   Or Time's slow malediction, came to be undone.   (SP, 240)

The moral commonplace of rural America speaks obviously to the survivors: be prepared when your own time comes. But the mysteries of human motivation remain inexplicable, even for "uncomplicated" poor whites. A later poem, "The Day Dr. Knox Did It," is no more helpful. A nine-year-old hears about a suicide, queries a grandfather, inspects the hayloft where it occurred, and speculates on who "had cleaned up the mess," before fleeing to immerse himself in flowing water; the adult, years later, muses that "there is / no water to wash the world away." The world simply "gets too much" for some people, explains the grandfather, but as an adult the speaker decides that "We are the world."

The recollection of past incidents disturbs the equanimity of Warren's personae, who are haunted by images of peril, trauma, or initiation. Recurring like nightmares, they possess talismanic significance *because* their precise meaning cannot be ascertained. Moreover, the struggle to understand is intensified because the context of the recurring images is so often domestic or benign, arising frequently from explicitly pastoral or rural settings. The speaker in "Court-Martial" remembers his grandfather's story of summarily hanging bushwhackers during an incident in the Civil War; in the imaginative reenactment he sees his grandfather as a young man ("Captain, cavalry, C.S.A.") riding away from the hanging "ornaments" of rope:

The horseman does not look back.
Blank-eyed, he continues his track,
Riding toward me there,
Through the darkening air.

The world is real. It is there.   (SP, 232)

"Boy's Will, Joyful Labor Without Pay, and Harvest Home (1918)" is a stunningly precise evocation of threshing day on a Kentucky farm, but the scene releases itself to the imagination more distinctly than its meaning to the intellect. The farmhands' killing of a blacksnake is a matter-of-fact action performed according to age-old rural custom—letting the stoned snake writhe on the tines of a pitchfork until it dies—but to the boy the deed is inexplicably brutal. It deprives him of sleep on the immediate occasion and of an easy accommodation thereafter to what is irrational and evil in the world. More than thirty years later, in the comfort and beauty of a European setting, he ponders helplessly on the summoned-up scene:

And the years go by like a breath, or eye-blink,
And all history lives in the head again,
And I shut my eyes and I see that scene,
And name each item, but cannot think
What, in their urgency, they must mean . . . .   (SP, 267)

What the clarity of the vision can do is to offer man something considerably humbler than the urgency of meaning—the real, though transitory, "heart-stab blessed past joy or despair." For better or worse, the source of such heart-stabs is the imagination that transfigures the purely human: "the shirt sticks cold to the shoulder blade, the overalls hang on the back of a chair / To stiffen, slow, as the sweat gets drier." Human inadequacy—too little wages for too much work, too much ignorance and blind custom—must be memorialized because it is human. Warren's subtle point thus becomes, like that in so many passages in James Agee's *Let Us Now Praise Famous Men*, the necessity for respect of the only human, bereft of sureties based on religion, philosophy, or history. Like so many of the poems about childhood moments whose significance is mysteriously peripheral to the situations themselves, "Boy's Will" asserts *its* meaning peripherally and with the cumulative force of related poems and poems in the same sequence.

Such a reenactment as "Dark Woods" takes place, dreamlike, in pantomime dominated by "a field full of folk" refusing "in their spooky connivance" to tell their secret to the speaker, who must continue his search for meaning. Rummaging about the discarded objects of the past, "a broken toy or rusted tool," can be a dangerous act for a sensibility whose tears "might mean more than the thing you wept for but did not understand." In the delicate act of return "Truth is always in balance, and / *Not much* can become *too much* so quick."

In "Fox-Fire: 1956" the speaker uses the grammar—the book of rules signifying directions for order—as emblem for inadequacy of human knowledge. Neither the old yellowed grammar from boyhood nor his "own grammar, / Unopened these thirty years," now side by side on the shelf, can satisfy the cry, "I want to understand." Those kinds of certainty can only be "Awe-struck and imbecile" when faced with "History's vice and vacuity . . . ." The call of an owl in Italy reminds the speaker of an earlier Kentucky scene; "between owl-call and owl-call, / Life's bright parenthesis," meaning is elusive, but life as it is lived in the necessary context of time and space must be accepted. "There once was a time when you thought you would understand / Many things, many things, including yourself," the speaker reminds himself in "A Real Question Calling for Solution"; "There is only one way, then, to make things hang together, / Which is to accept the logic of dream," that is, to forget the strivings of reason—"There must be / A way by which the process of living can become Truth" ("Does the Wild Rose?").

Edging the pastoral environment and the security of the small town that, in the naïveté of the child, exist as givens are subsistence farmers, mad druggists, and tramps whose obscure despairs often erupt into violence. These images of domestic loneliness and psychic maladies recall the small-town solitaries, eccentrics, and pinched husbandmen that Whittier foreshadows in "Among the Hills" and that in the regional portraits made memorable by Robinson and Frost come to represent the general human condition. If in Warren's similar portraits motivations for distorting and damaging acts remain mysteriously locked up, the acts themselves—the poor white farmer's and the well-to-do physician's—tend to nourish the speakers' moral urgency to cherish that frail integument that man is.

"Summer Storm (Circa 1916), and God's Grace" suggests very tentatively that endurance is a virtue in a world of naturalistic intensity. The circumstances of this poem, along with those of "Dark Night of the Soul," are the same ones Warren fuses in his most accomplished short story, "Blackberry Winter." If "Summer Storm" suggests that man is at the mercy of nature, "Dark Night of the Soul" suggests that man is at the mercy of man. That "we're all one flesh at last" is not a lesson very amenable to a twelve-year-old boy who discovers the violation of his father's property by a grizzled old tramp: "Lost and face-less and far," taking refuge against the "world's bright vacancy" in a thicket of elder and honeysuckle, he is disturbed:

> Old and spent, but heaves up his head,
> And our eyes thread the single thread
> Of the human entrapment . . . .   (SP, 247)

Then, off again, walking in the world on a "track no man would have planned," the old man is not conceived as an object of easy sympathy and pathos but transfigured into a stern object lesson, the very image of Man moving in the "dark air" of a homeless universe, his head gleaming "with the absolute and glacial purity of despair," wander-ing "in joy past contumely of stars or insolent indifference of the dark air." The mature speaker ends his account with a prayer: "May we all at last enter into that awfulness of joy he has found there." Given such cosmic uncertainty, the continuity of flesh is doubly important.

If the intensities of social and political upheaval exert any compelling shift in Warren's verse of the 1960s, as some have argued to be the case with some of his contemporaries, it is difficult to detect. Indeed, if anything, his movement has been in the direction of more and more privacies. The "Mortmain" sequence of *You, Emperors, and Others*, with its extended investigation into the emotional circumstances oc-casioned by his father's death, is followed by the "Tale of Time" sequence in *Tale of Time* (1966), an equally detailed study of the effects of his mother's death. There are further assays into the need for "a new definition of virtue" ("Shoes in Rain Jungle"), as well as explorations into the recurring problem of living a life in the proper way ("Notes on a Life to Be Lived"). Even the poems that are super-ficially more public are finally one man's engagement with the private matter of "learning to live." In one of these poems, "Dragon-Tree," Warren writes: "Have you thought that the headlines are only the images of your own heart?" That rhetorical question continues the as-sumptions of such quasi-public poems deriving from the political cataclysms of the late 1930s. Domestic sounds (a cat's squall, the drip of a faucet) are potentially as ominous as nature's (the thunderous booms when the ice-locked river breaks up in spring thaw), and the headlines of the 1960s are no more reassuring, or any more cataclysmic, than they were thirty years earlier. If news from Asia is bad, the news from the human interior equals it; and some of the evasions that man is so adept at fashioning—such as those enumerated in "Infant Boy at Mid-Century"—still offer themselves:

Some study compassion. Some, confusing
Personal pathology with the logic of history, jump
Out of windows. Some walk with God, some by rivers, at twilight.
Have you tried to just sit with the children and tell a tale
                                    ending in laughter?[15]

The poems of the 1960s reveal increasingly less shock at natural catastrophe and human pathology and more surprise that laughter and joy are possible. Despite the fact that the human heart is a dragon tree, happy tales may still be told. In "Ways of Day," for all his convulsive and cantankerous nature, the poet of the night can be enlightened:

I am the dark and tricky one.
I am watching from my shade.
Your tousled hair-tips prickle the sunlight.
I watch you at your sunlit play.
Teach me, my son, the ways of day.   (SP, 162)

And in "Chain Saw at Dawn in Vermont in Time of Drouth," the speaker contrasts his own problems of learning how to live with that of a dying man in the village who is thinking "*I have not learned how to die . . . .*"

Among the familiar Warren images of flowing water, mirror reflections, immensities of sky and darkness, the sounds of birds and animals that comment on man's condition, comes a new directive, to eat human flesh, appearing first in "Dragon-Tree," a poem in which the geographic and the chthonic meet. As a dry fact that might have appeared in *National Geographic* in the early 1960s ("the Belgians sure mucked up / The Congo. Human flesh is yet eaten there, often uncooked"), the directive is followed by an allusion to one of Stephen Crane's most famous parable poems: "Have you sat on a hillside at sunset and eaten the flesh of your own heart?" In the next sequence, "Tale of Time," the image is associated with a mother's death and signifies a shift from self-pity and cynicism to empathetic grief. A smaller sequence, "The Interim," attempts to define love through the parallel instance of the death of a black woman, a surrogate mother, the loss of whom becomes a more manageable one for the son to sustain. The final poem of this subsequence begins:

But the solution: You
Must eat the dead.
You must eat them completely, bone, blood, flesh, gristle, even
Such hair as can be forced. You
Must undertake this in the dark of the moon, but
At your plenilune of anguish.   (SP, 148)

Although as image the eating of human flesh carries some deeply private meaning, its ritualistic suggestions are clear. The act is symbolic assimilation, an attempt at both recovery and preservation—recovery of the past, of the kind of self the self ideally projects, of fullness of identity; and preservation of all that makes up the human fabric. We must learn, says the poet in a related poem, "The nature of being, in order / In the end to be . . . ." Eating the dead at the "plenilune of anguish" is a macabre directive for learning the nature of being, but its ritualistic constraint transforms it from nightmare into something psychically useful. Striking as this homoeopathic metaphor is, it is merely an extravagant variation on other metaphorical expressions of a persistent theme in Warren's work: the conviction that only an intense possession of the past can provide life with meaning in the present. Here it says: to possess the past is to become it or to have it become you. On one level the concept is akin to ancient Indian rites in which the hunter absorbs the virtues of his victim by ritualistic cannibalism; the victim is honored by having his virtues transmitted, in continuity, into the body of the hunter.[16] Given Warren's frequent bouts with the claims of the past, the image is no doubt intended to be ambiguous; but it is also one that celebrates man's necessity to know and revere the present, which means cherishing human relationships; and the injunction to "eat the dead" is, as one critic has put it, "an osmotic eucharist" similar to the flesh-devouring hogs of "Ballad of a Sweet Dream of Peace."[17]

In "the public and private mania" of our "maniacal century," Warren more and more explores the means for accommodating his inner vision to the several faces of the soul and its progressive rebirths, just as he learns to accommodate his eyes to the "new dark" that descends after heat lightning. That exploration is more and more of the poet's own past.

The obsessive recurrence with which Warren rifles his past carries with it the obvious temptation toward nostalgia. Insofar as nostalgia is not so much a feeling about what has passed as it is a feeling about the "pastness" of the past, Warren sometimes goes no farther than the documenting of astonished wonder in his contemplation of past moments. More frequently, however, it is not that he finds that the past is unrecoverable—creative memory assures its recovery—but that its meaning resists human efforts, even those made through that imaginative sympathy that we see frequently in the poems about the parents. In these, recovery of the past takes the shape of remembered and imagined scenes that though tantalizingly clear in mass and line are portentously opaque in meaning. These are poems in which the speaker summons up certain past moments not as memorializing acts (as in "Founding Fathers") but as ratifying searches: these moments may contain answers to questions being asked in the present. While poems about dead parents are always personal in the sense that they are familial acts of homage, those of Warren's are personal also in a more egoistic sense—as exercises in spectral pedagogy in which Warren's "I" reaches out to the customary wisdom figures for intelligence that would help the life lived in the present. For the son's anguish, sentimental memorializing of the parents is not enough.

In those poems dealing with the death of the mother (and its companion piece on the poet's visit to his dying black mammy), Warren skirts easy sentimentality out of personal need and in so doing protects his poems against their own generating events. On a simple level, the emotional content of the poet's response to these moments is governed by candor rather than simple piety. The speaker recognizes his grief over the parent's death as selfish because he perceives that the dead parent is forever indifferent to the child's deprivation:

> the living remember the dead only
> Because we cannot bear the thought that they
> Might forget us.

The desperation of the speaker, the frustration that is at bottom selfish, is articulated in language that reflects the frustration rather than the customary homage. The emotional register of loss and grief is frequently juxtaposed against a verbal register of material calculation, of commercial profit and loss. In the early poem on the death of the mother, "The Return: An Elegy," we also find two opposing registers: the conventionally elegiac is offset by the conventionally impious, and the mother becomes "the old fox" and "the old bitch." In that poem both registers are variations harmonized by the poet's unrelieved naturalistic vision. When more than two decades later Warren returns formally to the same subject and the same moment for his "Tale of Time," the elegy has become a suite of poems. The dominant register consists of homage, grief, awe, and anxiety that can be released through precisely reconstructed scenes, and the ironic register undercuts the first through such punctuated reminders as "Death is only a technical correction of the market," "There are factors to be considered in making any final estimate," and "Your whole position must be reconsidered."

Finally, Warren avoids elegiac sentimentality even while retaining a conventionally reverential subject and tone by transposing the generative events into *imagined* re-creations, the most successful of which project the joy of innocence and the frustration of experience. In two poems in the "Tale of Time" suite, he imagines his mother as a child and himself as parent. Although he can only wonder what she was thinking as she lay "lost in the long grass," he reminds her that he too as a child lay "in the grass of that same spot," and they are united in intimations of mortality, signified here, as in most of Warren's poems, by such phrases as "sober recesses of cedar," "beyond the dark cedars," and "Darkness of cedars." The son parentally reaches out to protect the mother-as-child from those inevitable encroachments, to preserve her in what he believes to be her innocence ("I am older than you will ever be"). His foreknowledge matched against her innocence, he guides her back from the dark recesses of impinging mortality to the momentary haven of her father's house.

Even when the tone shifts from the desperation of "Look, look at these—" as the speaker tries to demonstrate his piety by gesturing to photographs he keeps in his wallet—to the colloquial punning of

> And as for you, and all the interesting things
> That must have happened to you and that
> I am just dying to hear about—   (SP, 151)

the burden of the poem is the uncompromising truth of the incommunicable dead. The poet is finally only "a balding stranger" to whom the dead mother will not confide the "intimate secret of death." If the "future is always unpredictable," "so is the past." Despite all the inadequate maneuvers undertaken, however, hopefulness survives.

This act of imaginative reconstruction is the same as in the final poem of "Mortmain," in which Warren sets down his father as a boy "poised between woods and pasture." For the son, "A Vision: Circa 1880" contains even greater frustration than "Tale of Time." The son cries out from his subsequent knowledge: *"Listen!* Say: *Listen! I know—oh, I know—let me tell you!"* Unheeding, the father-as-boy "in patched britches and that idleness of boyhood / Which asks nothing and is its own fulfillment," goes his way toward the shadowy woods with one backward glance, "grins once, / And is gone." Child is bound to parent and parent to child, but both are bound to Time; and even when the great corridor is breached by imagination, the linkage that would reveal all, reconcile all, is frail and tenuous. But if "Hope dances on the razor edge," even those tentative, temporary connections are to be cherished. In "Tale of Time" the symbol of that hope is in the son's experience after the vision, when the stars are reborn; in "Mortmain" it is the stirring of an oak leaf, freshening "to the favor of rain." The images of the father and mother confirm continuity, which even in the incompleteness of knowledge is a source for hope.

In Warren's reconstructions of personal events the psychic intersection always lies in the poet himself, in the here and now; and the backward and forward glances—the visions and the projections—are efforts to give dimension to what the poet sees in the present moment. The energy or tension varies, however, from poem to poem. In certain pieces—especially in "Tale of Time" and "Mortmain," those condensed narratives of filiation—Warren openly confronts the burden of the blood. In other poems—such as "Founding Fathers" and "Ballad of the Boxcars"—the epiphanous moments are almost willed into existence, and so are distanced and generalized; stripped of "spooky connivance," they possess less power to hurt, and their reenactments more easily assume the shape of images culturally and mythically meaningful.

In both kinds the extraordinary density of the reconstructions, scenes built by the meticulous naming of parts and their spatial placement, does not make them any less a species of daydream in the sense in which E. M. Gombrich uses the term; indeed, the pictorial method is suggested in the very titles of some of the poems and in the "progress" of their structure. But in the less urgently personal poems pictorial and verbal art tend to merge much more conventionally, as they do in some of the genre pieces in Whittier and Longfellow.[18] The daydream necessary for their action is clearly an exercise in recovery more cognitive than emotional. What is recovered in both kinds is of course strongly shaped by what is expected: Gombrich's principle of "the interplay between expectation and observation" applies equally to the personal and impersonal reconstructions and to those lyrics that attempt only to reenact a thought or an experience in the just-barely past.[19] All are skirmishes in the struggle to understand, to know one's precarious identity in a context of both a society of human construction and a nonhuman, nonsocial world that reveals its connections to man through emblematic manifestations only faintly glimpsed and sporadically set in perspective.

If memory complicates that identity in some of the most crucial poems of the early 1960s, the concern for human continuity is not diminished in *Incarnations: Poems 1966–1968*. The noticeable emphasis in these poems, however, is personal rather than communal, visceral more than filiative:

> We cannot love others unless
> We learn how to love
> Ourselves properly . . . .

On one level these poems constitute a reversion to Warren's earliest fascination with naturalism; on another they transform the bleakness of that doctrine into awe and respect for the very fragility of man puzzled by his own treacherous flesh and threatened by the nonhuman, nonsocial world with which he is forced to traffic. Despite a few local and topical details of a technological world (a prowling jet, a fume-track, the *tat-tat* of jackhammers), *Incarnations* concerns the effects of the intractable world and flesh on the sensibilities of speakers who would will their incarnated meanings into usable moments of knowledge. The first and third parts of the volume ("Island of Summer" and "Enclaves") exploit contrasting topographies that mutually comment on each other, the world of dense, constituent actuality with that of abstract, spiritual transcendence: Mediterranean lushness as against Alpine austerity, sun and sea against snow and fog. But the unremitting emphasis of the strongly positioned central section, "Internal Injuries," is man's vulnerable flesh, and that theme reverberates in such a way that no simple polarities are possible.

Warren's crucial signals come first in the two epigraphs, one from Nehemiah ("Yet now our flesh is as the flesh of our brethren") and the other from the familiar ballad of "John Henry" ("John Henry said to the Captain, 'A man ain't nuthin but a man' "). The biblical allusion refers to the people's cry against their own officials who had usurped their vineyards and fields by exacting interest, and it is an assertion of equality of worth, of common humanity which is threatened by man's exploitation of his fellow man. John Henry's statement to his captain, which says "A man ain't a machine," is an assertion of man's strength, dignity, perseverance; its human context suggests that his very limitations can be suitably celebrated because they also make man what he is. Behind both epigraphs is the image of man working, exercising the power inherent in his talents. But behind both is also the more sober evidence of man's betrayal of his own: the captain who displaces his efficient worker by bringing "the steam drill 'round," and the entrepreneurs who exploit their Jewish brethren while they rebuild the great wall of Jerusalem. These juxtaposed images establish in an uncommon way a common view of man the mixed creature, alternately blessed by such virtues as industry, strength, dedication, and cursed by such frailties as envy, ambition, greed. That common view is explicitly underscored by the first poem in the volume, "What Day Is." The long perspective of history reveals man's glory and his greed, his need to build and his urge to tear down. The "incessant effort" of cicadas is a chorus, commenting on that inextricably intertwined nature—the enterprising Phoenicians, Celts, and Romans who constructed and the "Monks, Moors, murderers" who later destroyed.

On an unnamed Mediterranean island, the poet imputes a kind of rank fatality to his golden world. The brightness of the sea threatens to "rinse out your eyeballs"; the ivy "assaults the wall"; the touch of a plum may "burn you"; Paul Valéry is imagined standing on a cliff facing "the furious energies of nature"; anonymous human faces on a café *terrase* are "Washed white as bone" in the sinister silver light of a moonrise; an old, bikini-clad, hunchback woman stuns the youthful, timeless beach world in a "Botticellian parody"; the mistral brings suffocation and unwelcome dreams; an unforgiving mullet, harbinger of mortality and indifferent natural continuity, confronts the speaker in a dark shoal; and figs, plums, peaches, and grapes are described in foreboding, rich sentience:

> The plum, black yet bough-bound, bursts, and the gold ooze is,
> Of bees, joy, the gold ooze has striven
> Outward . . . .   (SP, 117–18)

> the peach
> has released the bough and at last
> makes full confession, its *pudeur*
> has departed like peach-fuzz wiped off, and

> We now know how the hot sweet-
> ness of flesh and the juice-dark hug
> the rough peach pit . . . .   (SP, 106)

> the fig,
> Motionless in that imperial and blunt
> Languor of glut, swells, and inward
> The fibers relax like a sigh in that
> Hot darkness, go soft, the air
> Is gold.

> When you
> Split the fig, you will see
> Lifting from the coarse and purple seed, its
> Flesh like flame, purer
> Than blood.   (SP, 104)

These are, in brief, further assertions that the world is "real," that it is "there"; but the poems in this first section show the commonplaces of natural history heightened into an exacerbated awareness of their relation to man. The effect is something like that of a Hakluyt voyager,

famed for his graceful and imaginative excursions into unnatural natural history, suddenly translated onto Darwin's *Beagle* moored off the
Galapagos Islands. It is Warren's own variation on the pathetic fallacy,
in which nature is not merely a reflector of man's changeable moods but
a realm in its own right, not susceptible of man's casual manipulation
but as richly varied as man's own condition and competitive with it.

For all the languor and semitropical ambience of these scenes, and
for all the peaceful connotations implicit in such a characteristic situation as "I sit and meditate," the really operative verbs in the "Island
of Summer" poems are *scream, boom, burn, clash, assaults, shudder,
burst,* and *dies.* One poem, "Natural History," posits a web of life and
death in which human bodies, mostly anonymous ("like the world"),
are eaten by "dogs, gulls, rodents, ants, / And fish," and in which even
"the root / Of the laurel has profited" and the leaf of the live oak
"achieves a new luster" because of this inexorable interdependence.
Furthermore, it is a relationship in which man is centrally involved:
the poet's son finds a Nazi helmet, a tiny hole at the left temple and,
on the right, at its "egress [a] large, raw, exploding outward . . . ."

On its simplest level, *Incarnations* is secular: these are poems about
bodily nature and form. But they are also poems of personification in
which figs and plums suggest human flesh in a kind of perverse emblem poetry. And perverse in a substantive way, too: though the volume
carries no specific statement on the theological meaning of the Incarnation, the great Johannine text which explains it hovers suggestively
throughout the book—"For God so loved the world that He gave His
only begotten Son that whosoever believeth in Him should not perish
but have everlasting life." The Son here, however, is dispersed throughout nature, and the end of "Masts at Dawn" is a significant measure of
Warren's departure from biblical text: "We must try / To love so well
the world that we may believe, in the end, in God"—that is, from
God's resolution to man's struggle for resolution, from *so loved the
world* to *try to love so well the world.* The sometimes desperate speculations fall into irony and paradox. That which the Word supposedly
effected—the redeeming of the world—is seen in piecemeal incarnations throughout a world that is yet unredeemed, recalcitrant, contingent. Both history and nature "may have mercy, / Though only by
accident." Despite the struggle for spiritual answers to metaphysical
questions, the context is still the naturalistic world that has always fascinated Warren. More often than not, nature holds out manifestations of
man, not God. The peach, wanting to suffer, has "suicidal yearnings."

The ivy dreams of peace. The red mullet is unforgiving. The plum aspires to innocence.

If the poems of *Incarnations* are dense with natural objects in a strange surfeit of oppressiveness, as if the melons and vines of Marvell's "Bermudas" throw themselves at and entangle man for malevolent reasons, man must still make his way in such a world. The crow seemingly calls to man in a "tatter of cold contempt," and as the sun has burned white the gull droppings on the fig leaf, so does it threaten to "Burn our bones to chalk . . . ." Most of the poems in the volume are about *flesh*—plant, animal, human—as if man's survival in his most fondly willed dreams is a chancy thing, tested alike by now fire now ice, now glut now want. The "only human" or "merely human" threads the verse in *Incarnations*.

The terror of blankness and whiteness is equal to the treachery inherent in the seductive golden world of the summer island. Fog and snow frustrate accustomed expectations and familiar orientation quite as ominously as the dense richness of sun and sea burns and drowns them. The sun-dazzling, surf-clashing world of summer is dense with images suggesting the frailty of human flesh amidst a surfeit of fleshly reminders; the world of snow and fog, on the other hand, has too few reminders—the human heart hangs suspended in the "Blank mufflement of white / Brightness . . . ." The "luminous but / Blind" landscape of Alpine mountains is "contextless"; the "blaze-brightness" of the island landscape is one of glut. In both the purely human is haunted, threatened, unredeemed.

In one of the last poems in *Incarnations*, skiers with the "motion of angels" appear in the distance perfectly adjusted to their white world, but on the "flat," where the white world is "Trodden and mud-streaked," they

> Are awkward, not yet well adjusted
> To this world, new and strange, of Time and
> Contingency, who now are only
> Human.   (SP, 136)

The world for Warren is of course always characterized by Time and Contingency, a view that informs the familiar sojourn, exhaustingly compromised by feints and dodges, that so many of Warren's personae undertake. "Riddle in the Garden" ends with the line, "The world means only itself." "The World Is a Parable" contains as its core statement,

> The world
> Is a parable and we are
> The meaning.

The first is an expression of Warren the naturalist (in both senses of the word); the second of Warren the moralist. The drive for meaning continues along a track parallel, here as in previous volumes, with the assertions of meaninglessness, or meaning ontologically self-contained and thereby excluding man.

The counterpart to the haunting poems on the cloying sentience of the "flaming" flesh of Mediterranean fruit is the middle segment of *Incarnations*, two sequences of which are visceral celebrations of fragile human flesh. Both the title poem, "Internal Injuries," about an old Negro woman struck down by a car in the New York streets, and "Penological Study: Southern Exposure," about a grizzled old convict dying of cancer in the state penitentiary, are explicit examples of the seeming naturalistic doctrine that reduces the human body not to its constituent elements but to an in-between stage—as an irrelevant commodity which an indifferent dispatcher is trying to schedule for delivery ("So load the finished product and go"). Such results are more chilling than the abstract, somewhat ethereal annihilation feared by the poet in an earlier poem—the prospects of going to "a place where / nothing is"; and they are a kind of answer to the prayer in another poem for the preservation of the body against the power of the sun:

> it would
> Burn our bones to chalk—yes, keep
> Them covered, oh flesh, oh sweet
> Integument, oh frail, depart not . . . .   (SP, 113)

Even when the sweet, frail integument betrays, as it does in both sequences, the speakers instinctively shape the same urgent appeals. Old Jake sits in his cell in a humped posture to try to ignore "the pumpkin [which] grows and grows" deep inside, for only in that posture can he "half-believe, / Like you or me, like you or me, / That the truth will not be true." The wounded old woman in the street notes the traffic beginning to move again even while she waits helplessly for the ambulance, "and meaning / In my guts blooms like / A begonia . . . ." This sequence ends as she speculates on the meaning of her flesh just as she is about to give it up, an urgency to

> know all the slithery functions of
> All those fat slick slimy things that
> Are so like a tub full of those things you would find

In a vat in the back room of a butcher shop,
    but wouldn't eat, but

Are not that, for they are you.
Driver, do you truly, truly
Know what flesh is, and if it is, as some people say,
    really sacred?

Driver, there's an awful glitter in the air. What is the
    weather forecast?   (SP, 134–35)

The fleshly consciousness that dominates this middle section literalizes the metaphor that dominates the first, with its reiterated emphasis on flame-red flesh of overripe fruit; and this visceral level gives way to the frail and tentative transcendence of the final section. How, asks the poet,

May I know the true nature of Time, if
Deep now in darkness that glittering enclave
I dream, hangs? It shines.[20]

Although the germ for *Audubon: A Vision* dates from the 1940s when Warren was researching *World Enough and Time*, the temper of the poem, its formal properties, and its thematic dispositions are all characteristic of the poet's later style. The gestation was difficult and long partly because, as in the case of *Brother to Dragons*, a form appropriate to the subject was so elusive.

Just as he discovered that the ballad form that had suited the Billie Potts material so well was inadequate for the radiating complexities of the Lewis tragedy, so for the Audubon story Warren was unable in the 1940s to find "the frame for it, the narrative line." The triggering event came in the 1960s. During his rereading of Audubon for *American Literature: The Makers and the Making*, Warren saw how to write his poem: "in fragments, sort of snapshots of Audubon" (*Talking*, 235, 276). In a sense Warren had set his own example for that literary discovery in his poems of the 1960s, in his poetic suites—related poems which are emotionally incomplete in themselves, which require for their completion mutual reinforcement and gradual accretion among the separate poems. Like *Audubon*, such suites as "Homage to Emerson," "Tale of Time," and "Ballad of a Sweet Dream of Peace" are formal and technical embodiments of Warren's thematic stress on relatedness and complicity.[21] He began to see the naturalist, says Warren, as "a man who has finally learned to accept his fate. The poem is about man and his fate—all along, Audubon resisted his fate and thought it was evil—a man is supposed to support his family' and so forth. But now he accepts his fate" (*Talking*, 235).

What the poem is "about" is fully enclosed by its structure: all the segments avoid the direct dramatic clashes characteristic of Warren's earlier narrative poems—or even the kind of severe internal conflicts that erupt into violence and self-destruction. The poem quietly dramatizes the acceptance of, not the resistance to, fate. Meditation, reverie, and an earned delight mark the poem, linking it generally with Warren's later poetry: "And then in the end the poem is about Audubon and me." Just as personal disclosure dominates the later poetry, with a structure fashioned for that major purpose, so *Audubon*. The long poem consists of captured moments of the naturalist's career projected as imaged panels (Audubon's contemplating the heron and the bear in earlier poems, Audubon's serene acceptance of his life in the later ones); a long central episode that focuses the dramatic process of a consciousness coming to know itself and the world ("The Dream He Never Knew the End Of"); and, interspersed, abstract segments in which Warren involves himself and the reader in explicit application of what Audubon learns and, as a life made myth, of what Audubon is. "I have moved more toward a moralized anecdote," Warren explains. "I would like to show the problem of the abstract and the concrete in the construction of the poem itself" (*Talking*, 231). In this sense the construction of *Audubon* is as revelatory as what the structure holds.

Anterior to the poem is the ethical conflict between the artist as artist and the artist as man, since the responsibilities of the one are not necessarily those of the other. Warren's private struggle with these opposing terms directly dictates the shape of the "Mortmain" and "Tale of Time" sequences and the later "I Am Dreaming of a White Christmas"; in *Audubon*, however, the working dialectic is fused and distanced in such a way that *Birds of America* becomes symbolically equivalent to the poet's own *Selected Poems*. The artist's justification is in a sense outside morality; responsibility for the creation of beauty may require the destruction of beauty. Understanding, respect, duty, deference, and other conventional human pieties may for an artist be imperfectly exercised in the sensuous immediacy of the world's body— in Warren's case, the parents and the values of their world—as sacrifice to the perfected artifact, which Conrad Aiken once asserted was the ultimate good and the ultimate obligation of the creative mind. Both in substance and structure *Audubon* is a quiet celebration of artistic victory—of Warren's as well as the naturalist's. "Tell me a story of deep delight" is the final line of the poem. The mythic tale of Audubon, hunter, naturalist, scientist, artist, is just that story; but it may also be read as the ratification of what this particular poet is and has done.

Audubon comes down to us as an appealing blend of the artist and the scientist, a man of both passion and reason who participated in the violence of the hunter's cultus without losing his capacity for love. One measure of his success, both personal and public, is the harrowing process through which he won fame and his own self-respect. He not only had to conquer a recalcitrant and indifferent world; he also had to learn to apply his innately modest talents to their most appropriate forms, transforming in the process crippling weaknesses and only desultory strengths into disciplined, maximum advantage. Although his achievement is the earnest of his heroic stature, his indomitable certitude is its antecedent. The signal fact of Audubon's biography is success earned through struggle.[22] It is a record, moreover, which rings the changes on an American pattern of heroism, one affecting baseball players and songwriters as well as industrialists and inventors. The materials of this particular victory are appropriately American—the birds and mammals of North America—but so also are the resolution and independence of their celebrant.

Warren would have liked Audubon because of his minor role in Kentucky history and his major role in America's mythologizing impulse; in many respects, however, the naturalist is not merely a congenial historical figure for Warren, but his character and career come down to us almost preshaped as one of Warren's fictional protagonists. The configurations of an unprepossessing but cosseted youth who strives mightily for heroic stature seem ready-made for the creator of Amantha Starr and Jeremiah Beaumont: not innately endowed with heroic nature, as, say legend tends to make Daniel Boone, Audubon works toward heroic stature primarily through efforts for increased self-knowledge: deprived of paternal protection, the youth falls into the insecure world of others whose very ordinariness demands that he prove himself extraordinary; against the intractability of the world he strives toward the fulfillment of his own ideal image whose effective projection is made possible only through an artistic process of softening, heightening, and selectivity.

What is at first unusual about Warren's protagonist is the portrayal of heroism *achieved*, of Audubon's sense of being at ease in the world. In this poem the world is just as resistant to a hero's dream as it usually is in Warren's works: petty malices, snobberies, material and spiritual threats are measures of a fallen order where evil is not a chimera but an active force. The usual Warrenesque hero, however, also finds himself at some crucial stage recognizing that the fallen order of society, and even the fallen state of nature, are projections of his own evil with which he must first come to terms before he can make his peace with the world. Warren's Audubon is not only more serene than Jefferson in *Brother to Dragons*; he is also more serene than the historical Audubon. Nowhere does Warren suggest an emotional intensity in the naturalist's love of birds matching Audubon's own almost frenzied identification with them. The terms of the struggle in Warren's figure seem suggestive merely, as if certain vital aspects of Audubon had been deliberately excised. Is the serenity the price of preferring a mythic to a tragic protagonist? What is the function of Warren's selectivity in discarding certain of the naturalist's traits and using others?

Audubon ascribes his lifelong love of birds to a childhood experience, when a pet parrot is killed calmly before his eyes by a pet monkey ("probably thinking the bird presumed upon his rights in the scale of Nature"); indirectly, the example of a superior animal's "rights" suggests something of Audubon's later pride as a marksman and his philosophical composure while affirming that skill. His writings are filled with admiration for Kentucky riflemen; on his rambles through the woods Audubon takes along, with revealing priorities, "my gun, my notebook, and my pencil." In New Orleans when he meets a gentleman artist the talk is more about a new percussion lock on his rifle than about birds. He talks of his twenty years of "vicissitudes" but attributes them in part to his "struggle against the will of all, except my wife and children, who in that period called themselves my friends." Seemingly aware of his ambiguous phrasing, Audubon adds: "Anyone unacquainted with the extraordinary desire I then felt to see and judge for myself would doubtless have pronounced me callous to every sense of duty."[23] The implications of such concessive language reveal qualities in the man that are as egotistic and self-indulgent as they are heroic. More disinterested accounts in fact underscore the less attractive aspects of his character. He is assailed and duped by what he calls "splendid promisers and very bad paymasters," but his own unpaid debts, lawsuits, and shady financial deals were marked by conscious deception as well as bad luck and the connivance of enemies. One biographer suggests that John Keats's last chance to marry Fanny Brawne was indirectly destroyed by Audubon's bad-faith gulling of George Keats in Kentucky.

In his desperate search in Europe for subscribers to his *Birds of America*, Audubon records how his "friendly good will" is rebuffed; he may wait humbly on a "soit disant Gentleman" and his lady in a hotel anteroom, but he uses his letters to vent his rage for such insults. The letters reveal a sensitivity to social slights when he is "reluctantly received, mostly ignored, but, at least, fed and lodged" at wayside inns; he records his humiliation of being a dancing master in Louisiana and of being embarrassed by creditors even after his fame begins to grow. To his son Victor, Audubon writes, "*I paddle my own canoe* in the face of the storm, and against strong contrary currents, but no matter—," and to his wife Lucy he admonishes, "We have nothing to expect from any one in this World" but that "the name of our sons will be a passport through the World."[24]

Only a firm belief in one's own worth can account for the persistence with which Audubon pursued his career. His pocket is picked not once but twice, a kind of paltry loss that becomes emblematic of something larger: to his collaborator in 1835, after success has been assured, he writes, "it has been my good fortune to be cheated by the World, that I have become habituated to it." By this time he is characteristically referring to "our great Work" which "the World" will be forced to recognize, though "in all probability only after" his death.[25]

Prickly, egoistic, eccentric, solitary, proud: these are the qualities of the historical Audubon—and they are qualities that often mark the typical hero in Warren's works. In *Audubon*, however, such full-scale struggles with both the self and the world are reduced to traceries along the edge of the portrait. The poem becomes a series of panels—of action and meditation upon the action—representing achieved victory. The *fury* of achievement is dropped into the interstices of the poem, although the *cost* is subtly preserved in its several segments.

Louis L. Martz was the first reader to point out how Warren modified the episode of Audubon's near murder by a frontier woman and her sons (recorded in "The Prairie" in his *Ornithological Biography*). In "The Dream He Never Knew the End Of" Warren most decisively caps the threatened violence of the recorded episode with actual violence—and to reinforce the action with appropriate local effects he changes the setting from summer to winter. The liberties that Warren takes here with his historical sources are not new, of course—his most famous alteration is his redoing of the conclusion of *The Confessions of Jereboam O. Beauchamp* for *World Enough and Time*. And, as Martz observes, Warren is fully justified, like Aeschylus or Ovid, in "re-imagining a myth," especially here since "Audubon truly is an American legend and folk hero."[26] But the significance of Warren's choice is farther reaching than this.

The sixty "Episodes" of the five-volume *Ornithological Biography*, dealing mainly with events and observations of life along the frontier, particularly the Ohio and Mississippi valleys between 1808 and 1834, were devised by the canny Audubon to relieve the tedium of a purely scientific descriptive ornithology: one intercalated sketch appears approximately after five articles describing the birds, except for the final two volumes, where these articles of a general nature had to be sacrificed.[27] Many of these articles draw upon Audubon's memory of experiences, and, especially in those describing his early adventures in the West (from about 1808 to 1818), he was, says a biographer, "wont to humor his fancy." "The Prairie" is one of these: though there is little reason to question the substantial truth of the episode, it still contains a "certain amount of invention."[28]

Warren chooses an episode, then, that is already preparing its hero for legend: its links are metaphorically and culturally with Daniel Boone, whose one chance meeting with Audubon is enlarged by the naturalist through repetition over the years into a central and meaningful association. What Audubon stresses in the episode is his foresight, skill, and calm demeanor in the face of danger. Alerted to that danger, he goes outside "on the pretext of seeing how the weather might point for the morrow," and prepares his rifle for action: "I slipped a ball into each barrel, scraped the edges of my flints, renewed the primings, returned to the hut . . . drew my gun close to my body and—to all outward appearances—fell fast asleep." After two "stout travellers" providentially appear, the "infernal hag" and her drunken sons are tied up; the next morning in the manner of "Regulators," they march the miscreants off into the woods, fire the cabin, give the "skins and implements" to a young Indian, and continue "on our way." The episode concludes with an admiring salute to the Regulators, self-appointed vigilantes who roam the frontier as private keepers of the peace.

What Warren is dealing with, then, is not quite the raw materials of a poem but a projected image of a man who is not only talented and ambitious but who is himself also sophisticated in the manipulations of a "fair name." "The Prairie" does not end with a spectacular frontier hanging, but the psychological scaffolding is already there waiting, as well as the hunter's undergirding values that sanction it: these are what Warren sees and enlarges upon, so that in his own episode he aesthetically completes what is ethically present in the source.

He of course does more. He gives his hero a more explicit self-knowledge than is readily apparent in Audubon's writings, though the transparent agonies, raw ambitions, and undisguised emotional responses to the ways of the world in the letters and journals are sufficient indicators of the difficult achievement of moral maturity and serenity that we see in the Audubon of Warren's poem. The seeming firmness of personal identity laced with doubt is another element of the historical figure that Warren transforms in his characteristic way. As Warren notes, "legends accreted" about Audubon without his help, but being a "fantasist of talent" he often aided the stories of his origin. If the tales that he was the lost Dauphin of France gained their dubious ground only after Audubon's death, when they were too tall to be true, others were created and passed along with Audubon's blessing. Even the names he went under smack of the shiftiness of frontier confidence games—Fougère, Rabin, LaForêt. Even as John James Audubon (itself an anglicization) he can conceive of his modest success in England in such suggestive terms as these: "my name is gradually creeping up in this extraordinary London."[29] As for the struggle for self-identity that Warren so often details in his other fictional lives, in *Audubon* the issue develops by metaphorical equivalents: to know the great heron, the bear, the trumpeter swan, the tusked boar, the eagle, is finally to know oneself. Warren's Audubon becomes a confirming image of that special kinship between man and animal in nineteenth-century America, the manifestations of which we see in cultural icons and literary texts alike. Both the gentleman and the backwoodsman exhibit this relationship, the first through elaborate codes and rituals of the hunt, the second through the impulse toward mythical aggrandizement, simultaneously anthropomorphic and supernatural, by which the chief quarry, the bear, is elevated in stature and status. As early as 1847, in a review of Audubon's books, one critic went so far as to specify the symbolic kinship between hunter and hunted: birds, he wrote, represent "the imagination or the soul" and the quadrupeds represent man's appetitive instincts: "[I]t is as brave of us, and as necessary, that we should be true animals, as that we should be true angels. Our mingled being can as yet be neither one nor the other wholly, but must wisely compound between the extremes and be simply what we are—men!"[30] For Warren's Audubon, to "walk in the world" is to acknowledge both his link with nature and with other men: the former ratifies the latter. He is the hunter who kills to know, his head bowed low over his quarry— "But not in grief."

In the opening segment, as he leans on his gun watching a bear yawn, he thinks "How thin is the membrane between himself and the world." The thinness of that membrane is even more striking in the central episode. The man participates in the great natural world he walks, and images of unmediated nature underscore what Warren has elsewhere called the osmosis of being. The dawn is "Redder than meat"; the bear's tongue "bleeds the black blood of the blueberry"; the bee's wings glint "like mica"; the clearing around the woman's cabin is "a wound rubbed raw in the vast pelt of the forest": all certify that special relationship between Audubon and the world of birds and mammals. But the membrane, though thin, is still there: "We are only ourselves"; his discovery of his fate, to transact an identity in both the natural world and the social world, allows Audubon to move toward that fulfillment in a simplicity without masquerade: "His life, at the end" is simple in that

> it had to be,
> Simply, what it was,
> In the end, himself and not what
> He had known he ought to be.
> The blessedness!—.   (SP, 94)

The predation of both hunter and quarry does not disturb the surface of the poem very much. As if both birds and Audubon had already undergone their passion, they are caught in a static tranquility, purged of the rawer excesses of creatureliness. If the hard, stoic killer spirit that D. H. Lawrence detected in the American character is a part of this hunter-naturalist, Warren cannily condenses it in one unit, the long second segment, so as to isolate and contain it. But even in this episode of frontier violence, barely suppressed lust, and *ad hoc* justice —built on fictive outlines drawn by Audubon himself—Warren restrains his customary exploitative gusto. If the slight and gentle retardation of dream governs the movement of *Audubon* as a whole, it functions even more decisively in "The Dream He Never Knew the End Of" (SP, 86–93).

The sting in the brutality of the hanging is eased by Audubon's vision of the woman's face, but imagistically the entire episode, for all its cruelty and horror, moves in the quietness of dream. Significantly, the cawing of a crow is the only sound in the forest as Audubon walks through the clearing to the cabin. "The hand / Strikes wood. No answer. He halloos. Then the voice." The active agent, the voice saying something, must wait; there are, first, the imaginative moment in which he visualizes the "nameless face" and muses that "The dregs / Of all nightmare are the same, and we call it / Life"; then from the "unspecifiable / Darkness of a cave" the materialization of that "Life," the woman herself. The Indian looks (from his one good eye), gestures, and moves his lips soundlessly; the breathing of Audubon's dog, the sloshing of the jug, the grinding teeth of the sons as they devour their food, and the soft whisper of a sharpening blade on the stone: such sounds in a context without the human voice not only heighten suspense on a purely narrative level; they also drag, delay, retard the climax: "Everything seems far away, and small." Even the providential entry of the travelers is recorded without urgency because Audubon, whose experience is internal as much as it is external, knows that the customary scream that breaks the spell of dream will not come because he does not yet know the end of the dream.

The technical feat by which Warren manages to transpose predictable expectations inherent in a subject dominated by passion ("What / Is man but his passion?") into the terms and conditions of serenity is perhaps finally not susceptible of analysis. But some of the local effects that contribute to that creative triumph can be seen in their accretive, repetitive emphases. For much of the poem the images are those of silence, slow-motion enactment, frozen stances anticipating meaning. "He was sometimes seen to stand / In perfect stillness, when no leaf stirred"; he stands at dusk on a bluff; he looks as bones whiten in hot daylight; and, as his flute and brushes finally lay untouched and dry, he sleeps, dreaming of birds. Perhaps the most stunning—and most subtle —example of retardation is the multileveled use of the word *hang*. Warren has always believed in what he calls the "participation" of elements in a poem (SE, 282)—the notion that images and words gather meaning by increment, even though those words and images recur in different contexts and with varied connotations.
Section C begins:

> The face, in the air, hangs.

The suspended phrase breaks up the normal prosaic order of the sentence ("the face hangs in the air"), suggesting how Audubon's mind takes it in fully, in momentary delayed perception, measuring the actual image against the one he has merely imagined in the preceding section ("What should he recognize?"). Linguistically the first sentence of section C quietly sets up the importance of the word *hangs*. The first use of the word comes in section A, when Audubon approaches the cabin door: "His hand / Lifts, hangs." The verb intrudes again: "Against the gray skirt, her hands hang." They are the same hands that reach out for his gold watch: "She hangs it about her neck." Finally the accumulated reiteration of this neutral word culminates in an image that is both precise and literal on the level of immediate action and chillingly predictive. The physical posture is given the full value of a separate line: in her lust for ownership, "Her body sways like a willow in spring wind like a girl." The moment transforms the cavelike woman into a shy girl receiving a gift from her lover. To Audubon the face "Is sweet in an outrage of sweetness, so that / His gut twists cold. He cannot bear what he sees." In the parallel moment in sections J and K, he can, however, bear to see it. In her rage of will as she dies hanging, he sees her face "beautiful as stone," and he acknowledges the erotic, and thus the human, impact of the violence.

Segment V ("The Sound of That Wind") is a kind of collage of Audubon's life: preserved moments of achievement and insult interspersed with quoted matter lifted from Audubon's own writings. Here are allusions to the temptations—of quick fame and easy wealth—that he ignores for the carrying out of his great project. His patient discoveries and their painstaking recording, the impressions that come from his desire to see the world and to acquire its Knowledge: this is the section of apotheosis of the hero-saint who finally lies down in old age in "his earned house." Warren gives us a brief glimpse of Audubon's being struck by "the splendor of God" in the Indian ("free from acquired Sorrow"), then moves into a passage—

> Below the salt, in rich houses, he sat, and knew insult.
> In the lobbies and couloirs of greatness he dangled,
> And was not unacquainted with contumely . . .—   (SP, 97)

which consciously echoes Christ's progress in the world as Isaiah's Man of Sorrows. He is so fortified by his inner faith that he need not receive the recognition in the street from haughty patrons or the condescension of the mighty. He enters into his reward—the love of a mourning world—because he has concluded that though wicked enough, the world he has known "is *perhaps* as good as worlds unknown."

The tentativeness of that conviction is of a piece with Audubon's experience in and of the world. But it indicates something of Warren's experience, too, especially the measure of how far the poet has walked in the world, from the *yanqui* observer in Mexico admiring the fatalism of the peach-gumming old man who says, "Viene galopando . . . el mundo." There can be no accommodating mystic surrender of the human to the world, but neither can that world of the other, nature and society, be rebuked or ignored. Though the membrane between the self and the other is thin, it is a membrane still. Resisting definition, a recalcitrant world requires instead intuitive understanding, from which then comes acceptance of its inclusiveness ("the human filth, the human hope"). "Osmosis of being" certifies connection, not dissolution.

Warren also asserts the high value of human connection in his other poetry of the 1970s, and, suggesting the difficulty of that seemingly simple virtue, he also resorts to the techniques of the frozen moment and the dreamlike retardation of movement. The governing theme of *Or Else—Poem / Poems 1968–1974* (1974), *Now and Then: Poems 1976–1978* (1978), and *Being Here: Poetry 1977–1980* (1980) is continuities: of blood, of time, of the world. The common protagonist in this trilogy is the poet himself, who searches for meaning in those continuities.[31]

Warren's fondness for dialectic play is reflected in the title of *Or Else*, and even the directions for reading this volume are playfully handed over to the reader, who must decide: is it a six-year collection of diverse poems now collected for the first time? or is it a single poem conceived as a sequence? It is something of both. In a prefatory note Warren states that *Or Else* was conceived "as a single long poem composed of a number of shorter poems as sections or chapters," some of them written prior to 1968. Structured as a kind of internal dialogue, twenty-four poems, most of them forty lines or longer, are irregularly interrupted by eight briefer "Interjections."

Although this latter group formally lends to the volume the air of philosophical discourse, the poems throughout *Or Else* openly traffic with philosophical speculation and debate; their texts are dense with *evidence, existence, will, logic, real, fact, proof, know, perception, principle*, and their variants. Few of the poems are as lyrical as those in *Incarnations*, and they continue some of the harsh naturalistic observations of nature in that volume. *Or Else* is unique in Warren's canon in that the governing tone is set by its weakest poems, those nakedly structured as premises, conclusions, objections, second thoughts, stripped of much specific context and dominated by unconciliating skepticism. Moreover, the pervasive thump of heavy-handed irony does little to rescue this bald poetry of statement. The worst in the volume ("News Photo," "Bad Year, Bad War: A New Year's Card, 1969") join topical comment (white racism, Vietnam) and intricate, abstract inquiry (individualism, heroism, innocence, guilt). Other poems pursue links between self-identity and egoism ("Interjection #5: Solipsism and Theology"), time and will ("Interjection #2: Caveat"), identity and reality ("Time as Hypnosis"); some, like "Stargazing" and "Vision

Under the October Mountain: A Love Poem," proceed with a succession of abstractions relieved only fitfully by a striking image; others, like "There's a Grandfather's Clock in the Hall" and "Interjection #7: Remarks of Soul to Body," while engaging ontologically related subjects of time, identity, perception, and meaning, project an uncertain tone—now grave, now flippant—that undercuts their claim to be taken seriously. We are clearly intended to see, for example, the pain behind the speaker's bluntly realistic account of his mother's death in "There's a Grandfather's Clock in the Hall," but the scene is overpowered by the same overly aggressive gestures for avoiding sentimentality that weaken parts of "The Return: An Elegy," an early poem on the same subject. Consider the concluding lines:

> Nothing happens, nothing happens, then suddenly, quick as a
> wink, and slick as a mink's prick, Time thrusts through
> the time of no-Time.   (SP, 66)

This final sentence emphasizes verbal ingenuities at the expense of not only compassion but also the tangled relationships of innocence, experience, and the mystery of eternity.

The strongest and most vivid poems of *Or Else*, however, explore from various angles and perspectives the problem of human understanding in the face of mortality. Most of these are personal recollections projected in dreams and quasi-mystical states of experience ("I Am Dreaming of a White Christmas," "Folly on Royal Street Before the Raw Face of God," "Reading Late at Night, Thermometer Falling"). While the specific locales of the poet's youth are as strong here as in earlier volumes, they paradoxically become less relevant to Warren's primary theme: "we must think of the / world as continuous," despite the fact that we know we exist "only, oh, on- / ly, in discontinuity" ("Interjection #2: Caveat").

That statement is given concrete embodiment in the most impressive poem in the volume, "I Am Dreaming of a White Christmas: The Natural History of a Vision." Like so many of his poems about his parents, this poem has its origins in what Warren has called "symbolic" memory. Unlike "narrative" memory—"the unspooling in the head of what has happened, like a movie film with no voices"—symbolic memory may center upon nothing more consecutive than a single well-defined image—of, say, a face with a characteristic expression which in the economy of dream represents a merging of character, personality, and shared experiences whose specificities are now lost to the past.[32] The dramatized dreamscape of "I Am Dreaming of a White Christmas" materializes through a slow, unhurried movement and a surreal shifting of focus within an almost naturalistic frame. This is a world of stasis, the *was* of the poem, which, like scenes from a wax museum, is both soundless and motionless. In juxtaposition, two segments of a noisy cityscape—Times Square, a jostling summer crowd that constitutes the inescapable *is*—shatter the dream without resolving the mystery of their connection. In the penultimate segment, the speaker attempts to bridge the *is* and the *was* by the imaginative act of memory: he recalls how, though summer is not yet over in West Montana ("Or is it Idaho?"), it will be snowing "tonight." And though the Kentucky winter and the New York summer, the past and the present, are linked by the Nez Perce Pass, certain questions cannot be answered. "Will I never know / What present there was in that package for me, / Under the Christmas tree?" In the final stanza, the speaker nevertheless can affirm that dream, reality, and memory all "belong in the world / In which all things are continuous . . . ." He is still trying "to discover the logic" of the original dream, a process to be cherished because it is the way in which

> pain of the past in its pastness
> May be converted into the future tense

Of joy. (SP, 34)

Another memory, beautifully evoked, is the burden of "Rattlesnake Country," set on a western ranch but peopled again by the merely human: ranchhands who drive horses down from the mountains for the guests to ride, a hare-lipped Indian who perfects a method for incinerating rattlesnakes before they reach the safety of their rockhole, a businesslike host with a beautiful wife and twin daughters, the speaker himself absorbing both the wonder and the transience of his western experience. The vividness of the past is, predictably, not nourishing enough for the speaker: "What was *is* is now *was*. But / Is *was* but a word for wisdom?" If what is completed has a logic not possible for the as-yet-incompleted, it may be wisdom; but Warren's persona here, as elsewhere, is not content with that kind of wisdom. Those frozen moments of that "long-lost summer," caught in precise gestures, cannot, except by artifice and will, be complete. The twin daughters are now dead, the beautiful wife is engaged in an adultery not her first, the husband is "totally cynical" or perhaps dead, the Indian is in the penitentiary for murder. The re-creation of that summer and the speculation about its consequences, admits the speaker, do not by themselves announce their significance. He does not

Know what it all means, unless the meaning inheres in
The compulsion to try to convert what now is *was*
Back into what was *is*.   (SP, 50)

Whereas *Or Else* is dominated by a series of narrative portraits and
situations interspersed by "Interjections," *Now and Then* is structured
by more portraits and situations presented as "Nostalgic," which are
succeeded by a series of "Speculative" poems in which the speaker
struggles to reconcile rational assessment of the past and the knowledge
it brings with more tentative and subliminal assertions of meaning
experienced in dream states and near-mystical moments. The structure
is more direct and more appealing than the debate format of *Or Else*,
and the tone of the poems is consistently less strident. The poems of
"Nostalgic" recount from the perspective of age once-significant persons and events from the past, most of them a Kentucky past and most
of them centering on the poet as a boy. The diminishments of time,
which the speaker suspects are the same as loss of meaning in human
experience generally, are illustrated by his meeting after sixty years an
old boyhood friend, "the best shot in ten counties," who never realized
his big-league ambitions ("American Portrait: Old Style") and, after
fifty years, a hometown beauty he had admired from afar, now "a grisly
old dame" with sausage legs ("Old Flame"). While time's ravishment
of flesh and dreams seems naturalistically complete and even though
he must ask, "Can you say—when *all-to-be* said is the *done?*" the speaker is reluctant to pronounce as meaningless those situations "Where
old dreams had once been Life's truth."

The spirit that dominates the poems of "Nostalgic" is the wonder of
the mysteries of love and human hope ("Boy Wandering in Simms'
Valley"), the birth of sexual awakening and spiritual guilt ("Amaz-
ing Grace in the Back Country"), and the attempt to distinguish reality
and dream ("Red-Tail Hawk and Pyre of Youth"). Many of the
poems here duplicate the dream or trancelike states of mind so frequently used in earlier poems when individual consciousness seems almost to merge pantheistically with a natural environment (lying in a
trench in a field at sunset, by a cool spring at night, or in a country
graveyard overlooking a town), as if questions of being might better
find answers in such potentially transcendent moments than in the play
of logic. Indeed, when the reasoning mind takes over, uncertainty and
wondering are the best that can be imagined ("And stood wondering
what life is, and love, and what they may be").

Although the second section more directly confronts such mysteries, the "Speculative" poems come no closer to satisfying positions. The speaker listens to the sounds of birds, a moonlit stream, a forest storm, and seabreakers, straining to learn the secrets of the self; he lies awake trying to separate things that are true from things that may not be, desperate because "I couldn't be sure something precious was true"; he speculates on whether "a *now* or a *then*" exists and broods on the treacheries of memory. These poems, like so many in *Or Else*, reveal the self grappling with such abstractions as truth, God, and reality, but without so many of the cynical ironies that lace the earlier volume; the approach, if not engaged with more hopeful anticipations, is at least more affecting, reaching out to the reader with a minimum of guile or pose. One of the most direct of the speculative poems, "Identity and Argument for Prayer," manages to avoid the sterility of abstract meditation not through an anchoring to narrative specificities ("Space and Time our arbitrary illusions") but through the simple presentation of the speaker's vulnerability to fear, anguish, and finally compromise:

> But whatever I am and Truth is, I
> Have stood on a high place, yearning
> To know what logic of years, and of
> Whatever stride, clamber, climb,
> Had brought me here to be what I am . . .
>
> . . . .
>   and all
> I recall is the shadowy thought that
> Man's mind, his heart, live only by piecemeal, like mice
> On cheese crumbs—the cheese itself, of course,
> Being locked in the tin
> In God's pantry.   (*Now and Then*, 67–68)

At the end the speaker can arrive at an undefinitive, frail, but inevitable position as he stares from his bed into the "coagulate darkness,"

> Thinking now that at least you are *you*,
> Saying *now*, saying *now*, for
> Now *now* is all, and you *you*.   (*Now and Then*, 68)

Whatever delusions and illusions may surround them, it is this coming to terms with *self* as it can be known in a *world* as it is experienced that ushers in the poems of *Being Here*, the very title of which announces its—and finally Warren's—major theme.

Warren projects a passion to know the world—persons, places, things both past and present—as if the rage to possess it cognitively will eventuate in those moments of moral understanding usually reserved for mystics and transcendentalists. The coercive world invariably promises, beckons, betrays, revenges, giving Warren's speakers cause for pronouncing naturalistic credos; and their relentless mission seems always to try to understand why they should have to truck with the world at all. In Warren's own naming of parts, in which man finds his necessity and his dearest pain in the cataloging of nature, an astonishing number of the features from the natural world carries suggestions of taint, terror, or dumbfounding mystery, as if the gull or the hawk or even the stone possesses a knowledge of relationships superior to man's. Some—the owl and the spider, say—strike fear because of their bland disregard of man, but more sinister is insentient nature, like the "ovoid horrors"—the furred peach or the overripe plum or mango—to which the speaker attributes malevolent godliness.

In *Or Else* and *Now and Then* particularly, the poetry depicts the natural world with ambiguity: hawks, bats, kestrel, partridge cock, muskrat, minnow, field mouse all function in their world according to preordained, self-fulfilling patterns of instinct and purpose; but they also serve as rebukes to man, who, uncertain of his own instinct and purpose, feels vaguely envious of creatures whose inner natures and outer contexts are perfectly accommodated. The vole can boast "neither theology nor / Aesthetic": "Poor thing, he has only himself. And what do you have . . .?" Because they know "the path of pathlessness" and the joy of "destiny fulfilling its own name," a flock of wild geese in "imperial utterance" arrows the wheeling sky as the speaker watches; knowing time and distance "but not why I am here," he can only imaginatively follow the geese with "unwordable utterance."

More threatening than geese or voles or hawks, however, is inanimate nature, whose implicit rebuke to human consciousness more and more threads Warren's poetry of the past two decades. The sky "shivers with whiteness" or has "murder in the eye"; the world swings into shadow, and the earth grinds on its axis; a spruce wants "to hide the house from the moon," whose "intentions have never been quite clear." The fact that Warren carries the anthropomorphizing tradition beyond customary poetic logic or tact testifies to the growing intensity with which the poet conducts his search for every clue in great nature that might reveal correspondences—in the Emersonian sense—between the rational self and the psychic self. Increasingly those clues seem to lurk in inanimate nature, even man-made objects, as often as they do among birds and mammals. Not only do mountains "moan" or "lean" or "watch" and moraine boulders "grieve"; both nature and artifacts take on new purpose: stone, leaf, and chewing gum pity the human for being lonelier than they. The earth twitches, the sun jerks about, a fragment of crushed rock glitters and "screams / in an ecstasy of / being." Expensive cowhide luggage "glints with a sense of its own destiny." A rod-reinforced oak tree is "trying to tell you something," but even more modest and familiar objects participate in such adumbrated colloquies: a clock is "trying to make up its mind to strike," a chain saw "sings" in bloodlust, and a telephone "keeps screaming its little black heart out." The secret of at least one way to heal the divided self would appear to be, in such poems as "Dream of a Dream" and "Identity and Argument for Prayer," in learning this mysterious language—the voices of the singing stone and the prophesying surf as well as the calling owl and declaring thrush.[33]

Is communication needed, asks the speaker in "Star-Fall," between lovers who, lying at midnight on a cliff, hearing the sea and watching the falling stars of August, are "each alone"

> sunk and absorbed into
> The mass and matrix of Being that defines
> Identity of all?

No, since even lovers must be aware of their mutual separateness. But the larger question is, can the individual know the language of that mass and matrix into which he is absorbed? Probably not, but the only possibility lies in the sacramental submission of the recalcitrant self to the subliminal self, a process often represented by the poet's strenuous but faltering efforts to ally himself to the birds and beasts of nature. In "Heart of Autumn," that process is symbolized by the experience in which the poet, with his "unwordable utterance," undertakes to comprehend the "imperial utterance" of wild geese wheeling south. In "The Mission" the speaker speculates that his lost mission is perhaps to understand the "possibility of joy in the world's tangled and hieroglyphic beauty." The adjectives denote precisely the poet's notion of the self's relationship to the ambiguous Other and signify something of Warren's frequent invocation of "joy."

With its publication coinciding with Warren's seventy-fifth birthday, *Being Here* is the finest of the trilogy; the poet-as-searcher again probes all the mysteries shrouding the self's relation to the Other, but with a sustained urgency seen previously only as articulations of specific moods. In no previous volume do we see ontological and existential issues converging from so many directions. *Who am I?* is a question threading many works throughout Warren's career; the uses of memory as an imaginative aid in answering that question, the answer to which inevitably entangles his own being with that of those he loves, have been subjects of exploration since *Promises*; the ineradicable erosions of time haunt even the poems of joyous celebration that seem more intense in the poetry since the 1960s; and the nagging speculations about Truth—does it exist? can it be known? intuited? how and in what circumstances?—are philosophical burdens that both dignify and encumber much of the poetry early and late. *Being Here* brings together intertwined versions of all these momentous themes enunciated by a poetic voice stripped of the impatient querulousness and much of the wise-guy irony so often heard in *Or Else*; it is also a voice that significantly fails to deck itself with the tremulos of achieved wisdom, that sound both elegant and tedious that we hear, say, in the later work of Frost and Eliot. While it is unmistakably the work of an aging poet, *Being Here* is very much the work of a man still searching for answers.

While it is always tempting to read a poet's latest volume as a summing up, a rounding off, of his characteristic themes and forms, Warren himself, in a rare "Afterthought" that closes *Being Here,* invites us to do so with this volume. The ordering of the poems, he explains, is "played against, or with, a shadowy narrative, a shadowy autobiography," which is to say, the *internal* record of his chief metaphysical concerns.[34] Thus, the large issues of Time, Truth, Identity are all here engaged by a poet who has (presumably) done so in poems written in a three-year period, but they are issues familiar enough by now from earlier contexts. Further, Warren says, the "thematic order—or better, structure—" is built into five sections that comprise the "shadowy autobiography" of the poet from childhood (section I) through old age (section V). But "shadowy" in another way, too. These poems, like all of Warren's poetry, are in his own words "a fusion of fiction and fact in varying degrees," an authorial reminder that, however urgent and personal, they aspire to the level of generalization. *Being Here* is not another volume from the confessional school but, as Peter Stitt puts it, a record of one poet's speculations on "the process of life as all thinking people know it," a single "narrative," which, expanding outwardly, mythically, achieves its generalizing impulse through the skillful use of various distancing techniques: the more frequent use of dreams and the refinement of *you* to refer to the poet himself.[35] Yet, for all the generalizing effects, *Being Here* is decidedly the product of personal need. The voice we hear of the speaker who refers to himself as both *I* and *you* is Warren's voice speaking of and for himself, not the expression of a dramatized persona that we might encounter in some High Modernist poem.

Certain recurring images here are not merely the formal signals of aesthetic purposiveness; they assume configurations of personal urgency, perhaps even obsession. The familiar Warren exploration of self within a time-bound world takes various forms—the fascination with caves, flowing water, woodland clearings, ditches and ravines, enclosed spaces dark and damp. In "Speleology," its most dramatic instance, the young boy seeks out the absolute darkness of a cave where he is forced to feel the self in relation to the ongoing, immemorial Other. As he feels his heartbeat merge with "a pulse of darkness and earth," he wonders *who am I?* and how it would feel to "be here forever"; that cry of identity, on the potential verge of extinction, is counterpointed by the "silken and whispering rustle" of a swollen river far below the ledge where he lies half-dreaming. In this poem the state of being "Lulled as by song in a dream" prepares the self to speculate on "What would it be like to be, in the end, part of all," and in darkness the young boy asks "*Is this all? What is all?*" This is the kind of preparatory state duplicated in such poems as "On Into the Night," "No Bird Does Call," "Tires on Wet Asphalt at Night," "Timeless, Twinned," "Anatomy: Time and Identity," and "Acquaintance with Time in Early Autumn." Sometimes the experience is of a dream state; sometimes the speaker is mesmerized by chasm, pool, or waterfall; at other times the musing, questioning mind achieves a near-mystical moment of insight into the nature of time and the self that is hostage to it.

The other major group of images, conveying whiteness, brightness, distance, and silence, suggests a way out of the contingencies of place and time; these occur primarily in those situations in which the poet attempts to make certain other phenomena emblematic of transcendence, of escape into timelessness. The speaker may be fixated by stars or far ranges on the horizon ("Snowshoeing Back to Camp in Gloaming," "Night Walking"), or he may be alone on a mountain ridge in "the world of glitter and dawn-cold whiteness" ("Preternaturally Early Snowfall in Mating Season"); in either case the speaker psychologically faces timelessness (or "no-Time"), a realm which he wants to see as the source of answers to the questions of time-bound flesh. The promise ("unworded revelation") must be deciphered, however, and the same tokens that may signify order and meaning—the moon at its zenith, a cloud or star, the far horizon, an eagle spiraling beyond peaks and clouds—may also signify cosmic emptiness, as in "Snowshoeing":

> So starward I stared
> To the unnamed void where Space and God
> Flinch to come, and where
> Un-Time roars like a wind that only
> The dead, unweeping, hear.   (*Being Here*, 28)

In the poems of *Being Here*, the byplay of Time and Timelessness, of identity and extinction, is both intellectual and emotional. Warren, who has admitted to being both skeptic and yearner, may search the distances for confirmation that man is more than grass, and his memory for ratification that man learns wisdom from experience, but the realm that embraces both aspiration for the future and redemption from the past is simply the sensuous world. Although in loneliness and anxiety he may doubt its actuality, and though he occasionally images himself as the "world's dream," Warren never quite sacrifices the only ground he can know, the world in all its specificity. The conclusion of his seven-part "Synonyms" sums up this kind of middle position:

> There are many things in the world, and I have seen some.
> Some things in the world are beautiful, and I
> Have seen some. But more things are to come,
> And in the world's tangled variety,
> It is hard sometimes to remember that beauty is one word for reality.
> (*Being Here*, 100)

The tentativeness of Warren's middle position in *Being Here* is structurally emphasized—literally italicized—by the paired poems bracketing the five sections as prologue and epilogue. In the formal chronology of the book the first of the bracketing poems, "October Picnic Long Ago," lies outside the time scheme. Thus, section I, an evocation of and meditation on boyhood memories, is preceded by an event summoned up from the aging poet's recollection, one that seemingly offers few of the resistances that characteristically help to generate such poems. The family group on an outing is as secure in its contentment as the era itself—1910 or 1911—fixed by the remembered details of the Negro-driven surrey and the parents' clothing ("My mother's skirt was blue serge, long and close-fit. / My father's suede shoes were buttoned up high, and a Norfolk jacket"). The picnic is as "predictable" as any similar event in "that old time," with the idyllic scene prepared by a nature as beneficent as Father himself. It is a time of modest pleasures, of kinship, held in place by memory alone:

lunch, the baby asleep, children gone
But not far, and Father and Mother gone, hand in hand,
Heads together as though in one long conversation . . . .

Even though it projects familial love and security, this poem of memory
also manages to suggest the very fragility of those values. Bathed in
"golden October light," a reminder of autumnal depredations despite
the pastoral suspension of time, the scene fairly proclaims its momen-
tariness through the diction of magic:

Out of town, *clop-clop*, till we found a side-lane that led
Into woods, where gold leaves flicked a fairy shadow and light
That changed the known shape of a nose or face or head
Till we looked like a passel of circus freaks crammed tight
On four wheels, while the flickering nag was steered by a witch's
sleight. (*Being Here*, 3)

The benevolence of the scene is thus threatened from the beginning
by an undertow of change, the transforming power of time, an effect
achieved partly by the double perspective: a seven-year-old's impressions subtly complicated by the aging poet who remembers—and interprets—those impressions. Even the picture of parental happiness is
undermined by this double perspective; the mother cries out in joy,
connecting the beauty of the woodland spot with personal satisfaction
of her lot (" 'What more would I want,' she now cried, 'when I love
everything I now see?' "), but the father, perhaps making-do with
second or third choices, clouds that spontaneous outcry: " 'My ship
will come in yet, / And you'll see all the beautiful world there is to
see.' " Though the mother sings on the ride back home, the poet observes that the shadows "Leashed the Future up, like a hound with a
slavering fang"; whereas the sleepy seven-year-old hears only the song,
the poet peers into a devouring future of losses.

It is that devouring future which the final bracketing poem com-
memorates with the lonely image of "Passers-By on Snowy Night."
From the "golden October light" of the intimating first poem, with its
focus on the full complement of family, the poet closes with "coni-
ferous darkness" (a link with Warren's usual association of cedars and
death) relieved only by a snow-track of a trail and a "skull-white"
moon illuminating the scene. The focus is now on the separated self:

Alone,
I wish you well in your night
As I pass you in my own.

The mother's poignant song of the past is now replaced by the crack of snow-burdened boughs and "the owl's benediction" of the present.

The shapeliness of the poems of *Being Here* reminds us again that formally as well as thematically Warren is working at the top of his talent. The conversational syntax of "October Picnic Long Ago," with a flow appropriate to a recollection partly mused, partly told as tale, is restrained by the stanzas of five end-rhymed lines whose extra foot in the fifth line of each emphasizes formal closure; both the flow and the restraint reflect perfectly the substance of the memory. Most of the poems, in fact, are structured in conventional stanzaic forms, some (like "The Moonlight's Dream") moving stately to regular rhymes, others (like "On Into the Night") having the visual appearance (the tetrameter quatrains) if not the aural effect of Housman. There are couplets, triplets, quatrains, octosyllabics; magisterial verse paragraphs recalling Wordsworth and Arnold; and irregular stanzas in which line lengths and stanza lengths are determined by the intensity of experience they recount.

The accommodation of form and content is perhaps most subtly effective in "When Life Begins," another of Warren's poems centering upon his maternal grandfather. Like "Court-Martial" (from *Promises*) and "Safe in Shade" (also from *Being Here*), "When Life Begins" presents first a static image, the old man seated in the summer shade of a cedar, his blue eyes rapt by distances, the poet as a child nearby waiting for him to "come back." The loose iambic tetrameters, gathered in the quiet regularity of five-line stanzas, are well-chosen to carry the reverie of the old Confederate; though that reverie is a thing mostly of silence, abstract gaze, and mythic distance, it is given substance through the grandson's participating imagination—a kind of ur-poet's instinct that the lapsing smallness of the ordinary should somehow be redeemed by "passionate / Endeavor." As the military engagement of long ago is imaginatively reenacted once again, the formal stanzas explode into peremptory long and short lines punctuated with the hard diction of warfare before subsiding into the final two stanzas, a return to the meditative regularity of the beginning.

"Poetry wants to be pure, but poems do not" (SE, 4). With his own famous distinction firmly before him, Warren has invariably titled his collected volumes (and subtitled his individual volumes) *Poems*—as if to ratify with the products of his own creative labor his critical dictum of 1942, that the "purity" to which *poetry* aspires is always compromised by certain "impure" elements out of which *poems* are made. His catalog of impurities—"cacophonies, jagged rhythms, ugly words and ugly thoughts, colloquialisms, clichés, sterile technical terms, headwork and argument, self-contradiction, clevernesses, irony, realism"—is a virtual guidebook to what would constitute his own characteristic verse beginning with "The Ballad of Billie Potts." Unlike all previous volumes, however, *Being Here* is called *Poetry*, not *Poems*. Is this new preference a variation too subtle, or too accidental, to be significant?

Being Here is blessed with as many of those impurities that tend to spoil idealized visions of nature as any other volume of Warren's verse. It is filled with scenes of man in nature—mountain pools, nighttime beaches, snow peaks, waterfalls and gorges, caves and coves—and though the speaker often wants to believe that nature conspires benevolently with human need, most of the specific phenomena are overwhelmingly neutral, indifferent to the poet's persistent habit of wresting meaning from his environment of meditation. The volume has scarcely a trace of that "garden purity" that Warren once found, and dismissed, in Shelley and Tennyson in "Pure and Impure Poetry"; rather, what he termed the "enemies" of garden purity—realism, wit, intellectual complication—are in control. No less than his earlier poems, these are conceived and executed under the aegis of Mercutio. If a poem must come to terms with its own resistances to justify itself, as Warren argued in 1942, that principle is amply illustrated by his own poems in 1980.

But *Being Here* also betrays a yearning for one kind of perfection— the purity of timelessness—even in the midst of doubt that it exists. The same speaker who is haunted by human limitation is preternaturally alert for any sign in nature that consciousness itself may be transcended, any intimations that the self, rapt by distances, high peaks, and stars, may enter into an eternity that those natural phenomena often symbolize. In "Snowshoeing Back to Camp in Gloaming," the poet finds himself on a high mountain staring at a westward expanse of "white alabaster unblemished" and the "peak-snagged horizon":

> So I stood on that knife-edge frontier
> Of Timelessness, knowing that yonder
> Ahead was the life I might live
> Could I but move
> Into the terror of unmarred whiteness under
> The be-nimbed and frozen sun. (*Being Here*, 27)

In that it is dense with the specificities of the world, *Being Here* fulfills the promise of its title, but in that it is a late product of an old poet, more sensitive than ever before to the fact of his mortality, *Being Here* entertains the possibilities of immortality. There is actuality, and there is reality; and often, even when he risks being humbled by reason or experience, the speaker willingly engages such risks to speculate on the nature of that reality: could it be the same as timelessness, the all, eternity, immortality? and can the individual consciousness ever become part of that reality? Admittedly, Warren is too much the skeptic to be Christian, a spiritual posture rhetorically reinforced by the high incidence of interrogatives in the five sections of *Being Here*.[36] In searching for reality in actuality the poet may find that the latency of signs in nature may be finally more discouraging than reassuring: a distant horizon can suggest a void, a snowy crag metaphysical silence. In "Language Barrier" a mountain shelf falters and plunges to a blue cirque far below, becoming

> Torment and tangle of stone, like Hell frozen, where snow
> Lingers only in shadow. Alone, alone,
> What grandeur here speaks? The world
> Is the language we cannot utter.
> Is it a language we can even hear?   (*Being Here*, 72)

But the questioning, the speculating, the desperate guessing of the unseen from the seen continues, as if the poet must hear the world's language and must struggle to translate it into the language of eternity. It is in this sense that *Being Here* is *poetry* as well as poems.

If Warren's most recent poetry lacks the formal excitement of the experimental line length of the late 1950s and early 1960s, as well as the rough energy generated by a heavily accentual diction reminiscent of Hopkins, it has not returned to the metaphysical densities of his earliest. It is a technical development—a matter of aesthetic choices—but the later stage reflects an emotional proficiency too, a quieter level of judgment and calculation. While the lines of many of the recent poems continue to be variable, they are also less showy, and the familiar compounds (*jag-heave, love-stung, wet-waisted, snag-edged*) tend to be less obtrusive, rhetorically adjusted to the more formal demands of the line; the frequent reappearance of regular rhythms and rhyme schemes shows both relaxation and economy, the token of a poet who betrays little need to strike out for an experimental territory where he has already been.

The very configuration of Warren's poetic career has its own logic. Its notable mark from the mid-1950s onward is the creation of forms the integrity of which comes from the artist's greater openness both to personal risk-taking and to formal experimenting. Each volume, from *Promises* (1957) to *Being Here* (1980), publicly celebrates the private discoveries of maturity in which the poet meditates on and speculates about the distribution and use of his powers to love, to question, and to evaluate what is left. *Brother to Dragons*, the major transitional work, leaves behind the metaphysical model, with its metaphorical densities, its compressed, clotted intensities of syntax, its stern control of line and meter, and opens the way for freer forms, the longer even prosy line, the more direct appropriation of the personal (indicated by the increasing frequency of first- and second-person pronouns), the use of unrelated images juxtaposed rather than integrated, in sequences of poems that are themselves only loosely related, and the strident insistence upon moralized abstractions as internal interpretations. In each of the later volumes the hectoring interlocutor of *Brother to Dragons* appears as a querulous but vulnerable speaker: the lyric "I" is guarded by fewer spaces of distancing between poet and reader, and the narrative "I" becomes a passionate and more demanding interpreter of those knotty events that resist interpretation. Strict metrical forms, though they do not wholly disappear, take their place in a context of casual forms whose line lengths are governed by natural syntactic units, eye rhymes, assonance, and innovations in conventional patterns of rhyme.[37]

This larger scheme, however, though it is corroborated by the jagged gaps in the publishing history, should not obscure what is perhaps just as important in Warren's development as a poet: that the growth was evolutionary. "Bearded Oaks" was once the anthologists' favorite Warren poem, but its impeccable metaphysical imitations are no more derivative than the Eliotic mannerisms of "History" and "The Return: An Elegy." The poetic suite, now associated with the later phase, actually comes early with the Kentucky Mountain Farm sequence and the Studies in Naturalism. The sometimes bewildering shifts in tone from the academic to the colloquial were bewildering first to the readers of "Billie Potts." The fondness for "you" as direct address does not suddenly emerge in *You, Emperors, and Others*; and the obtrusively didactic, while it may mar more recent poems than early ones, has been from the beginning a consistent temptation to which Warren has frequently succumbed.

From the perspective of his entire career as poet we can now see that the beneficiary of that great sense of release evident in *Brother to Dragons*, *Promises*, and *You, Emperors, and Others* is a kind of "breathing" pace that permits quasi-narratives to be told more leisurely. Such a technical discovery has had substantive implications. Predetermined meanings of reconstituted events, the primary impression of "The Ballad of Billie Potts," give way to meanings discovered in the aesthetic act of reconstitution; and the interstices—what cannot be precisely placed— become as significant to meaning (or the search for it) as those nagging details lodged in the memory. This newer way of recalling events has also affected Warren's way of *imagining* events: just as his poems on Valéry (*Incarnations*), Audubon (*Audubon: A Vision*), Flaubert and Dreiser (*Or Else*), and Mark Twain (*Now and Then*) emerge out of the conjunction of biography and imagination, so are the poems about himself engendered by the union of autobiography and imagination. These more personal poems, as Warren admits in *Being Here*, are "a fusion of fiction and fact in varying degrees and perspectives." We can only guess, since he has never been comfortable with the nakedly confessional mode, that most of the personal poems since the technical breakthroughs of the 1950s result from that same fusion.

If his naturalistic orientation tells Warren that great nature is fallen, that it resists man's fondest attempts to make it correspond to his moods and beliefs, his reluctance to accept the external world as blank, mechanistic, or grimly unreadable is just as romantic as that of Coleridge or Emerson, who, dissatisfied by mere response to nature, celebrate the human need to make the Other more rewarding, or even minimally bearable, by what has been called "active emotional projection." Only when the natural world has been "enlivened by the projection into it of human passions does it become a source of wonder, of solace, of joy."[38] The great Romantics could rest more easily than Warren in the satisfying spectacle of nature in effect molded, shaped, and selectively rearranged, since it testified to poetic power, the imaginative uniqueness that in little imitates the Creator's.

The tensions in Warren are obvious. On the one hand he is orthodox in his conviction that man is separated from both nature and God, a realist who, if he were a churchman, would see heresy in such romantic ideology, but, since he is not, sees compulsive human presumption. On the other hand, being a moral realist does not lessen the need either to see pattern and meaning in the ruck of nature or to impose them on nature; presumption may be necessary if the sliding brokenness of things is to yield up meaning that men require. Sights set too high bring only disappointment when meaning cannot match the expectations of the creating imagination; sights set too low bring only cynicism, the grumpy denial that any meaning in a contingent universe is possible.

Warren's psychic and moral resolution of such tensions, where there is resolution at all, depicts chastened man's accepting the probability that the world is finally unreadable but that, by acknowledging his responsibility to the self and his entanglement with the Other, he will read it anyway. Through an "osmosis of being" he may receive the satisfaction of a creator who is able to make sense of "what is left" by ordering and shaping the fugitive scraps and tattered fragments of his experience. Thus the note of "joy" which recurs desperately, especially in Warren's later poetry, is visionary, but it is not dissociated from what Jeremiah Beaumont calls "the moil and clutter of the world," that fact of imperfection which consciousness can only observe and lament. Even in those lyrics incorporating the trans- or preternatural state, in which dreaming dislocates images of the daylight sensibility into patterns whose referents defy rational design and purpose, evil and confusion are not ignored but subsumed.[39] If it is true, as Karl Kroeber has claimed, that the English Romantics insisted upon the "unified indivisibility of moral action" and demanded that it be judged "in terms of its own entirety, as a total process," then Warren is a latter-day Romantic. To him, as for his predecessors, "good and evil, innocence and experience, sensual passion and spiritual passion are definite, irreducible components out of whose interactions the processes of human experience arise."[40]

The constant play of energy accounts in part for the remarkable vitality of Warren's poetry. From "abstracted passion" to "passionate inquiry," the growth over nearly six decades shows flexibility within a disciplined intelligence that very early found its congenial themes and their articulating techniques.[41] *"This is the world"*: it is a discovery which comes to speaker after speaker in Warren's poems. That world refuses to go away, and the discovery must be lived with in varying states of doubt and tentative belief.[42] Even when the emphases shift, as in the later poems when there are transcendent moments of love or joy or hope, those values are always anchored in the reality of a complex and fallen world. In a world that is never irrelevant, even joy is a necessary discipline.

THREE

Discourse as Art

Warren's Nonfiction Prose

Only by pressure and in pain is man "routed" into a knowledge of his fate, and into whatever triumph, however limited and qualified, is possible in it.

—"Melville's Poems" (1967)

Whatever integration may come to mean, it will mean a great change; and change, however deeply willed, is always shocking; old stances and accommodations, like the twinge of an old wound, are part of the self, and even as we desire new life and more life, we must realize that a part of us—of each individual person, black or white, has to *die* into that new life.

—*Who Speaks for the Negro?* (1965)

VI. Pure and Impure Criticism

Warren's place in American criticism is not so dominant as John Crowe Ransom's, so cerebral as Allen Tate's, nor so ingenious as Cleanth Brooks's. Warren invented no new terms in the lexicon of the New Criticism and broached no new theories worth the name. From the first he considered the writing of criticism as a spare-time activity —"part of my social life," like "talking" (*Talking*, 287)—and most of the early essays he chose to preserve in *Selected Essays* (1958) began as book reviews.[1] Even the ambitious and perceptive later essays reflect his primary interest in specific matters (American writers, the writing of poetry and fiction) and often seem to originate as commissioned lectures or as exploratory byways of more major projects—such as the task of assembling, ordering, and glossing the major documents in American literature, which resulted in *American Literature: The Makers and the Making* (1973), an ambitious anthology on which he collaborated with Brooks and R. W. B. Lewis. Despite this apparently peripheral interest, Warren has established himself as one of the most perceptive practical critics in America.

For various reasons—convenience, the academic impulse to categorize according to schools and movements, the fact of friendships and associations—Warren has always been linked with the movement that carries the name given to it by his friend and mentor, John Crowe Ransom; and, because he has been an enunciator and defender of the single cohesive principle that holds all the so-called New Critics together—the supremacy of the text—he has never strenuously sought to disengage himself from that influential movement. Indeed, though he has referred to New Critics as "they" more often than as "we," there is no substantial evidence to indicate that he should so disengage.[2] He believes that content and form in poetry are inseparable, and he has insisted that poetry is separable from ethics (and from religion, politics, and science). The poem itself is both greater than and different from the materials that go into its making and the effects that it subsequently has on the reader; it is a made unity incorporating diverse and often contradictory impulses. Warren is interested in affirming the importance of ambiguity, irony, complexity, multivalent connotation, tension, and paradox—not only because he thinks these are constituent elements of all serious literature but also because he thinks they characterize the true nature of human experience. And he is aware that we violate the richness of the poem as it is experienced when we talk about the text discursively. If his criticism shows a remarkable lack of interest in "the poem," "the play," or "the novel," it reveals a considerable interest in the idea that literature is a form of knowledge—a commitment shared but argued more theoretically by Tate, Ransom, and Brooks. Because of his role in the pedagogical revolution in the teaching of literature, Warren has in a sense been the tactical field commander of the New Criticism. Since 1938, when he and Brooks published what was essentially a revision of their syllabi as *Understanding Poetry*, his provocative analyses and shrewd judgments have been an important generative basis for literary criticism of the most diverse kinds. In his preface to *Selected Essays*, Warren disavows any aspirations to construct "a complete theory of criticism," observing that what has been called our Age of Criticism is really noted "not for a massive and systematic orthodoxy, but for the variety and internecine vindictiveness" of critics who find little in common "except their enemies" (SE, xi–xii).

In calling for an untiring and commonsensical scrutiny of the text, Brooks and Warren were able to sidestep any explicit promulgation of poetic theory. While *Understanding Poetry* may have been the result of certain cherished theories about the making of poems as a human act and the poem itself as a tangible human artifact, its real and immediate contribution was the shattering of the mystique of the poet as possessor of impulses, sentiments, and intuitions too rarefied to be understood by ordinary men. The poet as ethereal alien and the poem as untouchable talisman were assumptions virtually unquestioned before 1938; further, these popular notions were not disabused but abetted by academic guardians who, avoiding poetic analysis, ended their responsibility by setting both poet and poem in their historical continuum. Just as the influence of *Understanding Poetry* and its later generic companions was pedagogical, so was the method itself. If a poem was a thing to be studied rather than an art object to be reverenced, then the image of the poet as some mysterious genius unrelated to anything more than the category poet could be replaced by the more realistic image of the poet as craftsman, maker, artisan. It is sometimes forgotten that, however truculent and iconoclastic we imagine Brooks and Warren sounded, their methods for worrying a poem until it yielded up its significance were rhetorically casual, reiterative, and varied.[3] Their major aim was not ideological but practical: moving the governing theories and practice of six or eight critics out of the little journals into the classroom.

The spirit of that eclecticism can be seen in all of Warren's critical work, from the merely journalistic to the most conceptually ambitious. Again, it is sometimes forgotten that in Warren's case the autotelic integrity of the text, the doctrine for which the *Understanding* books were said to be manuals, was antedated by at least a decade by a deep interest in and practice of history and biography. Warren's taste in reading has always tended not toward authors of theoretical and abstract ideas but toward those fascinated by the clash of rival ideas and their effect on circumstances: William James, Machiavelli, Dante, Shakespeare. Warren has no single volume that can stand as a major document in the triumph of formalistic criticism, no *Well-Wrought Urn* or *The World's Body*, no *Seven Types of Ambiguity*. Indeed, he has no single essay that can stand as an exemplary landmark in the development of a methodology, as I think we can so designate "A Poem Nearly Anonymous" and "Tension in Poetry." If we compare the most celebrated essay by Ransom, Tate, or Brooks with a comparable one of Warren's, Warren's would have to be "Pure and Impure Poetry," an essay that nevertheless resists the use of new terms and tools for analyzing and evaluating poetry. Lurking behind it are *structure, tension, paradox*, and especially *irony*, but any sign of theory is firmly subsumed by the practical business at hand: to show how human experience modifies, or fails to modify, poetic impulse, the special gift of perspective conventionally assumed, sometimes by poets themselves, to be insulated from "unpoetic" experience that is amenable to the poetic only through the use of special formulas, diction, and appropriate "attitudes." Even "Pure and Impure Poetry" is a genial expatiation of certain suggestions and principles out of *Understanding Poetry* and Cleanth Brooks's attack (in *Modern Poetry and the Tradition* [1939] and elsewhere) on the Arnoldian notion that no poem should contain any word that seemingly contradicts the poet's main purpose.

Warren's criticism finally reveals less the rigidities of formalism, including the doctrine of autotelic art, than an older notion of art as a complex function involving biography, history, other art forms, religion, and psychology. Respect for the text is not lessened thereby, but appreciates insofar as it is regarded as the product of a maker who is not aesthetic man only. Without benefit of theoretical superstructures, Warren reveals his bias in the concern for the sundry pressure points whose intersections tug and push a writer into certain definable modes and strategies. Warren finds the world that Dreiser accepted, for example, one of "morally undifferentiated experience," exhibited in the novelist's twin obsessions—compulsive veracity and compulsive lying. The poles of Melville's thought and art he finds to be nature and spirit, but the abstract philosophical question—"What meaning or reconciliation could men find in nature? What in the spirit?"—is preceded, determined, and illuminated by two very material adventures, the early flight into a Pacific Eden and the 1856 journey to the Holy Land. Poetic power or value is not a simple thing, says Warren, "but always a resultant of forces, a compound of elements" (HM, viii). Passionately desiring a fur coat, as in Dreiser's case, can be as contributory to the shape of an artistic text as hearing a lecture on the Dahlgren gun, as in Melville's. In both instances, the episodes converge with other urgencies, contributing to general dispositions of themes and patterns of imagery. It is not enough to exhaust the possibilities of meaning within a text; the text itself is a complex of forces articulated and formalized.

Warren was a debunking biographer before he was a New Critic, and his easy use of primary documents and secondary scholarship and his alert attention to factual ironies have been sufficiently exercised ever since the writing of *John Brown*. Biography, history, sociology, psychology, philosophy have served him well in essay after essay. The uses of learning of any kind, not merely the most obvious disciplines relating to literary criticism, are evident in Warren's series of essays on American literature, which stylistically are the most graceful and effective of all his criticism.

"John Greenleaf Whittier: Poetry as Experience" is a characteristic later essay. Structured on the chronological career of its subject, with set pauses for analyses of key poems, it is textured by juxtapositions of selected interests, anxieties, vanities drawn (inasmuch as they can be determined) from the poet's inner life, along with their sometimes speculative relationship to the poems. This essay, like most of his discursive writing, frankly incorporates subordinate topics that are as relevant to Warren's own interests as they are to Whittier's. In a sketch of Whittier's family background, Warren devotes two paragraphs to a succinct discussion of *peasant*: our contemporary confusion of this term and "poor farmer," Jefferson's clarity on the matter, the psychological nimbus of the word, and the use of folk elements by sophisticated poets. At the proper structural place in the essay, as he must do, Warren defines *abolitionism*, but the nine-paragraph excursus becomes a brief history of that political and moral movement in relation to emancipation, Christian theology, the concept of the higher law, antinomianism, American individualism as a national ideology, and "the democratic process." Lying behind Warren's revealing discussion of one of Whittier's finest achievements, "Letter from a Missionary of the Methodist Episcopal Church South, in Kansas, to a Distinguished Politician," is everything Warren knows about the preparatory stages of the Civil War, particularly the struggle between the proslavery and free-soil partisans for control of Kansas. Such raw information Warren had as early as 1929, but in his book on John Brown that information is also a tonal weapon, useful for the young southerner hostile to the arrogance of Yankee moral snobbery in the twentieth century. In his evaluation of Whittier, abolitionism is seen in a more balanced light, especially when it is informed, as in Whittier's case, by a Quaker commitment favoring human as well as doctrinal values. It is that stout commitment on Whittier's part that actually supplies a second layer of irony to what Warren calls the "ventriloquism" of the poem. This southern Methodist becomes not simply the evil man cloaking himself in the language of the good (the formal irony of the poem); he may in fact be good, if misguided, a moral insight on Whittier's part that turns into an aesthetic effect: the rendering of "the fundamental irony of the relation of evil and good in human character, action, and history" (JGW, 32). Thus, for Warren, church history, conflicting doctrines, and politics merge not merely to lend resonance to a poem but to invest it with its most basic significance.

Warren's eclecticism in critical writing is not, as some readers have believed, a late development, a mea culpa response to the widespread reaction in the 1960s against the ingenuity of the New Criticism, just as his later more open poetry is not a response to the influential "Confessional" movement. His famous and controversial essay on *The Rime of the Ancient Mariner*—still his virtuoso piece—was written in 1945–1946 as a lecture and published as an introductory essay to a special edition of Coleridge's poem in 1946. "A Poem of Pure Imagination: An Experiment in Reading" appeared, then, when most of the formalist victories had been won, and that date has some bearing on the curious way in which the essay is both old-fashioned and premonitory.

Warren displays an academic's thorough knowledge of Coleridge's criticism and poetry because he had consulted essentially the same texts, memoirs, and letters that scholars of English romanticism had always used for their understanding of the poem; moreover, he builds upon scholarship rather than dismisses it. The uses to which he puts it, however, result in the most imaginative reading of the poem ever advanced.

It is ingenious criticism that is also creative scholarship. Warren's use of John Livingston Lowes's methods in *The Road to Xanadu* (1927), itself a scholarly breakthrough long regarded by admirers as sui generis, was remarkably discreet and tactful. Warren saw, along with the other admirers, that Lowes's adaptation of a long-honored and pedantic method of literary study—source hunting—was brilliant; but he alone saw that Lowes's methods were static; they were unable to show how Coleridge's reading, though transmuted into the texture of the poem, contributed to "imaginative meaning," how the books the poet read became organically related to the meaningful structure of the poem (SE, 272–73). Warren adapts Lowes's subtitle—*A Study in the Ways of the Imagination*—for his own title; but his very procedure is an imaginative extension of Lowes's landmark work.

He admits that *The Rime of the Ancient Mariner* may well reflect "internal conflicts" in the poet (that is, Coleridge's alienation from the purely physical world or his sexual drives or his struggles with opium addiction) and that pointing them out has its own values: "a poignant chapter of biography," for example, or an affecting image of "human suffering and aspiration." But Warren is not primarily interested in Coleridge's poem for purposes of reconstructing such a chapter or in establishing such an image. If a poem reflects personal motives (even in disguised form), it also tends to "transcend the personal problem, to objectify and universalize it." And this particular transcendence is his interest.

To his homework in the *Biographia Literaria* and the contributions of John Livingston Lowes, Earl Leslie Griggs, Lamb, Wordsworth, John Muirhead, T. M. Raysor, and others, Warren adds his knowledge of psychological archetypes and conventional Christian symbols to buttress an interpretation of the poem that runs counter to that of earlier Coleridge scholars. Briefly, this is the conviction that *The Ancient Mariner* possesses "a relatively high degree of expressive integration" and that it is a moral work far different from Mrs. Barbauld's sense of the term, a complex but logically fused work of art despite the opinions of Wordsworth and Southey, and a work of art freely using the supernatural for effects quite beyond the gothic *frisson* felt by Marius Bewley. Furthermore, Warren finds the poem "central and seminal" for Coleridge the philosopher as well as for Coleridge the composer of "magical lines"— central both for the poet, and "for its age, providing, not a comment on an age, but a focus of the being and issues of that age." This opening out of significance, the idea of a poem as something more than a complex tissue of images related only to themselves, makes this ambitious exercise important for Warren as critic. It is his one earlier essay that anticipates the larger interests of his later work on Melville, Whittier, Dreiser, Hawthorne, and Mark Twain. Part of its importance is Warren's boldness in advancing himself as a "symbol-hunter," that degenerative specimen of New Critical ideology that literary historians and philologists had been scolding for years. Sometimes concessive, sometimes adjunctive to the colloquial impatience that marks *John Brown*, Warren's essay and the notes in which he debates the others' positions betray one of the few demonstrable principles of his criticism: that every conceivable resource available to the critic is potentially a useful tool. If his reading derives more from theology than psychology, from the great religious formulations that for Coleridge were equally relevant to Belief and Poetry, Warren does not hesitate to rely on the related but diverse methods made familiar by archetypal criticism, symbolic logic, and aestheticism; he dips into necessitarian philosophy, Kantian phenomenalism, and Hartleyean associationism when they seem relevant.

If "A Poem of Pure Imagination" is remarkable criticism because Warren insists upon seeing a text normally considered "pure" or "self-contained" opening centrifugally, becoming itself a signification of a historical moment, *Homage to Theodore Dreiser* is remarkable for quite the opposite reason. For most of his essay Warren ignores the critical article of faith that has determined the ambiguous status of Dreiser in our literature—that his is a poetics of pity whose effectiveness comes not from artistry (that is, his style) but from some mysterious emotive power inherent in iteration and accretion. Warren matter-of-factly assumes the unity of the uneven works, especially as they are projections of twin obsessions (Dreiser's conviction of his own uncommonness as a man of superior worth and his surety that all actuality, even his extraordinariness, was illusion). But despite the way he sees the novels as fictional enactments of the novelist's biography, both factual and imagined, Warren finally defends Dreiser's "art." He believes that *An American Tragedy* can be admired as a documentary record of a particular moment in our history, "the half-century in which the new America of industry and finance capitalism was hardening into shape and its secret forces were emerging to dominate all life" (TD, 112). But this documentary quality, Warren says, derives from the more important fact of Dreiser's experience in this historical moment, an experience which is felt in his greatest work as *materials*: "in the strange metabolism of creation, they are absorbed and transmuted into fictional idea, fictional analogy, fictional allusion. The book is 'created,' and therefore generates its own power, multiplying the power implicit in the materials" (TD, 113). In Warren's corrective lens, *The Rime of the Ancient Mariner*, a "pure" poem, is a significant text for revealing the "being and issues" of its age; Dreiser's "impure" novels are significant indexes to an artist's transposition of personal-public materials of an age into fiction whose own patterns and rhythms make for an independent power.

With his sexual insecurities and drive for power, documented in his biography and transferred boldly to his novels, Dreiser would seem to invite the diagnostic ministrations of the psychological critic. But, as any committed reader of the little journal *Literature and Psychology* could point out, Warren is not a very orthodox psychological critic; in his reading of Dreiser there is no systematic Freudian or Reichian body of truths shaping his observations either early or late. The raw, pretentious checklist of terms usually clogging the argument in psychoanalytically derived criticism—the turgid parade of *urethral*, *phallicness*, *anal*, and the rest—is notably scarce in Warren's work generally; even *repression* and *sublimation*, terms that by now have been domesticated by literary critics and television personalities alike, seldom appear in his criticism. Nevertheless, the psychological intricacies involved in a writer's conversion of autobiography into art do interest Warren, especially as they can be seen in American writers. Warren is fascinated by certain continuing premises operable in the writing of Americans: the quality of success in America, the thrust and drag of individualism as opposed to community, the interchangeable calculus of commercial and moral values. "Melville's Poetry," "John Greenleaf Whittier: Poetry as Experience," *Homage to Theodore Dreiser*, and other essays all show Warren's interest in the American writer's respect for fact, that of his own life and the life of his nation; in the multiform continuities between the public life and the private; and in the covert transposition of what Warren calls private "inwardness and shadows" into theme, character, image, even the structure of artifact (JGW, 7). These are interests whose affinities most readers would agree to be psychological; yet Warren's usual method is to convert the appropriate terminology into the idiom of more conventional critical discourse.

To cite only two examples of Warren's strategy: in most ways dissimilar, both Dreiser and Whittier are public men of letters whose best work comes when their deepest source, private anguish, is channeled into those public forms—novels, ballads, and nostalgic autobiography—most conducive to the widest response. Awakening to the harshness of a Darwinian world, young Dreiser agonizes on what he will be: a

superman, an autonomous predator, or another will-less chemism buf-
feted by chance and nature. The answer to his question does not lie in
his work, says Warren: "It *is* his work" (TD, 19). *Sister Carrie,* the
Cowperwood trilogy, *An American Tragedy* enact facts of being—
the incontrovertible facts available, on both conscious and unconscious
levels, to the "outsider, the rejected, the yearner." In Whittier's case,
throughout his massive and compulsive production of verse between
1843 and the Civil War, the young poet blunders into growth, not in
technical skill (which he matter-of-factly achieved early on) but in
choosing or being chosen by congenial subjects "that might release the
inner energy necessary for real poetry" (JGW, 34). The abolitionist
verse, because it was "hallowed—and disinfected—expression," was
not enough, observes Warren, to discharge a much deeper sense of
grievance: that could come only when his greatest poetic power was
released through his greatest indignation, more intense than with most
men, of having lost his childhood Eden.

   Without the crutch of a borrowed lexicon Warren balances himself
between a kind of borderman's canny common sense and an exegete's
sophisticated insights. Without once using the term *nonfiction novel,*
for example, Warren defines it in his book on Dreiser and gives that
stumbling genius credit for "trying to invent a genre" long before
Truman Capote's elegant expediency; moreover, he does so not by fierce
theorizing but by the logic of cultural and literary history. *The Financier*
reflects other American realists' interest in using art to celebrate the
actual, rendering the "material of fact" with "the airs and graces of
fiction." The novels about Yerkes became that kind of fiction "in which
all the outer facts are certified and the inner facts are imaginatively ex-
trapolated from that evidence, and the whole, outer and inner, is offered
as a document" (TD, 76–77). Warren respects both the power of
personal experience and the impinging historical moment when they
conspire to produce a poem or novel, when both are submitted to what
he calls "the strange metabolism of creation"; but his greatest involvement in the work of other literary men characteristically occurs when
he observes how the pressures of inner disharmonies issue visibly in
the artifact.

   For John Brown, a kind of "found" protagonist, that expression is the
biography itself, a life of unambiguous action and ambiguous motives.
For Dreiser, it is the balanced compulsion "for both self-indulgence
and self-scrutiny" (TD, 75). It is a pattern that Warren himself repeats in the divided heroes of his own fiction. In the case of Robert
Frost, the internal conflict between the acknowledged fact and the

seductive dream issues forth in such superb poems as "Mowing," "Stopping by Woods on a Snowy Evening," and "After Apple-Picking." For Conrad, a noble vision is contaminated by action to which mature men are nevertheless committed, an insight resulting in a series of novels without moral or political resolution: "some hope" is one term; "they shall all be pitied together" is another. For Dreiser, the oscillating convictions that he was nobody and that he was destined for special achievement become the governing fables of all his novels.

When Warren says that "internal consistency"—all the elements operating together "toward one end"—is the basis for interpreting a literary work, he does not offer this directive as the ultimate one that helped to fashion an entire generation of classroom critics. He reminds us that internal consistency as a criterion is subject to distortion and the subjective fancies of the free-wheeling critics unless it is corrected and tested by "external consistency": consideration of the intellectual and spiritual climate of the age in which the poem was written, the overall pattern of the writer's work, the writer's thought which can be gleaned from "non-artistic sources," and the ineradicable facts of the author's life (SE, 269–70). The insistence upon the bringing together of both criteria as applicable guides for reading a literary text is notably free of arcane theorizing and is rational in its argument. It seems made to order for the common reader. But as the product of such a critical procedure, "A Poem of Pure Imagination" demonstrates not the ease but the difficulty of coming to terms satisfactorily with a great text. It shows the necessity for going beyond both the level of mere appreciation and intuition and that of hermetic linguistic analysis. When several years later Warren turns for the second time to the study of Melville's poetry (his first attempt, "Melville the Poet" dates from 1945), he follows the same guidelines he laid down in his essay on Coleridge. What counts, he says, "is not the degree of consciousness (or of clarity of intention) that the writer actually had during the process of creation, but the degree (or clarity) of expressive integration in the work as delivered" (HM, 77). That "expressive integration" is arrived at, in the case of *Clarel*, by consideration not only of the internal cohesiveness of thematic, narrative, and symbolic elements in that long poem, but also of their relationship to Melville's other works (*Pierre* and *Battle-Pieces* especially), the biographical circumstances (the sense of failure, poverty, emotional strain) and the context of intellectual and literary history (the place of *Clarel* vis-à-vis *Childe Harold*, *In Memoriam*, and "Dover Beach").

Most of Warren's criticism is an implicit plea to the reader to take a text at least as seriously as he takes his own notions about that text, a task requiring hard work as well as sensitivity. This kind of critical activity is a mimetic parallel to what Warren stresses as significant in the creative activity of the writers he respects. Dedicated labor is commensurable with the high role of the artist and confirms his claim to that calling. Without it, the artist is merely potential; his actualizing comes only through the disciplining of his diverse impulses and winning the right to make his work succeed by using his resistances, by incorporating his own divergent needs. Poems are impure; that they contain more of the world's dross than they "ideally" should is indicated by the frequency of *self*-marring imperfections: "cacophonies, jagged rhythms, ugly words and ugly thoughts, colloquialism, clichés, sterile technical terms, headwork and argument, self-contradictions, clevernesses, irony, realism—all things which call us back to the world of prose and imperfection" (SE, 4–5). Warren's own famous essay of 1942 is repeated the following year, with some variations, in Slim Sarrett's essay on Shakespeare in *At Heaven's Gate*: "The pure cry of pain is not poetry. The pure gasp and sigh of love is not poetry. Poetry is the impurity which an active being secretes to become pure. It is the glitter of pus, richer than Ind, the monument in dung, the oyster's pearl" (AHG, 196). The process of *striving*—the clues to a writer's effort to make sense of his own recalcitrances—is what Warren characteristically looks for in literary texts. To be remarked is the frequency with which such words as *test* and *earn* appear in Warren's critical writing.

A poem, we are told, "to be good, must earn itself"—that is, it must come to terms with "resistances" represented by "the materials of the poem." The poet "proves" his vision, refines it, "by submitting it to the fires of irony"—one form of the earning process—in the hope that his vision will be earned, "that it can survive reference to the complexities and contradictions of experience" (SE, 29). Proust, Eliot, Faulkner, even Dreiser, remained faithful to the complexities of the problems they dealt with; in so doing, they defined the context in which and the terms by which "faith and ideals" could take on aesthetic integrity.

The language of striving dominates *Selected Essays*. For Warren the importance of Conrad's men of natural virtue lies "in their being, not in their doing," but when they reach their moments of salvation, the spontaneous act which verifies it "must have been earned, and only by the fact of its having been earned" is the act significant. If "the process of the earned redemption" is the theme which engaged Conrad most fully, it is clearly a theme in other writers that engages Warren. In examining "Stopping by Woods," he speaks of "the beauty and peace" not in the scenic surrender of Frost's woods but in their promise at the end of the speaker's journey, an anticipation of "earned beauty stemming from action." Warren points out that the resolution of Katherine Anne Porter's *The Cracked Looking-Glass* is provisional, one that the young Irish girl must "re-learn and re-earn every day." Miranda of *Old Mortality* "must earn" the truth of a family legend by which she can live only "in the process of living." Warren admires Porter's "dialectical approach to matters of definition" largely because it results in a narrative forced to "test its thematic line at every point against its total circumstantiality" so that the theme is "validated" by experience both real and total.

This principle in effect becomes Warren's own "test" that certain writers fail. Despite, for example, the lyric power of Hemingway and his compelling symbolic response to our age, Warren detects a limitation: the "scruple of honor," of Hemingway's heroic ideas, is "submitted to the test of relatively small area of experience, to experience of a hand-picked sort, and to characters of a limited range" (SE, 117). And Warren locates the source of Thomas Wolfe's failure in the easy seduction to "the mysticism of the American idea," a tendency he finds more blatantly dominating Carl Sandburg, Stephen Vincent Benét, Hart Crane, and other poets of "the hortatory moment, the fleeting symbol, and the affirmation." Their weakness lies precisely in their rage for smoothing out all the kinks and jags of human experience, seeking the "Word" that will "clarify all the disparate and confused elements" of America (SE, 180–81).

For all his eclecticism in the practical matter of analysis and evaluation, Warren's work shows a clean line of interest. The isolated poem or novel is rarely seen as the self-containing object that yields its meaning through contemplation. Warren is a critic of continuities and contexts. He is more interested in perceiving the central principles operating throughout a writer's canon than in discovering the autotelic integrity of one work within it. Even in those essays originating as reviews of single titles (as in Eudora Welty's *The Wide Net* and Thomas Wolfe's *Of Time and the River*), his method is invariably to show by contrast or comparison with the writer's earlier titles how the vision and the technique have been extended, refined, or otherwise altered. It is a critical method that seeks to make sense of the total writer, and the simple expedient of chronology facilitates the discovery of the distinctive thrust of a particular writer. Warren appeals to what he calls the "principle of presumptive coherence in development, the fact that, despite waverings and false starts, a writer's history usually shows us a basic line."[4]

Conrad, he finds, employs a fable as his "central fact," a fable that is the "story of awakening and redemption." The fact of isolation "provides the basic situation" in Eudora Welty's stories. The "conflict between past and present is a constant concern" in Faulkner, and "recognition of the common human bond, a profound respect for the human," is the "central fact" of his work. Katherine Anne Porter's fiction is informed by "the fact drenched in God's direct daylight" and to "the inwardness of character." Abolitionism, because it is "the central fact of Whittier's life," generates the chief engagement in the poetry: "personal fate as an image for a general cultural and philosophic situation" (JGW, 59).

That observation about Whittier can serve, I think, as a general indication of Warren's critical interest in other writers. In the essay on Coleridge is an acute passage on the creative process, a passage whose air of authority depends upon the personal experience of a writer who has himself participated in that enterprise. The process of discovering what a poem means to a poet varies, says Warren. It may begin as "a phrase, a scene, an image, or an incident which has, for the poet, a suggestive quality—what for him in the light of his total available experience, we may call the symbolic potential" (SE, 268). The process is a curious interchange of the willed and the unconscious, of the poet as private man and public man, of the reason and the intuition, of incorporation and enlargement and rejection and revision. In its deepest sense, says Warren, poetry is rational—that is, it has a structure "that reflects, embodies, and clarifies the secret structure of the human soul and human experience" (SE, 281). By the exercise of intelligence, tact, discipline, honesty, sensitivity, that structure is made perceptible and meaningful. If Warren's principle of composition, which one critic has described as "search and discovery," requires such a massive outlay of energy and commitment, his principle of criticism requires nothing less.[5] Warren has displayed little patience for those writers or critics who are narrowly aesthetic, who compose or appreciate "magical lines," well-made plots, virtuoso metaphors, or the intensely charged style which betrays only the naked sensibility. Even for the most divided and disorganized poet, the poem he produces is not so much a reflection of his merely personal disorder, but an object that "brings to focus and embodies issues and conflicts that permeate the circumambient society, with the result that the poem itself evokes mysterious echoes in the selves of those who are drawn to it, thus providing a dialectic in the social process. The "made thing" becomes, then, a vital emblem of the struggle toward the achieving of the self, and that mark of struggle, the human signature, is what gives the aesthetic organization its numinousness" (DP, 69).

Early and late, Warren's critical observations have thus been set in larger contexts—historical, philosophical, cultural. Poet and novelist, Warren has also been the critic as scholar, performing his homework dutifully and imaginatively. In his later essays, however, there is a perceptible broadening of even these tendencies in ways reminiscent of Van Wyck Brooks or Edmund Wilson: a new respect for biography and its revelatory possibilities of national moods, concerns, and values; an alert eye for the dramatic or eccentric anecdote that is symptomatic of more fundamental issues; and an almost compulsive need to place figures and their works in a historical continuum. Hence, the importance of "reconstructions" of families, including the use of genealogies, dictionaries of biography, literary histories, letters, diaries, and other documents. Out of the basic social grouping—the family with its intricate interdependencies—comes one kind of self-definition and one kind of self-estimate: the atomic self measured in both love for and hostility toward other members of the family. Such an impulse, I believe, lies behind Warren's vast deployment of materials in forging a kind of spiritual history of the Civil War, for Warren the most stunning and meaningful event in our history. Out of such participation—willing or otherwise—in this public event come another kind of self-definition and another kind of self-estimate: one group self measured against another. The derivation of this larger grouping is essentially the basic one of family, among whose varied dispositions of virtues and vices, traits and taints, the single self finds his place.

Snow-Bound, Warren remarks, is a summarizing poem for Whittier, but it also appeared "at a summarizing moment for the country"— the end of the Civil War when the poet could foresee "the victory of the cause to which he had given his energies for more than thirty years and which had, in a sense, served as his justification for life and as a substitute for other aspects of life" (JGW, 46–47). The forging of an identity, then, always comes at great familial cost; it is not occasioned by the success of a private role alone or a public role wholly, and the grappling in both spheres brings about, consciously or otherwise, an often troubled struggle with time and change. "All are caught in Time" is a repetitive pattern always drawn; "what can survive?" is the poignant but not answerless question.

In his discussion of what he calls the third "perspective" of *Snow-*

Bound, the one that ends the poem, Warren gets to the nub of Whittier's work, and in so doing to his own work in all genres: "What is the relation between the dream of the past and the obligations and actions of the future?" Not surprisingly he finds the answer in "the sense of continuity of human experience." At the same time that one may discover "the meaningfulness of obligation and action in Time," he also discovers in specific memories and images from the past an articulable and larger image "for the values out of Time" (JGW, 53). Warren finds that Whittier's personal discovery of how "to make the past nourish the future" is enacted aesthetically in the masterwork of one of our great public poets: "Whittier undertook to see the problem of the past and future as generalized rather than personal, as an issue confronting America, not only himself: furthermore, to see it *sub specie aeternitatis,* as an aspect of man's fate. And he came to see that man's fate is that he must learn to accept and use his past completely, knowingly, rather than to permit himself to be used, ignorantly, by it" (JGW, 56).

The later critical essays illustrate the striking fact that Warren's sensibility has become at once both more personal and more public. As I mentioned earlier, Warren was never much inclined (outside the textbooks) toward isolating texts for analysis. He nevertheless subscribed to the same virtues of critical discourse—succinctness, concision, firmness of judgment—enunciated and practiced by such friends as Brooks, Tate, and Ransom. In his early essays the diction within the tightly controlled and logically compressed syntax is crisp and precise; in the essays after 1958 the diction loses some of its precision, just as the syntax accommodates a certain desultory expatiation. Stylistically the critical prose comes to resemble the thinking process verbalized, with considerable dependence upon accretive statement, clarification (sometimes involving cancellation and substitution), and the use of the "near appositive" to suggest a slight increment of meaning over the original statement.

The recent criticism also reinforces the sense of transparency so evident in Warren's later work, generally. Whittier, Melville, Dreiser, Hawthorne, Mark Twain: all American writers. But what else in common could attract Warren to write at great length and with no little research behind the writing? The answer lies in the first paragraph of *Homage to Theodore Dreiser,* in which the critic stresses the intricate and inevitable relation of life and art—how configurations of one's life show up, sometimes in secret patterns, sometimes in obvious ones, as art. Furthermore, all these writers are particularly susceptible of such an inquiry. Warren, uncommonly fascinated by figures whose real-life urgencies can be seen informing their work, is interested in the process—psychological, creative—by which this transformation occurs.

The tendency toward the personal can also be seen in Warren's often frank use of his own past—in the sense that he has a story to tell, a yarn to pass on, an assorted bag of reminiscences to open: about what Ransom expected of fledgling poets or how Frank Owsley told him a real-life chiller once on the Cumberland bluffs. But it is private in another way—in the sense that opinions, even whimsical asides, are more easily dropped in passing (perhaps in the very midst of an impeccably "objective" reading), without the felt necessity to offer customary corroboration of a judgment just loosed upon the reader. In this sense his recent criticism can be seen as a guide to his own recent poetry and fiction. The casual pace, the additive structure, the sleuthing inquiry into the puzzling ways in which long-buried memories, anecdotes, and images are unearthed, demanding form and meaning: all coalesce visibly so that the form of the later essays gradually reveals itself as another expression of the qualities of mind and temperament that inform Warren the novelist and poet.

Arnold Stein once began a subtle explication of Wyatt's "They Flee From Me" with "I may as well admit that I love this poem."[6] Warren rarely expresses his personal affection for literature quite so disarmingly, but the gradual loosening of his critical prose—which chronologically parallels the loosening of his poetic line—has allowed for more private expressions of preferences, even biases. The fuller, less constrained syntax supplies its own tonal openings for such expressions, which are reinforced not so much in nuggets of immediate demonstration as in the total functioning of critical intelligence and taste.[7]

This strong personal imprint, so evident in the shape of the essay, the frank use of the self, and the inner movement of the discursive prose, can also be seen in Warren's scrupulous respect for and use of "objective" history—biographical, regional, national. The careful use of history and biography has not always been congenial (or even possible) in the work of many fine American critics from Poe to R. P. Blackmur. In still others, notably Edmund Wilson, the very facts of the life-and-times approach constantly threaten to submerge the critical conclusions they are meant to illuminate. What keep the objective record from becoming inert lumps of authority in such an essay as the introduction to his *Selected Poems of Herman Melville* are Warren's own deep attraction to and respect for the record itself that date to the very beginning of his career. The relationships of father and son, brother and brother, cousin and cousin; the deployments of massed men in fratricidal battles; the significance of minor, faceless figures lost in the shadowy recesses of known records, coincidences, or accidents: all these have interested Warren as deeply and as long as have the aesthetics of writing poems and learning how to talk about them.

The "facts"—however highly they must be respected—are in Warren's work never wholly sufficient to account for the compulsions of human nature. Though they cannot be scorned they are more often corroborative than seminal in Warren's kind of criticism. Between "Melville the Poet" (1945) and "Melville's Poetry" (1970) Warren consulted various states of the author's texts, manuscripts, letters, and other documents, but that scholarly digging only underlined the intuitions and judgments of the earlier essay; and the central poems that he felt worthy of notice in 1945 are those he returns to in 1970, with more detailed explication: "In a Bye-Canal," "The March into Virginia," "On the Slain Collegians," "Malvern Hill." In 1945 he is already exploring the nature of the tenuous resolutions attempted in the best poems, notably Melville's insight into the way the human act is "poised on the verge of history" and the way human passion is poised on the moment when it is about to "disappear into time" and the stuff of legend. The later essay is a full-scale proving of early convictions and intuited readings of the poems.

On the eve of the Civil War Centennial, C. Vann Woodward issued a challenge to his fellow historians to remember in their commemorative volumes their obligation to "sobriety and fidelity to the record." Whoever writes in that spirit, he added, "will flatter the self-righteousness of neither side."[8] It is precisely that posture which Warren takes in his little book for the centennial; *The Legacy of the Civil War* seems in one sense a direct response to Woodward's challenge. It demonstrates a great deal of its author's mastery of the prodigious literature about the war, much of which Warren had read and assimilated for many years. One historian calls it a "distillation" of thirty years of reflection on the subject; and certainly Warren is scrupulous in his citation of authorities, which range from soldiers' letters to official histories. In his readiness to interpret the historical evidence, however, to render judgments, to weigh men and their ideas in scales now moral, now political, Warren goes far beyond the kind of history most favored by professional historians.

Despite a stern respect for the "record," Warren never allows the record to use him. "I can show you what is left," begins the historian of *World Enough and Time*. But reconstructions, either factual or

fictive, also require intelligence, logic, and sensitivity to the interstices
of the record—to what is not left. Authoritative facts must sometimes
be enlarged and interpreted by the conscientious, speculative man who
would understand the past and therefore the present. It is not surprising that Warren should see the Civil War in terms of "the American imagination," or that he should assert that prior to it Americans
had no history "in the deepest and most inward sense," or that the
words *validate, test,* and *cost* all appear on the very first page of *The
Legacy of the Civil War.* As we might expect from his subtitle—
Meditations on the Centennial—the book is an assessment of "what is
left" a century after the event, mulled over and articulated by a man
of letters whose major concern is the divisions, contradictions, anxieties,
even the conflict of convictions, within the self. The high cost of en-
forced self-awareness, one theme shaping the moral growth of many
of his protagonists, here is raised to a national level. The tragedy of
the Civil War has a definable arc that parallels the trajectory of the
individual lives recounted by Warren the novelist: it begins in innocence (with the Founding Fathers' dream, untested by the real, inward dilemmas), peaks in a bloodletting (because antithetical principles
will brook no corrupting compromise), and ends with an ambiguous
resolution with far-reaching consequences (that there is some glory in
the "human effort to win meaning from the complex and confused
motives of men and the blind ruck of event" [LCW, 108]).

The language in *The Legacy of the Civil War* is typically Warrenesque: the heavy iteration of such terms as *validate* and *anguished scrutiny*; the pragmatic assumption that virtuous action is *earned* and that
vision must always be submitted to the refining fires of *experience*; the
fascination with the theory of history as the discharging of polarized
tensions—the *deepest and most inward* commitments unable to be resolved except in violence; and the firm conviction that both the noble
ideal and its corruption issue from the same imperfect human source.
Warren's meditations are neither revolutionary nor quirky. Out of them
are advanced no new theories about the "causes" of the war, its conduct, the cost of the conflict in lives and property, or the question of its
inevitability. The topic upon which Warren meditates the longest is, un-
surprisingly, the emotional costs of the struggle and their influence in
the shaping of a national identity. Out of the clash of absolutes and the
rigid political stands that they nourished came pragmatism, which in
Warren's lexicon means a suspicion of abstractions even when they are
named good; the restriction of means to achieve ends however noble;
and the recognition of the fallibility, incompleteness, and probable

failure of schemes that promote comprehensive solutions to universal human problems.

The Legacy of the Civil War is interesting finally, then, for what it reveals about Warren's art—in fiction and poetry as well as in his discursive prose. His arraignment of the abolitionists, particularly those infected by transcendentalism, is succinct and persuasive; but when he observes "the joyful mustering of the darker forces of our nature in that just cause," in which the lust for blood and the love of liberty conspire "to forbid self-scrutiny," what strikes us most is that the psychology of the idealist, rendered obsessively in Warren's fiction, is validated by a shrewd reading of century-old history. The Great Alibi and the Treasury of Virtue—those deft psychologies that served both sides in the war and after and which became a substitute for historical realism and self-criticism—are concepts not yet worn thin, as history in the last twenty years has so depressingly shown. More interestingly, however, they are states of mind, what Raymond Williams would call structures of feeling, which Warren has for many years captured in such poems as "Terror," "Pursuit," and "Original Sin: A Short Story," and in moment after moment in *All the King's Men, World Enough and Time,* and *The Cave*: the exercise of all the ingenious dodges that can be summoned to stave off self-awareness.

VII. *Public Stands and Private Journeys*

1.

"I think it would be very interesting," remarked Cleanth Brooks in 1969, "if somebody had discernment enough, enough knowledge of history and certainly enough knowledge of the South to write a reassessment" of the southern agrarian movement in the twentieth century: "Obviously the Agrarians were misunderstood in many ways. Obviously they themselves misunderstood the situation in many ways. On the other hand, they certainly had something—very much had their hold on something which today we are going to face more and more."[9] The central document of that movement, *I'll Take My Stand: The South and the Agrarian Tradition* (1930), has not gone begging for reassessors, though the discernment and sense of history that Brooks asked for have not always been plentiful. As Louis D. Rubin, Jr., has reminded us, *I'll Take My Stand* was only moderately successful in its original sales and it soon went out of print; but it has nevertheless remained a focus of controversy: "Ridiculed, condemned, championed, it has been everything except ignored"; no writer about the modern South "has failed to mention and discuss it."[10]

Collectively, the Twelve Southerners—to its core of four Fugitive poets were added another poet, two fiction writers, a professor of literature, two historians, a newspaperman, and a psychologist—were waging their war on two fronts. Their older enemy was the sentimental myth of an aristocratic South, now "the ruined homeland," whose generals were the United Daughters of the Confederacy, countless compilers of genealogies, historical archivists, and various cultural arbiters such as those represented by state garden clubs and poetry associations. A newer enemy, which by 1930 was no longer very new, was considerably more potent in its strength and more efficient and resourceful in its strategy: the "New South" movement, whose chief goal was to erase sectional backwardness through progress—that is, industrialization. The activating assumptions of the New South partisans, says one historian, "were the ideas of economic regeneration, national reconciliation, and adjustment of the race question."[11] If such were the purposes of the first wave of "progressives" in the 1880s, it took little imagination for the commonest observers in the 1920s to see that the ambitious programs of Henry Grady, Richard Edmonds, Henry Watterson, and the others had not been spectacularly successful. If the planter, the politician, and the preacher were the three great culprits in the South's material and intellectual impoverishment in the nineteenth century, as Walter Hines Page insisted in 1902,[12] the region in the 1920s was still dominated by farmers who stubbornly followed archaic notions of land use, rapacious and cynical demagogues, and a disproportionate number of clergymen who clung to fundamentalist doctrines undiluted by "modernism," by which was meant the Social Gospel. But if the South had not lived up to its promise as the El Dorado of American Adventure or the New Canaan rosily predicted by aggressive editors at the turn of the century, it had changed enough to worry the Nashville Agrarians. Even its inertia was being used to hasten the day when the South would be no different from any other region. Like the rest of the country, the South was slowly becoming more homogeneous, and in a particularly debased way. Native crafts were being replaced by machine-made Yankee gew-gaws. As man himself became more materialistic, he also became replaceable. Loss of identity was no longer a mere personal matter; it was looming as a sectional threat. Such was the feeling among the Twelve Southerners.

I'll Take My Stand is an extended manifesto, and it is unabashedly ideological. Warren, in fact, preferred another title: *Tracts Against Communism*. Its governing impetus is conservative (in all the meanings of that word), anti-industrial, Christian. It supports an image of man that resists fragmentation because his entire activities are merely an extension of his spiritual wholeness. A widely heard charge in the early 1930s was that the Twelve Southerners could not speak with much authority on such matters as politics and economics. Such charges, repeated on occasion in the intervening years, are of course valid.[13] But the Agrarians' basic assumption in their manifesto is that man is indivisible: not merely a political animal or economic counter. Hovering behind every essay in *I'll Take My Stand* is the old-fashioned concept of the author as humane man of letters, the man who transcends professional specialization and the necessarily narrow vision that such specialization requires. Further, the literate observer of the southern scene insists that he has not only the talent to assess its impulses and contours and the right to make that assessment known, but he also has the duty to resist any piecemeal vision based on expertise because, enthralled by science and the scientific method, expertise tends to reduce man to piecemeal impulses and functions.

Any critique of *I'll Take My Stand* is in one sense supererogatory. The essays of course fail to measure up to standards set by sociologists, geographers, economists, political scientists, even many historians.[14] But in more general ways, some of the commitments and postures strike us as thin and questionable in our historical perspective; the contributors themselves misunderstood the situation, as Brooks remarked.[15] One valid objection is that the common version of the southern past—that it was a hard-scrabbling but satisfying agrarian life in which all its members operated in harmony with the environment—is itself as much a myth as W. J. Cash's sardonic version of an aristocratic cloud cuckoo-land, an earlier and more solemn view of which the Agrarians were trying to correct.[16] Something of the idealizing romanticist can be seen in nearly every essay, the sense of an image creatively cultivated often in defiance or absence of fact, which is to say that this book resembles most other works of ideological stamp; this one projects the impassioned quality of pastoral rebuke.[17]

But *I'll Take My Stand*, for all its polemical abrasiveness and heavy irony, continues to attract readers. If the imagined society of the Agrarians fails to fit historical fact, as it sometimes does, the image of that society is an accretion of values that we see more and more argued. Again, Rubin has made the point better than anyone else. The Agrarians' image of the old South, he says, "was a society that *should* have existed—one in which men could live as individuals and not as automatons, aware of their finiteness and their dependence upon God and nature, devoted to the enhancement of the moral life in its aesthetic and spiritual dimensions, possessed of a sense of the deep inscrutability of the natural world."[18] This perceptive insight into the synoptic appeal of *I'll Take My Stand* comes close to describing the moral thrust behind Warren's art, not merely the single contribution to that volume, but the several modes which Warren makes his own after 1930. All of his novels and many of his poems are set in the South, involving men both past and present whose struggle to realize themselves in their environment constitutes the striking "eventfulness" characteristic of his work.

Warren's acceptance of the biracial southern network of labor, responsibilities, even personal attributes in "The Briar Patch" is easy to cite as evidence of the moral bankruptcy in the Twelve Southerners' polemical defense of a discredited system; but more to the point, that specific acceptance is merely one manifestation of a more general acceptance of a social status quo that radiates throughout Warren's contribution. There is no cutting edge in his essay, no visible respect for human finiteness or joy for human individuality, no evidence of the searing clash within man of ethical alternatives, and only the most simplistic sense of the "inscrutability of the natural world." There is, in short, no human drama that plays so prominent a part in almost every other of Warren's essays.

"The Briar Patch" has sometimes been read as Warren's guilt-ridden defense of segregation in the South, an interpretation to which Warren himself has misleadingly contributed. It is both natural and comforting to so read it from the perspective of *Brown* vs. *Board of Education* a quarter-century after *I'll Take My Stand*. Perhaps Warren should have been more imaginative; perhaps he should have foreseen the possibilities of the bettering of the Negro's condition beyond an inherited system of social segregation. His essay makes no such bold leaps, however. The argument cited and explored there assumes segregation as the *sine qua non* of southern society, and for this reason "The Briar Patch" is not a relevant statement, or even a relevant speculation, on the status of the Negro and his chances for improvement.

Readers both black and white can fairly bristle at the presumption and snobbery inherent in the suggestion that vocational training for Negroes, rather than higher education, is the proper preparation for a better life in the future. And the suggestion that the Negro should cultivate his own garden may be impeccable agrarian doctrine until we realize that for most Negroes that means cultivating the gardens of more prosperous whites. On the land, says Warren, the Negro has fully demonstrated his "capacity to achieve a certain degree of happiness and independence," whereas in the northern cities he gains freedom at the expense of becoming as impersonal and characterless as the white industrial worker.[19] Warren's alternative is not only sentimental but also at odds with considerable sociological evidence to the contrary. The consolidation of ethnic sections of the great cities no doubt has contributed to general urban problems of justice, but social cohesion and a sense of communal values must surely be considered at least as valuable as the inherited order of rural and small-town white communities in the South. On the other hand, it must be pointed out that the sentimentality and dubious sociology of Warren's essay are no more damaging to the truth than the extravagant and expedient scrambling of reformists both black and white in the

1960s, with their inflammatory and sloganeering rhetoric. Applause for reformist sociology should not obscure the virtues that do exist in Warren's modest little essay.

If the major assumption behind "The Briar Patch" is the existence of segregation as a permanent structure within southern society, a second assumption informs it and the whole of *I'll Take My Stand*: the superiority of agrarian over industrial life. If in Warren's view the Negro "by temperament and capacity" is a "creature of the small town and farm," so is the southern white, poor and otherwise. Throughout his essay, however, Warren especially links the needs of the southern Negro with those of the poor white. Both groups are victims of the old slave system, individual violence such as lynching stems from this linkage, and rampant industrialization in the South tends to aggravate that situation. "The only way out, except for a costly purgation by blood," says Warren, "is in a realization that the fates of the 'poor white' and the negro are linked in a single tether. The well-being and adjustment of one depends on that of the other" (ITMS, 259). In a very tangible sense such a linkage extends to all southern whites, especially landowners. "With all the evils which beset the tenant system in the South there is still a certain obvious community of interest between the owner and the 'cropper'; profit for one is profit for the other" (ITMS, 262). And the notion that such a relationship encourages "personal contact" between economic classes and races, though it has been fiercely challenged by sophisticated northern blacks, has been confirmed by the experiences of several spokesmen since 1930, notably Malcolm X and Ralph Ellison.

Warren also considers the issue of Negro self-respect, one that in 1930 was prophetic. Those blacks a generation later who confronted the issue with black-is-beautiful slogans while sporting Afro hairdos and dashikis rejected, of course, Booker T. Washington's milder schemes to secure for the Negro the conditions for self-respect. In "The Briar Patch" Warren correctly foresees the basis for that rejection, though he then could not agree with it: simply to anticipate a black society able to respond to the needs of its members is a "feeble compromise." And it may be that Warren could not have foreseen the manner in which his plan for a general and dynamic self-respect would be later implemented; that, he predicts, "is to be expected when, and only when, the negro is able to think of himself as the member of a group that can afford an outlet for any talent or energy he may possess" (ITMS, 255).

"The Briar Patch" is not a great contribution to either the evolving solution of racial strife or Warren's own artistic stature. In structure and style, as in content, the essay is unremarkable. In places it is pedestrian—something which the contributions by Ransom, Davidson, Tate, Stark Young, and especially Andrew Lytle are not. But Warren's inability to imagine the southern Negro in a context not informed by segregation does not invalidate his specific observations, some of which are acute. He correctly saw that the professional Negro's flight from the South stemmed from lack of opportunity and discrimination. The explosive issue of the Negro within organized labor is, if not satisfactorily resolved, at least recognized in 1930, when it was generally and genially ignored in the North. Warren's observations that interracial conferences are poor substitutes for racial harmony and that organized philanthropy for the benefit of southern Negroes is only a pernicious distraction are opinions that are at least worthy of notice. Moreover, Warren's essay at least recognized the role of blacks in terms other than agrarian. And when Warren cautions the agents of industrialism to absorb the Negro into their schemes in the role of "the citizen and not of the conqueror," he seems to be tacitly acknowledging the inevitable victory of industrialism. As much as his grappling with the "Negro problem," even in delicate ways, such hints that Warren might be resigned to the hated industrialist as conqueror of the South explains, I think, the shock and disbelief that "The Briar Patch" occasioned when it was received in Nashville. It contained, thundered Davidson, " 'progressive' implications" inimical to the group's principles: "The very language, the catchwords, somehow don't fit. I am almost inclined to doubt whether RED ACTUALLY WROTE THIS ESSAY!"[20]

I would suggest that the writing of later books—*Band of Angels* and *Wilderness* as well as *Segregation* and *Who Speaks for the Negro?*—is less an act of restitution for lamentable early views expressed in "The Briar Patch" than it is a conscientious exploration of a race and its problems, a response both moral and aesthetic to this writer's own cultural situation as a child and young adult in which the Negro simply did not occupy a central place. In terms of mere population, blacks in the Kentucky and Tennessee of Warren's early years could exert little of that massive and pervasive *presence* which figures so prominently in the growing-up experience of youths in Mississippi and the other states in the lower South—a cultural difference that in turn informs the work of many southern writers contemporary with Warren. These later works of Warren represent an awakened consciousness more than they do a ravaged conscience.

We can speculate, finally, that Warren's myopia in regard to segregation is of a piece with his nonideological but residual faith in the beneficence of agrarianism. His observations about the human components in an intricately complex society suggest a good deal of tough realism about man's nature and condition—a realism that constitutes the superstructure of all of Warren's writing.[21]

The shared sentiments that make *I'll Take My Stand* a unified volume—and it is a group effort in a way that collections of Fugitive verse are not—find their echoing sympathies in Warren. Although he was in England when he wrote his essay, he, like the other contributors, subscribed to the beliefs enunciated as the "Introduction: A Statement of Principles." "The Briar Patch" bears many affinities with the other essays: the aura of defensiveness that clings to the very citing of facts and the working out of arguments, the scorn for consumer-prodding advertising, the respect for the yeoman farmer who was neither aristocratic planter nor illiterate poor white, a quickened sense of history, and a keen relish for the homely metaphor.

The shared sentiments are hardly surprising. Warren had known many of his fellow contributors, including their biases against science and their quiet championing of traditional religion. He was already familiar with Ransom's theory of the South's "Europeanism"—that is, its "self-sufficient, backward-looking, intensely provincial communities" as opposed to the "urbanized, anti-provincial, progressive, and mobile" society in the North and East;[22] and something of Ransom's influence can be seen, I think, in "Literature as a Symptom," Warren's contribution to the Herbert Agar–Allen Tate collection of 1936, *Who Owns America?* In that essay Warren rejects proletarianism as a literary program because of its worship of abstraction and because it results most often in mere propaganda. More positively, he promotes the idea and practice of regionalism, which he associates with the concreteness of place and people and the vital interpenetration of past and present.[23]

Certain specific attitudes, positions, and prejudices scattered throughout *I'll Take My Stand* strike responsive chords in Warren's later writing: Ransom's warning that we must retain "the humble sense of man's precarious position in the universe"; Davidson's sketch of the low-keyed way of life of the old southerners, whose manners "did not require them to change their beliefs and temper in going from cornfield to drawing-room, from cotton rows to church or frolic"; Owsley's observation that southerners favored reading about the Romans of the early Republic because they "reeked of the soil, of the plow and the spade" and "wrestled with virgin soil and forest" and so became the historical precedent that justified their own concepts of the right life; Lanier's low opinion of Dewey's "public socialism" and its "dubious prospect" for remaking human nature; Tate's simplistic notion that the Western European mind in "its American form" is characterized by an "ineradicable belief in the fundamental evil of nature"; Lytle's vivid story of how the southern yeoman, "the plain man," lost his economic and political independence and so became "the hookwormed illiterate"; Young's conception of what aristocracy in the Old South meant—self control, "mutuality of interests," an innate code of obligations, and "a certain openness of life."[24]

There are differences, too. Young's inflated notion of antebellum aristocracy, along with its arrogance and snobbery, is an orientation alien to Warren's cast of mind. Warren was never to become, like his friend Tate, obsessed with Anglo-Catholic orthodoxy, nor would he ever write prose quite so tortured, oblique, image-heavy. His reading of American history was to produce a version of the Civil War considerably more complex and less revisionist than that of Owsley. And, perhaps more important, Warren was never to view the status of letters and the shoddy place of the artist in America with the gloomy alarm evidenced in Davidson's undifferentiated polemic against mass culture, romanticists, realists, and local colorists.

If the appeal of I'll Take My Stand comes primarily from its general evocation of a mythic, even utopian, image of society, the appeal of Warren's work comes from a quite different stimulus. For Warren, fresh from his conclusions about John Brown and the destructive tendencies of the visonary idealist, even the evocation of a utopian image of society would carry grave risks. Throughout his career Warren has consistently traced the debilitating human effects of such thinking and such image-making. More than Ransom or Tate or Davidson, certainly more than Wade or Young, he has sought actively to demythicize those elements of the southern past most receptive to wish-fulfillment and nostalgia. This process can be seen not only in his versions of the southern past in World Enough and Time and The Legacy of the Civil War, but also in his reconstructions of the very different kinds of pasts for such writers as Melville and Whittier and Dreiser. In fiction and nonfiction alike Warren typically stresses the contradictions, the internal tensions, the gaps between aspiration and achievement, and even the healthy uses to which such jarring flaws may be put. This does not mean that his images of the past, in their variform testimony, are not mythic. Warren recognizes that even a mythic image is a human construct, and even its imperfections provide resonance for the human mind that contemplates it.

2.

The racial aspects of the inevitability of historical entrapment, questioned and tested in *Segregation* (1956), are explored first in *Band of Angels* (1955) about as explicitly as fiction allows. The lesson proposed in the case of a white planter's daughter by a slave is that integration is a matter primarily of individual will, that being trapped in history is not divinely or even socially ordained, that psychic splits are the great source for the failure of one's identity. The world sees Amantha Starr as white (which means that it offers her options open only to those Negroes who can pass)—a rather special case whose ambiguities work better for Warren the novelist than for Warren the sociologist. But even *Band of Angels* suggests that the social problem, accommodation between the races, is finally a psychological one. It is a suggestion made explicit in *Segregation*, the subtitle of which contains its thesis: *The Inner Conflict in the South.*

In this "report of conversations," Warren speaks candidly of the southerner's impulse to flee the "reality" of the South, a reality that he specifies as "self-division." It is a division not merely between man and man in society, crucial as that is, but within the individual man. The secret self so often explored by Warren in other contexts—the bestial, sin-drenched, fallen man in every breast—is here identified honorifically by a Tennessee editor as the "fifth column of decency" at work throughout the white South. When Warren specifies some of the "lines of fracture" in the white southerner, we see, first, that they are valid and, second, that they are the very substance that in one form or another has attracted Warren from the beginning of his career. Some of these issues of self-division reveal the lines of continuity harking back to "The Briar Patch" and looking forward to *Who Speaks for the Negro?* (1965):

> It may be between his allegiance to organized labor and his racism—for status or blood purity. . . . It may be between his sense of democracy and his ingrained attitudes toward the Negro. It may be between his own local views and his concern for the figure America cuts in the international picture. It may be between his practical concern at the money loss to society caused by the Negro's depressed condition and his own personal gain or personal prejudice. It may be, and

disastrously, between his sense of the inevitable and his emotional need to act against the inevitable.   (S, 94–95)

And from *John Brown* to *The Legacy of the Civil War*: "It may be between his own social idealism and his anger at Yankee Phariseeism . . . . It may be between his social views and his fear of the power state. It may be between his social views and his clan sense" (S, 94). When Warren incorporates all these possible combinations, they add up to one thing; "a deep intellectual rub, a moral rub, anger at the irremediable self-division, a deep exacerbation at some failure to find identity" (S, 95). These "rubs" are, of course, the impetus behind much of the poetry and most of the fiction; genres meet in Warren's own moral engagement.

Even as sensitive journalism, *Segregation* is a modest book. It makes no claim to represent a cross-section of opinion in the South in the years immediately following the Supreme Court decision; indeed, spokesmen from Alabama, Georgia, North and South Carolina, or Virginia are not even represented. But there is no question in Warren's mind that what he finds in the remaining southern states is a fair and undistorted representation of "the inner conflict." In his own interview with himself which concludes the book, Warren faces some of the most troubling aspects of the conflict: his conviction that the Treasury of Virtue (a coinage that had to wait for *The Legacy of the Civil War*) is constantly being dipped into by northern editors and readers and bureaucrats, that the southern problem is not learning to live with Negroes but "with ourselves," that the red-neck is only the cutting edge of white violence and that responsibility is a "seamless garment," that desegregation is one episode in the long battle for justice, that we should not worry about racial amalgamation in the future since the problem is "our historical moment," and that the South may be able to make a precious contribution to the national life—an achievement of "moral identity." The undespairing note with which the book closes is hardly unalloyed optimism, but it is hopeful, and it is earned because of the uncompromising struggle with the realities which Warren finds—not merely social, but psychological realities. These are personal aspects that he uses again, with more controlled effects, in the more ambitious *Who Speaks for the Negro?*

Big and sprawling, this latter book structures its materials with a deceptive lack of urgency. Except for the final chapter, "Conversation Piece," a summary meditation on the meaning of Warren's findings for American society generally, the chapters present dialogue between

Warren and various Negro leaders; their separate statements on such subjects as Lincoln, nonviolence as a viable tactic, white participation in the civil rights movement, and positions and remarks of other black leaders; passages from Warren's working notes presumably made at the time of the interviews; and expository and descriptive transitions that supply contexts.

The author functions as a concerned but disinterested observer resisting the temptation to exploit or imitate the built-in emotionalism of his subject. Because the interview itself is the organizing form, Warren risks tediousness, as interview follows interview, out of a scrupulous regard for some personal equal-time policy; but the inevitable repetition of positions and programs is, from the standpoint of dramatic interest, matched by the sniping rivalry among those who attempt to carve out distinctive niches for themselves within the movement. But *Who Speaks for the Negro?* is very much Warren's document, which is to say that it is not *merely* edited. The spokesmen are grouped not in any random order but according to consensus logic: the very center of the book is reserved for what Warren calls "The Big Brass" (Adam Clayton Powell, Roy Wilkins, Martin Luther King, Jr., and Malcolm X) and "Leadership from the Periphery" (a sampling of opinion from a judge, a banker, a journalist, a psychologist, and two writers)—that is, leadership that is public and political and that which is social and intellectual. Just as these two chapters are the heart of the book, so are they the most revealing and significant.

They are flanked by chapters dealing with representative "local" problems posed and discussed by dedicated but faceless Negro community leaders, an account of the Mississippi Summer Project of 1964, an examination of some divergent attitudes from "The Young," and the final essay, rich in historical background and psychological insight, on the prospects of a "changed" society. It would be forcing the text to insist upon any more intricate structure to *Who Speaks for the Negro?* It has, to use the terms from old textbooks on narrative writing, rising action, followed by maximum complication, and falling action or resolution, although in the narrative of the Negro Revolution the complexities are more vastly entangled than even Warren can order, and any achieved resolution lies far beyond the final pages of his book. Neither is there any evidence of the blatant journalistic device of ironic juxtaposition (of, say, King's interview alongside Malcolm X's); even the sequential arrangement fails to fit any easy progression of categories (from Uncle Toms to Whitey-haters). One of Warren's unifying devices, however, is the reminder of an earlier statement suggested by another spokesman for purposes of amplification or contrast.

There are other reasons why this book is very much Warren's. While he generally allows his spokesmen their own formulations, he does not hesitate to editorialize or even moralize. He permits, for example, Adam Clayton Powell's biographical sketch, prepared by a public relations aide, to stand on its own, and its extravagant pompousness, in a style as lush as the image-building subject it describes, needs no ironic undercutting. But in his interview with Wyatt Tee Walker, one of King's former lieutenants, he admits recoiling in "a cold flash of rage" at Walker's moral condescension. He suggests that the Negro Movement in general needs "*humor: And not only self-humor*" (WSN, 232). At another time he laments the scarcity, at least in some of the leaders, of charm and courtesy. At one point in an interview he underscores his role as something more than indifferent questioner when he introduces a portion of a transcript with the words, "Here is one more passage of our dialogue." He admits being somewhat disturbed by Charles Evers' "officialized" rhetoric that seems to have replaced direct speech. He is not hesitant in showing his admiration—as it emerges, for example, during Whitney Young's incisive discussion of the social, economic, and geographical gap between lower-class and middle-class blacks, and in Bayard Rustin's rejection of a social movement based on past sins and the promotion of one based "on the collective needs of people at this time, regardless of color, creed, race" (WSN, 241).

Warren says in his Foreword that *Who Speaks for the Negro?* is not "a history, a sociological analysis, an anthropological study, or a *Who's Who* of the Negro Revolution," but simply a documentary comprised mostly of transcripts of taped interviews. But it is not simply a documentary. Like most of the other examples of "the higher journalism" of recent years and like many of his own books in other genres, *Who Speaks for the Negro?* is a record of personal discovery.[25] It is not merely a compilation of what his informants think of themselves, their mission in the movement, and the priorities of issues; it is an account of what Warren thinks of all these things, too. "It is a record of my attempt to find out what I could find out," he says, including his own feelings. Superficially, it is his most objective book, coming as close to being a discursive volume as anything in his canon; but in its structure, its internal patterns, and its textural "voice," *Who Speaks for the Negro?* speaks for Robert Penn Warren.

It is very much Warren's book primarily because of its variations on and continuities with themes and techniques in his work in the major genres. Both admirers and detractors have frequently commented on the remarkable cohesion seen in his work. It is not surprising that Warren should characterize the Negro revolution as a quest for "identity." Indeed, given the almost obsessional quality of his commitment to that theme in his poetry and fiction, it would seem strange if his journalism, that other way of reporting the world, did not reflect his general vision and sensibility. At the beginning of *Who Speaks for the Negro?* Warren announces the importance that the word *identity* will have throughout:

> On this word will focus, around this word will coagulate, a dozen issues, shifting, shading into each other. Alienated from the world to which he is born and from the country of which he is a citizen, yet surrounded by the successful values of that world, and country, how can the Negro define himself? There is the extreme act of withdrawing as completely as possible from that white world. There is the other extreme of "self-hatred," or repudiating the self—and one's own group. Clearly, neither extreme offers a happy solution. Yet there is no simple solution of half-and-half, for the soul doesn't operate with that arithmetical tidiness.   (WSN, 17)

With that statement Warren might have been formulating the central situation in most of his novels, in which spiritually each protagonist is a Negro. His introduction to the segment on Martin Luther King, Jr., could easily be an extract from one of his first-person fictional narrators on a favorite subject, the anguished relationship of human will and historical necessity: "An event is never single and isolated. It is not a bright unit gleaming before the eye of God. It is a complex of various factors. It is hard to know where accident comes in. It is hard to know where necessity comes in" (WSN, 202–203). When Warren says of one black lawyer that he knows that change takes place in time and that there are "no solutions without cost," he might be commenting on one of his fictional heroes.[26] Although he finds considerable resistance among his subjects to the notion that merely passage of time, evolution in both status and attitude, was necessary for the Negro Revolution of the 1960s, Warren nevertheless thinks highly of that idea: as a theme, time as a matrix in which moral as well as social issues evolve has always been important to him. Roy Wilkins is seen in the same light that Warren might see a Conrad character, the man who, though he lives with the discrepancy between "practicality" and the "idea," knows that the strain and distress for so little obvious gain is part of the human process, and his "willingness to pay this excessive cost is the fundamental glory of the human effort." What Warren sees in an old Negro who is being registered to vote for the first time is what he has always seen as the unlettered man's need to "hang on to the specificity of things"; the "image in his head, not any written word or abstraction, is his fundamental contact with reality" (WSN, 10).

The alert ear and the educated eye of the novelist serve Warren well in the cameo vignettes that appear throughout *Who Speaks for the Negro?* A young black lawyer whose large hands "don't seem to go with his stature" grips a pencil "with unnecessary pressure" and doodles ferociously on his yellow pad. When he speaks briefly in defense of the New Orleans city fathers, Warren tries to assess the statement: "There is always something edging the words that Mr. Elie utters, quivering and licking along the edges like new flame along the edge of a piece of newspaper in sunlight, too pale yet to be seen" (WSN, 31–32). And here is Warren's observation of a white cab driver in Jackson:

> The driver is a youngish, burly man—seeming fat at first glance, but with that hard, smooth-faced, small-nosed fleshiness that you often find in the deep South. The belly of such a man bulges, but bulges with muscle. This man lolls back in his seat, drives the cab with only two fingers of the left hand on the wheel, and lays his right arm along the back of the front seat. I look at the hand. The flesh bulges on the hand, and the fingers, in repose, do not lie together, side by side, because the flesh bulges up to the first knuckle joint, forcing the fingers apart. The hand looks, somehow, babyish, awkward, indolent, but you know that it can move fast. The back of the hand and the back of the chubby, powerful baby-fingers are sprigged with coarse black hair. He is from the country, he says, but since Korea has been driving a cab in Jackson. He has done right good, he says.   (WSN, 44–45)

Punctuating the formal presentation of portraits, commentaries, and reportorial observations is also a miscellany of allusions to and parallels with situations and themes in Warren's other work. A succinct and moving two-paragraph sketch of Warren's father bears a revealing kinship with the poem, "Founding Fathers, Nineteenth-Century Style, Southeast U.S.A." There is a glimpse of the author's postcollege "romantic fascination" with tenant farmers, hill people, blacksmiths, and moonshiners, because they seemed then, he says, more of a piece, "in self and in fate," than he could ever be. That explicit confession reveals much about the similar longings of such protagonists as Perse Munn, Jerry Calhoun, Adam Rosenzweig, Brad Tolliver, and Jed Tewksbury. Warren states that his work on John Brown, though flawed, was nevertheless his real introduction into an awareness of the "dark and tangled problem of motives and values." There is a penetrating little inset essay on "Samboism" and the vexations of whites who struggle to distinguish "the true from the tactical Sambo"—the very perplexities projected onto Brad Tolliver's assessment of Jingle Bells in *Flood*.

On a purely personal level this book is (and undoubtedly was intended to be) a tangible sign of its author's capacity for growth. Warren recalls his self-conscious "humaneness" toward the Negro when he wrote "The Briar Patch" thirty-five years earlier. Although he suspected *no* system of segregation could be humane, it never occurred to him then—as a student in England—that "anybody could do anything about it." One suspects that the very distance, educational and physical, separating Warren from his subject helped to foster his image of the South as massively immobile, as a usable symbol of the "unchangeable human condition, beautiful, sad, tragic." In the shattering of that image Warren discovers the vast complexities of human arrangements that made race a national rather than a regional concern. *Who Speaks for the Negro?* is personal in its exploration of freedom and fate, motive and act, the contingency of events and the exertion of will, the paradoxes of history, identities both private and public, the pragmatic uses of an idea, the psychology of the reformer: in brief, the subjects and themes that account for the aesthetic integration of Warren's work as a whole.

Who Speaks for the Negro? appeared at the cresting of the Negro Revolution. By the time of its publication in the spring of 1965 the impetus behind Martin Luther King's nonviolent movement was faltering, and the spokesmen for alternative strategies, most of them to the left of King's Southern Christian Leadership Conference (and some of them candidly opposed to cooperation with white liberals either in or out of government), were making their separate appeals to the disparate elements of what had once been conceived as a monolithic bloc. In one sense Warren's book was dated by the time it appeared: *the* Negro, though he had always been an abstraction, was by 1965 showing little sense of being even a comprehensible classification. In another sense, however, the book was prophetic. It is no accident that Warren's very title is ambiguously both an interrogative sentence and a rhetorical question. Not that we have reason to doubt the author's motives that he wanted "to find out what [he] could find out" about the leadership and informal governance of the largest minority in our society; but it must have become increasingly clear to him, as it does to the reader who follows his record, that one possible title for his book is *Nobody Speaks for the Negro*. The implied answer to the rhetorical question has a further ambiguity. If nobody speaks for the Negro, it is just as true that everybody speaks for the Negro. Widespread concern for an entire race, whether because of self-interest among the blacks or guilt among the whites, carries a human danger comparable to lack of concern, the danger that people may be conceived only in terms of group identity, that individuality may be devoured by insistent community.

What one New Orleans lawyer perceived about his city ("we don't have a community to work with, we have only a population") is, for effects good and bad, what this book *as a book* perceives about blacks throughout the country. Though the relatively small proportion of response among blacks to their leaders may be the result of apathy, as some of their spokesmen claim, Warren hints that the reason may be more complex, that people of whatever color make their choices on the basis of immediate needs that vary widely at different times and in different places. Of all the spokesmen, Adam Clayton Powell, as appropriate to this self-styled "elder statesman" among the black leadership, is the smoothest in his casual references to "the masses"; but all the leaders, whatever their formulations, seem equally aware of the distance between the leaders and the led. That awareness accounts in part for the overlapping, merging, and splintering of Negro organizations and, therefore, the competition among their spokesmen for loyalty, money, and headlines. The matter is acknowledged as a substantial one by most of those interviewed: too much "in-fighting," according to James Forman, or competition based "on the fastest footwork," according to James Farmer. The competition, however, says Farmer, "keeps us on our toes." Wyatt Tee Walker asserts bluntly that he thinks no person "speaks for the Negro community—not even Martin Luther King, Jr." Of all the leaders interviewed, only Whitney Young named as "one of the tragedies" of the movement the inability of the whites "to distinguish significant Negro leadership." The implication is that the majority of blacks have been able to do that. Reaching the illiterate and the inarticulate becomes the real challenge for those spokesmen who would lay claim to "significant" leadership.

Warren permits to pass without obvious comment some of the cynical manipulations of "the masses" and the large vocal segments within them—Adam Clayton Powell's slick accommodation to youthful black activists, for example. Powell admits that he once used semantic tricks on them, and "they ate it up." And James Farmer admits that the crowds had such a minimal sense of cohesion that their "amorphousness" allowed cheers of the same indiscriminate lustiness for both Malcolm X's speech on separation and Farmer's own on integration. But Warren does allow himself to comment on the massive Negro registration drive in 1964 in Mississippi. He sees that Summer Project not so much as an effort to be judged by the actual number of potential new voters (which was disappointingly small) as an "elaborate educational process, a process involving . . . the rudiments of English syntax, of the syllogism, of American history, of political organization, and of the simple business of planning and working with other people—this last a capacity that some analysts claim the Negro American has sadly lacked." The men who ran the project, Warren says, "were good enough psychologists to understand that a mass base is not created by preaching abstractions; it is created by involvement, by acting" (WSN, 116–17). The terms he chooses, in obvious admiration for the leaders' efforts, are typically Warrenesque.

The strongly felt presence of the interviewer, as might be predicted, lies behind the questions Warren asks of his informants. Time and again he brings up the matter of "responsibility" as a parallel *quid pro quo* for more Negro "rights" (a favorite position of conservative news columnists in the 1960s) and the rejection of nonviolence and cooperation with white liberals as tactical developments in the movement. Although he is sympathetic with those who must tack with the wind in a climate that constantly changes, Warren clearly detects their tacit approval of irrational destruction, either by mobs or conscious programs; and he suggests that the go-it-alone postures of the more militant black groups, often marked by scornful superiority, represent a willful pride that, however compensatory in its origins, impedes rather than advances self-identity. Running like a ground note throughout his account is the assumption of the Negro's likenesses to the often difficult experiences of all Americans, rather than the Negro's differences from them. Here is his comment on the potential development of a violent wing in the dominantly educative mission of the Mississippi Summer Project: "the wild impulse to destruction, and self-destruction, lurks in even the wisest and best of men, and circumstances of protracted tension invite it forth from the dark oubliettes of human nature" (WSN, 123). It is a fair enough observation, one that informs most pertinently and most nakedly his first two books, *John Brown* and *Night Rider*, and it is absorbed as the moral *donnée* in most of his succeeding works.

In *The Legacy of the Civil War*, Warren formulates the respective political and emotional rigidities of the North and South as the Treasury of Virtue and the Great Alibi, phrases that sum up all the various dodges and rationalizations which that great ideological war brought forth as justifying "causes." The dialectical sensibility operating in that little book shows up again in *Who Speaks for the Negro?* Aligning the ranks of the Treasury of Virtue here, Warren finds, are those liberals of easy sentiment who self-righteously and irresponsibly promote the Negro, because of his "betterness," as our society's redeemer; and he assails those sentimental grand-pappy pieties, rife among the voices of the Great Alibi, that blacks naturally love white folks and that sour racial relations can be traced to the occasional "bad nigger" and the outsider (the "Jew Communist" becomes an updated carpetbagger). In the South the Negro is recognized, but his rights are not. In the North the rights of the Negro are recognized, but he is not. The danger in both regions, Warren reminds us, is condescension.

The tonic hopefulness of *Who Speaks for the Negro?* has little to do, finally, with blacks or whites. It stems in large part from a moral and aesthetic bias that sets great store on the sense of community viewed in its most comprehensive way, as the seamless fabric of "humanness," the tearing of which threatens an always precarious individuality with alienation and spiritual death. Despite the occasional irresponsibilities voiced to him, Warren concludes that the energizing motive behind the civil rights movement was a revolution aiming not "to liquidate, but to join," a society. He is cheered by James Farmer's assent to the notion that the generative issues are moral rather than political, placed in "the context of the human condition," and that most Americans still subscribe to "the possibility of human change." Warren speculates that even Malcolm X, from the spring of 1964 to the time of his assassination a year later, was "bit by bit, purging himself" of violence and working toward a "rapprochement with the integrationists, with the white man himself" (WSN, 263).

For Warren *integration* is a richly resonant word that cannot be exhausted by its specific racial connotation; indeed the modern usage, because it attests to the relevant and living nature of metaphor, appeals to Warren in both aesthetic and moral ways. In the most fundamental sense, the lack of integration accounts for the malaise of Jack Burden just as surely as it does for the irritable agony of Amantha Starr. Fragmented man is no twentieth-century invention, as Warren has himself demonstrated in his essays on American writers whose texts are testimony to the enduring fear of the bloated ego, the separated man, the victim of psychic distortions. The matter is perhaps most clearly the obsession of Melville and Hawthorne. Though one is no longer able to purge his malady, Bartleby's dead-wall reveries and Ishmael's hypos are equally illustrative of the dangers of a "November of the soul." From Wakefield to Ethan Brand, from quiet quirkiness to radically willed separation, the lesson is clear: any break in "the magnetic chain of humanity" dooms man to moral death. And despite the more sensational rhetoric celebrating the "infinitude of the private self," the "acme of things accomplish'd" and "encloser of things to be," and the superiority of men over towns, the matter is just as crucial in the tradition we associate with Emerson and Whitman in whose works the unified soul and man's extended sympathy for his fellows are prime themes.

We know from history, says Warren, "that you do not achieve an ideal spiritual condition and then set up a society to express it" (WSN, 413). We know it from our literature as well—from Emerson's 1840 journals as well as Hawthorne's *The Blithedale Romance*; and we know it from Warren's own novels. "Ideals grow out of the act of living, out of the logic of life; and in a long dialectic, even as they grow, they modify living." We may think of integration, says Warren, as that process "by which we exercise our will to realize and explore, individually and institutionally, in the contingencies of life, that ideal of mutual human recognition and appreciation" (WSN, 413). Warren would also agree with James Farmer's definition of integration as simply the "maximum opportunity for significant choices." *Having choices* is one of Warren's convictions about man—that his glory lies in exercising choices even when he makes the wrong ones. It is also the conviction that supplies the necessary edge to the other term in his dialectic: the *blindness of history*, the "fatedness" of fate, which indifferently includes man in the unrolling of its own logic. Warren insists that the word *integration* itself is multivalent: "It refers to a shifting, shadowy mass of interfusing possibilities. It refers, in short, to the future." It involves change, which, however deeply willed, is "always shocking; old stances and accommodations, like the twinge of an old wound, are part of the self, and even as we desire new life and more life, we must realize that a part of us . . . has to *die* into that new life" (WSN, 414–15).

Warren also detects an ugly aspect in the drive toward integration on the purely material level: a suspicion of a rapacious industrial society and its fostering of a devitalized homogeneity. We can see Warren's quickening alertness to those black spokesmen who reject the "melting pot" ideal for American society and his responsive sympathy for James Baldwin's rhetorical question, "Who wants to integrate with a burning house?" (WSN, 254). Drab, conformist, materialistic, mediocre:

the burning house of contemporary America is most visible in the dismal cityscapes of the North and East, those sections most unaffected by the Jeffersonian agrarian dream. In the years since the Twelve Southerners' pronouncements, however, their fears that the South might too fall under the sway of impersonal, sometimes absent industrialists have obviously been realized. The white southerner, says Warren, has in himself a "household traitor" who has sold out for the "gauds and gewgaws of high-powered Yankeedom." Both white southerners and blacks are minorities who have most dramatically resisted the invitation to "be totally devalued, gutted, and scraped before being flung into the melting pot" (WSN, 426).

Warren's instinct in linking southern white and southern black is perceptive, and the dilemma is just as acute for Warren as it is for James Farmer: what is needed is community, even if it is one plagued by a surfeit of shoddy. One of the unsympathetic positions that Warren and most of his interviewing subjects skirt is the charge that such quasi-agrarian sniping at and revolutionary attack on middle-class America and its values are hypocritical: both minorities aspire to, and often achieve, the very conditions which they say they deplore. At one point, however, Warren does recognize the difficult goal of achieving community—integration—without the corresponding loss of individuality. Is it possible, he muses, to retain pluralism and variety in the very midst of standardization, to foster both "social and individual integrity"? Like Whitman, Warren clearly has doubts about an affirmative answer to that question, but his work of the last several years on balance affirms the necessity for believing in *yes*. He is too much the historian to rest for very long in the easy claims of any particular age to social and cultural uniqueness, including Baldwin's apocalyptic glimpses. The image of America as a burning house, though perhaps more cyclical in its application, has its own history to match that of America as melting pot. Despair and hope: they are human responses to social as well as metaphysical distress. Both visions appear in earlier times before they do in ours, and both coincide with social upheaval—war and famine, depression and repression.

The questions Warren asked in 1961 and to which he returned in 1980 in *Jefferson Davis Gets His Citizenship Back*, were pegged to issues that he has consistently seen as emerging from the Civil War in an era which produced our first modern notions of "inwardness" of character, notions which carry the visceral reality of the struggle to define clear aims and certain commitments "in the complexity of life." The embodiments of that inner struggle in larger-than-life heroes draw us nostalgically to the realization that for all their complications and inner divisions they "made the simple cutting edge of action" and by moral awareness achieved identity. Thus their "images of integrity" cannot fail to contrast with our own uniformity, our public relations images. And to this "old-fashioned concept of the person," our nostalgia extends itself to the notion of community, "the shared place" made coherent and vital by "shared sentiments."

Nostalgia implies self-criticism, says Warren, and what is being criticized is the lapse of a society no longer able or willing to engender those Civil War men, the famous and nameless alike, who out of their internal struggles achieved a sense of themselves in a society, at once distinct from and at ease in the commonality. He cites our mobility, our look-alike Main Streets, our hucksterel substitution of togetherness for community. But even in that sobering estimate of our time, Warren says that there is yet, in the nostalgia, hope: "hope that somehow in our modern world we may achieve our own new version, humanly acceptable, of identity and community" (LCW, 92). Warren is the one after all who most recently has reminded us of Dreiser's "rabid and incoherent" book, *America Is Worth Saving* (1941)—a product not so much of a very real cultural crisis as of an ailing mind that, engulfed by overlapping ideologies, crusades, hates, and paranoia, was so uncertain of its subject that until the last minute the title was *Is America Worth Saving?* (TD, 141). While it is inconceivable that Warren should ever write such a book with either variant as a title, his answer to the interrogative version would be a qualified but necessary *yes*.

FOUR

The Lying Imagination
Warren the Novelist

I was almost ready to learn
What imagination is—it is only
The lie we must learn to live by, if ever
We mean to live at all.
> —"American Portrait: Old Style" (1978)

The philosophical novelist, or poet, is one for whom the
documentation of the world is constantly striving to rise to the
level of generalization about values, for whom the image strives
to rise to symbol, for whom images always fall into a dialectical
configuration, for whom the urgency of experience, no matter
how vividly and strongly experience may enchant, is the urgency
to know the meaning of experience.
> —" 'The Great Mirage': Conrad and *Nostromo*" (1951)

Politics and Morals

Irving Howe has argued that many American political novels fail because their authors do not see politics "as a distinctive mode of social existence, with values and manners of its own." But Joseph Blotner disagrees; they fail, he says, because their authors see politics "too much as a distinctive mode" and because the action of such novels "is removed from the context of life and set down in another where the governing elements are not so much the constants in human experience as parliamentary procedure, the tactics of the back room, or the milieu of the campaign."[1] Blotner's observation applies to dozens of forgotten and forgettable novels whose most common thread is the meager craft of their authors. Works of more pretension—such as those by Upton Sinclair, John Dos Passos, and John Steinbeck—tend not to dwell on details of parliamentary procedure, backroom tactics, or the campaign trail but on ideology, doctrine, the morality of choice, intellectual searching and discrimination: in short, all those characteristics that we normally associate with another subgenre, the novel of ideas.

The political variety of the novel of ideas tends, even more than the potboiling novel about the mechanics of politics, to be "removed from the context of life" and set down in a context considerably more abstract. Its propelling energy is belief; its formal configurations are tractarian. Conversion and counterconversion, backsliding and expulsion, soul-searching and soul-sickness: the metaphysical texture proclaims politics as transposed religion. Such otherwise disparate books as Sinclair's *The Jungle*, Jack London's *Martin Eden*, Sinclair Lewis' *It Can't Happen Here*, Steinbeck's *In Dubious Battle*, Lionel Trilling's *The Middle of the Journey*, and Norman Mailer's *Barbary Shore* all take their place in a continuing tradition. Although Warren's first three novels share characteristics of popular political fiction, with its rich details of practical campaigning and strategic applications of power, they are finally versions of the novel of ideas, with its emphasis on moral choice and conflicting ideologies.

All the King's Men (1946) is the work of a moralist who casts in political terms the great spiritual debate about man's condition and the likely prospects of improving his lot. Integration of the self, not the merits of the political strongman, is the chief concern. If Willie Stark's aim is to fulfill others, Jack Burden's is to be fulfilled by Willie, a man of too much direction completing a man with too little. Both voices, active and passive, announce the same dilemma: a radical spiritual sickness. Warren dramatizes this moral issue so well in *All the King's Men* partly because of his earlier efforts to concretize the theme in character and narration. Percy Munn and Jerry Calhoun in *Night Rider* (1939) and *At Heaven's Gate* (1943) are only the most important figures who suffer psychically; they are flanked by others, some stronger, some weaker, who share the modern disease of an empty and diffused consciousness.

Percy Munn is Warren's first Hollow Man, but, like Jerry Calhoun of *At Heaven's Gate*, he is ineffectual in resisting the blandishments of other Hollow Men skilled in the ruthless use of others for their own selfish ends. The Brotherhood in *Night Rider* is political; that is its tangible manifestation. But it is more importantly a metaphor for the abuse and misuse of community, and this study of the perversion of community is moral rather than political. Thus, at the very beginning of his career as a novelist, Warren continues a tradition solidly established by Hawthorne and James. In certain fictions of Hawthorne, in which the selfish use of others takes its appropriate horror from perverted idealism (which results in "experimentation") and misapplied principles of brotherhood, the authorial judgment is most powerfully delivered in terms not of the violated but of the violator: Chillingworth, Ethan Brand, Aylmer, Westervelt. In much of James, the telling horror is widened to include the victims of experimentation as well as its perpetrators: Daisy Miller, Maisie, Catherine Sloper, Milly Theale.

In Warren's works, violator and violated typically converge in the same character. Self-hate, self-distrust, self-division are at once anterior to and derivative of man's inadequate response to other human beings. A pattern of moral import in Warren most often emerges in the refusal to show much concern for others, a disinclination to shoulder responsibility, to accept blame, to acknowledge one's contribution to the events that convulse the world. "Passion and slaughter, ruth, decay," all the conditions attendant upon flawed humanity, are reluctant truths that most of Warren's protagonists are finally compelled to face: "We live in time so little time / And we learn all so painfully . . ." (SP, 309).

Warren's first three protagonists—as well as many later ones—are be-

set by passion, slaughter, ruth, and decay which they in large part engender. Glimpsing their own emptiness is a sight too horrendous for
them; they may shudder momentarily, but they try to forget what they
have seen through psychic refuges—abstraction (Percy Munn), inarticulate passivism (Jerry Calhoun), cynicism (Jack Burden). Munn fills
his emptiness with somnambulistic activism and self-absorption; Calhoun allows his will to be converted into another man's legal tender;
Burden attaches his own rootlessness to someone else's purposefulness.
These are, Warren makes clear, diversionary or surrogatory actions, of
the kind anatomized often in his poetry of the same period. The gritty
political infighting so brilliantly recounted in Willie Stark's world is
balanced by assessments of its moral costs, and such assessments come
not merely from the spiritual drifter Jack Burden but occasionally from
the Boss himself. However meaningful the re-created milieu of regional
political interests is to historical credibility in *Night Rider*, both the tobacco wars generally and the problems of the protagonist specifically
cannot be disengaged from Warren's controlling moral design. Even
the world of *At Heaven's Gate*, dominated as from a distance by the
cool manipulations of Bogan Murdock, is inhabited, as one critic has
put it, by "figures from a moral bestiary."[2]

It would be simplistic to label Warren's first three extended narratives "political novels," since politics is less the substance than the
context for the substance. But it is not simplistic, I think, to say that the
vitality and felt life of the themes are realized through Warren's engagement with man as a political animal; and part of the resonance of
these early fictional worlds comes from Warren's urge to show that
man's behavior as a political animal is inseparable from larger philosophical dilemmas that hound him. They are among his strongest novels
because the grand moral issues of will, freedom, self-knowledge, complicity, and mutual responsibility are grounded solidly in a tangible
world, and Warren has always rendered such a world most successfully
in terms of human power—its distribution and manipulation.

Some of the affective thinness of the later fiction can be traced to
the writer's decreasing interest in political man. When Warren attempts
the evocation of a time and place primarily through historical event,
manners, dress, speech, and the often rich concatenation of tools,
weapons, instruments, and implements, the result is often a lesser
achievement—evocation merely, the exercise of an accurate eye. At its
least impressive, it fills out the substantial but limited circumferences of
the local colorist and the antiquarian. Even such a major work as
World Enough and Time, which has its own special strengths, grows

realistically thinner as the moral journey of the protagonist recedes farther and farther from the intrigues of Kentucky politics that contribute so richly and so fatally to his personal intrigues. Although in *Band of Angels* the actual conflict of the Civil War raises localized political impulses to the highest level, as the chief historical event that war also must bear the most intensely freighted symbolic significance. While at one end of the spectrum politics leaches out into domestic sociologies, at the other it is raised to abstraction and moral generalization. *Night Rider* (as well as "Prime Leaf," the early version of it) concentrates, for all the talk of men seized by an "idea," on *men*; the emphasis in *Band of Angels*, for all its remarkable density, is on *idea*.

But even the account of Amantha Starr's dilemma, which in the latter half of the novel tends to be identified with the historical convulsion of war and reconstruction, is novelistically rich in both narrative and local effects compared to Warren's later tale of the Civil War. In *Wilderness* the protagonist's entire career—including his prime motivation —is fablistically conceived; Adam Rosenzweig's "idea" dominates every encounter with circumstances engendered and promoted by human beings, and all sense of a world is stripped to only those factual essentials which can lend symbolic texture to the protagonist's thematic function. In terms of our conventional expectations, the later fiction suffers as its worlds grow less political: the vastly distributed personal urgencies in *The Cave*, the fablistic moral progress of one man in *Wilderness*, the clash of jarring aesthetics in *Flood*. All of these contexts serve to highlight Warren's usual moral enterprise; all are competent and some are extraordinarily imaginative. But compared to the resonances of the political contexts of the first three novels, they are thin.

The scaffolding of the first three novels is clearly political, but their substance is man's moral struggle toward regeneration. Warren examines the possibilities of community, of the healing effects of love on atomized men adrift in their own confusion, contradictory drives, and self-delusion. The verdict is not cheerful. The possibilities seem slender indeed, although there is a detectable progression from *Night Rider* to *At Heaven's Gate* to *All the King's Men*. In the first novel, only the hero of the interpolated story, Willie Proudfit, can be said to have passed from a negative state of violence and confusion to a positive state of self-knowledge; the overall vision is nihilistic. In the second novel, the self-knowledge of Ashby Wyndham is so unremittingly radical and fundamentalist that it virtually debases the self rather than lifting it up as a model of growth for others; but the protagonist,

Jerry Calhoun, though he has by the end of the novel endured humiliation and defeat, at least survives, taken in hand by a loving and humble father in whose care lies the possibility of regeneration. Cass Mastern in *All the King's Men* constitutes a plausible model for his twentieth-century kinsman, who in his own story survives spiritual drift and betrayal (his own and others) long enough to pick up the pieces of a casually violent life. Only in the first novel is the prospect devastatingly grim.

VIII. Night Rider
An Adequate Definition of Terror

Night Rider, Warren's first novel and the winner of the first Houghton Mifflin Fellowship, has usually been considered something of a paradigm work in its author's career. It demonstrates Warren's relish for regional history, particularly the central Kentucky-Tennessee border area of his childhood. It shows an extraordinary sensitivity not only to border state nature—its seasonal variations, its prodigal richness, its ambiguous association with moral innocence—but also to border state man—his elemental needs, his sense of justice, and his penchant for violence. Warren's great themes—the clash of the ideal and the actual, the effort to ratify the dream by the act, and the painful crawl toward self-knowledge—are from the first incorporated in the substantial narrative of a time and place most congenial to his imagination. In technique, too, *Night Rider* establishes certain standard Warrenesque dispositions: delight in action, resourceful manipulation of language, conscious distancing between narrating voices and narrated actions, reliance upon metaphor and image that are more poetic than novelistic, creation of secondary characters and situations that functionally parallel major ones, even the use of the interpolated tale that, as precedent and model for alternative handlings of moral dilemmas, serves as ironic contrast to similar dilemmas of the protagonist.

In short, *Night Rider* is a finely realized, well-made novel, a notable first effort. Unlike the succeeding fiction, however, it is severe and chilly. If none of his subsequent novels shows Warren so determinedly in control of his abundant materials, in none does the author so dispassionately trace a protagonist's career and so disinterestedly articulate human failure.

1.

As many readers have observed, the spiritual division of Percy Munn is suggested structurally by the contrast between his daytime activities and those he performs at night.[3] This pattern of action delineates both the quality and the intensity of Munn's moral confusion.

By day the young lawyer is almost a somnambulist, performing his duties without clear purpose or conviction; at night he functions with energetic decisiveness. Ransacking Negro cabins, scraping tender tobacco plants in their growing beds, burning warehouses, taking secret oaths, directing violence both ceremonial and actual: only in these activities does this Young Goodman Munn come close to feeling fulfilled, as if he can end his cold isolation only by submitting himself to a brotherhood whose reality is confirmed chiefly after sunset.

Complementing this structural pattern is the thematic reinforcement of key words that suggest Munn's alienation. The informing images in *Night Rider* are those of distance, emptiness, vacancy, and blankness—appropriate ones, certainly, for depicting a hollow man; and they recur with such frequency, even in those parts of the novel that are not symbolic transcriptions of Munn's anguished isolation, that they come to suggest the shape and texture of the world in which hollow men must act.[4]

We find some version of these images on nearly every page. Empty fields curve away into the distance; lowering skies presage spiritual deadness as well as a snowfall; the footsteps of the night riders' board of directors resound "hollowly"; several directors are given to "rapt and distant" expressions; sentences hang "unfinished in the air"; Munn observes how his wife retreats "into an impersonal and ambiguous distance"; others as well as Munn fix their gazes into "absolute emptiness"; the autumn landscapes encourage a "sense of recession and finality"; Munn sees the sky consistently as "empty" and comes to loathe the "emptiness" of sexual contact with Lucille Christian; in hiding, he feels "hollow," while in flight he sees natural objects in stark "emptiness"; finally, at Proudfit's, his vision of his natural surroundings fades "aqueously in the shadows and in the uncertain striations of mist and dim light."

Although the context is not unrelievedly nihilistic—nature, however abused, is still green and good, and a few characters preserve honor and integrity—the narrative seems so because it is so resolutely Munn's. To the blankness and emptiness of the rendered world of his narrative Warren specifically adds the inarticulateness of his protagonist. As long as his confusion lasts, which is to say throughout his career, he is unable to tell others how he feels. More crucially, he signally fails to clarify the sense of his experiences even to himself. That failure to communicate is a radical one, the most significant indicator of his endemic failure to find communal salvation. Emptiness breeds vacillation, and vacillation breeds inarticulateness.

Munn's unstable feelings for the tobacco farmers whom he would lead are symptomatic of a more general confusion. As their spokesman he is alternately filled with contempt and compassion. In Bardsville, gathered though they are for a high purpose, they strike him as "no better than any other crowd," but he is temporarily excited by his mission when his eyes fasten on a single face and what he takes to be the human need behind it. Warren systematically links his protagonist's lack of integration—shown by a spiritual state alternating between bouts of depression and exaltation—with Munn's desire to "tell" what he knows (or hopes or wishes) to be the truth.

In trying to give to his wife, and thus to himself, something of his sense of exaltation when new members join the tobacco farmers' association, Munn fumbles the words and receives dutiful but noncomprehending encouragement. What begins as an effort to formulate and preserve those moments that seem enlivened by transcendent meaning ends in embarrassed futility. The need for naming the meaning of an event becomes merely the most necessary of his many compulsions, since to name his exaltations is to justify his role. Though he tries desperately to explain himself and his feelings to others, notably young Benton Todd, it is his failure to explain himself to his wife that is most serious. Stimulating rather than retarding the growing abstractness of their marriage, it leads directly to their separation. Munn finally labors alone on his farm, seldom choosing to go to his office, "almost glad for May's absence." His private failure with May prefigures the public failure of his career and parallels the hollowness of his liaison with Lucille Christian. Appropriately, Munn's subsequent sexual affair is conducted without the necessity for language: the characteristic image of this relationship is that of the shadowy figure coming to his room cautioning silence with her finger on her lips.

Since *telling* the experiences which elate him is unsuccessful, Munn turns to the oath, the formal ceremony of words that initiate a new and violent phase in the brotherhood and Munn's final absorption into its corporate authority. His real struggle to achieve self-definition is now subsumed in the easy assent to a ready-made integration. In the oath-taking ritual at the old mill, the ceremony itself becomes for Munn a kind of talisman that promises success, changing "the relation of all those men to each other there beside him" in the darkness. The anonymity, the secrecy, the silence before and after the ceremony all point to the oath as a confirming seal of impersonal violence to come.

The oath is implemented in the raid on Bardsville. As the air swells with the blast from the warehouses, Munn feels that at last, in concert with a thousand others, he may have discovered one "reeling moment of certainty and fulfillment." Even after finding the "one thing seizable and namable," however, its definition dissipates in self-defeating acts, culminating in the death of young Todd. From this moment on, Munn's ability to seize and name becomes more and more impaired, while his compulsion to fulfill himself in violence is heightened.

This compulsion is evidenced in several ways. In the isolation of his final fugitive days, Munn tries to remember the name of the old Negro whom he had caused to be hanged for the murder committed by his client Trevelyan. His obsessive attempt to remember the name leads him to reconstruct a complete, though imaginary, history of the man. He recounts with abnormal sensitivity the complete details of his office and his associates, repeating aloud "the very words" of greeting. Once, as he falls exhausted in the mud of a stock pond, Munn fights the feeling of indefiniteness that threatens to engulf him, and out of a heaving vision of familiar objects—"an emptiness, an innocence, a primal namelessness"—he sees light: "His mind named that: light." It is almost an unconscious will that chooses to seize and name the element that can give back definition to objects once familiar to him— trees, barn, fences, bluff. And his desperate attempt to define objects rather than self further emphasizes the loss. It is at this moment that the verbalizing of Willie Proudfit might have halted Munn's disintegration; but Munn, whose alienation is now complete, passes off Willie's story as the self-gratification of a man reliving a more glorious past. And although Willie's story exercises only a subliminal influence on Munn, the parallel is clear. Munn's journey from the desolate, waterless Proudfit land to Senator Tolliver's Monclair is comparable to Willie's journey from the western plains to the green lands of Kentucky. Munn moves into an area where the undergrowth is lush, where the tilled lands are prosperous and ordered in geometrically precise rows of corn and tobacco, where fresh groves surround the barns and houses. Like Willie, Munn comes home to a familiar landscape. In his return, also couched in a kind of splendid indifference and detachment, Willie at least knows regeneration. Even in the end, however, Munn does not know why he has returned. He cannot kill Tolliver, now a pathetic spent figure on the bed, who says insistently, "A man never knows what he is, Perse. You don't know what you are, Perse. You thought you knew, one time, Perse. When we were friends, Perse." The repetition of Munn's name becomes an incantatory plea from an alter ego who knows Munn as he knows himself. But though Munn says, "It came to me, Do it, do it, and you'll not be nothing," he chooses not to act. That he cannot complete this final wrong act is not so much a tribute to a late-blooming virtue as it is a signal of his final collapse into inertia. In his final plunge to escape, the last things Munn can identify are the voices of his pursuers calling, and, even in death, he names them, the "seizable" and "namable" objects, now metaphorically rather than literally: "the voices of boys at a game in the dark."

Although all of his acquaintances call Munn by his first name, Warren's narrator never does. We always know him as "Mr. Munn." The third-person point of view emphasizes the fact that most of the other characters finally know Munn as well as he knows himself. The narrator's slight distance is both structural (between narrator and protagonist) and thematic (within Munn, the difference between self-knowledge and almost self-knowledge). Both structure and theme are supported in the narrative texture by the stress on words, naming motives and defining acts.

Like the attainment of any other virtue, the gift of saying can be the mark of genuine achievement. The two men who have the greatest conscious influence on Munn, Captain Todd and Doctor MacDonald, have no difficulty in verbalizing. Munn admires Todd for what appears to be his "deep, inner certainty of self, his caution and detachment and tolerance in regard to the world outside himself," and he observes that MacDonald laughs "easily and softly, easily like a man who finds the world hung together right and himself at home in it, and softly like a man who finds part of his pleasure always in the privacy of himself." The fluency of both men is the objectification of their integrated personalities. The commanding figure who has the greatest initial influence upon Munn, Tolliver, is finally a lesser man than Todd and MacDonald, but he is still superior to Munn, whose personality comes to be objectified in neither his private nor his public speech.

Given the verbal deficiencies of Munn, it is not surprising that most of the significant communication in *Night Rider* should occur as symbolic gestures. In Todd's resignation from the association board, for example, the actual announcement says less about either Todd or the present state of the organization than the gestures attendant upon it. Surrounded by the other board members arguing simultaneously, the old man holds up one hand "as though he wished to speak or as though, perhaps, to ward off a blow." This impression comes, of course, from Munn, who appropriately perceives the connection between that moment and the one a few weeks later in the old mill, as Todd's son, hand raised, advances in lantern light to take his oath as night rider.

The parallel gestures dramatize both similarities and differences. The first shows maturity's double responsibility strained in an agony of will: the dissolution of loyalty to a group in favor of a commitment more personally justifiable. The second shows the failure of the father's gesture for the immature and idealistic son. Just as the earlier defection of Tolliver, Munn's surrogate father, fails to say anything to Munn more complex than *betrayal*, so the later gesture of Todd fails to communicate itself as significant to young Benton Todd. At its best, the message is the bracing one that the son must make his own commitments and risk their consequences; at its worst, it is the nihilistic one that nothing is ever learned, that atomie rules all.

Munn never quite sees such symbolic gestures as moments that might supply clues for his own future action. His realization comes only after he has thoroughly denied the kind of moral commitments represented by Todd and Tolliver. The latter's defection embroils Munn in ambiguous needs that are not to be filled even when they lead him to Monclair to kill Tolliver; and Todd's defection embroils Munn in the same ambiguous needs, by now even more urgent, that eventuate in young Todd's death.

Bunk Trevelyan's career is the most striking example of how a commitment to the abstract "justice" supposedly inherent in the brotherhood leads inevitably to corruption. Although indifferent to the purpose of the organization (he admits that his small tobacco crop "ain't worth a toot"), Trevelyan is useful to it just as he cunningly sees how it can be useful to him. As the complexion of the association changes, he comes to represent its growing expediency and lawlessness. Trevelyan attempts to blackmail another member, and the night riders, for corporate self-protection and discipline, must punish the member who has violated their rules. The responsibility for that punishment is delegated to Munn, whose determination to kill him, however, issues not so much from the corporately impersonal mandate of the group as from personal motives. Munn's most decisive act is his murder of Trevelyan on the brink of a quarry. The scene is Hawthornesque: against a backdrop of masked men in a semicircle, stands an outcast whose guilt is merely a heightened version of their own: "It seemed to him [Munn] that only the hands holding the pistols, not those blank, cloth-shrouded faces that could not be seen, were alive and real. At that moment the mask was suffocating to him. Its privacy was hideous, cutting him off from everything, from everyone. From all the world. He lifted his left hand, slowly; then, as though stifling, he tore the mask from his face, and took a long stride toward Trevelyan, and thrust out his head and called, 'Trevelyan!' " (NR, 199–200).

Since the actual murder is ritualistic, the most significant aspect of it is Munn's equally ritualistic response to that necessity: tearing off his mask suggests his reawakening moral sense, a feeling that he must not compound his guilt by committing the act anonymously. His compulsion is in marked contrast to the natural act of another rider who, after Trevelyan's body slips over the rim into the quarry below, removes his mask, sticking "it into a side pocket with the easy gesture of a man who crams his handkerchief into his pocket." Munn's act is the logical—almost simple—result of a full commitment to a corporate order; but the horror of the act is not that it is committed by impersonal fiat (inherent in any quasi-fascistic order) but that Munn chooses to play the role of impersonal executioner from wholly personal needs.

The night riders' oath is a major commitment, contrasted as it is with the promise Munn lightly makes to his wife:

> 'Do you love me, Perse?' she demanded.
> 'Sure,' he said, 'sure, I love you.'
> 'Love me, Perse. Love me always,' she pleaded.
> 'Always,' he promised, and turned away down the overgrown, mossy brick wall.   (NR, 163)

His ideological allegiance and its gratifications of personal needs drain away the energies available for more immediate responsibilities. Although his wife senses their gradual alienation, May's attempts to dispel her husband's deep gloom are futile. Munn shudders at the thought of her hand on him, rejecting her puzzled and tentative attempts to understand what is happening to him. Significantly, he rapes his wife after he kills Trevelyan: the key act committed in the name of the corporate order in effect supersedes an earlier commitment to a personal and familial order. His numbing identification with politics carries him into a proportionate withdrawal from the privileges and duties of the personal.

In repetitive physical patterns of action condensed into the language of hands, Warren dramatizes his protagonist's shift in loyalties. Along with his wife's ineffectual, pleading touch, Munn rejects the paternal gestures of Tolliver; and he accepts as their replacement the muscular grasp of a fraternal hand: Christian, the intuitive, pragmatic man of action always establishes contact with the reserved Munn by a plump, hearty palm on Munn's shoulder or back and by his bluff verbal punctuations. Time and again we hear that Christian's hand "bore down on his shoulder," "and urged"; at other times the heavy hand had slapped

Munn's back "so hard that the flesh stung under the impact." This masculine camaraderie is contrasted to the persuasive and cultivated touch of Tolliver: "He stretched out his hand paternally and laid it on Mr. Munn's shoulder . . . and patted Mr. Munn's shoulder." Munn, pleased "by the words and by the hand on his shoulder," is at the same time "a little embarrassed," as if the special concern he feels cannot be equaled or understood by even the most congenial friend.

Tolliver's paternal, persuasive touch is temperamentally of a piece with May's gentle touch, just as Christian's masculine, fraternal hand is paralleled by his daughter's sensuous, seductive one. Ironically, the May-Tolliver gestures, which should find the most natural response in Munn, turn out to be inadequate to his deeper, ill-defined needs. Although his response to Christian is always forced, and his relationship with Lucille superficial, Munn chooses to be completed by the mechanical instead of the familial. Munn's commitment, unsatisfactory as it finally becomes, is to the Christian rather than to the Tolliver bloc. Believing that he holds more in common with Christian than with the senator furnishes Munn with another frustrated motive for striking back at the "traitor" Tolliver. For all his attempted reversals of identification, his efforts are still exploratory, still tinged by a haunting irresolution. Munn is too discriminating to carry the burden of an ideology and insufficiently intelligent to come to terms with any responsibility more personal and particular.

Unlike some of Warren's later protagonists—Jack Burden or Jeremiah Beaumont, for example—Percy Munn is neither vital nor very verbal: further, he lacks any driving curiosity about the real nature of his problem. He drifts vaguely, without much direction, waiting for the right event which will clarify his own nature. He dies without self-knowledge, running toward the darkness that has always been his most comfortable operating medium, perfunctorily firing at his pursuers "without thought" and "without concern for direction."

That *Night Rider* is so absorbing, says John L. Stewart, "is a tribute to the excitement and historical significance of the events and the skill with which Warren reveals his character in behavior."[5] Stewart's first reason is dubious, and the skill that insures the reader's absorption is not merely one of characterization. The general skill of *Night Rider* is that of a writer already using technique—and occasionally surmounting it—more than he is being used by it.

2.

The terms of the novel are established overtly (and covertly in

minor ways as well) in the very first paragraph, itself a small master-
piece of narrative economy. Standing in the aisle of the crowded, smelly
train to Bardsville, without sufficient experience for bracing himself,
Percy Munn bears the brunt of the *jarring* brakes, the *grinding, heavy
momentum* of the crowd, the *gathering force* that lurches him into
his neighbor. When he does act—when he steps on a man's foot—
it is because of the *wave* of other bodies that pitches him against the
man. The train trip is an appropriate means for depicting a spiritual
journey that is unusually passive. In this premonitory vignette, Munn
is at the mercy of forces that have their own momentum; he does not,
nor can he, muster clear direction, destination, pace. Further, although
he is engulfed in these forces, that passive state does not prevent his
engulfing others.

Despite his legal training and his long residence in the area, Munn
is alien to the normal experiences of other men, detached from their
material and spiritual poverty. His fellow passengers, those to whom
he will later speak, suggest a vast herd of cattle waiting for roundup
by those political wranglers with the right tone and pitch. Though
he lacks the natural gifts to qualify, Munn learns quickly enough and
is rewarded. Without understanding these men with whom he is to
deal (they are alternately an "inhuman" crowd and individuals "not
like anybody else in the world"), without understanding even his own
motives or desires, he assumes the role of a leader. Nauseated by the
smell of whisky, sweat, and lye soap, the sound of raucous laughter and
conversation, the sight of the moiling crowd surging through the
streets, the feel of hot damp flesh pressing on other flesh, he is so
far removed from the tangibles of this world that he can comfort himself only with intangibles: "justice," which vibrates about him, "hope
and loyalty," which he feels certain that these men carry in their hearts,
an "idea" coalescing individual farmers into an effective force.

Also established in the first chapter is an architecture of physical and
spiritual levels that symbolically positions Munn in relation to the
people he would lead. Although he is nauseated on the train, he is
caught by a "sudden surge of excitement" just before he leaves the
coach, when he looks over the faces "upturned toward him," and he
is quick to observe occasional marshalls on horseback surveying the
crowd "arrogantly and detachedly" like officers. From a commanding
position on the speaker's platform, he detects again the "tremendous
emptiness" on the faces gazing up expectantly. And later, in his curtain-
drawn hotel room on the top floor, he peers down on the "idle and
aimless" stream of bodies on the street below, abstractly raising an arm

"as though to address a great multitude and tell them what he knew to be the truth."

Given such a protagonist who is also the governing point of view character, the vitality, direction, and definition of the novel are remarkable. Out of what can only be called a recalcitrant central intelligence, Warren draws a perspective that, because it incorporates both Munn and a disinterested narrating voice, becomes a supple narrative technique for advancing his theme. Even when that technique falters, as it does on several occasions, the results are never perfunctory. The narrating voice of the first chapter establishes the cool disinterested tone that will continue for the most part throughout the novel. It is a voice that accompanies Munn's very eyes and mind, partakes of them, yet is not synonymous with Munn. Everything this protagonist is or will become is inherent in what the voice says about Munn's observing, thinking, and saying.

At times this narrating voice is at a further remove from Munn, as in Chapter 2, when he transmits briefly what has transpired among the board members of the tobacco growers' association. As the chapter progresses, this intervening presence sometimes resembles the narrator of early radio plays, attempting a kind of tonal neutrality but betraying a position by the very frequency with which he merges with the protagonist's voice. There is this, for instance: "Mr. Munn's common sense, his logic, had conspired with his friends to force his acceptance. Such chances to get along didn't turn up every day to a young man of thirty. He had better grab it." This is a paraphrase of Munn's own rationalization, more flexible and economical than a first-person version could be with Munn as his own narrator; Munn is alone, almost as object, while the detached narrator, speaking for him rather than through him, hovers nearby.

This slight tonal coloring, which is to mark the quality of the narrating intelligence for the rest of the novel, recurs in mild, nearly neutral, statements: "For the new activities more and more engrossed him, and he lived in a state of excitement that precluded the question of happiness or unhappiness. All fall he traveled much around the section." When Munn interrupts the old Negro, whom he successfully charges with murder, "petulantly and resentfully," the adverbs are exactly right, but they are not Munn's self-estimate of how he sounds. They are judgments of an observer, a separate felt presence.

Something of the flexibility that Warren achieves with this narrating voice—it functions similarly to the "effaced narrator" that Caroline Gordon detects in *Madame Bovary*—comes from the occasional appearance of the narrator as stagemanager-chorus.[6] In Chapter 7, for example, he telescopes time in a kind of generalized summary of the night riders' activity in the spring. He sets the situation before us ("all of the tobacco . . . was sold") and then the special fact ("the first plant-bed raids occurred"), before painting a nostalgic, poignant picture of how the tobacco seeds sprout and leaf in the protected rich earth. Then he itemizes the number of plant-bed raids on "one night" only in a clipped series of simple sentences. The matter-of-fact quality of the prose, here as often in Hemingway, intensifies the horror of the act.

The "agrarian" voice of the narrator opens Chapter 9 with a similar description: the tobacco stobs protruding from the hill, the stooped field hands, the bony heads of the mules, the thin odor of burning, the swarms of crying grackles. Again, the voice complements the mood of Munn, rather than supplanting his thoughts or speeches. It is also the narrator who observes for us that Munn "was much alone now, and by choice." The flattened-out prose becomes useful when the narrator gives the succeeding account, beginning "There were burnings all fall. As soon as the tobacco in the barns began to cure, the fires began. At first there were only a few, then there were the letters. Then there were many fires" (NR, 253). This account is sprinkled with expressions of shifting perspective: "It was reported that," "it was assumed," and numerous uses of the impersonal communal "they." This tone is important, for it fits precisely the picture of tobacco farmers waiting with guns by night to defend their crops from the raiders—a futile watch, since there come nights of "confidence or weariness," and the barns would be burned as always. Overdrawn or overstressed, these pictures could mar the usually laconic style of Munn and the consistently lean style of the narrator. But when Warren uses this flattened-out style he achieves a poignancy and a cautious, highly manipulative emotional response. And when his prose becomes more abstract, it reflects the intellectualizing of Munn.

Sometimes the reach of this narrator extends outward, functioning like the lens of a panning camera. In Chapter 11, just before the night riders' march on Bardsville, this cinematic perspective begins with a casual survey above the streets and rooftops of the town; then it closes in to the streets and along the fronts of the hotel lobby and the saloons, picking up in soundless activity the averageness of the people inside; floats further along the streets, picking out, with contrasting sounds, loiterers laughing under the arc-lamps, isolated figures clicking their heels along the pavement, and the crowded depot just before the train clanks to a stop. Only after this prolonged cinematic scene-setting are we suddenly shifted to MacDonald standing on the outskirts, hidden by an elder thicket.

The same technique is less successful in Chapter 12, since it is almost overburdened with obvious "significance." With the arrival of the state militia, the narrator chooses to signal its seriousness by mirroring the event first in children's eyes, then in the eyes of the divided townspeople. The contrast implicit in the fact itself carries the faint irony. The mayor welcomes the military commander, but the affair is mostly summarized by the narrator, who incorporates the ponderous interplay of clichés abstracted from the speeches ("thriving community," "fair name," "kind words," "sacrifice will not have been offered up in vain," "firm stand in favor of law and truth and right"), all punctuated by noises from the crowd, some people clamoring to hear, some heckling, but all taking the situation less seriously than either the mayor or the major. Finally, the narrator returns to Munn, who is merely one of the spectators in the crowd.

Warren's first novel is not flawless. It contains segments that are serious lapses in point of view and narrative balance. The first of these occurs in Chapter 4, when the narrator freezes the action (a house party at Monclair) while for about six pages he gives a detailed account of Senator Tolliver's career. The sudden omniscience draws attention to the narrator's voice detached from Munn, but it fails to assert its own special claims. The material is important—an unflattering portrait of an expedient politician—because it forestalls any unearned sympathy for Tolliver, and though it is information that Munn could plausibly have, to have attributed it any more closely to Munn would have risked marring his otherwise consistent lack of curiosity about people, his almost bovine apathy.

More organic are two other segments, occurring in the same chapter. One concerns Munn's memory of Ianthe Sprague, whom Munn had visited when he was a law student in Philadelphia. This distant cousin had achieved a cold self-definition by resisting the knowledge of anything that was *not* fragmentary and irrelevant; at a time when his disintegrating world leads him to find nourishment in random and meaningless details, Munn thinks of her "cold, unhuman" discipline that could so successfully reject any event in time that "pretended to a meaning." It is his curse to try to fit his random fragments of memory into some systematic consistency. Another example of a kind of cold perfection which Munn can never achieve is Miss Lucy Burnham, his wife's aunt who wills her life to the grim service of a father and niece. Both Ianthe Sprague and Lucy Burnham are figures of reproach to Munn at this crucial stage. Although both women achieve the horror of a death in life, they do so through the exercise of will. Munn simply drifts into his horror.

The most sustained narrative excrescence in *Night Rider*, however, is Willie Proudfit's story, Warren's first embedded tale. It is a colloquial tour de force that cheerfully ignores for most of a chapter the governing presence of the narrator. Its position is wholly dramatic. Proudfit, who does not even enter the narrative until it is nearly over, tells his long, rambling story of sin and regeneration to a distraught Munn, whose moral collapse has gone too far to enable him to see in his host any parallel to his own life. This situation becomes the culmination of a lifetime in which Munn has failed to see connections. Proudfit is no *deus ex machina* and his story provides no illumination for the protagonist. Warren's technique is simply to let Proudfit talk; the moral relevance emerges, despite Munn's inability to see it, in recreated narrative.

This story is the most obvious example in *Night Rider* of parallel narratives, what has been called *exempla*, used to complicate and enrich otherwise tidy narratives.[7] In a strictly formal sense, Proudfit's story is more of a flaw than Warren's later *exempla* are in their narratives; but for all his critical reputation, Warren has never shown much fondness for the formal perfections of a story. He would doubtless agree with Percy Lubbock, who argued that any inherent weakness "plainly admitted and recognized," asserted and emphasized, can be fashioned into "a new kind of strength."[8] Although some of the flaws of Warren's first novel cannot in any way be elevated into new kinds of strengths, the inset story here, as that in *All the King's Men*, is a decided enrichment. Proudfit's story is the final gathering together of moral patterns that pervasively inform the massive spiritual failure of Percy Munn.

Since Warren's first protagonist dies unenlightened, the view of life that the novel enforces is, as Eric Bentley long ago observed, "inferred from a whole complex of situations and relationships."[9] MacDonald, Todd, and Proudfit by contrast highlight the lesson that Munn fails to learn; Tolliver (along with Ianthe Sprague and Lucy Burnham) does the same by parallelism. But, however more enlightened some of the other characters are, Warren chooses to center his tale in Munn himself. And Munn possesses a built-in discrepancy. The narrator, however subtly attuned to the mental blocks and tangential vision of Munn, succeeds in correcting Munn's view for us. He does this by the understated quality of his reportage and by occasionally moving away from Munn to pick up details of a larger picture that Munn presumably never sees. With a limited point of view, Warren executes a number of maneuvers to vary the angle and, with the angle, the quality of the vision.

Munn's lack of clarity about what he wants and needs is the paramount aspect of his character that we comprehend throughout. Intellectually, we see the isolated individual yearning for human community, which might be real but which, when joined, turns out to be the false solidarity of a secret and violent organization, an absolutist political group that subsumes all individual moral choice.[10] Yet we do not see that situation merely intellectually. The fate of Percy Munn comes to us not in what Warren has called "the poverty of statement" but in "terms of circumstance and experience," in the total exercise of the artist's faculty: "the delicacy of phrase, the close structure, the counterpoint of incident and implication" (SE, 154–55). Because of this "total circumstantiality," we detect gradually and cumulatively the dilemma of Warren's first protagonist.[11]

Despite its flaws, *Night Rider* is impressive, not because of its author's theme, however important that is for this novel specifically and for Warren's work generally, but because the theme is realized through the sustained and generally subtle deployment of techniques that had, in fact, been long in the making. In an extraordinary way this novel fuses the local realism of setting and character (without which such a narrative would become sheer fable) with its generalized theme of moral significance (without which it would remain local-color storytelling). Except for his recent fiction, Warren has never been accused, even by his most severe critics, of having a deficient sense of dramatic action involving recognizable characters in likely places; nor has he been charged with lacking a grand moral theme. On the contrary, Warren shakes the superflux so vigorously that he often produces melodrama and homilies in only lumpish suspension. In *Night Rider* there is a sustained merging of dramatic action and its thematic burden. For a first novel, the result is credible and imaginative art.

IX. On the Politics of the Self-Created
At Heaven's Gate

Warren's first two novels have often seemed better as the trying-out of *All the King's Men* than as novels in their own right. Certainly, as studies of the nature and uses of political power, *Night Rider* and *At Heaven's Gate* are anticipatory. Both touch on big bossism in its corporate and individual forms, and both dramatize the dangers to the morally insensitive individual posed by abstract embodiments of power: the Association of Growers of Dark Fired Tobacco in one, Bogan Murdock's financial empire in the other. And compared to the firm assurances of the third novel, both seem tentative: they lack a particularized, sensuously immediate politician whose motives and acts are examined in a context of rich circumstantiality, as well as an engaging figure who is articulate enough to justify his credibility as a man both morally aware and expediently knowledgeable. Willie Stark and Jack Burden, for all their foreshadowings, had to wait for *All the King's Men*.

Although we occasionally still hear opinions that *Night Rider* is Warren's best novel (opinions that become more assertive with successive appearances of Warren's later work), only one critic to my knowledge has suggested that *At Heaven's Gate* is even his *second* best.[12] I do not believe that *Night Rider*, for all its precision and control, is Warren's finest novel, and at least two later titles can rival *At Heaven's Gate* for second place. But neither of his first two novels is apprentice fiction—we know that there were two earlier attempts that did not reach print—and both are works that deserve recognition without the inevitable use of *All the King's Men* as some kind of ultimate model.[13]

There are flaws aplenty in *At Heaven's Gate*, not the least of which are the undisguised threads stitching the various segments together like a patchwork quilt. There are occasional spurts of fancy writing, and the more self-conscious stylistic effects are obviously derivative and uncertainly controlled. (The derivation is mostly from Faulkner: there

are detectable echoes from *The Sound and the Fury, The Wild Palms,*
and perhaps *Sanctuary.*) The whole of Chapter 13, which contains the
most pretentious writing of the novel, is also a technical shambles. In
it are wasted closeups (for the first time) of Dorothy Murdock, who
scarcely matters in the thrust of the plot, and the young Negro house
man, Anse, who matters only in the final few pages because he is false-
ly accused of Sue Murdock's murder; this chapter also contains scenes
of Sue's final break with her family, which are jaggedly ineffective,
even as melodrama.

Despite all these flaws *At Heaven's Gate* is finally more interesting
than *Night Rider.* Its stylistic modulations, its scattergun point of view,
and its deployment of multiple narratives can be seen as both untidy and
typically Warrenesque. For the first time we see the rich profusion of
favorite words and phrases—"the blind, unqualified retch and spasm
of the flesh, the twist, the sudden push, the twitch, the pinch of ejec-
tion and refusal"—and the lengthy segments of second-person idiom,
faintly ironic and precisely detailed, straight out of the tough-guy
and private-eye tradition of the 1920s and 1930s. And, in its more
discursive moments, *At Heaven's Gate* achieves a kind of lyric naturalism that becomes a hallmark of Warren's prose: periods of closely
observed details strung out in an evocative rhetoric which invites
nostalgia for a specific time and place or which invokes awe for a
mythic history that seems to explain national and even human urges.

John M. Bradbury once noted that *At Heaven's Gate* is Warren's only
"city-bound" novel.[14] In a technical sense this is true. But it is also
the closest Warren ever came to writing an agrarian novel. The values
associated with southern Agrarianism—integration of personality, mutual responsibility, and a general harmony of man and nature—are
conspicuously missing in the lives of the major characters, but their
very absence is a measure of their importance.[15]

The urban setting (a city like Nashville) and the time (the 1920s)
suggest strongly that Warren's second novel establishes the New South
as a homegrown wasteland. The novel is studded with physical and
spiritual images of disease, perversion, filth; and its characters are
dominated by movers and shakers who keep one eye on public relations
and the other on schemes for maintaining wealth and power through
abstract finance. *At Heaven's Gate* is Warren's only work in which the
combined effects of technology, finance capitalism, and political power
are examined so explicitly, even obviously. Bogan Murdock, the chief
symbol of power, is a hollow man; and most of the other characters are

fragmented people spiritually awash in a milieu stripped of the values that presumably once obtained in an agrarian mode of life.

The countryside is seen almost totally as remote, though not remote enough to escape victimization by urban greed. Surrounding land is foreclosed for commercial exploitation by functionaries within Murdock's empire. The solidity and specificity of the land are absorbed by abstract capitalism and retained only as ironic pastoral names of the major interlocked Murdock enterprises: Massey Mountain, Happy Valley, Pretty River. Mr. Calhoun is the only genuine countryman in the novel. Quiet and ineffectual, he is a reminder—hardly even a backdrop for important scenes—of simple and profound human values and an implicit model by which the lapses of others, including his son's, are contrasted. That standard is unobtrusive but pervasive.

The "Jesus-struck" hillman, Ashby Wyndham, is the only articulate spokesman for rural values, but it is only a secondary interest at best since the chief concern is the moral failure in his role as wandering evangelist. His earlier sin is in striking his brother, who wants to retain the family farm despite Ashby's eagerness to sell, get his share of the money, and be off to the urban fleshpots. But one of Ashby's themes is the general decline in the quality of life after the coming of "newfangleness." The immediate source of his spiritual sloth he cites as "abominations under the ridgepole of the Lords house," but he also looks back to earlier days before "the change of time," when the woods were "full of varmints yit, and squirrils fat in the trees, lak apples when the limb bends and turkeys gabblin . . . [and] the skillit never groan[ing] empty" (AHG, 76). Jerry Calhoun's great-uncle Lew raves about land grabbing—a very real thing, since Murdock is engaged in seizing commercial advantage out of his apparent gift of a forest preserve.

The entire rural environment is threatened by "development." Massey Mountain is seen in terms of mines, timber, resources; and the promotional phrases for justifying its exploitation are "expansion and development," "haven't scratched the surface," "bold enough and farsighted," and "free flow of financing." Sweetwater, the union organizer, puts the matter bluntly: "They took the iron out and cut it over and blew the rock out and starved the folks to death and the ground's washed away." He is right in his charge, of course, though his function at Massey Mountain is just as manipulative as the capitalist owners. The total result is, predictably enough, radical dehumanization.

Given the lapse of necessary and sustaining values in *At Heaven's*

Gate, what is left is manner—watching and learning "methods." The novel is a brilliant example of Warren's insight into the manipulative uses of technique. The roles his characters play are desperate, and the techniques of their playing serve to mask, distract, or deceive. The major psychological patterns of the novel involve rejection and repudiation, often in violent ways. In most cases what the characters react against is the continuing relationship of the individual with the home, the past, and tradition. In Warren's own Unreal City the uses of technique are necessarily efforts to remake the self after new images, to fill the gaps left by repudiation, to heal what Jack Burden of *All the King's Men* will later call the terrible division of the age. What usually results in these efforts to create the self anew is to widen the division and make it all the more terrible.

Warren returns again and again to the notion of how Bogan Murdock operates in abstraction without concern for human involvement. His manner with his subordinates is assured, cool, detached—and effective. Jerry becomes head of the securities department of a new Murdock bank *because* he knows as little about its operation as Private Porsum, the president, knows about banking generally. Jerry's decision to reject a career in geology (a science based on the tangible manifestations of nature) for the abstractions of speculative finance is symbolically confirmed at his graduation.[16] There his geologist mentor meets and chats with Jerry's father; Murdock, glimpsed in the crowd, is mysteriously unavailable—and even unseen except by his future employee. And when Jerry becomes engaged to Sue Murdock, his cynical accountant friend, Duckfoot Blake, suggests that he ask for a cash settlement: "Cash, not paper. Not a scrap of Bogan's paper. Or some day you will be using it in the back house." (It is the prescient Blake who explains to Jerry: "Bogan is a solar myth, he is a pixy, he is a poltergeist. . . . When Bogan Murdock looks in the mirror, he don't see a thing.")

Around this hollow man are gathered associates and even members of his own family who serve only as adjuncts to his power. Enormously polite, Murdock has a bland exterior that is of a piece with his speech patterns, a compound of clichés drawn from patriotic oratory and idioms drawn from indulgent parental lectures. This rhetoric and manner are tools, says his daughter, to make people do what he wants. And most people are gullible enough to be taken in by what Duckfoot Blake calls "the voice of the charmer" and "the smile of the Crucified Redeemer." Murdock is Warren's single most explicit exhibit of how substance has been reduced to salesmanship, and Jerry Calhoun is his fullest development of those figures who are unable to distinguish the difference.

Like Percy Munn of *Night Rider* Jerry Calhoun is unable to communicate to others what he is like or how he feels. To dramatize the state of the spiritual drifter, Warren shows how, almost unconsciously, Jerry falls into the styles of living that insure a blind security without the burden of human responsibility. Vaguely dissatisfied with himself and with only a blurred sense of identity, Jerry seizes upon certain kinds of patterns that lend him a feeling of greater inner clarity and security. As a football player he cherishes certain plays because they permit him to be caught up into "a pure, rhythmic, fluctuating but patterned flow of being" that momentarily protects him from "the disorders and despairs of his life." Later his homework in the banking business—reading books and reports which Blake recommends—offers him something similar: "It was so clean and sure, that flow of unheard voice off the page—a guarantee that the world was secure, was a pattern which you could grasp and live by."

Jerry rejects the past because it is not a guarantee of security; his father's house, in fact, embodies the truth of man's financial precariousness and his physical imperfections. Only painfully does Mr. Calhoun make the family farm minimally productive. Within the household are two people, one embittered and lame, the other almost vegetablelike in her blindness and immobility. And the most painful sight for Jerry is his father, who performs simple chores clumsily, then goes about his tasks of caring for these people whose actual relationship to him is only through marriage. Such visible evidence of insecurity and imperfection is revulsive to Jerry, whose only alternative is withdrawal from all human relationships that demand responsibility. He therefore rejects his past because he equates it with inadequacy, imperfection, failure. To accept it would be to accept what he most fears. In denying that responsibility he also denies the mutual warmth and closeness that could purge his fears. There is, then, always a chilly impersonality in his friendships among the other Murdock boys, and Sue rightly detects that their affair is loveless and mechanical.

The past rejected (or, more precisely, avoided, since he is too passive to reject outright), Jerry has only the present, and, because he cannot endure meaningful relations with others, even that present is delicate and precarious. He moves smoothly on the surfaces, adopting the bland Murdock's speech patterns, gestures, attitudes, along with his New York tailor. Murdock is his model not merely because he is the top man but also because, psychologically, Murdock so successfully ignores the problems of emotional entanglements, a problem that the long-suffering Mr. Calhoun never acknowledges as a problem. Murdock's coolness is unruffled, his concern itself devoted only to making others help him to perpetuate his power. Jerry cherishes the present world, and he is discomfited by anything in it that recalls his past and the human imperfections associated with it: Blake's bumbling parents, for example, or Rosemary, Sue's painfully crippled friend. Particularly reproachful to him is the warmth of the Blake house: for hours after a visit he suffers from "elegiac melancholy" and "diffused despair."

Jerry Calhoun never knows with any precision who he is. In our first glimpse of him he is rehearsing available definitions ("Bull's-eye Calhoun," the boy who "brought back the bacon from New York") until his very name echoes in his head "like a set of nonsense syllables." And at the last scene he has become, literally, what Sue Murdock once accused him of being, an "emotional cripple" in the house of cripples, like Aunt Ursula and Uncle Lew, under his father's care. In between, to compensate for his avoidance of human involvement, he cultivates the manner of the progressive businessman on the way up.

Warren devotes most of Chapter 5 to Jerry's training for his job. While he studiously learns the basic principles of economics and the technicalities of investments and securities, Jerry is most adept at learning the required amenities of getting along in his new milieu: what to wear, what to say to associates, where to live (Blake tells him that the smell of cabbage will cling to his clothing if he lives in a boarding-house too long). And, most important, he learns the trick of successful behavior with potential customers:

> It was all easier than he had imagined. . . . If they asked him questions or asked for his opinion, he would answer not too discursively, nodding slightly, his manner respectful but authoritative. He was not afraid to disagree with them. He knew football and fishing and hunting; and they knew that he knew those things. When the men talked to him about business or politics, he listened in the same way; and when they asked him a question he replied in the same way, rather briefly, respectfully, not afraid to disagree, not afraid to say that he did not know, nodding almost imperceptibly, with a slight corrugation of the strong, glowing flesh between his straight brows.
>
> (AHG, 76)

These are the resources of a not especially intelligent man whose fragmented identity is supplemented by a reliance on self-conscious tricks, manners, gestures.

His affair with Sue Murdock ironically undercuts Jerry's best efforts to achieve a harmonious, well-regulated, and "healthy" position within her father's organization. For Sue, like Jerry, is also repudiating home, past, tradition. Her restlessness, her refusal to accept an understood place in her family circle, is marked by several instances: her insistence on sexual intercourse at the most dangerous times and in the most dangerous places; her perverse taunting of Jerry, her brother, her father, her mother, and her grandfather. Moreover the second world that Sue enters impinges uncomfortably on Jerry's plans. It is precisely the phony world of the university and the little theater, the functions of which suggest the diverse and the tangential, that threatens the routine niche that Jerry is laboring to carve out for himself. Sue's strategies are more desperate than her lover's: having rejected an unsatisfactory definition of herself, she is still searching for a satisfactory one.

If Chapter 5 shows Jerry learning the techniques necessary for a new self, Chapter 7 and its extension in Chapter 19 describe Sue's efforts. At play rehearsals Jerry wonders to what extent her reciting of fictional "sentiments and passions" is her own; even the "familiar fluent movement from the waist and shift of the shoulder" are convincing. But he is quick to detect the artifice of her special language which she uses with her new friends: "Oh, she was the queen, all right, Jerry thought. Bullying them and saying, 'Darling, darling, blessed one,' in that phony voice he hated, which wasn't her voice, which was a voice she never used except when she was with these phonies."

Under the tutelage of Slim Sarrett, Sue progresses from the early state of being unable "to put it into words" to that state which Jerry so despises: the carefully learned, calculated repartee which she develops by skimming through current issues and fads and applying to them fragments of wit and breathless pauses. The technique never wholly satisfies her, but since her goal of self-definition is so hazy, she must concentrate on the method to get as much as she can from the immediate moment. With cues from Sarrett she polishes her techniques:

> Something is *like* something else—oh, just like something—the "just" was important—and you shut your eyes and it popped into your head and you said it, and they would laugh. But you yourself did not laugh. You just sat there with your face straight, just as straight as you could make it. Unless nobody laughed at first. Then you looked off to one corner of the room, and smiled just a little bit to yourself, like you knew something, and then—it always worked that way—somebody laughed, like he knew something too.
>
> (AHG, 239)

It is ironic that Jerry, who perceives the artifice and the special language of Sue, takes Murdock's speeches and gestures at face value. The easy, seductive conversation, the confidential intimacy, the calculated show of emotion, the very stock speeches stitched with parental and political clichés: all are part of his actuating rhetoric, and all make Jerry "relaxed, patient, and strong." Sue's conversation and mannerisms simply make him nervous; but his failure to discriminate between the ploys of the political corrupter and those of the desperate searcher is radical.

One of the wiles of the political corrupter is the appeal to social egalitarianism. Murdock, who is pleased with his lack of snobbishness, reminds Jerry of one of his favorite stories. "I think that the Emperor Tiberius was right in his reply to the courtiers who remarked on the poor birth of the favorite Rufus: Rufus is his own ancestor. I have always thought that a noble remark." *Man as his own ancestor*: both the concept and its verbal justification in anecdotal ancient history come easily to Murdock. The notion has always had special relevance for the American, of course, ranging from political and social independence to spiritual Self-Reliance, and to their economic vulgarization in the phrase *self-made man*. Murdock is the perfect manipulator of the doctrines of the New South apostles, his rhetoric a symbolic union of traditional sectional pieties and the promotional slogans of national big business. In Warren's context there is a further declension: the spiritual implications of the self-made man are both extensive and gloomy.

Their reliance on techniques betrays a fundamental lack of substance in Jerry and Sue. Warren's emphatic and iterated references to calculated effects, artifice, rhetorical patterns, deployment of manners and gestures, tricks of phrasing and bons mots, and cultivation of personal images for public consumption all point up the plight of the fragmented self who is not at home even in the world it tries to make. In an urban milieu liberated from the demands of family, past, or tradition, values that celebrate man's responsibility for man are few and fragile. Techniques can only oil the machinery of an impersonal, dehumanized, and abstracted society.

Except for Sue, who searches for a real human involvement outside the sterile managerial atmosphere of her father's house (and her options are less varied than they appear to be), all the great users of technique in *At Heaven's Gate* shirk any mutual responsibilities: Murdock, Slim Sarrett, Sweetie Sweetwater, Jerry, and Private Porsum, another of Murdock's less apt pupils. Sue's successive loves—Jerry, Sarrett, Sweetwater—share a desire to revise their imperfect pasts, and for Sue all come to be in varied ways reflections of Murdock, who himself has revised the past (his father is a political murderer) into a chapter of heroism and local patriotism. None of them is a true alternative to her father; all three are merely fragmented replacements. All are moved by abstractions no less than Murdock: Jerry (like Porsum) is a poor boy turned hero, and the nature of his success is as mysterious as his identity; the dehumanization of her other two lovers is suggested by their obsessive devotion to abstract systems—Sarrett to aestheticism, Sweetwater to Marxism—and both share Murdock's talent for manipulating others.

During the same evening that Sarrett tells Sue, fresh from a dispute with Jerry, that she had created a version of Jerry to fit her needs, as well as a new version of herself to accommodate it, he tells her the version of himself and his past that he needs. It is a rich romantic story of the precocious child of a riverboat captain and a New Orleans prostitute. Once on his own, this young Sarrett knocks about the country, instinctively honing in on wealthy and influential patrons; "how easy it is," he tells Sue, "once you get the trick." Although the details of the narrative are fabricated, the governing motives are clear enough. Sarrett has so denied his home, past, and tradition that he must manufacture replacements; but his present world is not one in which he can immerse himself. He is too much the director, watching over the intricate interrelationships of his world. He is Warren's most dramatic case of alienation until the creation of Isaac Sumpter of *The Cave*. His actors—graduate students, professors, foundry workers, newspapermen—perform regularly, and he observes them with clinical dispassion. Though he mingles, he mingles to manipulate, pressing here, encouraging there.

One of the clearest examples of Sarrett's technique occurs when Sue tries to compare acting to her own personal development: Sarrett completes her simile ("Like first menstruation?"), and she agrees; Sarrett then congratulates her on that "subtle and precise" comparison, concluding: "You say very subtle and precise things, sometimes." But even Sue, for most of her association with Sarrett, is nothing more to him than the most important fixture in his studio world. Just as she is his biggest triumph, so she becomes his most significant failure after his past is exposed by the homosexual Mr. Billie Constantidopeles. As an impurity that has corrupted the pure world of his own creation, she must be either "remade" or removed utterly.

When this world collapses, she turns to Sweetwater; and for all his differences, he follows the same pattern as Jerry Calhoun and Slim Sarrett. In rejecting the world of his preacher father and his certainty of belief, Sweetwater eventually comes to duplicate it and can apply his father's proverb without irony: "A man cannot believe in himself unless he believes in something else." As a vehement unionist, Sweetwater plays his role with a fervor worthy of his father. Fleeing from rigidity, he embraces rigidity. He demands rights as a husband despite his principle that a mission as labor organizer precludes marriage.

Sue is attracted to both Sarrett and Sweetwater because they exercise discipline and self-control and because they have goals. The price is high for a woman with only an impulse toward independence. Sue has no external goals and little internal discipline; her lovers, no less than her father, supply her with the outline (and as much substance as they can) for the creation of a new self. They can mold new images for her, but they cannot offer her what she most desperately needs: the full unreserved commitment of love. Although it is Sarrett who murders her, in the context of mutual responsibility Sweetwater must also share the guilt. In the context of a rapacious world, however, both escape such judgment. As in most of his novels with strong political strains, *At Heaven's Gate* is not about Warren's views of politics—even Agrarian politics—or politicians. It is a study of individuals who in the "blur of the world" strive to find a focus in their own shape and weight, apart from such piecemeal definitions as economic man or aesthetic man.

I have spoken of the gloomy implications of Murdock's example in this novel. One of them is that those who have successfully defined themselves are precisely those who fulfill a fragmented, specialized category; those who fail do not achieve even that. One of the maxims in the novel says that "no one who has succeeded in fulfilling his nature, whatever that nature is, needs sympathy. The man who has not fulfilled his nature is the man who needs sympathy." Although it comes from Sarrett, the crisply detached intellectual, the statement is ratified by the action of the novel. As monstrous examples of the self-created, Murdock, Sarrett, and Sweetwater need no sympathy; Jerry and Sue, whose natures are never fulfilled, are pathetic cases of individuals who ache for a human wholeness but who learn merely shallow skills for a kind of protective adaptation in the world of the self-created.

Ashby Wyndham, of course, is the one character who lacks even protective adaptation. In a world dominated by the self-created, his only tack is confrontation. And though he casts in relief the spiritual failures of the major characters, his career offers still another variation on their pattern of repudiation. Ashby's sin is in seeking his individuality outside the context of familial responsibilities; but, unlike the major characters, Ashby seeks help by holding his sin before him as a constant reminder of man's creatureliness. He succumbs to pride even in this, but he does achieve an identity less blurred than the others', and his sense of responsibility serves as a moral yardstick against which the other characters are measured.

Sarrett and Sweetwater (and to a lesser extent Sue and Jerry—lesser only because they are less intelligent) are merely dissatisfied with what they have been. Out of their dissatisfaction they manufacture by their own wills, and in totally secular contexts, new personalities for themselves and new functions which are merely (and perilously) grafted onto the old. Self-convicted, Ashby knows precisely what is required for reclamation: a reconstituting of the self from the inside out. Of all the characters he is least equipped, socially and intellectually, to ease his way through the urban world of the self-created by judicious use of technique. His public role—a combination of the Ancient Mariner and the southern street preacher—and his general theme—"the pore human man"—are possible only because of private experience: the transformation of man's evil ("a hog hollerness and emptiness for the world's slop") into righteousness through traditional Christian regeneration. To use a phrase from East Tennessee fundamentalists, Ashby "preaches mad." He is no mincer of words, no carrier of balm, since the burden of his message is the wrath of God upon sinful man. His role is not that of priest (representing man to God) but that of prophet (representing God to man). "He made the world and what walks on it," Ashby writes, "and it out of pure love." For him the world in all its variety is no place where the self can be defined in purely secular ways. His statement is his proof that the self is God-created.

As a confessional tract Ashby Wyndham's Statement is markedly free of rhetorical technique. "The Lord led me, and He laid the words on my tongue. I named them, and it was ample." Since the words are by inspiration, the style inevitably is unvarnished: "I will put it down, spare not, fear nor favor, and I will write it as fair as I can." But it is of course unvarnished only from an urbane point of view. In his hill-country way Ashby Wyndham is among the most articulate of all the characters: his script may be crabbed, but the rhetoric abounds with figures that accord perfectly with the man's earthiness, his deep involvement with other sin-prone men and women, and his abiding respect for the mysteries of God's love. At the farthest remove from Ashby's vivid specificity is Bogan Murdock's rhetoric of bland abstraction and generalization. In each case the rhetoric is an index to character, particularly the depth of concern of one human being for another. For Ashby Wyndham death and violence around him stimulate a profound reordering of his own life; for Bogan Murdock they become occasions for further political opportunism.

At Heaven's Gate posits no easy solution to the problem of self-definition. Those who are most in need of solving it—Sue Murdock and Jerry Calhoun—are confounded by the complexity and try to accommodate their urgencies with the stopgap measures of surface technique. Slim Sarrett tells Sue that people talk about themselves not out of vanity but because "they are mysterious to themselves, and they talk just to find out something about the mystery." But even at the end, when Sue is murdered and when a broken and bewildered Jerry is returned to his father's house, neither has learned much about the mystery. On the other hand Ashby Wyndham accepts the mystery because man is not his own creature. "A man don't know, for he is ignorant," and he "don't know, nor was made to." God's will, he explains, "runs lak a fox with the dogs on him, and doubles, and knows places secret and hard for a man's foot. But a man wants to know, but it is his weakness."

Those who use technique most outrageously to manipulate others—Murdock, Sarrett, Sweetwater—continue their lives apparently without much readjustment of their personal goals and methods. In the world of rapacity, the ruthless rule, mouthing their rhetorical clichés so patly that the mask becomes the face. Swearing by the portrait of Andrew Jackson (or by theories of poetry or politics) comes to be the real as well as the fake, the goal as well as the technique.

Murdock, Sarrett, Sweetwater: Their respective stewardships are all perverted because they avoid the high penalties for human responsibility. Jerry Calhoun and Sue Murdock suffer the pathos of failure. Only Ashby Wyndham emerges with anything resembling tragic stature, and that because he pays dearly for a commitment which seems anomalous to the urbanized denizens of the Waste Land. His career anticipates that of Cass Mastern in *All the King's Men*, and his folk formula foreshadows Jack Burden's spider-web theory of complicity: "When a man ever does a sin he ain't done it secret and him private. He has done taken his own sin on his shoulders, but another mans sin too to bear him down. You throw a rock in a pond and it don't make one splash but they is ripples runs out from it."

X. *All the Burdens of* All the King's Men

1.

Warren reports that he "stumbled" into the writing of fiction when he was at Oxford, where he sought to put down on paper some of the "tales" he had once talked about with his friend Paul Rosenfeld. "Fiction was for me," he remembers, "a way of reliving life that I was separate from—3,000 miles away from." Those oral tales became "Prime Leaf," and this early version of *Night Rider* reflected the imaginative "reliving," not of narrative lines (whose literal events occurred about the time Warren was born), but of the human circumstances of the action readily available to the amalgamating memory of a young Rhodes Scholar: people whose characteristic principles and behavior were recognizably human because they were first true to the place that nurtured them. If poetry is what Warren calls "a more direct way of trying to know the self, to make sense of experience—freer from *place*" than fiction, both modes are imaginatively generated from "an observed fact of life," which then invites an "ethical issue" that will invest the fact with significance.[17] From "Prime Leaf" onward, Warren's fiction reveals the double predilection of a writer who imposes ethical patterns on the felt life of a place he is separate from.

By the time *All the King's Men* appeared in 1946, Warren had already explored the hardy theme of the conflict between the public and private self, the actual and the ideal, commitment and disengagement—primarily by concentrating on the uses of political power. In both *Night Rider* and *At Heaven's Gate* he had tried to transform relatively abstract embodiments of power (the tobacco growers' association in one, Bogan Murdock in the other) into particularized, sensuously immediate politicians whose motives and acts are set in a context of rich circumstantiality.

That brand of circumstantiality is most decisively apparent in his third novel, in which Warren was able to give credible life to a political organization, as he was not able to do in *Night Rider*, and to a flesh-

and-blood political boss, which he was not able to do in *At Heaven's Gate*. Warren's tenure at Louisiana State University (1934–1942) encompassed both the kinetic atmosphere of Huey Long's awesome and sometimes comic domination of state politics and the corrupting aftermath of the Kingfish's assassination. There is no doubt that Warren's residence in Long's Louisiana constitutes the generative base of his most popular novel, and *All the King's Men* is not merely an extension of the compositional pattern of the "observed fact" and the "ethical issue" which is evident in the first two novels; it is also an intensification of this pattern. *Night Rider* is the re-creation of events of his father's generation—a collocation of regional history and family legend centering upon the Black Patch Wars; *At Heaven's Gate* has at its center a fictionalized version of Luke Lea, a Tennessee financier the peak of whose shady career coincided with Warren's undergraduate years at Vanderbilt. *All the King's Men*, despite its publication date, is in the most explicit way a fictional ordering of events and motifs crucial to Warren's maturity—events transpiring in his day-to-day activities at "Huey Long's university" and motifs of profound relevance to a Great Depression society of which he was still a part. For the first time in his career, that relevance in the actual world of the 1930s—politically, psychologically, philosophically, and culturally—intersects with Warren's most significant aesthetic and moral concerns.

Just as Huey Long was not merely another in the familiar class of southern demagogue, so Willie Stark is given the insight, procedural skill, and innovative intelligence lacking in such real-life demagogues as Theodore Bilbo of Mississippi or "Pitchfork" Ben Tillman of South Carolina. The career of Warren's politician generally follows that of Huey Long, not some conflated history of the southern demagogue. *All the King's Men* is of course more than this, and it is unsurprising that, faced with so many literalist sensibilities, Warren has always been prompted to deemphasize the convergence of his fiction and modern Louisiana history. His explanation, however, that Long provided him merely with atmosphere or "myth" should not obscure the nature of that convergence.[18]

In addition to the literal pattern of similarity, there is the pragmatic base of end over means in Long which becomes a central philosophic issue in Warren's novel. "You sometimes fight fire with fire," Long is quoted as saying. "The end justifies the means. I would do it some other way if there was time or if it wasn't necessary to do it this way."[19] As recounted in T. Harry Williams' superb biography, certain details about

Long's career are also reflected in Warren's account of Stark—Long's practice, for example, of requiring political appointees to sign undated resignations (Williams, 294), or the aristocratic conservatives' opposition to most of Long's measures partly because a boor was proposing them (Williams, 298–99).[20] Warren's Sugar-Boy bears a striking resemblance to Joe Messina, Long's devoted but unintelligent bodyguard (Williams, 322–23). Long's matter-of-fact assumption that every man had something in his past worthy of concealing is dramatized in Stark's pungent doctrine of man, and Jack Burden as Stark's chief investigator of opponents' secrets dramatizes Long's well-known practice of keeping a lockbox stuffed with damaging records of and affidavits on potential enemies that could be used when the governor thought it necessary (Williams, 751). Warren's fictive economy shows up in the case of Tiny Duffy, a conflated and concentrated example of many figures in Long's retinue. "He liked to break people, especially the strong, and then build them up again," intimates reported of Long; "then they knew their place" (Williams, 751–52).

That Willie Stark strongly resembles Louisiana's potlikker *tyrannos* would be, finally, a contention of little moment were it not for the fact that it simultaneously seems so obvious to so many and so critically disreputable to so many others. Most of the early reviewers made much of the resemblance and waxed moralistically because of it; later critics of *All the King's Men* have tended to see Huey Long almost as an accidental ingredient in the novel's genesis. Neither position should be ignored, though Warren's entire career, from which perspective we can see a persistent personal engagement with his own past, suggests that the author's Baton Rouge years—coming at the end of the era of Long's hegemony—should not be underestimated in their contribution to what Warren has called "the coiling, interfused forces" that go into literary decisions.[21]

Warren tells us that worrying his politician into shape began in the winter and summer of 1938 in Louisiana and Italy (in a verse drama called *Proud Flesh*), resumed in the summer of 1940 and in the spring of 1943, and only gradually emerged as the protagonist of *All the King's Men*. Into this study of a southern demagogue, whose name was changed from Talos to Stark, went not only the example of Huey Long but also Warren's wide reading in Dante, Machiavelli, Elizabethan tragedy, American history, William James, and his observation of the very real day-to-day melodrama of depression in America and fascism in Italy.[22] Like so many American works written in the shadow of World War II, *All the King's Men* is infused with the theme of power, its distribution, ethics, and consequences.[23]

The urge to dramatize the Willie Stark story was not lessened by the enormous critical and popular response to the novel nor by its author's winning of the Pulitzer Prize. Warren was not yet done with his politician. The tinkering and reshaping of the by now multiversioned drama resulted in numerous theatrical performances, most of them short-lived, from 1946 to 1959. Finally the text of *All the King's Men: A Play* appeared, presumably in the dramatic form that satisfied Warren.[24] The weaknesses of these versions are apparent: stilted dialogue, old-fashioned artiness in the Eliot manner, abstract moralisms imposed upon the action, belabored polarities too categorically parceled out. But the most obvious reason for the dramatic failures was the generic necessity to deemphasize Jack Burden, the narrator of the novel. This diminishment looms over all, changing all. Burden's transformation from a nearly undifferentiated bystander to chief among the king's men, from mere observer of the spectacle to narrator of and participator in the Willie Stark story, is, as most critics now agree, the peculiar strength of *All the King's Men* as a novel.

2.

The fleshing out of Burden was from the start, as Warren himself has pointed out, a technical choice. The novel fairly cried out for a more sensitive consciousness than that of the politician whose story had to be told. Call him Ishmael or Carraway, Burden is another in a long line of American narrators who by dint of their special positions in the stories they tell end by telling their own stories as well.[25] The case of Willie Stark readily invited naturalistic treatment, but the "impingement of that material . . . upon a special temperament" allowed Warren "another perspective than the reportorial one," and it also provided the basis for "some range of style."[26] Both author and narrator finally agree that the story of Willie Stark is also the story of Jack Burden.

Almost alone among the earliest critics, however, Norton Girault was able to see the focus of the novel in the character and sensibility of Burden, in his language of rebirth, in his halting, stumbling movements from ignorance to knowledge.[27] Though the progress from Cousin Willie to Governor Stark may be the tale told in the book, it is Burden's revelation of that progress that is the experience of the book. And *revelation* in two ways: first, his discovery of the meaning of Stark's rise and fall and of his own identity through these events, and second, his articulation of those meanings in a long I-narration. Perhaps no other modern novel so clearly demonstrates the fact that a happy technical choice alters the very meaning of materials that it must shape.

Nothing is more naturally dramatic or susceptible of significance than Willie Stark's story, the hard narrative facts isolated and untouched by a consciousness other than the author's. But both the drama and the meaning of that story are significantly redirected and heightened by having those facts experienced and related by an intervening consciousness. As a man of imagination and intelligence, Burden's own drama is, as James observed of Lambert Strether's, "under stress, the drama of discrimination,"[28] the shucking off of first one, then another, alternative to meaning until he *sees* and in the seeing allows the reader to follow the painful progress to moral awareness. From the desire to remain innocent, to resist the costly maturity of rebirth, Burden moves through even more costly immersions into experience, which he misinterprets and revises until he is forced to acknowledge his portion of evil.

Burden is a most unlikely learner when we meet him. Smug, astute, world-weary, he could almost pass for a New South variety of Conrad's Decoud in *Nostromo*. But the empty *boulevardier*, who scribbles his self-regenerative letter in the focus of battle, has pushed a habit of vision to its limits; Burden's memoir is itself the symbol of regeneration, a product of, not an ingredient in, his moral education. Such a memoir is *All the King's Men*, produced by a man who, after having arrived at a certain stage of self-knowledge, reenacts the costly process. We are constantly aware of growth as something both achieved and being achieved. But however insistent the interweaving of product and process—the necessary impingement of present attitudes on past beliefs and acts—the shaping perspective is that of the educated Jack Burden, the "legal, biological, and perhaps even metaphysical continuator" of the earlier king's man.

Burden's change has sometimes been thought phony or self-deceiving. It is true that Jack Burden is no Cass Mastern; neither is he a Scholarly Attorney. He has nothing of the humility of the first nor the radical spirituality of the latter. But in his learning Burden does achieve a measure of both humility and spirituality. If we are tempted to think of Burden as unchanging because he does not become either a Cass Mastern or a Scholarly Attorney, we might well speculate on the novelistic failure of *All the King's Men* had Burden's conversion taken on the obsessive coloration of those two figures. One of the thematic constants in Warren's fiction is that single-mindedness of whatever sort destroys human balance; it leads to a warping of man's need for community as well as for personal identity. Hence, the narrator's slower progress. If with his customary brio Burden calls Trollope "Anthony," it is only good craftsmanship to make the new Burden in certain tangible ways consistent with the old. Even the disasters tumbling in profusion about him cannot rout the tendencies of a lifetime—the easy cynicism of the newspaperman grafted onto the floating romanticism of the graduate student.

It is also true that the narrator seems callous in episodes that, upon proper assessment, require sensitivity; and he turns unduly sensitive at times when we would prefer the Hurt Young Man to be less touchy in his garrulity. But we are offended, and properly so, by his on-again, off-again, hard-boiled detective moods interspersed with debilitatingly romantic fancies. Hemingway demonstrated long ago that the modern stoic tough guy hides a sentimental idealist. Warren suggests such a functional split in Burden by vacillations between pretentious philosophizing and wise-guy witticisms. The split in his narrator serves in fact as a trope, compacted and made interior, for the entire novel. If a study of its theme and structure shows anything, it is that *All the King's Men* is one writer's concern about "the terrible division of [our] age," explored not only through explicit antitheses (man of idea/man of fact, means/ends, science/nature) but also through the subtle and pervasive doubling of characters: Stark/Burden, Burden/Duffy, Irwin/Mastern, Stark/Irwin, Stark/Stanton.[29] Burden, with his problems of spiritual integration, is the front-and-center figure within the play of larger, if not more meaningful, antitheses; furthermore, we know him only through a narration that reveals qualities which in actual people we could just as well do without. Tough guys and ersatz philosophers in our own time can be just as tiresome as the efficient housekeepers and virtuous companions of Victorian fiction.

As the twentieth-century wise guy who has put his learning to work for him, Burden must take shape, more imperatively even than Stark, literally through his own words. As public figure, he is in-the-know; as private figure, he seeks to know. His rhetoric, both as narrator and as character, reflects this split, appropriately embodying the strain between Burden as Sam Spade and Burden as Stephen Dedalus. He is alternately garrulous and noncommittal; he is cynically efficient, always prepared to "deliver" or to "make it stick." Privately, he belittles his efficiency, and we become increasingly aware of his real distaste for the particular person he has become. He chides himself frequently, referring to himself in the third person. With cocksure stridency he announces "the curse" of Jack Burden: "he was invulnerable." But even as he talks, he shows how vulnerable he is—to nostalgia, sentimentality, and those tangential events that nudge him into newer versions of himself and reality.

The Burden who remains after the fall of the king is a different person from the king's man; indeed, after those ambivalent and tentative loyalties, he takes a stand similar to Cass Mastern's. Partially responsible for at least three deaths and several lesser disasters, he comes to accept them fully in the "awful responsibility of time." He ends with a healthier respect for flawed humanity, extending to both Judge Irwin and Willie Stark, and with discomfort even sees his connection, spiritual as well as physical, with such a hack as Tiny Duffy. As acting son and stenographer, he cares for the Scholarly Attorney in his last days, and instead of condescending toward his marriage-prone mother he shows an admirable if low-keyed compassion. He devotes himself to the long-delayed editorial task of publishing the diary of Cass Mastern. He refuses to say the word to Sugar-Boy that would destroy not only Duffy but Sugar-Boy as well. In marrying Anne Stanton he wins a belated victory over the paralyzing image of purity that he holds of her throughout much of the novel. Perhaps most important, he even hints of his return to active politics in some future administration.

Burden is a conscious artist, scrupulously constructing his story from an open position, manipulating the early versions of himself from his newer one of control, growth, and moral self-evaluation. Although he perceives more at the end than at the beginning of the novel, he is careful in his verbal reconstruction to permit his earlier self full rein to maneuver within those limited terms.[30] If he occasionally sounds hysterical or even absurd, that impression is one that the narrator who reconstructs himself is the first to recognize. Such is the risk that the educated Burden willingly takes to present honestly the learning Burden. Certainly the final position at which he arrives is neither absurd nor hysterical. It is, in fact, a measure of his integrity that he can submit an imperfect image of himself with only such sporadic glossing as "that was the way I argued the case back then."

Burden's rhetoric throughout maintains certain characteristics: wisecracks, fancy metaphors, self-irony, the mingling of the elegant and the colloquial. His general diction and syntax do not change substantially, since the entire story is a memoir of events from 1922 (and occasionally earlier) to 1939, told in the language of the latest stage of his growth. Just as there is no dramatic physical alteration in

Burden—he presumably looks much the same in the late 1930s as he did in the early 1920s—so there is no obvious change in the physical shape of his words. The changes in Burden are philosophical and psychological, and the changes in his language are largely tonal. The mature Burden still clings to the wise-guy idiom of his Great Twitch days, but more important is the fact that the tone of that idiom shifts perceptibly. Here is the typical early Burden style:

> In a town like Mason City the bench in front of the harness shop is—or was twenty years ago before the concrete slab got laid down— the place where Time gets tangled in its own feet and lies down like an old hound and gives up the struggle. It is a place where you sit down and wait for night to come and arteriosclerosis. It is the place the local undertaker looks at with confidence and thinks he is not going to starve as long as that much work is cut out for him . . . . You sit there among the elder gods, disturbed by no sound except the slight *râle* of the one who has asthma, and wait for them to lean from the Olympian and sunlit detachment and comment, with their unenvious and foreknowing irony, on the goings-on of the folks who are still snared in the toils of mortal compulsions.
>
> (AKM, 56–57)

The subject, courthouse characters, is not an unusual one for the narrator at any time; neither is the feeling of bemused superiority which seeps out of his own Olympian syntax and the brash imagery. But if the subject and the observer's clear-eyed view of it do not vary greatly during Burden's education, the tone does. Here is a similar passage from the last chapter: "And I sat for hours in the newspaper room of the public library, the place which like railway stations and missions and public latrines is where the catarrhal old men and bums go and where they sit to thumb the papers which tell about the world in which they live for a certain number of years or to sit and wheeze and stare while the gray rain slides down the big windowpanes above them" (AKM, 443). In his final phase the narrator's wisecracks become muted, the tough line relaxes, the naturalistic observations become a trifle lame, the superiority itself undergoes chastening: all these changes reflect the sadness and near-inertia of an exhausted man.

Warren has said that the key device for making his narrator work satisfactorily was finding his "lingo" (*Talking*, 60), and certainly Burden's striking shifts from pretentious philosopher to streetwise pol attest to both his literal position in the narrative and the symbolic self-division of a character whose moral drama claims its own share of our attraction. But there is also a quieter, less intrusive verbal pattern in

All the King's Men that is shaped more directly by the author himself than by his narrator. There is, for example, the steady accretion of the contrasting images of ice and water, corresponding to emotional states of, on the one hand, rigidity, stasis, and purity, and on the other, immersion, flowing, drowning. Fixity—psychological and ideological—means protection from the contingence of actuality. Both Adam Stanton and Sugar-Boy are significantly linked by the image of ice: the bodyguard stares at Jack in the library "through the last preserving glaze of ice," and Adam's smile is described as "the stab of an icicle through the heart." Primitive purity and lethal innocence find common spiritual ground. Burden's dominant image of Anne is that of "some clean bright and gold leaf" buried in the clear ice of a frozen stream; later that image "breaks up" as in a spring thaw, which then threatens to sweep him under, to engulf him in "the moving stream of time." The thaw of Chapter 6 continues in later chapters as "the full dark stream of the world," "the flow," "the flux," "the current," and "drowning in West."

Such informing images verbally reinforce the narrator's efforts to close his emotional and intellectual gaps. Burden's struggle for spiritual unity is in fact reinforced by every aspect of the larger scheme of the novel. Consider, for example, the title of *All the King's Men* and its Dantean epigraph. With these juxtaposed elements Warren establishes, anterior to the novel itself, two apparently contradictory positions that suggest the basis of the conflict in Burden's difficult progress to self-knowledge. The title, with its nursery-rhyme allusion, connotes a pattern of thought and behavior dominated by acquiescence to the phenomenal, the factual, the way things are. The factual motif is posited by Stark's own proverb: "Man is conceived in sin and born in corruption and he passeth from the stink of the didie to the stench of the shroud." Like older tragic protagonists, Willie Stark falls from the clash of opposing motives. His doubleness cannot be erased; he is now tyrant, now hero, alternately damned and praised. As Burden finally and reluctantly discovers in his Case of the Upright Judge: "There is always the clue, the canceled check, the smear of lipstick, the footprint in the canna bed, the condom on the park path, the twitch in the old wound, the baby shoes dipped in bronze, the taint in the bloodstream." And that discovery brings Burden around once again to his kinsman's final vision of "the common guilt of man." These conclusions are further reinforced by the Scholarly Attorney's tract statement that "the only way for God to create, truly create, man was to make him separate from God Himself, and to be separate from God is to be sinful." This pattern, in short, asserts the natural depravity of man, the way—whether he likes it or not—man is.

Against the shattered world of Humpty-Dumpty, Burden comes to juxtapose his own experience in that tragedy and to conclude from it that he has not only been affected by the tragedy but that he has also affected it. As a Student of History, he must accept Cass Mastern's insistence upon personal involvement in the guilt of others; as a student of human nature he must share the blame in an affair that takes the lives of his two best friends and almost wrecks the life of the woman he loves. The deterministic resonance of the title, however, is counter-pointed by the fragmentary epigraph from the *Purgatorio—Mentre che la speranza ha fior del verde*. The hope that survives the Stark story may appear more gray than green, but it is hope nevertheless.

Acceptance of the way things are, without hope, may be merely sentimental complacency. As a graduate student Burden had flippantly visualized his future in some junior college "long on Jesus and short on funds" where he would have watched "the slow withering of the green wisp of dream," but later he can find a green wisp in the most basic fact of all: "there were some of us left." Since he halts further bloodshed by a willed silence in his last meeting with Sugar-Boy, survival is earned. He and Anne read Trollope together, uncurious about how equilibriums are changing; caught in a "massive and bemusing tide," they accept that tide's own "pace and time." Acceptance is earned. Seeing the grandson of Stark, Burden agrees with Lucy that she must believe that the Boss had been a great man even though the "greatness and ungreatness" had been so mixed he could not tell them apart. History is neutral, but man, working through history, is not. For all the ruck of irresistible fact that conditions him, man must still exercise his will. There is fact and there is hope. Certain theological and psychological benefits may be gained from accepting the way things are; but whatever his nature man still lives in a defective world with other defective men, and mutual responsibility involves more of his energies than a posture of weary resignation. Picking up the pieces may not put together another king, but the reminder of human fragility may stimulate the survivors to cherish what virtues remain.

These opposing attitudes associated with the factual and the hope-ful are established, then, before the novel begins, in its title and epi-graph.[31] Within the novel they are developed through the metaphorical possibilities of *rest* and *motion*. The way things are, man's depravity, the familiar pattern of failure after great effort: all these suggest rest, the state of certainty, the problem solved, the contest won (or lost).

The possibility of hope even in these terms, the perpetual testing of values, the willingness to risk becoming reconciled after grandly repudiating: all these suggest motion, the trying-out of grace, direction if not destination. The confident Burden is the cocky newspaperman who pursues the embarrassing deed out of the past to "make it stick," the cynical observer of the political animals at play, the Student of History who exchanges without undue upheaval his brass-bound Idealism for the positivism of the Great Twitch (and is perfectly certain that in each case he has arrived at Truth, or at least truth). In one of his definitive acts—his flight West—he says, "meaning is never in the event but in the motion through event." This assertion that, for man, "direction is all" is confirmed in his theological parries with the Scholarly Attorney. "Life is motion," Burden repeats several times; "if the object which a man looks at changes constantly so that knowledge of it is constantly untrue and is therefore Non-Knowledge, then Eternal Motion is possible." But these statements of self-assurance come from the king's man; in the end Burden affirms the truth of both rest and motion.

The famous final paragraph of *All the King's Men* is a capping rhetorical union of these two patterns. With its emphasis on depleted energies, memory, and nostalgia, the emotional associations are with rest; but the syntax and diction suggest motion: *to walk down the Row, walk down the beach, diving floats lift gently, footfall, we shall move, we shall go out, and go into.* The substance of the final paragraph is that even nostalgia will have no easy time of it; even that indulgence "will be a long time from now." The price of seeing things as they are has been high. Burden has seen his two friends, Stark and Stanton, "doomed," but they have also been men of individual will. Thus the burden of Jack Burden is what he learns to bear: man, though he accepts inscrutable providence, cannot luxuriate in inaction because of that surety. The tone of the later Burden cannot be called optimistic. He no longer rests his case in the firmly bound, well-labeled file folders of the private eye. Except for his acknowledgment of man's situation "in the world in which we live from birth to death," he comes to see all other judgments as tentative, judgments that therefore require retesting to be continually relevant.

Our pervasive sense of this work's political context in its largest sense, the great world in which personal values are ratified, extended, distorted, or extinguished, accounts for the special poignancy of the final chapter of *All the King's Men*, particularly its sliding weariness of nuance that reminds us of the frightful toll that the public life extracts from the individual. The shattering of private lives is the most obvious sign of that toll: in the inner narrative, that of Cass Mastern, his adulterous partner, and the slave Phebe, a physical and moral collapse which images forth the great public issues of slavery, secession, and war; and in the central narrative, the lives of most of Jack Burden's friends who are caught up in the swirling issues of demagoguery, dictatorship, and the political testing of personal loyalties. The sad waste dramatized by the deaths of the governor and the doctor is not completed in that violent moment but is extended through days of anticlimax. Sadie Burke vegetating in the sanitarium, a purposeless Sugar-Boy idling his time away in the public library, Tiny Duffy eagerly assuming the stained mantle of Willie Stark: all become visible analogues for Jack Burden of his potential fate. What is notable about Warren's ethical denouement is that, despite the treacherous impact of public life on private identity, *All the King's Men* is finally not a preachment against the bruising and corrupting world of politics and the mixed rewards of social reform.

Jack Burden is a most battered man at the end of the novel, yet the most poisonous influence has not been Willie Stark's pragmatic political programs or the sour rankling between the partisans of Mason City and Burden's Landing. Jack Burden suffers most from a sense of self-betrayal. He himself pictures for us how easy it was for him to live with a fuzzy self-definition before there was a public context to his life: his lazy tennis-and-swimming summers with Anne Stanton, his professional drift, his self-indulgent marriage to Lois. Subliminal discontent, however, like a faint toothache, can be tolerated without substantial disruption of the psyche; not so the blatant daily barrage of conflicting principles and loyalties. Burden's victory in coming through the Willie Stark years with self-respect is obviously limited. Salvaging honor in purely personal ways is an understandable resolution to this protagonist's dilemmas, and the most engaging of his acts after the deaths of Stark and Stanton are acts of reclamation in personal relationships: becoming a husband to Anne, serving as stenographer and nurse to Ellis Burden, understanding his mother. Important as they are, however, two other decisions suggest that for Jack Burden the merely personal is not enough for the satisfactory definition of the self: leaving Irwin's house and selling the family property that is now legally his, and his tentative interest in reentering politics, this time under the aegis of the honest Hugh Miller. Both decisions imply that there is no *achieved* self-definition possible, that it is only *process*, and that such a process necessarily requires the continued testing of the self in the great world. Thus, like Warren's view of Conrad, the lesson of Jack Burden is the human necessity to go "naked into the pit, again and again, to make the same old struggle for his truth." Like *Nostromo, All the King's Men* dramatizes "the cost of awareness and the difficulty of virtue" (SE, 58, 48–49).

If Burden achieves a victory, it is in recognizing that the self must be submitted to motion, that it must act upon the slender green hope in the face of defeat. One of the achievements of Burden's memoir is that it can reveal the victory while simultaneously celebrating the often debilitating movements toward it. While in the tentative rest of the final period the tone of the narrator is less patronizing, less dogmatic, the basic thrust of his rhetoric is the same. Burden as narrator never allows even his guilt, rooted in the magnitude of recent events, to paralyze his ability to tell his own story effectively; and although he reconstructs his own past with as much detachment as he does the whole Stark era, he still bears the personal marks of that ordeal. His name, we can see now, suggests his vital centrality in that general reconstruction. Thematically he bears his past with difficulty, heavy obligation, and great expense. And even the future must be borne. Structurally, and here the musical signification of *burden* is pertinent, his story carries the "ground" for the more obvious pattern of Stark's story—those obligatory measures in the novel. When Burden permits the learning character to catch up with the narrator who has learned, he admits how tempting it has been to try to shoulder the least painful parts of his burden. He is denied, for instance, the "inexpensive satisfaction in virtue" when, upon trying to give what is left of Irwin's estate to Miss Littlepaugh, he finds she has died.

At the end of *All the King's Men,* Burden is both his own judge and his own accused who, deprived of many of the intellectual and emotional conditions that he formerly demanded, must now accept his own burden of being man. He is like Bunyan's Christian at the beginning of the journey. But for Jack Burden that journey lies beyond the confines of the novel, beyond 1939, in the "convulsion of the world" where, we may assume, his own travail will be convulsive before his burden can be rolled away.[32]

3.

When *All the King's Men* appeared in 1946, most readers saw it as a political novel, and most of them were not overly concerned that the fictive testing of its philosophical assumptions resembled spiritual autobiography more than it did fiction by Upton Sinclair (who was still writing his Lanny Budd novels) of John Dos Passos. More serious readers, however, directed us properly and acutely to the moral import of the novel.[33] So successful were they that most of us now tend to regard *All the King's Men* almost solely as a moral fiction. But its original reception was not wholly misinterpreted; the political base of the novel is firm. I have already suggested that for those readers who do not remember the Huey Long years, T. Harry Williams' definitive biography suggests the revealing parallels of Warren's novel and this historical moment as well as some equally revealing divergences. Despite Warren's own exasperations with having such links pointed out, logic will have its say.

But there is another logic at work, too, one that is both farther reaching in the political implications of the novel and more narrowly relevant to the story of Jack Burden's struggle for moral identity. This logic is located within the novel itself, both what is put in and what is left out. If Jack Burden can at one point muse on the curious and unsettling feeling that he is like God brooding on history (during the impeachment proceedings), it is also true that overall, at all points, Warren is like the historian, another surrogate God, brooding on history.

When Jack writes on the last page, "So by the summer of this year, 1939, we shall have left Burden's Landing," we are suddenly jolted by the specificity of the date (more than a year has passed since Stark's assassination in late 1937). The narrative sequence in the last fourth of the novel requires no such specificity: only the sequence of deaths and their causes are required. After the profusion of losses, Jack and Anne slowly regain their "perilous equilibrium" in the lemon-pale sun of late autumn, reading Trollope, and submitting themselves to the "enormous drift" of events that knows "its own pace and time." But then the pace and time pick up. Jack's final meeting with Sugar-Boy in the public library occurs in February. In May, Jack goes to see Lucy Stark in the country. In "early summer" he returns to Burden's Landing for a final visit with his mother. When she remarks vaguely that she had originally intended to go to Europe, Jack responds with "You better stay out of Europe. . . . All hell is going to break loose over there and not long either." This seemingly is Warren's only direct allusion to the events that were to crowd and jostle each other until their eruption on September 1, 1939.

Despite the rhetorical dying fall of the last several pages of the novel, despite the exhaustion and weariness that hound Jack Burden in his fragile task of picking up the pieces of at least two shattered lives, the moral note suggested by these pages is a curious compound of wary hope and nostalgia: that is, the *text* of the novel looks both forward and backward. And in the interstices of the text we can read the larger implications of a regional story of morality and politics.

Although the composition of *All the King's Men* stretches from at least 1940 to 1945, the action of the novel ends during the year before the first stage of composition. Thus, what is omitted from the story is the convulsion of the world *beginning* with 1939. Jack Burden stands at the threshold of World War II, but his creator stands at its conclusion. Warren's strategy is a rhetorical one, incorporating within the experience of the novel, as one critic has put it, "the knowledge of a reader who has lived through what it anticipates."[34]

The confused moral principles working themselves out in such violent ways in a southern state in the 1930s, especially as they are registered on a tortured sensibility, have their louder political resonance in the ideological debates in Europe. In fact the story of Jack Burden, the divided man who after spiritual drift and moral paralysis finally comes to do the right thing, reads like a conflation, a miniaturized history, of the larger political and moral story of the late 1930s. Warren, no less than his contemporary W. H. Auden, knew the truth of what 1939 was like:

> In the nightmare of the dark
> All the dogs of Europe bark,
> And the living nations wait,
> Each sequestered in its hate;[35]

a similar registering can be found in some of Warren's poems contemporaneous with the early composition of the novel and preserved in *Selected Poems: 1923–1943*. One of the recurring themes in these is echoed in Warren's theory that the man of power is powerful only because he responds to the blank needs of people around him. What is missing in these poems is the explicit man of power (though Fascist leaders lurk in the shadows); what we see instead are the confused and compensatory acts of those cursed with "blanknesses and needs": Harry L., whose "heart bled speed" in a plane; some "whose passionate emptiness and tidal / Lust swayed toward the debris of Madrid"; and still others awash in Europe's greater tidal lust who continue to "sink / To rest in lobbies, or pace gardens where / The slow god crumbles and the fountains prink. . . ." Both the flight to surrogate commitments and the heedless pursuit of transient pleasures are seen as postponements of an inevitable reckoning. For the personae in these early poems, self-confrontation cannot be denied:

> Till you sit alone—which is the beginning of error—
> Behind you the music and lights of the great hotel:
> Solution, perhaps, is public, despair personal,
> But history held to your breath clouds like a mirror.

(SP, 285, 286, 288)

On the battlefield or on the beaches of fashionable watering places, the spiritual state is the same.

For the narrator of *All the King's Men*, the Great Sleep and the Great Twitch are psychologically definitive gestures of a man who cherishes his innocence and his spiritual stasis all the more urgently as events nudge him into facing truths about himself and his involvement in those events. Jack Burden's political experiences, no less than his personal ones, turn out to exemplify the truths he would shun. Evasions, feints, and flanking actions are not necessarily easier maneuvers than headlong confrontations; but they are partial, inadequate, and finally dishonest.

Self-confrontation means holding history to your breath; the personae in these early poems and Jack Burden in *All the King's Men* must admit their participation in history—and thus their responsibility to it. If, as Warren knew, betrayal stained so many lives and careers in a political machine in the South, betrayal on a grander scale, as he knew equally well, was to become the name of diplomacy in all the Mason Cities of western Europe. Behind Warren's sonorous abstractions —"into the convulsion of the world, out of history into history and the awful responsibility of Time"—are those specific public convulsions that give resonance to and that perhaps are the literal referents of these abstractions: Spain, Poland, Czechoslovakia, France; the Channel War, Dresden, Belsen, Stalingrad. These public eruptions, varied as they were militarily, demonstrate a common fact, the inescapable entanglement of the moral and the political—which is also the inescapable lesson that Jack Burden learns. History is neutral, but man is not. Breathing the very air of depletion, Jack Burden muses on his own lately recognized responsibility; in the retrospection of recent history, Robert Penn Warren suggests that the bouts of European Great Sleeps and European Great Twitches merely postponed the reckoning.

Romance and History

William Styron calls *The Confessions of Nat Turner* (1967), a book that his friend Robert Penn Warren admires, a "meditation on history" rather than a "historical novel." It represents an attempt both to be more precise about his motives and methods and to separate himself from those ranks of novelists once favored by book club members. Warren has also resisted the label of *historical novelist* simply because he thinks he does not write historical novels. "I hate costume novels," he says, and that resistance, which begins with his first novel in 1939, owes something to traditional prejudice among those serious readers and critics who systematically deplore the crude, mechanical, and exploitative habits of the popular practitioners of that variety of fiction.[1]

Arguably, the depression and war years in America constitute something of a record in the popularity of historical fiction. Hardly a publishing season went by without spirited internecine rivalry among the leaders: Samuel Shellabarger, Thomas B. Costain, Daphne DuMaurier, Frank Yerby, Inglis Fletcher, and Gladys Schmidt; and these professional ranks were on occasion breached by an amateur such as Kathleen Windsor. By 1939 Warren was quite aware that the literary staple in the larder of the post–Reconstruction South—the self-conscious reenactments of the glamorous legends of what W. J. Cash was to call Cloud-Cuckoo-Land—was undepleted.[2] The plain fare of the actual South by imaginative compensation seemed paradoxically to nourish the richest of fantasies, the kind that Warren and his fellow Fugitives had rejected fifteen years earlier. It was, if anything, intensified by the commercial success of two novels better than the usual run: Stark Young's *So Red the Rose* (1934) and Margaret Mitchell's *Gone With the Wind* (1936).

Warren's relationship to the historical novelists of his day bears a certain but restricted resemblance to Hawthorne's relationship to the writers of romance in the middle of the nineteenth century. Just as the appropriation of "romance" by popular authors was much lamented by nineteenth-century medieval scholars, twentieth-century historians, before Georg Luckas' influential study made it respectable, often questioned the very existence of that elusive form called the "historical novel." More frequently, however, it was agreed to be that species of the novel which "makes history come alive," and, more often than not, it seemed that in our time female novelists took more sprightly to their task than did their male counterparts. If by 1850 Hawthorne felt compelled to rail (privately) against what he called "that damned mob of scribbling women" who sensationally and profitably were working the same generic vein as he, the very popularity of *Gone With the Wind* and *Forever Amber* insured the historical novel against serious consideration by an entire generation of critics.[3] Hawthorne's strategy was at once shrewd and defensive. Acknowledging that the limits of his temperament prevented his entering the heartier ranks of novelists who flourished in the medium of a beef-and-beer actuality, he redefined the terms and circumstances of the frailer genre, elevating it out of a shabby and trivial status into one that could satisfy the demand that it be serious. From 1850 onward, Hawthorne glossed his own practice with the theoretical terms in light of which his work was to be read, terms that could fairly claim to be serious both aesthetically and morally.

In the writing of his first extensive piece of fiction, Warren, unlike Hawthorne, refrained from any theoretical challenge to the mob of scribbling historical novelists. Directly, he announced that *Night Rider* was not a historical novel; indirectly, the novel itself served as a challenge to the popular species. Because of the quietest exploitation possible of materials usually considered appropriate to the historical novel, *Night Rider* maintains a firm, cool distance between those materials and the author's shaping of them. The melodrama, violence, and emotional eruptions are muted by a ritualistic restraint and a prose style closer to Hawthorne than to Hervey Allen. The novel derived from the writer's own near-memories of the tobacco wars of Tennessee and Kentucky in 1905–1906. These stories, still fresh in Warren's growing-up years, took their place in the continuum of family and regional history stretching back to include the Civil War adventures related by a Confederate grandfather who had ridden with Bedford Forrest.

If *Night Rider* is not a historical novel, its status is more ambiguous than Warren's prefatory disclaimer at first appears: "Although this book was suggested by certain events that took place in Kentucky in the early years of this century, it is not, in any strict sense, a historical novel." Does this mean, for instance, that in Warren's view a historical novel must conform more completely to known facts than does his first novel, which was only "suggested" by these facts? Does the retelling of historical events in narrative that is faithful to them qualify as a historical novel in the "strict sense"?[4]

The issue is never quite settled in Warren's career. A keen interest in history and the practice of fiction overlap in several ways. In a "strict sense"—as almost anybody would define that slippery and concessive term—*Band of Angels* and *Wilderness* are certainly historical novels; that is, they recount the interaction of events and characters in a multireferential, reimagined world of the past. *World Enough and Time* is a less pure example because of its contemporary frame, but that temporal level is dependent entirely upon the century-old events that it encloses. No one would seriously call *All the King's Men* a historical novel, although its major action is conceived to be morally coextensive with its secondary action of two generations earlier, and in certain ways the major action aesthetically duplicates that earlier one.

Warren's ambiguous attitude toward the fictionalizing of history can be seen in his first book. *John Brown: The Making of a Martyr* (1929) is important, but not because it gives us an objective portrait of John Brown to replace the distorted and mythic images of previous biographers. For the writing of this book Warren acquainted himself with the considerable secondary literature, much of it biased—accounts of old Brown written to buttress larger causes. Warren's procedure was to sift through these accounts, looking for contradictory uses of the same factual evidence and the selective process by which some facts were cited, some authorities quoted, while others were ignored. Warren tries to make his subject more complex than either of the opposing figures projected by the partisans and enemies—that is, Brown is neither saint nor madman, but an ambitious failure who makes the most of his middling talents, a charismatic leader with a paltry knowledge of tactics, and a self-deluded idealist indifferent to the most commonplace moral and ethical standards of his day. As a result, Warren's account of John Brown is perhaps more interesting than any other, but it can hardly be termed objective. The tone is breezily irreverent, a kind of countrified version of that brandished by such Tory rebels of the 1920s as Lytton Strachey and Aldous Huxley; some facts are unsubtly reiterated to reinforce certain observed propensities in Brown's character; and, most important, Warren imaginatively reconstructs events as the historical novelist was required generically to do, supplying dialogue and dramatic interest, and emphasizing symbolic correspondences between early and late episodes and between states of mind and nature. If the figure of John Brown anticipates the typical protagonist in Warren's fiction, especially that obsessive man who willingly embraces dubious means to bring about moral ends, the actual process by which Warren engages himself with the rich materials, the visible struggle with his subject, anticipates his willingness to use biography and history for larger imaginative purposes.[5]

Such a choice is not of course unique with Warren. As recent scholars have demonstrated, imaginative manipulation of historical fact began with the first historical novelist, Sir Walter Scott; it was a literary tactic that was executed by succeeding practitioners who, almost without exception, thought of such latitude in regard to factual history as their generic right as opposed to the responsibilities of formal historians. We now know that the use of that latitude—Hawthorne finds the word useful—is not only one of the keys to distinguish the romance as a fictional genre from the novel but is also the defining characteristic of any historical fiction. Thus the historical novel really is the historical romance. In a process of conflation, the romance in the nineteenth century came to mean any fiction removed from its time of composition either spatially (the far away) or temporally (the long ago).

When Melville, after his success with two "narratives of voyages," determined to write a "downright earnest" romance, the terms become fascinatingly ambiguous. If *Typee* and *Omoo* are not proper novels, neither are they proper romances—but they are, in the words of his preface to *Mardi*, narratives "received for a verity." That description makes them closer to the conventional novel than *Mardi*, which clearly represents for its creator an unshackling of imagination, a release from mere "verity" to a trafficking with the verities, the appropriate field for the real artist. Melville had long thought that Polynesia was rich in romantic materials that, "to bring out suitably, required only that play of freedom and invention accorded only to the Romancer and poet," but only with his third book could he frankly indulge his appetite for imaginative latitude. The eventual products of such freedom and invention were both *Moby-Dick* and *Pierre*. For Melville's friend Hawthorne, there never seems to have been a choice between the narrative "received for a verity" and that accepted for its extraordinary departure from the usual course of things. He was never to produce a work that would follow Scott's definition of a novel—a narrative in which events "are accommodated to the ordinary train of human events, and the modern state of society."[6] Even *The Blithedale Romance* was not quite that.

But if the penchant for using, even distorting, historical and biographical facts for larger imaginative purposes tends to be accepted as a matter of course in the cases of the great nineteenth-century writers, it is more often resisted by a younger generation of historical fictionists. And although there have been recorded occasional murmurs of discontent at such manipulation by Ellen Glasgow, Willa Cather, even Faulkner, critics have been considerably more vocal in their disapproval of those writers who use historical materials as a baggy portmanteau for smuggling in modern issues and fashionable dilemmas.

Developing a suggestion by Lion Feuchtwanger that historical novelists are really treating contemporary matters, Floyd C. Watkins remarks: "The thinking of an author in our time may be of such value artistically and philosophically as to justify even the deliberate invention if not misrepresentation of history." He cites Warren and William Styron as writers who have such value.[7] But Walter Sullivan, using *Band of Angels* as his chief exhibit, excoriates the modern novelist who violates the past by imposing on it the philosophical or ideological errors of the present—and for Sullivan that means Existentialism, "the most damaging sort of anachronism." Sullivan doubts that teenaged Kentucky girls of the 1850s—or anybody else back then—"troubled themselves much about the problem of identity." He goes on to elaborate: "Whatever reappraisals and revisions the historians might make, the novelist is obligated by the demands of his craft to keep to the truth in its simplest form. That is, he must be faithful to the spirit of the time. His characters must share with their now dead, but once actual counterparts a common view of life and its sources, the way it should be lived, the ends it should serve."[8] One wonders if such a program is even possible —or, if a novel written to its specifications would be worth the enormous energy, the stringent and possibly misplaced discipline that would be required. Parodists, I suspect, would be the most enthusiastic applauders of Watkins' position, but only the most dedicated antiquarian could find much pleasure in writing his work according to Sullivan's prescriptions.

Most examples of this maligned subgenre are neither as radical as Watkins' remark might suggest nor as reactionary as Sullivan's. One historian believes that the whole purpose of the historical romance is, as he bluntly puts it, "to score some point about the present or to settle some score about the past."[9] Warren comes close to this position in a somewhat different tone; he says his historical fiction is meant to be "a sort of simplified and distant framed image, of an immediate and contemporary issue, a sort of interplay between that image and the contemporary world" (*Talking*, 129). One can be dedicated to an accurate reconstruction of history—if it can be known—but one cannot write as if he had no knowledge of his own time and place and all that has transpired after the historical moment he has chosen to recreate.[10] Unless he aspires to literary forgery, there is of course no reason why a writer should want to extirpate all signs of his own period.

As in any other kind of fiction, we are inevitably pulled back to another vague word—*serious*. It is finally a quality of mind that emerges in the intricate building of the artifact. We can have serious love stories, serious novels of manners, even serious "narratives of voyages." Historical novels often sound silly or shallow for the same reasons that novels generally sound silly or shallow: they simplify and make tidy—and thus offer sham versions of a reality that resists easy representation. Reductionism is the enemy of serious historical fiction. Whatever else may be said about the difference between *Gone With the Wind* and *Absalom, Absalom!*, a display of reductive solutions to human problems cannot be said to typify the Sutpen story at any stage in its telling. Finally, the issue is not even a matter of relevance—that a novelist make the past more palatable by investing it with problems and issues similar to his own time—it is simply a matter of the individual sensibility of the novelist, his informing compulsions, and his skill in rendering what Eudora Welty has called "the achieved world of appearance." Perhaps even more than Warren, Welty has invested her world of appearance with the stuff of history, legend, fairy tale, folklore, and community gossip; but fiction, as she insists, "is properly at work on the here and now, or the past made here and now; for in novels *we* have to be there."[11] If feeling and meaning of the writer's life are intensely held, they will permeate even the historical fiction.

His memories of tales told by his grandfather and other relatives and his early fondness for reading history, a preference that continued into adulthood, account, Warren says, for his particular evocations of times and places past in those of his works that most readers regard as historical. An undeniably vivid memory and a natural predilection for history, however, do not quite account for the felt texture of such works as *Band of Angels,* just as these same admirable gifts cannot account for the texture of *The Legacy of the Civil War.*

What books were read on the Kentucky frontier? How did Jefferson's nephews murder a slave? What kind of education did Oberlin College offer a young girl before the Civil War? What were the day-to-day conditions in New Orleans under Beast Butler? These and dozens of other questions require for their answers specific information, details, concrete data—all of which appear in Warren's novels and all of which contribute to the textured credibility of those reconstructed worlds. Such specificity is rarely available to mere memory. Warren may not be a researcher in some vague pejorative sense that he associates with the historical novelist. His attraction to and skill in scholarly research, however, are a matter of record: in his essays on *The Rime of the Ancient Mariner*, Melville's poetry, and Dreiser's career (the use of manuscripts, historical background, biographies); *The Legacy of the Civil War* (the use of official records and Civil War histories); *Segregation* and *Who Speaks for the Negro?* (the use of taperecorded interviews, sociological data).[12] The production of an impressive anthology required of Warren, no less than it did of Cleanth Brooks and R. W. B. Lewis, a systematic reading and rereading of thousands of pages of both primary and secondary sources in American literature.[13] Given this record of acknowledged research in his nonfiction writing, it is naive to think that the unacknowledged kind in his fiction has been any less conscientious and thorough.

The nineteenth-century South draws Warren as compellingly as the South Seas drew Melville or colonial New England drew Hawthorne. His fields of energy are moral idealism and politics, both of which are designed to call forth strenuous and often melodramatic action, intellectual conflict, and philosophical speculation. By the very nature of his construct, there are more flashes of psychic disunity than integration, more questions asked than answered. And always, the events and characters are most often given shape and purpose by what Warren considers the single great convulsion in the nation's history—the Civil War. The image of that conflict portentously insinuates itself, by seemingly unrelated issues, synecdochic parallels, and emblematic squabbles, in those fictions set before 1860; and the shadow of that war hangs over his postbellum people, whose memories stretch out through the century and beyond, even to those unborn who will ultimately be forced to pick their way perilously through the rippling consequences.

Such continuities in *World Enough and Time* and *Band of Angels* suggest one of the underlying premises of most practitioners of historical fiction since Scott: that society is dynamic rather than static, that the consistently contemporary aspect of a society seen in such eighteenth-century novels as *Tom Jones* and *Humphry Clinker* reveals a sensibility conceptually unable to think of society, in one critic's words, "as the product of past experiences and traditions which are in the process of becoming something different."[14] From Scott onward, except for the purely meretricious hacks, the historical novelist only superficially dredges up a past era for its picturesque and remote effects; rather he enlivens it by reconceiving it as an era humanly like his own, a period beset by stresses, crises, and competing modes of belief and action, circumstances that compel alignment by those who may or may not be aware that some aspects of their society are flowering while others are dying. As his characters' actions depend upon shifting tensions among persons and groups, so in the depiction of those actions the novelist asserts his belief that society is perpetually in the process of casting off certain traditions, prescriptions, and hierarchies and assuming certain others. At bottom the historical novelist, by applying the biological principle of organic growth to society, affirms that the present is always a world that embodies selective shreds of a relevant past and projects some bases for a usable future.

For Warren this sense of historical continuities is rarely cramped by a necessary allegiance to verifiable fact, and in his best historical fictions imaginative latitude and fidelity to known fact mesh almost imperceptibly. What Melville called "the play of freedom and invention" is first evident in Warren's biography of John Brown; but from the crucial occurrences at Harpers Ferry to the protracted battles in the Wilderness, Warren has chosen for his reimagination of historical events those which are seldom clear-cut, usually sensational, sometimes paradoxical, and always encrusted by folklore, legend, and myth. He has shown a special fondness for delving into issues that seem overburdened and unmanageable, events that are the least susceptible of rational reconstruction; similarly, any human effort to codify, simplify, and order is always held at some ironic distance, as if the coiling human soul can finally be known only to God. With the publication of *World Enough and Time* in 1950 Warren decisively and formally entered modern literary history as a writer of historical romances.

XI. Dream and Drama
World Enough and Time

1.

The subtitle of his fourth novel, *World Enough and Time*, casts into relief Warren's attraction to the massive complexities of the past, just as his choice of narrator emphasizes the urgency with which Warren regards the past: the necessity to acknowledge its moral densities, to unravel the tangled threads of human motivation and need, to make sense of those events that may yield a usable meaning for the present. "A Romantic Novel" signals its author's decisive acceptance of historical fiction as a valid aesthetic enterprise, since the raw materials upon which the novel is based are lurid and sensational, the very stuff of romantic melodrama.[15] This grand-operatic mode featuring a pair of aspiring, self-indulgent, and doomed lovers frankly absorbs some of the ingredients of nineteenth-century female romancers: inflated bombast, sensitized temperaments, derring-do transplanted from decadent Old World settings to the civilized peripheries of a rawer America. But Warren incorporates in his adaptation of the historical romance two familiar themes that hark back to the beginning of his career. He recounts the struggle of an egoistic idealist to reshape a recalcitrant world to meet the demands of his own shapeless dream, and he places that struggle squarely within political as well as personal contexts.

If for Warren's protagonist the effort to transform an intractable world into a realm uncontaminated by the ravages of time is frustrating, his narrator's need to understand those efforts, to see them as timelessly significant, reveals the urgencies for dealing with an unheroic present. As Jeremiah Beaumont in his private dreams anticipates the Jefferson of *Brother to Dragons*, so the narrator in his public manipulation of his subject anticipates the interlocutor R.P.W. of that work.

Given the nature of his "violent and lonely land," Jeremiah Beaumont is a paltry knight, both exasperating and comic in his ambiguous campaigns to "possess the wild land." He is also touching and a little sad in his efforts to bring that divergent world of early Kentucky around to his control: "In that world the leather hunting shirt and the broadcloth coat mixed at burgoo, barbecue, market, or hustings, and a man might wear both the coonskin cap and the two-story beaver in his time. . . . The dirk (of Spanish steel or made from a hunting knife or Revolutionary sword) and the Bible might lie side by side on the table, or Plato and the dueling pistols on the mantel shelf" (WET, 6–7). Ambitious, proud, snobbish, Beaumont would forget the leather hunting shirt and wear the broadcloth coat; but, more than that, he expects to find meaning in a gentleman's life. His career, however stumbling and misdirected, is primarily a search for inner wholeness that the public world will ratify. Characteristically, Warren uses the cultural fact to suggest a psychological condition. Indeed, Beaumont's story, both the self-chronicled parts and those summarized by the narrator, turns on the paradoxical relationships of *dream* and *drama*, the private plans and the public acts.

In order to live "as a human being against the ruck of the world," Beaumont prepares his ambiguous drama, which, though it "seemed both to affirm and to deny life," is to be the culmination of a long dream. Private as it is, however, the dream is as ambiguous as the drama that would complete it. The clues come early in the narrative. The first image that young Beaumont summons up in his dream derives from the picture of a young female martyr at the burning stake. His fancies give him three roles: rescuer, cosufferer, and persecutor. The shifting ambiguity of roles in his dream prefigures the relationship with Rachel, when he attempts to translate the dream into drama. Later, even the impulse to kill Colonel Fort, aside from its hesitations and vacillations, is characteristically split. In Frankfort, Beaumont insists that he has no desire for secrecy; he wants the duel to be known to the world. Yet he waits until Fort is alone to propose the duel because he wants "no interruption by the chance passer." He rejects one opportunity to punish Fort because he decides he will horsewhip the older man in the public streets "before the eyes of the town." He even plans to "lie in wait" and then "before all eyes" surprise Fort with the whip. What should be the private achievement of a long-nourished dream is really a bid to have that achievement publicly applauded. If Beaumont suspects the inadequacy of the self-contained, self-generating private gesture, then third parties will confirm its adequacy; but while the public enactment of the dream confirms the world's image of himself, it seriously damages his very right to act for personal reasons. By submitting the autonomous "pure act" to the applause of Frankfort, he exposes its ethical frailty.

In the long interim between the resolution and the act, Beaumont revives the Jordan farm and makes good crops. He becomes enamored of "the good opinions of honest and laborious men." He begins socializing at the tavern, sharing the jokes and gossip; he even joins his neighbors on a hunt into the western country. But political controversy embroils him, and he is accused of marrying Rachel Jordan for her farm. Beaumont records his confusion: "If a man lives by what he feels to be the truth in him, and discovers in a single instant that the tongue of the world says differently of him, there comes the fear and shame that what he had held to be the truth in him may not be the truth after all and there may be no truth for him but the terrible truth now given him by the tongue of the world. And if a man is robbed of his truth, and of a sudden, how can he know what he is?" (WET, 179). The syntactical convolution of his statement reflects his philosophical confusion. The *truth in him*, turning back upon itself, so countered by the *tongue of the world*, leaches away. Open charges of self-interest revive Beaumont's dream to defend Rachel—and himself— "against all the world." But, after reasoning that he "could not strangle the whole world," he retreats to the controlled flawlessness of his former dream. The solution to his dilemma comes more and more to depend upon Fort's death, which he foresees as "the perfect act, outside the world, pure and untarnished."

That act, however, cannot be so. The enactment of such a drama must be performed in the world's terms even as it is justifying his own private needs. Moreover, by now the dream itself is tarnished. Although Rachel would like to forget the pledge that Beaumont once forced her to demand of him ("Kill Fort!"), Beaumont must use it to soothe his private anguish. Caught up in these opposites, which both conflict and merge, Beaumont must act on the dream tarnished or not. Only sporadically aware of what he is doing, he accepts the ambiguous interplay of dream and drama and tries to fuse motive and act in a consistent script which he will both act out and direct. Henceforth, the chief image for Beaumont and Rachel becomes "that high and secret stage."

But while dream and drama may be fused, Beaumont's consciousness remains split. Imagining himself master of the doubleness, Beaumont thinks of himself living untroubled in both worlds, "speaking different languages, abiding by different laws, worshipping different gods, walking different streets, admiring different landscapes." When the two worlds blur, as they inevitably must, Beaumont finds himself playing simultaneously the outraged victimized hero and the witty confident villain. His on-again off-again niceties of distinction and his peculiar mixture of sincerity and practicality at times buoy him and at others betray him. Just before his trial, in the span of one page, Beaumont displays the wide range of these particular resources:

> Jeremiah Beaumont . . . was trapped in that anguish, was snarled in the thousand clinging threads of lies, was drowning in lies, and nobody could stretch out a hand to him, nobody would write him a letter. . . .
> But before the despair could overwhelm him again, the rage came. By God, he was what he was, and he was not ashamed. . . . He had tried to do all in the blazing sun of honor.
> By God, he had tried, but they had not let him. The world had not let him. It was the world's fault that he had come by night with a mask on his face. For that was the way of the world. . . .
> No, worse, by God, they came and laid a hand on your shoulder, they looked you in your face and called you a man of honor and took your word. . . . For that was the world's last trick, to torture and snare you by honor, till you almost burst out with truth. . . .
> By God, he hated them all. . . . He spat upon them, for they knew nothing.
> They did not know that the price of truth was lies.
> He was suddenly calm in that thought. He was himself, and could not be otherwise. He would regret no more, and yearn no more.
>   (WET, 320)

In all his moods, favorite words (*lies, truth, sun of honor, the world, man of honor*) whirl and tumble indiscriminately to support whatever image of the moment he happens to hold of himself. "He was himself" is an ironic phrase whenever it appears in the narrative, since Beaumont is at all stages of his developing self at once too sure and too indecisive.[16] In his long rhetoric of anguish, both his visions and his concrete acts are far removed from any real reconciliation. Just as his private world is rocked by internecine conflict, so is his public world variously wooed, appeased, threatened, and warred against. Faced with such a balky peace in each world, any entente is doomed to failure.[17]

Beaumont's first significant awareness of the gulf that separates him from the great world comes as he lies sunning on a spit in the river at Runnymede. In a near-drowse he hears music; a keelboat with a fiddler poles into view; Beaumont leaps up, "forgetful of nakedness," instinctively plunges into the water after it, but stops "kneedeep in the stream" watching the disappearing boat. This impulse to cast off one self and take up another recurs after he hears a Great Awakener, Corinthian McClardy. A "wildness of joy" comes upon him, and he runs "howling into the woods," stumbling, tearing clothes, and striking against trees. Finding himself face to face with "another creature," he has his first sexual experience. When it is over, he sees a smelly, half-breed "snaggle-toothed hag," and in horror flees toward the sound of running water. He was, as the narrator puts it, "still Jeremiah Beaumont, coming back to the three-room cabin, to the work in the field and in the schoolhouse, and to the world as it was, with which, if he was to live, he would have to make terms." The unfulfilled self has been completed neither in romantic gestures of abandonment nor in spiritual enthusiasm.

With the failure of such gestures toward a "real" self, Beaumont must seek that self in other ways. He can never be what William James called "the healthy minded"—the once-born man who "looks on all things and sees that they are good."[18] No traditional ritual of rebirth can release in Beaumont "the full flood of ecstatic liberation," and whenever that evanescent impulse approaches, it takes the form of pantheistic dissolution. Even as a McClardy convert, Beaumont's life is neither doctrinal nor moral. What really ushers in his new life is a series of natural phenomena: the coming of a great frost, the sun that makes the landscape glitter, and freezing snow that makes the trees groan and crack "like canon." Natural manifestation replaces the traditional patterns of the healed soul (prayer, Bible study, and the imitation of pious men). When Beaumont tastes an icicle which he breaks from a tree, he describes the mystical feelings that sweep over him: [M]y own strength seemed to pass away through my fingers into the very tree. I seemed to become the tree, and knew how it was to be rooted in the deep dark of earth and bear with my boughs the weight of glittering ice like joy. Then my substance seemed to pass beyond the trees and into all the land around that spread in the sunlight, and into the sunlight itself" (WET, 31–32). This kind of transcendence-through-dissolution emphasizes rather than conceals the separated soul. Beaumont grows further apart from the world that he alternately courts and spurns, partly because his private self is even more chaotically varied than that world. He cannot make terms with it until he first makes terms with his split self.

Paradoxically, in the world of human volition he can never succeed in merging idea and act; the dream and the drama remain separate, and his identity remains fragmented. All the gratifying moments are fleeting, and they invariably occur without plan or will. With these images of dissolution, transcendence, and pantheism, Warren prepares his protagonist for his final experience: existence in a world entirely removed from his will, a world that itself is conceived in terms of arrested movement and slow decay. This is the world of La Grand' Bosse.

A young T. S. Eliot wrote that romanticism "stands for *excess*" and splits into two streams: "escape from the world of fact, and devotion to brute fact."[19] As a study in the pathology of romanticism, *World Enough and Time* presents us with a protagonist as the man of excess taking both directions, first as a finicky Platonist, finally as a soporific Hobbesian. Whatever the literary debt, the excess of emotion recorded in Beaumont's love affair with Rachel, both before and after marriage, is psychologically apt, since such excess is possible for lovers who are also idlers with seemingly world enough and time for creating their special place to pursue the pleasures of art, philosophy, and passion.[20] The world they create, however, is not well lost for love. The larger world keeps impinging on their melancholy affair; the selfishness of their moral irresponsibility spills over into the actual political world of cross purposes, adding to the perplexity of a society already rife with competing sources of power. To the amorality of such a world the lovers contribute their own, at least for a time. They leave the ruined garden and the rotting plantation house, their cultivated space for permitting the free play of self-indulgent feeling, ending an episode that forms a prelude to the drama that must be enacted before the world as a kind of test of their joint emotional extravagance—just as the swamp of La Grand' Bosse will constitute a postlude to that drama. Both episodes are inversions, even parodies, of the great world from which they at first flee, then join fitfully, only to flee it again with finality.

Warren's concluding segment departs so substantially from its source that some readers, familiar with *The Confession of Jereboam O. Beauchamp*, have assumed that Beaumont's shabby last days in La Grand' Bosse's swampy empire are nothing more than another example of his author's penchant for violence and naturalistic melodrama. Unlike the originals, Beauchamp and Ann Cook, who, despite their botched plans for a romantic suicide pact, die more or less expectedly in the real Frankfort of 1826, Beaumont and Rachel cheat the punishment of the law by a last-minute rescue and are shuffled off to a new world, figuratively underground and literally ruled by a bestial dictator. Although there is a certain quaint dignity in the final days of Beauchamp, there is unrelieved degradation in those of Warren's protagonist. The land and the denizens under Ole Big Hump's rule are malarial, filthy, flea-ridden, fungoid, rotting. Rachel goes mad and stabs herself to death; Beaumont becomes a syphilitic, killing and ultimately being killed.

What could have been a narrative anticlimax is in fact the most vigorously conceived episode in the novel. For this new stage in Beaumont's degeneration, the writing has a sustained excitement and movement unequalled in the earlier portions. But the coda is neither a mere indulgence in Calvinistic naturalism nor a gratuitous appendage to the narrative. Internally, Beaumont's impulses logically culminate in Ole Big Hump's empire—the dreams of finding fulfillment "in the western lands" in Chapter 5 come bitterly true in Chapter 12. Conceptually, Warren plays out Beaumont's hand to the end to illustrate larger cultural truths: the entire final espisode ironically conflates diverse but related American themes that in their mingling of idealistic and commercial motives guided countless careers of the famous and infamous alike—West as the Land of Beginning Again, America as the New Garden, Self-Reliance, Individualism. The narrator can even say that with the coming of the steamboat, La Grand' Bosse, trader-thief of the keelboat era, came to be "simply the victim of technological unemployment."

Beaumont's sojourn among the swamp rats is also a culmination of his impulses toward pantheistic transcendence. Psychologically the journey which ends in a scrofulous Eden begins when the young lawyer crouches in the lilac thicket, outside Fort's house, lying in wait to kill his former mentor. At the time he fancies himself "growing into the ground," "setting root" like the plants, becoming "one of them groping deeper and deeper into the cold, damp earth with fingers of root and tentacles like hair." Remembering this scene as he lies in his pitlike cell in Frankfort, Beaumont himself names it as a prefiguring of his imprisonment underground, where the "cool, inward smell of earth's bowels" suggests his own, "pregnant with a secret life." From the dungeon Beaumont and Rachel are spirited away onto a keelboat in a "cubby with a smell like a latrine." The same feeling of having his identity seep away recurs instinctively, and Beaumont imagines his body absorbed in the "dark inwardness" of the river, "flowing on with the inner current, on and on." The moment triggers his first "intimation," when the keelboat and the fiddle urged him into the "deliberation of the river." The times before seem "foreshortened and fused" as if he had indeed fulfilled his initial impulse to surrender to a new selfless self, to be sucked away into the darkness. Moving to that final moment has for Beaumont been a descending rather than an ascending series of stages: from the healthy flow of the river in sunlight and in youth, to the icy glitter of egocentric absorption, to the lilac thicket waiting to murder, to the underground cell where night and day are the same murky gray, and, finally, to a keelboat cubby smelling of urine and drifting with the black current of the river.

And the descent is not quite over. For all his idealism, a scruffy world in stasis seems an inevitable destination for Beaumont. The torpid garden that Warren prepares for his couple is a rank world sustained by mere appetite, a backwash simultaneously primitive and decadent. This world is a kind of overstated corrolary to the Kentucky society that has formed Beaumont, a culture simultaneously frontierlike and genteel, marked alike by eye-gouging free-for-alls and the rigid proprieties of the *code duello*. Dilapidated huts, bear robes, deerskins, and dismembered keelboats take their place among silver and china, elegant furniture, and unread books hoarded and rotting in the fetid climate. Although this real place, with its distorted versions of the society the lovers leave behind, is an appropriate projection of Beaumont's psychic confusion, the total effect of this segment is vivid, sharply configured, even realistic. Indeed, its clearly delineated rendering makes the larger segments—Beaumont's activities in Kentucky politics and his trial and incarceration—seem hallucinatory by contrast.

Warren depicts the public world of frontier Kentucky as a highly articulate, complex civilization to whose sophisticated intricacies the heroic posturing of Beaumont falls victim. The conniving of politicians, the ideological battles between Old Court and New Court, the plots, counterplots, and intrigues, the sense of inchoate power follow the realistic lines of regional American history less than they do those of an early Renaissance court, with its murky and protean alliances. The great world that Frankfort represents is a shifting field of unloosed energies which sometimes match Beaumont's aspirations and needs and just as often blunt and challenge them, but he is never sure of their source, their channels of power, or their stability. That confusion may mask the give-and-take exigencies of coonskin politics or signal the appalling logic of a master plot, but he cannot know whether either is the reality.

Because it is a world which Beaumont never properly understands— he is baffled, tricked, hooked at every turn, especially at those times when he suddenly feels that all is clear at last—this central portion of *World Enough and Time* is rendered as nightmare. By contrast, both the prelude and the postlude, despite the heavy romantic trappings of the first and the naturalistic sensationalism of the second, have a relatively rational movement because the meaning of both experiences is clear to Beaumont. He *wills* himself into the role of *cavalier servente* at the Jordan house, and he *accepts* the torpid horror of swamp life in western Kentucky; in each he can make sense of his experience because it fully constitutes a self-generating and circumscribed world. Moreover, the prelude and postlude are mutually informing. Beaumont's courting visits to the "crepuscular world" of the Jordan farm and its house of "dampness and shadows" culminate cruelly in the loveless drama of runaway lovers in a remote and watery world—a stunning reminder of the gap between the Garden the lovers cultivate and the Wilderness they inherit. For the ritualistic etiquette in his courtship of Rachel, there is now casual wenching with diseased hags; for the stately Colonel Fort and his gentleman's affair with Rachel, there is now an old hunchback, half-breed Frenchman feeling Rachel's breasts and dismissing them with an insult; for Beaumont's politicking and hunting and socializing with his wary neighbors, there are now hunting and drinking with "louse-bit, yellow-skinned" men of the swamp.[21]

This Hobbesian world of the postlude is also more clearly defined than the larger segments in a moral sense, since this is the scene of Beaumont's final insight into his necessary salvation. By the time he can say "the crime is I," he has already driven Rachel to her madness and death and himself to a mindless immersion in what he calls "the blank cup of nature." His obsessive beliefs he now sees as abstract and self-deceiving: the idea will not redeem the world; neither will the world redeem the idea. With a "kind of knowledge that is identity," as he puts it in his manuscript, he begins his journey back to Frankfort, certain now that his salvation lies not in pardon but in expiation, not internally or privately but symbolically and publicly. He will "shake the hangman's hand" and call him brother.

And though he says that all he can now have is knowledge, it is merely tentative—there "must be a way," he hopes, to reconcile the private and public worlds, the dream of self and the drama of self-fulfillment. Even his provisional knowledge is cause enough for him to act, but what might have been a retrieved glory—shaking the hangman's hand—is itself thwarted by a hired killer, and so Beaumont's impulse toward a unified self is frustrated even in death. There is symbolic appropriateness in that end: his head severed from his body, and the narrative of his agonized search capped not by an assertion but by a question: "Was all for naught?"

2.

The single most important technical device in *World Enough and Time* is the author's choice of point of view. Beaumont is there, with all his psychic tensions leaking through his florid rhetoric; and he is aware of some of these tensions as he tells his story. But the enveloping vision is aggressively twentieth century, with Beaumont's story mediated by an anonymous historian. Warren once stated that one of his "objective" decisions in beginning a novel is the matter of "who is going to tell the story." About this "prime question" he says: "You have to make a judgment. You find one character is more insistent, he's more sensitive and more pointed than the others."[22] The case of *All the King's Men* abundantly demonstrates how such a technical decision affects substance as well as craft. The dispersion of Jack Burden's function into hectoring choruses of surgeons and scientists in the dramatic version accounts largely for its failure either as literature to be read or as play to be witnessed.

About *World Enough and Time*, Warren has said that the interplay between the "modern man writing the book" and the "set historical piece," the Beaumont story, offered him "the reality, the interest of the novel" (*Talking*, 118).[23] That is, the dialectical exchanges, the statements and counterstatements, the assertions and challenges form the heart of the novel. Its life consists neither in the romantic posturings of a deluded young idealist in the early nineteenth century nor in the skeptical, inquiring intelligence of a twentieth-century man of reason, but rather in the engagement between these two sensibilities.[24] The personality of Beaumont, primarily as he reveals it in his own journal, is rich, quirky, sensitive, and certainly "more pointed" than that of any of the supporting characters. He fairly cries out to tell his own story. But in a sense his point of view is almost too rich, too obsessively compelling; and Warren's method of inventing another first-person voice to supplement his protagonist's allows a simultaneous evaluation by another temperament, alternately suspicious and sympathetic, closer to the sensibilities of the reader.[25]

Warren's method of "correcting" his own protagonist's statements is not all to Beaumont's discredit or diminution. The historian-narrator's skillful interlineations paradoxically give Beaumont more substance than he would have without them. What amounts to a double first-person point of view results in more than a proportionate doubling of perspective. Part of the tonal complexity of this novel lies in Warren's refusal to slice away the narrative in layers now admiring, now ironic. Beaumont himself is not wholly self-admiring, even before his debasement in the later chapters; and his occasional ability to view himself with detachment and even irony is one of the reasons Warren permits authorial admiration as well as irony when the narrator submits Beaumont to his commentary. Author and narrator, in this respect, reflect some of the protagonist's contradictory moods and shifting images of himself, which constitute an important aspect in the shape of the novel. The structure is prestressed, as it were, to absorb the tensions of the theme.

Many readers react to *World Enough and Time* as if Warren had been at least betrayed by his penchant for philosophical speculation when he grafted it onto the factual melodrama of the Kentucky Tragedy. The speculations of the "I" that gloss the Beaumont narrative are so frequent that they can hardly be called intrusions; in fact the *kind* of narrator who is in charge of Beaumont's story is central to the novel. The technique constantly threatens to topple the substance of the novel, and certainly the reiterations and longeurs as well as the fatigued and fatiguing introspection help to make *World Enough and Time* the most rococo of Warren's works. But without the narrator who contributes so materially to this feeling, Beaumont's story would be merely antiquarian. The historian lacks the superficial cynicism and arrogance of Jack Burden, and *World Enough and Time* is not his story in the same way that *All the King's Men* is Burden's: the truculent Burden gives the impression of having unwittingly exposed his own recent wound while performing his autopsy of Willie Stark. Nevertheless, because the imposition of the historian into Beaumont's story is so persistent the very texture of the novel is affected—and with the texture, meaning. Distanced in time from the protagonist, he is also subtler in mood, reasoning, tone, and judgment.[26]

He is in fact a facile insinuator. He establishes himself not as spokesman for Beaumont, but as spokesman for our own better selves: we want to believe, despite our skepticism, that the historical reconstruction of a man and his era may be relevant for us in ours. "I can show you what is left": that filtering intelligence is the temperament that conditions Beaumont's own first-person segments and supplies the degree of authority necessary for us to come to terms with this complex romantic sensibility. He is "one of us," speaking for the values most twentieth-century intellectuals have come not only to accept but also to promote: common sense and the golden rule, psychological as well as physical fact-finding, expediency as well as idealism, fair play along with a fair amount of skepticism. These values, so easily assented to, lead us inevitably to think of the excessive Beaumont as quaint and slightly anachronistic even in that day when Kentucky was a frontier. Some portions of Beaumont's story, however, the narrator allows to stand; others he modifies, disputes, or undercuts with his own more representative notion of truth.

In the opening paragraphs this skillful narrator does more than persuade us that a trip through the jungle of Beaumont's motives and deeds requires a guide; he comes near to admitting that even with his help Beaumont's career stretches into trackless territory. Nevertheless, there he is, demonstrating his experience, adjusting our angle of vision, giving us his cartographic instruments to use, and tracing the premium off-beat paths for especially exotic viewing. The confusions that we willingly leave for our guide to straighten out he identifies as "pride, passion, agony, and bemused aspiration," those human tics whose explanations cannot be exhausted by the documentary record—newspaper clippings, diaries, letters, court records. The narrator is convinced that Beaumont's story is more than a colorful chapter in regional Americana and more than a civic-affairs text on the difficulty of democracy on the frontier. Hence the narrator's sometimes intense involvement with his subject; his premise is that the statistical and the superficially factual require selectivity and judgment, weighing and evaluation. Letting the record speak for itself has its own strengths; but given the fustian quality of this protagonist, a mediating voice, like Marlow's for Lord Jim and Kurtz, is not unwelcome.

But if the bare record does not exhaust the "truth," neither does its interpretation. Warren has defined history as "the big myth we live" and poetry as "the little myth we make," and the sense of both, he insists, "should not, in the end, be contradictory." (BD, xii). Both the imaginative historian and the poet with historical sympathies can explore "the human constant." If Warren believes that ultimate authority is attached to either the historian or the poet, it is at best provisional. Jack Burden, the Student of History, goes wrong about as often, though not as radically, as Slim Sarrett, the poet and critic. The exactness with which the historian compiles his records is not to be despised, but his definitiveness is suspect. Intelligence and conscientiousness require balanced sympathy and moral vigor. Although the anonymous narrator of *World Enough and Time* shows us these humanizing virtues, they are often enough canceled out by bursts of condescension and impatience. And though we must use him as our guide, we are clearly meant to be wary of placing utter confidence in him.

"To whom was he writing . . . his story?" asks the narrator, who confidently answers: "The answer is easy. He was writing to us." Despite the authority in the very syntax of his rhetoric, an authority that carries over into his own bemused tone, the issue is not really as clear as such assertiveness suggests. Although the "answer" may be "easy," the process by which the narrator carries us to such an answer is riddled by ambiguity and ambivalence. As "one of us," the historian tempts us into that unarticulated position of generational superiority from which most moderns instinctively regard the past, only to reprimand us for doing so. "We are complacent as we look back on those dunces," he writes, but "on second thought, we may be like the dunces." To look back on Beaumont's story, "so confused and comic and pretentious and sad," is finally, through the narrator's efforts, to assess our own confused struggles to define ourselves.

The narrator's devotion ultimately is to an ethical rather than to a historiographical principle, one that reveals another aspect of the man who lives and writes by it. "Puzzling over what is left," he writes, "we are like the scientist fumbling with a tooth and thigh bone to reconstruct for a museum some great, stupid beast extinct with the ice age." Insofar as he depicts Beaumont as a great if futile figure lumbering through his precarious world, the narrator's analogy is precise, although his most common metaphors are theatrical: "By turns abstracted and acute," Beaumont urges his calculated dream into a drama that he intends to be grand and "serious as blood," but that turns out to be a farce in which he fluffs his grand effects, improvises loutishly, and flees from the stage when the spectators' hoots and giggles overcome him at last. The pathos of farce is suggested by what the narrator concludes from "what is left."

Yet the historian cannot be merely that kind of scientific reconstructor; he must speculate, sympathize, admire, understand. And this dilemma within the narrator duplicates as structural tension the internal clashes within his subject and thereby complicates what would be untangled. As Beaumont's editor, he is no less mercurial than his subject. What might have been a straightforward ordering of a chaos turns out to be only sporadically orderly. And, lest we succumb completely to the narrator's authority, we should remember that for long stretches and for certain incidents Beaumont is remarkably self-contained and straightforward, and it is our guide who introduces the chaos—as if he believes that Beaumont can neither think nor act *except* under the intensities of ambiguity.

The narrator, then, stands between us and Beaumont, and we must always be aware of his perspective because this is the only way we can get to Beaumont. And to be aware of this is to be wary of the narrator. Highly charged, even misplaced valuations of Beaumont are inevitable, given the character and personality of such a protagonist; and some kind of "interpreted" Beaumont must of course emerge out of the ruck of his own words and the welter of the supplementary evidence. Warren's intervening perspective suggests the elusiveness of "truth" in any of our accounts of the past. In the process of clarifying the tangled issues in Beaumont's story, the narrator of *World Enough and Time* succeeds mostly in clarifying the fact that the issues are indeed tangled. He owes allegiance to his profession, which demands disinterested investigation, but he must also be true to his own humanity, which leads him by turns into subjective sympathy with and antagonism toward his subject. Thus *his* tensions between personal involvement and professional discipline parallel the tensions in Beaumont—between the private dream and public drama, the idea and the fact, the word and the flesh.

Like the anthropologist with his "tooth and thigh bone," the historian's attempt to reconstruct his subject is perhaps best demonstrated by the many excerpts, most of them from Beaumont's journal, that form the substance of the tale. To these are added impressive selections from more objective materials, such as court records. Lacing the entire narrative are the rubrics that the careful historian uses to stamp the sources of the reported acts, motives, and feelings, and in the more bizarre or perplexing segments these attributions serve as a kind of ethical *sic*. This is especially true in the first half of the novel, in which the historian, still establishing his authority, relies heavily on such formulas as *according to his report, we do not know why, we cannot be sure, in any case we know, we know this much, we have only his abbreviated account*. These are the marks of a professional who attributes information when it is known and, while admitting the many gaps in the Beaumont case, conscientiously strives for the educated, human guess.

The narrator as humanist frequently goes out of his way to avoid being strapped by twentieth-century notions of honor, propriety, and reason. Of Dr. Burnham's *Healthful Man's Vademecum*, with its unashamed mingling of prescriptions and poems, he says it is now "easy to smile" at the folksy remedies and the chaste Popean couplets which grace the book. Although they may strike us as being strange, however, they are probably no stranger than "our own verses or our own animadversions upon the meaning of life and our scientific speculations upon the relation of mind and body" will seem when a hundred years from now "some prowler" goes through our libraries. With little warning, however, his moments of playing fair with Beaumont can also become reductive: an overeager neutrality slips into sympathy, and an embarrassed sympathy shifts briskly into impatience. Noting Beaumont's public reactions to Fort's murder ("A most dire and disturbing event"), the historian appeals to sociology and literary criticism with a testy vigor that overvalues the parenthetical importance of Beaumont's remarks: "We can notice in the many instances in his narrative

where he records his own description of the event that he seems to take
relish in using terms of horror and condemnation—"dire," "distress-
ing," "heinous," "reprehensible," "damnable"—as though he would
cloak himself in the language of common report" (WET, 270). And
to the high peaks of Beaumont and Rachel's correspondence the historian reacts wearily, sarcastically. With his hindsight, he sees it as
recapitulating that degenerate form of the romance convention, the Victorian melodrama: "We can fancy them as high allegorical figures acting out their ritual. He puts his left hand on his heart and stretches
forth his right to her to importune. She lets her arms fall at her sides and
averts her face, shaking her head slowly, trapped in her own mysterious
distress. He kneels before her, and she smiles down at him with wonderful pity, but cannot speak the word he seeks. He kisses the hem of
her dress, and she covers her face with her hands, racked by grief"
(WET, 330–31).

Sometimes the historian becomes the professor of American Studies.
When Rachel shows Beaumont a copy she has made of an engraving,
the narrator admits that there is no record of what that engraving was,
but he imagines it anyway through generalization: "We know what they
were like, those pictures. But there are few in attics or old trunks or
Negro cabins now. And there are none in the museums where the
'primitives' hang to show us the tavern or the quilting party or the severe face of the Merchant from Nashville, those things which were
American, but were no more American than those things which were not
American but the things which America dreamed it was, but was not"
(WET, 203). And when Beaumont takes a certain route to Frankfort, the narrator cannot resist parodying the parochial pride of the
WPA guidebook: "Now the highways, 31W and 31E, glittering with
concrete or asphalt, slash north across the Knobs, and in no time you
can make it to Louisville (The Fall City), Bardstown ('My Old Ken-
tucky Home'), Frankfort (Historic Frankfort), or Lexington (The
Dimple of the Bluegrass)" (WET, 244).

With the rhetorical question, a device characteristic of Beaumont's
own style, the narrator is imaginatively caught up in his investigation of
the case and approximates that style perhaps oftener than he himself
would like. Many of the narrator's questions are simply paraphrased
from Beaumont's or Rachel's questions in the documents: "Did somewhere, in the unspoken depth of her mind, lurk the notion that he had
come to her for her lands?" or "But could you know? Could you know?
Was there a way to know?" Despite their repetitiveness, these para-
phrases emphasize Beaumont's self-aggrandizement, self-torture, and

self-doubts. But such rhetorical mimesis frequently slips over into the purely speculative, as when the narrator departs from his more-or-less faithful picture of Beaumont to reconstruct the thoughts of the principals, which are missing from the documents. When Rachel closes her diary with her father's death, the narrator questions her reasons: "Did she know why she closed it? Did she feel that now, having met her father at last, she now was truly bereaved and alone? That only when you are truly alone, can you begin to live? That when you truly begin to live you must construct your own world and therefore have no need for words written on paper, words that can only give the shadow of a world already lived?" (WET, 59). And when the imprisoned Beaumont says he has come to knowledge, the narrator takes issue: "He says that, but we can scarcely believe him, for if he had come truly to the knowledge, would he have sat down again the next day at his table and written down the account of all that Munn Short had said, and all that he himself had said, and the horror of his nightmare? With that knowledge what would have been the meaning of that act of recording?" (WET, 428).

But it is with just such speculations that the sketch of Beaumont becomes a full portrait. For all the filling in, of course, the ambiguity remains, and Beaumont emerges as a self-contradictory, confused, and wildly alternating character. Warren's technique is to add another layer of complexity to the figures and concerns of the past, a cushioning intelligence that disturbs rather than comforts. If the immediate function of the narrator is to point up the difficulty of knowing the *past*, it becomes finally a technical fillip for stressing an even more urgent theme in Warren's work: the difficulty of knowing the *self*. In Beaumont's story the difficulty is made apparent by having that young man's original difficulty in self-definition compounded rather than simplified by an interpreting historian.

For at no point are we allowed to forget that it is he who is showing us Beaumont. With all his brilliant editing and annotating, with all his devices allowing the principals to speak for themselves, we are always conscious that the Beaumont story comes to us only through him. It is he who decides which passages to quote, which passages can stand alone and which need further explication, when the "subjective" record needs balancing by the "objective" accounts, when the drama needs fleshing out with thumbnail biographies of the supporting players (Wilkie Barron, Sugg Lancaster, Percival Scrogg, Stella Fort, La Grand' Bosse), and when it needs a chorus or entr'acte commentary and diversion or a local-color display of his own claim to the sense of history.

The personality, technique, and shortcomings that the historian-narrator shares with his protagonist furnish us with the most important perspective on the Beaumont story. He becomes almost another character, as much *our* persona as he is Warren's, seeing and assuming what we would see and assume, hovering over his material in the stance of instructor, sometimes intruding impatiently in Beaumont's narrative. He makes yet another version of what is already a complex affair, and to attempt to understand the Beaumont story without him is like trying to understand the Sutpen story in *Absalom, Absalom!* without Quentin and Shreve.

3.

The moral anarchism of frontier Kentucky results from its temporal and spatial circumstances; the old-fashioned idealism of the Founding Fathers and the raw pragmatism of Jacksonianism are merely extremes on the scale. Ranging themselves between these extremes, most of the characters exhibit precisely what Warren sees in that history and geography—the representative diversity, complexity, and richness of human experience of any period, especially the creator's own.

Like Scott and Cooper before him, Warren in *World Enough and Time* faces the troubling dilemma of law as the foundation of civilized life. If clear-cut, abstract, and arbitrary principles are unable to respond adequately to complex actualities, how flexible should they become in order to benefit archaic or local ways of life threatened or ignored by more progressive ways? Can justice be trusted to survive the administrative disposition of law? "The rights and the law of things ain't exactly the same thing sometimes," says a character in Warren's first fiction, "Prime Leaf," and the issue is central to Willie Stark's vision of practical governance in the deep South of the 1930s as well as to the racking struggles between Old Court and New Court in Kentucky of the 1820s. All three narratives reflect their author's considerable observation of and meditation on the goals and tactics of Franklin D. Roosevelt's New Deal.[27] But the issue of abstract law and human need is context, not subject, in *World Enough and Time*. It is illustrative of a more comprehensive human problem.

In his little book on the Civil War, Warren discusses how nostalgically the modern American looks upon that conflict as the characteristic image of the "natural relation of man to place and man to man, fulfilled in worthy action." Not even the corrosive events since then can dash our hopes "that somehow in our modern world we may achieve our own new version, humanly acceptable, of identity and community"

(LCW, 92). The political complex of Kentucky in 1825 certainly offers one example of America's struggle for justice, but *World Enough and Time* is not "about" the clash between human need and legal order any more than the Cass Mastern episode in *All the King's Men* is "about" a similar problem a generation later. Both contain the problem of justice, but in both the focus is on an individual who faces, even if he cannot solve, this abstract problem while trying concretely to achieve self-definition. *Night Rider* illustrates clearly the dangers of empty allegiance to community without adequate personal identity. *Brother to Dragons* shows the results of an achieved identity without reference to community. So it is with Jeremiah Beaumont.

The choice of a narrator with his own frailties continues in actual narrative the irony only suggested by Warren's epigraph from the *Faerie Queene*. In three stanzas from the prologue to Book V, the theme of justice is announced, with appropriate gravity, in a lament over how the present times have sorely degenerated from the "antique" world, when "good was onely for it selfe desyred" and "When Justice was not for most meed outhyred, / But simple Truth did rayne, and was of all admyred." In the Beaumont story, the public world of the nineteenth century presumably engenders the "blossom of faire vertue," but the twentieth-century historian knows better and sets out to prove it. Beaumont becomes a pretentious knight with Hamletic indecisiveness, trying to stage a grand tragedy and succeeding only in starring in a farce of his own making. Beaumont's story "improved," the historian fills in the open spaces with his own interpretation. What is implied is the rather aggressive pragmatic resignations of the twentieth-century historian: our world is indeed "runne quite out of square," but it does not grow "daily wourse and wourse" since there never was a time when the world was not "amisse." From the dated view of a lapsed golden age comes the smug, albeit troubling, assurance that it was tarnished before its lapse.

We may be impatient with his tone, his manipulation of details, and his verbal mannerisms, but what the narrator sees as a modern specialist is roughly what we see as modern readers.[28] What his imperfections demonstrate is that our view, even if it were possible to see Beaumont straightaway, would likewise be distorted. The story of Beaumont remains as a record, but its meaning can ultimately be only conjecture. For this reason the narrator repeats as his final words Beaumont's own anguished question, "Was all for naught?" And the historian's dilemma is ours.

Apart from his persona as the historian-narrator, the one clear instance when Warren himself intervenes in the Beaumont story is the italicized portion that nearly concludes the novel, and it underscores with sarcasm the implicit irony of the Spenserian epigraph. For every Artegal there is his Talos; Beaumont is his own Talos as well as his own Artegal. Warren writes: *"In this fair land there is little enough justice yet, heart-justice or belly-justice, but that does not make Kentucky different from other places."* And he concludes: *"But men still long for justice."* The Beaumont search could not serve as the search for any kind of justice. The final knowledge that Beaumont does attain is that his crime has not been anything he has done, for the act and the elaborate motives are but manifestations of the real crime: "The crime is I." In Augustinian terms Beaumont affirms his share of Original Sin; his long search has been for a flattering self, and the contours of that journey preclude any real justice. Only when he identifies the real crime, and thus his self, is justice possible, and then only in the most humbling terms. He must return to shake the hangman's hand and call him brother. This is the only justice possible for Beaumont. In that instant he will achieve both identity and community.

A dream of justice, even by a wrong-headed dreamer, is not to be despised. Even to dream of justice is a tacit act of community. Beaumont is neither typical Kentucky frontiersman nor Everyman, but both his flaw and his virtue are human. Furthermore, the aspiration to extend oneself beyond his limits is partly what Warren calls elsewhere "the glory of the human effort." Although Warren ends his italicized segment with *"But men still long for justice,"* the very next words are his protagonist's: " 'I had longed for some nobility.' " The difference in emphasis is to be noted. Beaumont's *nobility* is more applicable to what he actually does, why he does it, and when he understands himself than Warren's *justice.* But in each case, the verb is finally the important word: men *long,* and in that longing lie both their glory and despair. For whatever reasons men seek to refashion the recalcitrant world, they must find it necessarily bounded by iron gates. The harshness of a world where dreams seldom come true demands rough strife to satisfy immediate pleasures; for the possible satisfaction of more permanent ones, the dreamer must submit his very dream to rough strife.

At one level, as an investigation into the truth and meaning of history, *World Enough and Time,* like *Absalom, Absalom!,* is a critique of conventional scientific historiography. The structural permissiveness of both novels allows the celebration of intuition, conjecture, and romantic self-indulgence, the very traits which Sir Walter Scott considered irresponsible in those authors who tended toward "wild excur-

sions of an unbridled fancy." Both Quentin and Shreve and the historian-narrator embellish a segment of history about which not enough is
known, and the motives in each novel are not so simple as Scott believed true in certain authors of his own day: "the simple tale of tradition had not passed through many mouths, ere some one, to indulge his
own propensity for the wonderful, or to secure by novelty the attention
of his audience, augments the meagre chronicle with his own apocryphal
inventions."[29] Neither the Sutpen nor Beaumont stories can be called
a "simple tale of tradition," of course. What we can perceive of the core
narrative in each case is complex even before the augmenter gets his
hands on it. In each, what the augmenter demonstrates is that "real"
history and hearsay are inextricably intertwined and ultimately resist the
best scientific hands that would separate them; and, since the truth of
history is difficult to know, imaginative reconstruction may come as
close to truth as we are likely to get.

But if Faulkner's example looms most immediately behind *World
Enough and Time*, so does an earlier book: *The Scarlet Letter*. Hawthorne was familiar with Governor Winthrop's and Samuel Sewall's
journals, Cotton Mather's *Magnalia Christi Americana*, as well as local
histories of Plymouth, Salem, and other Massachusetts towns. Warren
has said that *World Enough and Time* was the only work whose preparation included research, which in his case included local histories of
Kentucky. Both tales are, in part, explorations of a regional past and
what Austin Warren has called the "ancestral mind."[30] The Massachusetts Puritan claimed his settlements, as Hawthorne says, "with his
Bible and his sword"; the Kentucky frontiersman came armed with his
Plato and his dueling pistols.

Furthermore, the process by which the strands of the past are untangled, sorted out, and reknitted in "The Custom-House" functions
similarly to the sifting process in Warren's novel, just as the persona in
Hawthorne's introduction resembles the editor of Beaumont's documents. Two generations after the major events recorded in the Hester
Prynne case, Mr. Surveyor Pue, sensing something special in them, turns
scholar, gathering the known facts through an early version of an oral
history project, by interviewing ancient contemporaries who still remember the old woman from their youth. The story is committed to
"half a dozen sheets of foolscap" without being published; eighty years
after Pue's death, Mr. Surveyor Hawthorne discovers the narrative core
on which he imposes a wry and bemused "Hawthorne," who then
presents it to the public as *The Scarlet Letter*. As Hawthorne tran-
scribes, interprets, and enriches his story from the foolscap, so does

Warren create his historian, who sets about reconstructing the Beaumont case from his cache of tattered documents. In both re-created
narratives the author surrogates strive to lift the materials of the story
into meaning. Both deal with extraordinary events—an invitation to
"incredulity" as Melville might put it—the full meaning of which they
see is still shrouded in ambiguity. Pue must rely on a superstition-ridden
folk for much of the truth about their minister and the ostracized
parishioner: some say this, others something else. Warren's historian is
not so hampered: there are simply "lies and half-lies" and "truths
and half-truths."

If for Pue, a man at one with his society, the Prynne-Dimmesdale
affair contains its own self-evident truths, the "Hawthorne" who glosses
Pue is more self-consciously aware that in the very recounting of the
narrative both the discrepancies of "report" and the passing of time
can alter the general configurations and import of truth. For Warren's
harried historian, the truths are not self-evident; they overlap too much
with themselves and with lies. And what he thinks is required is
nothing less than a full-scale reproduction of "the times," a context
that might perhaps justify the motives and the acts and the truths and
the lies. The re-created Kentucky of the 1820s is not so much the
result of an antiquarian bent—though there is some of that, too—as
it is of satisfying a conviction that Beaumont's story recapitulates national, and human, patterns that should be instructive for modern man.

Although the internal historian sees that relevance in terms of the
universal search for justice, Warren makes it clear, from the external
perspective of the artifact itself, the entire book which encloses his
historian as well as Beaumont, that the primary relevance is a moral
issue transcending generational questions. However involved with one
historical moment whose salients and vectors may illuminate the meaning of the national experiment, Beaumont's search is specifically for self-
definition, not justice, and his search is conducted with a personal urgency no less intense than that of Jack Burden. His example suggests
the overwhelming complexity and difficulty of self-definition more explicitly than that of any other protagonist in Warren's works.

XII. The Slavery of Freedom in Band of Angels

One of Warren's constants in his several fictions is the massive reality of a public world with which his protagonists must deal in their veering search for self. Abstracted from the rich immediacy of narrative, the thematic burden of the first three novels is the integrity of one's humanity measured against political expediency; with *World Enough and Time*, Warren's first extensive excursion into the nineteenth century, Jeremiah Beaumont's struggle is toward inner wholeness set against a public world caught between the competing claims of law and human need. In *Band of Angels* Warren moves the relevant dichotomies away from the provincial arena of the 1820s onto what he believes to be the central stage of American history: our fratricide of the 1860s.

Like much of his work, *Band of Angels* reflects Warren's fascination with the Civil War as a cultural symbol of the nation's most intense struggle for clarification of its own being; aesthetically, that national event, with its tangled causes and decisive effects, serves as a confirming image for his philosophical penchant for dialectic. With his choice of protagonist, a well-bred planter's daughter who on the eve of the Civil War discovers that she is a mulatto, Warren for the first time merges his most durable theme, the search for personal identity, with the larger issue of national identity. A woman divided against herself conducts an agonized search for psychic unity within the resonant context of a nation divided against itself. Conceptually, *Band of Angels* is more ambitious than *World Enough and Time*, a fact that makes its aesthetic failure all the more regrettable.

1.

As a species of the *Bildungsroman*, *Band of Angels* is a companion piece to *All the King's Men*. Jack Burden, a well-born, literate, and cynical young man knocking about in his twentieth-century world, momentarily adjusts his own ironic perspectives to fit its ironies until such time when he can permanently find himself satisfactorily placed, which is to say, morally placed, in that world. Amantha Starr must accommodate herself to the duplicities and accidents of her heaved-up nineteenth-century world, presumably as any cosseted young lady of leisure might have done once that antebellum milieu was shattered. Although tonally different, these stories of Warren's principal first-person narrators are both recitals of anguish; theirs are voices of pain retelling the struggles to come to terms both with their often conflicting desires and with a harsh actuality that will not suffer too much bending for their benefit, both with the sins of the self and with those of the father, history, and time.

Except for a few demurrers, most readers agree that Jack Burden is not only an interesting character whose story is worth the telling but also that his particular rhetoric, consonant as it is with his personality, is effective. Except for even fewer demurrers, most readers agree that Amantha Starr is a tiresome character whose frail sense of discrimination puts the trivial and the momentous on a single egocentric plane and whose rhetoric sometimes reflects her shallow personality and sometimes egregiously speaks for her homiletic creator. But these two protagonists are similar, and the difference in our response to them lies partly in the linguistic fact that Burden's rhetoric is closer to us, is more immediately available, than is Amantha's. The heroine of *Band of Angels* is a whiner and a nagger, a spoiled, petulant woman who refines a talent for manipulating men, which she has cultivated at home and at school. By the time she tells her story she is rich in experiences and in her own way educated (though what she absorbs at Oberlin is a moralistic patina more than anything substantial). But the discourse shows that Warren realizes the central problem in the crafting of *Band of Angels* to be narrational, which is to say *rhetorical*. What Amantha must say is far too ambitious for her. A close examination of the curious language reveals something of Warren's efforts to resolve that narrational dilemma. Here is the way the novel begins:

> Oh, who am I? For so long that was, you might say, the cry of my heart. There were times when I would say to myself my own name—my name is Amantha Starr—over and over again, trying, somehow, to make myself come true. But then, even the name might fade away in the air, in the bigness of the world. The world is big, and you feel lost in it, as though the bigness recedes forever, in all directions, like a desert of sand, and distance flees glimmering from you in all directions. Or the world is big, and the bigness grows tall and close, like walls coming together with a great weight and you will be crushed to nothingness. Nothingness—there are two kinds,

the kind which is being only yourself, lonely as the distance with-
draws forever, and the kind when the walls of the world come together to crush you. (BA, 3)

Most of the stylistic excesses of this narrative are suggested in its
opening paragraph: the self-conscious exclamations, the inflated diction, the too-frequent dependence upon metaphor and simile to suggest
the anxiety of a somewhat ordinary sensibility.[31] Amantha's fondest
wish—shall we say her dream—is "to make myself come true." The
ontological implications of such cerebral turns are staggering. But while
the threat to credibility begins with the first paragraph, so also does
Warren's strategy for countering it. "Oh, who am I?" is not, for
example, a direct quotation, but is explicitly called "the cry of my
heart"—that is, what is felt but unexpressed is given a verbal shape
that approximates the feeling. It is one of those signs that Amantha,
unlike Jack Burden, is only partly the teller of her own tale. The double
I-narration of *World Enough and Time* has intervened, and though
Amantha's story, as well as her personality, is not complex enough to
warrant a second use of that device, something of its effect can be seen.
In a rhetoric hedged by a persistent conditional effect, the limitations
of her sensibility are compensated for by a shadowy author who intrudes
only halfway to supply an "improved" Amantha, by a secondary voice
that supplements the thin actuality of the primary Amantha. And if
"Oh, who am I?" is not a direct quotation in the conventional sense, it
is also provisional in a telling way: "you might say" is a lame metaphorical crutch ("the cry of my heart") which only accentuates Amantha's tenuous notion of self.[32]

Although such a smudging of point of view violates the dicta of the
strictest Jamesians (though it in fact conforms to James's actual practice
in *The Ambassadors*), the device accounts, I think, for the apparent
disparity between what Amantha does and the way she explains what
she does. Warren creates a more articulate narrator than the protagonist
who acts; the Amantha who experiences and the Amantha who relates
those experiences are not precisely identical.[33]

Like Marivaux's Marianne, Amantha tells her incredible story several years after its major events. At rest, the narrator of this *récit per-
sonnel* is one who is at last peaceful after nearly a lifetime of both
internal and external buffeting. The primary touchstone of emotion becomes *joy*. And though the extreme violence and shock of the incidents
glimmer just beneath the joy, the emotion is yet more affirmative than
that of Jack Burden at the conclusion of his narrative. The difference

lies partly in the fact that Amantha rests in the achievement of identity and Jack Burden stands only at the threshold of his.

John L. Stewart is surely right in stressing the archetypal quality of childhood trauma in Warren's work. Character after character reaches adulthood unprepared for the corrosiveness of living in time, resisting notions of either limitation or responsibility.[34] For Amantha this trauma is expressed in the shifting weights of meaning to be found in the words *freedom* and *slavery*. Socially, freedom means adulthood, responsibilities, acts of will; slavery means childhood safety, protection by a father, innocence. Psychologically, however, these values are reversed, and Amantha endures her long ordeal awash in the paradox. But even Amantha is fleetingly aware that these shifting terms signify something in the public world as well as in her private one, as states of being carrying cultural, political, and philosophical meanings that for too long bear little relevance to her deepest psychological needs.

Despite her proper education in the North, she is not equipped to face her dilemma intellectually. Her first thoughts, after she is seized for chattel at her father's grave, are not so much thoughts as brooding intimations: The whole affair is "an absurd mistake," which, however, can "always be rectified." And rectifying it means putting a very special kind of meaning on *freedom*, which is simply the return to her former state. It means nothing less than a fairy-tale restoration: the slave aboard the *Kentucky Queen* must come again into her rightful position as princess of Starrwood. But the act of restoration is the task of someone else: someone will save her since she is not "somebody without value, unloved." Even in her later dreams of rescue centering on Seth Parton, her manacles fall off, and she is on the verge of whirling away when her father spoils the rescue by confirming her black blood.

The novel is thick with images of flight. Early they appear as symbols of the natural order: swallows flaring in the sunset, ducks wheeling freely over the river, butterflies dancing over a blossoming tree. Later, such images suggest the escaped slave fleeing humiliation and the overburdened self escaping from its own responsibilities. One incident awakens Amantha to the elation of escape. When one of the other slaves on the boat plunges over the railing into the river, she interprets the act as a decisive act of will—he risks death to be free. She is chagrined when she hears his "oh, massa, save me!" Learning that he has only slipped, she feels "robbed of some deep confidence." It is a confidence, however, contingent upon an absolute line between freedom and slavery, which she unthinkingly accepts in their conventional definitions. The boat incident prefigures the blurring of that line in her own experience.

Once the property of Hamish Bond, Amantha begins storing away all her possibilities of flight. "I would observe everything. I would learn the city. I would be ready when the time came." Learning that a particular smile can soften Bond's face, she perfects this tactic as "oil on the lock" for some future time when the manacles will in reality drop off. She envisions a time when she will be confidently free, churning upriver on a great white steamboat. When the time does come, however, and Bond freely gives her the papers and money for her freedom in Cincinnati, she confronts anew the ambiguity of slavery and freedom. The terms become almost meaningless in their confusing reversal, and she rushes back down the gangplank to Bond, a gesture that says in effect, "oh, massa, save me!" For the first time she senses, though she cannot or dare not articulate them, the psychological dimensions of slavery, the ambivalent satisfaction in comfort, secure with a master who is more like her father than a new lover. If Hamish Bond does not quite make her the "Little Miss Sugar-and-Spice" that Aaron Pendleton Starr did earlier, he is just as careful to protect her against the world and is extraordinarily solicitous of her ladylike desires.

Amantha's emotions are further complicated by the attentions of two other men: Charles de Marigny Prieur-Denis, a kind of Creole courtier, and Rau-Ru, Bond's personal man hovering ambiguously in the background. The image of herself when she is with Charles is that of a white woman even more elegant than she had been before she was sold. When she is with Rau-Ru, the image is reversed, and she senses herself in his terms, as the slave who has been raised to a special status only by the grace of the master. With Charles she can practice French and learn the aesthetics of repartee. More, she can act out a surrogate freedom by horseback riding and, safely contained, enjoy "the surge and power, and the control of that power in the sway of the body and the light movement of fingers." Rau-Ru, both in his presence and his overt attitude, erodes this figure. Although his manner is not insulting, his nominal respect is tempered by an unspoken assumption that they are equals and that their equality is relative to Bond's pleasure. Both Amantha and Rau-Ru finally come to hate Bond not because he is a cruel master but because he is an indulgent one whose liberality further blurs the meaning of slavery and freedom. Framing precise definitions of these terms, which would thereby define her self, is Amantha's lifelong ambition and the source of her frustration.[35]

Structurally, *Band of Angels* reinforces the thematic paradox of slav-

ery and freedom. The novel begins and ends with the literal image of
a grave and the rich metaphorical values associated with life and death
as spiritual facts. Amatha Starr's mother, the slave Renie, lies buried
in "a grassy place" lined with cedars and willows—a spot that Amantha
sometimes confuses with an imaginative "grassy place, a place with
sun." How can two such places merge, she asks herself, "when the
place in my dream is a place of beginnings and the place in my true
recollection has a grave, the mark of endings? When the dream is a
place of freedom, the real place a place of immobility and constriction?"
This symbolic merging of a scene of freedom and a scene of constriction is rhetorically anticipated in the first paragraph, in which Amantha's sense of her unstable identity is rendered through a diction of
both dissolution (*fade away, recedes*) and constriction (*walls, weight*).
A lifetime later Amantha's regeneration occurs in a Kansas cemetery,
barely affected by the wide expanse of sky and land, above the con-
stricted rectangle of a grave marked "*Old man, colored, no name.*"

2.

Eventually, as her expectations of a speedy solution wither,
Amantha falls into the habit of thinking herself doomed. Amantha the
Victim resigns herself to the next easiest pattern of thought—expect-
ing that her self-definition will be completed in the simple thrust of
history. She thinks of herself as "an expression of History"; "you are,"
she says, "only what History does to you." Some of her fondest and
most desperate desires and plans she glumly compares to the "jerks and
spin of a June bug on a thread." Identifying oneself with history may
be an act of hubris (Jack Burden occasionally does it), but succumbing
to such a notion contributes merely to a mood of lethargy, a secular
form of acedia.

In time, Amantha tries to immerse herself in her milieu. By becoming a teacher to Negro children, for instance, she complements Tobias
Sears's command of a Negro regiment. But the gesture, made in the
spirit of a grim-faced social worker, shows traces of weary profes-
sionalism as she learns what she calls "the trick of sinking into . . . the
human commitment," and although she occasionally finds "promise
of happiness" in her work, it serves mostly as a temporary balm for
her own bruised ego. At times Amantha senses the futility of her recurring impulses toward "the human commitment." "I would flee into the
commonness of life, the life of people one saw on the street," she
says, "into the common meaninglessness, or meaningfulness, it did
not matter which so long as it was different from whatever had been."
And for all her efforts to sink into "averageness" or "dullness," her

fondest moments are those she can fantasize, the romantic and extraordinary moments in her dream when Tobias will again "step down from the golden mist, high-faced and smiling from his victorious cloud" and save her.

Such temporary accommodations with a world she still regards as indifferent and even hostile are punctuated by a restlessness that marks her moment of history. Manifest Destiny serves as a cultural endorsement of a personal psychological state. Since the East (Tobias' home) and the South (her own) have had their moments of promise and ascendancy, as history points West, Amantha sees herself being quietly absorbed in that great movement. If for many of her years flight has been the rhetorical burden of her speech and style, it now can be literalized. But, as is usually the case in Warren's works, the physical flight west occurs at a crucial stage in a character's search for inner wholeness. For Amantha, like Jack Burden and Jeremiah Beaumont, it signifies flight from self and thus militates against the urgent need for self-definition by postponements and surrogate tactics. Amantha's great removals—St. Louis, Sill's Crossing, Blair City, Kiowa City, Halesburg ("failing westward, you might say")—for more than twenty years establish a habit of dispersion and dispossession unconducive to self-examination. What she finally learns is that no place, no person, and no moment in history can release her from the ambiguity of the self; learning to accept that ambiguity means accepting her father and his guilt and Tobias and his idealism in the same terms: in their humanness. Amantha makes a ritualistic peace with Rau-Ru through the nameless old beggar in Halesburg; and Tobias, no longer the liberator, achieves his own definition ("brother to a coon") by participating in the restoration of Old Slop, the Negro garbage man. Both Amantha and Tobias come to involve themselves in that "commonality of weakness and rejection" from which they have fled for years.

In terms of temporal sequence, Amantha Starr's progress to self-knowledge is Warren's most protracted. Although the course of Jack Burden's full regeneration requires nearly a decade, its focus is limited to about four years; for Jeremiah Beaumont, that focus is hardly more than two. That it takes Amantha a lifetime to be redeemed in "joy" accounts in part for the static movement we sense in her narrative, as if the physical restlessness and geographical displacement that structure her career are almost irrelevant to her spiritual growth. The halting course of her regeneration is sometimes attributed to her passivity of character: if she is convinced that she is only what history does to her, history in its many guises can victimize her willy-nilly, without order or purpose she need bother to divine. But in fact her passivity is of a very special kind. She not only retains the childish self-image of "poor little Manty"; she wills it and acts on it because it is to her advantage that she do so. In her "slavery" she enjoys a latitude of freedom not merely to indulge herself but to enslave others psychologically for her own gratification. With varying success she tries to place in bondage Hamish Bond, Seth Parton, Rau-Ru, and Tobias Sears, acts that undercut considerably her fondest creed, that history, embodied in these and other masculine figures, is tyrannical and abstract. Her regeneration is so protracted because she is *not* strictly passive; she wills herself into human situations in such a way that self-knowledge is almost impossible for her to attain. Although she may submit to an abstract determinism she thinks the men in her life represent, she finds that she can subtly write some of the rules of the game they expect her to play.[36]

Amantha's observation that Bond has "kindness like a disease" has its echo later when she comments that Tobias has "nobility like a disease." The phrases reveal a consciousness already alert to the possibilities that all virtues have their built-in weaknesses which may be exploited. With that consciousness, "poor little Manty" is no longer a *cri-de-coeur*; it is an active weapon to use against even well-meaning rescuers. "If once you know what secret disease of virtue a person has in him," she boasts, "then you have more power over him than if you had spied his most concealed and disgraceful vice."[37] In her day-to-day, year-to-year struggle Amantha belies her own easy saw, "you are only what History does to you."

Amantha's fashioning of her own agony of will into an instrument of survival can be seen in several ways. There is her response to the world, more public than private, whose dominant note is a grim flirtatiousness. And there is her response to her own divided self, which carries unpleasant overtones of guilt and a masochistic need for punishment. Neither, of course, exists wholly in isolation from the other, for the truth is that the world *is* a slippery place and her position in it does shift uncomfortably. That her entire life is spent in dislocating and varying environments is suggested by the way in which people from her past reappear regularly, and often ominously, with different names and titles, identities that take their coloration from the most chaotic flux of any American moment. Amantha's father is not what he seems; he has whored and gambled away his estate, preserving only a surface image of Devoted Father and Benevolent Slave Owner. Seth Parton, whose piety and single-minded devotion to Truth doom his relationship with Amantha, finally betrays her by a falling away from his own code (by not telling Tobias of her "defilement of blood" as he had promised and by a liaison with Miss Idell). The fact that Bond's name is Alex Hinks bruises Amantha's sensibilities as much as his profession of African slave-trading. Miss Idell, who hovers over Amantha's quest for identity like an evil genius, is personal daemon in her several guises: Mrs. Herman Muller, when she is Starr's mistress in Cincinnati, and Mrs. Morgan Morton, wife of one of General Butler's colonels in the federal occupation of New Orleans. Rau-Ru, Bond's *k'la*, becomes self-righteous Lieutenant Oliver Cromwell Jones, a hero in a skirmish with Bedford Forrest's rebels, and is reincarnated (for Amantha, at least) as the old Negro beggar in Kansas many years later.

Given such a world, it is no surprise that Amantha has difficulty in knowing who *she* is. From the first, she lays excessive stress on her name. For her the name is character, the key to her place in the world. At her father's grave she must "state and affirm" that she goes "by the name of" Amantha Starr, but her protests that she "is" Amantha Starr are absorbed in the official voice of the sheriff, who affirms that she is "the issue of the body of one Renie, who was a chattel of Aaron Pendleton Starr, deceased." Legally, her identity is firmly established. Psychologically, the shock of the experience is too great to permit anything less than denial. Later the voice of Hamish Bond calling her "Manty" reawakens her sense of an earlier self and helps momentarily to ease the discomfort over her legal status.

Like Amantha, Bond also places unusual importance on both his name and the fact that she does not know who he really is. Following her compulsion, she insists upon knowing his, but knowing Bond's story helps little in her own self-definition. She continues to force responses from others to fit whatever version of herself she entertains at the moment. Sudden gushes of tenderness make her feel maternal, and sudden moments of resentment sharpen her sense of being "the favorite slave," at which time she preens herself competitively with Dollie and compares her own light skin favorably against Rau-Ru's blackness. If it is the lady of quality she wants acknowledged, she emphasizes her name and her former status; if it is Amantha the Victim, she prostrates herself physically, a submission both sexual and psychological.

When she asks to see and touch Rau-Ru's scars, she accepts his slap across the mouth because through physical contact with blackness she hopes to become reconciled to her Negro blood. And when one of her Negro students presses her hand into Amantha's to show how clean it is, Amantha admits her "nausea," her "sense of defilement." As she cries out, "Don't!—don't touch me!" she is startled by the child's sudden tears; but the spell is broken, and Amantha embraces the child, repeating words of endearment and pressing "desperate kisses" against the skin and "the coarse hair." Not until the ritualistic restoration scene years later, in which Amantha participates in the scrubbing of Old Slop, can she finally accept her own ambiguity of self.

The flight from self through most of her adult life means an imperfect acceptance of any black and any male, but the crucial test is her relationship with Rau-Ru, one that ends in her collaboration against him. With that repudiation she is forced to pick up remaining burdens. Continuing her efforts to adjust to the white world, she suffers the disillusion of Tobias and his infidelities. She must share the guilt in the death of Bond—especially Bond, who, as his name suggests, has been the one man who has tried to make the ambiguity of her blood more bearable. Although literally and symbolically he has been an agent of her bondage, he has also been a uniting agent, her link to both worlds, and he has acted as surety for her future freedom. Finally she must bear the heaviest burden of all: the betrayal of Rau-Ru, representative of the blood she has tried so strenuously to deny. Her torment over the beggar whom she insists upon calling Rau-Ru is not eased at his death or with the knowledge that his funeral has been paid for chiefly through her anonymous gifts. That freeing comes even later, when sitting in the little Kansas cemetery she has a vision of all the people in her past, black and white, lifting up their hands, beseeching.

Part of Amantha's difficulty, common to other Warren protagonists, is that she sees completion of self possible only through other people. She is a long time in learning that the "nothingness" of her being which she so deplores cannot be replaced by the strengths of others, whose identities are themselves sheathed in masks, illusory names, disguises, and facsimile selves. It is no wonder that Amantha, loosed upon a world that is only occasionally what it seems, learns how to use her confusion for survival in that world by the rigorous adoption of "pseudo-identities."[38] But survival is not enough. When she decides that she has not been wholly used by the world, but that she has also used it, she understands that nightmares are a part of living even in the "sweet commonness of life," then some reconciliation is possible.

3.

The transferral of roles—the pattern of the slave enslaving others—is Amantha's for most of her life. That psychological task fits a social fact: As an overt slave she is compelled to enslave covertly. Her experience with her "masters" is in small what the history of the slaveowning South is in large. But the use of her condition, no matter how immediately successful as maneuver, can bring no peace, much less "the perfect joy" promised her by Seth Parton at Oberlin. Amantha's most serious victimization is self-inflicted, and because she caresses her injuries for so long, her healing takes more than twenty years.

The sudden recovery, in the last few pages of *Band of Angels*, is technically the least credible segment of her long story. It is both too sudden and too unrealized dramatically. For most of her life Amantha denies the power of her own will (even when she uses it) and finds sufficient evidence in those around her that all present ills, public as well as private, have devolved inexorably from the power of the Father in its most comprehensive and symbolic sense. While Amantha's search for wholeness is the primary theme of *Band of Angels*, that theme is lightly, perhaps too tenuously, related to a series of related motifs. The pervasive damning of the father, announced first by the Housman epigraph, is not only a recurring issue with Amantha but one that is central to both Hamish Bond (who reacts against an ineffectual father as well as a domineering mother) and Rau-Ru (who in turn rejects Bond as father). Metaphorically it is related to "paternalism," the attitude that turns the pejorative master-slave arrangement into an honorific father-child relationship. By extension, the father is also generalized as the Past, as History. Amantha feels raped by History, which is another way of saying she has been ill-used by her father as an object of little worth. And, by further extension, the sins of the father are linked to philosophical enslavement of the will, a pietistic doctrine that drains the present generation of real purpose.

"I didn't make this world and make 'em drink blood, I didn't make myself and I can't help what I am doing." The mournful Bond, who excuses his profession with these words, passes on his creed of helplessness to both Amantha and Rau-Ru. When Amantha hears Rau-Ru's little rubric, "You're just the way you are," it is not the first time she has received such unhelpful advice. Rau-Ru's is an echo of Bond's formula, "Oh, Manty, we're just what we are." Taken together, these represent a sentimental determinism that places all present evil on prior agencies: a paternal past (the father) or a generic one (a predestinating Father). Amantha can escape the gloomy fate of such advisors only by denying the definitiveness of their doctrine, which is to say, by affirming her will.

Her characteristic cry—*who will save me?*—implies dependence upon others, and it is one that can only disappoint. In that disappointment Amantha accuses them of betrayal—her father, Miss Idell, Bond, Rau-Ru. The catalog would include most of the characters. Such an attitude is the inevitable result of a fundamental self-pity. As long as she thinks of History as one long rape and of herself as victim, she can enjoy the luxuries of determinism; but when she asserts will (and admits it), she becomes an active agent in the best sense, acknowledging her involvement in and responsibility to the "sweet injustices" of the world: "I had been involved in the very cause of the world, and whatever had happened corresponded in some crazy way with what was in me, and even if I didn't cause it, it somehow conformed to my will" (BA, 364).

This moment when Amantha conceptually understands and accepts her true role marks her long-awaited regeneration, and it is accompanied by a dream-vision that affectively confirms it. She undergoes a regenerative ritual early on at Pointe du Loup when, standing in the center of a group of slaves, she endures the purification of "finger-pointing" and "raise-up" ceremonies—formal measures that are preparatory exercises for full spiritual release, when "everybody would clap hands and stamp earth and chant in the common joy of restoration." Since this is only a "nigger" ritual, however, Amantha, who denies kinship to the slaves, cannot yet be restored. That rebirth comes, irrelevant of her name, many years later in a setting with another kind of formal coherence: the little Kansas cemetery. A static *memento mori*, the spot allows for the contemplation of mortality within the boundaries of a lucid order; the random contingencies of which death is the most solemn are aesthetically stabilized, placed, and so yield up the state of mind conducive to a humble coming to terms with chaos. And with that frame of mind Amantha is finally ready for the ritualistic summing-up dumb show:

> And then, with perfect clarity, I saw the people I had known, the people who had not set me free—my father, all of them—and they were crouching there on the sun-baked earth, a little distance off, and they lifted their hands toward me in some humble beseeching. And then it wasn't only they, it was other people, too, how many I don't know, thousands, millions, black and white, crowding the prairie beyond, people so ghostly you saw right through them, but they were looking at me, and they held out their hands. (BA, 363)

It is a moment of no little glory. Like so many of Warren's later poems, *Band of Angels* concludes in "joy," and its lyric affirmation follows the structural movement of the poem more than it does that of the novel. The resolution is dramatically forced because Amantha's rebirth is, in effect, collapsed into a moment, a mystical insight that replaces the discursive and dramatized stages of change common to fiction. Because mystical moments are virtually incommunicable, Warren must press rhetoric into service to announce the change that resolves his protagonist's dilemma. Deciding that nobody can set her free except herself is for the reader a belated discovery, but for Amantha the moment reverses the tendencies of a lifetime: submitting her will to the spirits of all those who could not set her free becomes an active blessing by which *they* can be set free of her enslaving appetite. Amantha becomes a Jack Burden projected beyond his entrance into the convulsion of the world, for it is by her fitful struggle through those convulsions that she can rightfully lay down her burden and accept a joy hard earned.

XIII. Wilderness: *An Inside Narrative*

Extravagant expectations, which so often comprise the idealism of Warren's protagonists, become in Amantha Starr almost indistinguishable from egoism pure and simple. Even the great drama that rages before and behind her she tends to appropriate into her own struggle for an identity that will match that preconception of herself which she carries about in her adolescent imagination. Resolution and conviction, those powerful stances of ideological will that continue to make the Civil War the most fascinating period in our history, are in her case bothersome interruptions, antagonisms that somehow impinge upon and frustrate her personal quest. In *Wilderness*, however, a more rational and intelligent protagonist appropriates the very terms of that national struggle for his own idealism; and although he comes to see that his idealism is also tainted by egoism, the process by which his destiny merges with that of America returns us centrally to Warren's enduring concern.

The conflict of convictions that Warren perceives as the major thrust in Melville's Civil War poetry is the intellectual matrix of *Wilderness*. Although it took him many years to conclude that the author of *Moby-Dick* was also a poet of subtlety and power, what he finally found as the interesting theme in the poetry, especially in *Battle-Pieces*, was the clash between common humanity and lofty idealism, "between the individual and ideology"—a theme familiar to readers of Warren's own work.[39]

Adam Rosenzweig is the first major Jewish character among Warren's protagonists, and, given his bent toward characters burdened by time and guilt seeking a satisfactory modus vivendi with the world, it is not difficult to see why the Jew becomes an attractive and useful figure for Warren. Unlike many of the earlier protagonists, Adam Rosenzweig experiences what he takes to be a rebirth at the beginning of his adventures, which subsequently turn out to be a series of tests of his convictions. As he lies dying, his father, Leopold, repudiates the idealism that in 1848 had led him to the barricades in Berlin. His older brother articulates the conflict in terms of his own orthodoxy: "You did not trust God. You trusted man." In the repudiation "Adam knew that, in the very moment, in that shadowy room, when his father's self had died, his own self had been born" (W, 9). That self, at the physical age of twenty-nine, is dedicated to a confirmation of his father's "blasphemy." Having been taught Greek and English, "the tongues of liberty," Adam in March, 1863, decides to go to America to "work for the day when the world will know Justice."

If the clash between inflexible Law and all-too-flexible Freedom is congenially symbolic for a Jewish immigrant, it is nothing new in Warren's fiction, in which many of his characters struggle just as ferociously within a similar dialectic. There is, if anything, a certain diminishment in Adam Rosenzweig's struggle; his problem shows up as more simplistically envisioned when compared to that of other figures whose psychological complexity commands greater interest. One of Warren's technical difficulties in *Wilderness* is in dramatizing Adam's psychological state. Unlike Jeremiah Beaumont, for example, Adam is always the passive spectator in his world. His lame left foot insures him against actual physical combat, and his assumed profession as sutler's assistant insures him against significant political involvement. His long search for his true self, while not entirely contained within the privacies of a canvas-topped wagon and hut, is severely conditioned by those mobile objects of his profession. Warren's conception of Adam thus discourages potential dramatic enactments of his personal search, which remains privately intellectual, privately emotional. Compared with every one of his other novels, *Wilderness* is a static work, one that symbolically extends the meditative genre of Warren's *The Legacy of the Civil War*, which appeared in the same year.

Both the narrative structure and the thematic texture of *Wilderness* suggest a kind of morality pageant in which ambiguous Good flounders in its definition and Evil accretes gradually and inevitably as the substance of human experience. The virtues—those abstractions like Justice, Truth, and Freedom that dog the steps of so many Warren protagonists—merely glimmer as potentialities through what Jack Burden calls the "twitch of the nerve and heave of the blood." For Adam Rosenzweig, as for his earlier counterparts, to earn self-knowledge is to come to terms with that flawed nature that resists massive conversion into ideal states. And in turn, once that knowledge comes, Adam must resist despair, the moral lapse that sees no likelihood that virtues are ever probable in a fallen world.

Adam's original dream is a romantic one, the context of which is determined by Mazzini, Byron, and the heroes of the European battles for human rights in the 1840s, but the dispute between the brothers Rosenzweig is articulated in terms perfectly consonant with American intellectual and religious life in the 1840s and after. Indeed, the older brother's accusation ("You did not trust God. You trusted man") is only a more bitter version of the charge that Mary Moody Emerson, a Calvinist of the old school, directed to her famous apostate nephew. But the ambiguity of Good in the first chapter of *Wilderness* is seen not so much in the dialectic between orthodoxy and liberalism; the older brother in his skull cap and the younger at the barricades are simply stark representations of one commitment against another. And both in Warren's scheme are flawed. The weakness of Leopold Rosenzweig's belief, and therefore that of his son, is its very single-mindedness that tends to simplify or even ignore the equivocalness of human experience. Fighting for an abstract good has its inevitable costs. For Leopold it means that the radical choice of standing "with the crowd in the Schlossplatz" rather than with his wife and son brings with it a legacy of unforgiving hate and a dubious model for emulation. Although he dies technically within the Law, he almost certainly dies in despair; and throughout most of his spiritual adventures in the New World, his son is constantly teetering above that same abyss.

Like Amantha Starr, Adam does finally emerge into a kind of "joy," which is to say an acceptance of men "in their error," for though in error, they (and he) are still men capable of the virtues to which his own life has been so undeviatingly committed. But the tragic complexity of man is a lesson that he is a long time learning—hence the narrative structure that Warren devises, for the first and only time, in *Wilderness*.

The journey is its most obvious and basic organization. The sea voyage is not only a narrative introduction to the central plot—the land journey from New York City to Virginia—but it also contains that plot in miniature. It is on board the *Elmyra* that Adam is initiated into a world that is to be his trial: the malignant hostility of the American, Duncan (reminiscent of Melville's Claggart in *Billy Budd*), the pragmatic condescension of the Dutch functionary, the bewilderment and amused scorn of the other German recruits, and the disinterested aid of the English seaman who brooks no speculations about his idealistic motives for showing Adam how to jump ship. The shape and texture of the world Adam experiences after his successful dash down the gang-plank are fleshed out, developed, intensified primarily in those same terms: hostility, expediency, puzzlement, ambivalent aid.

But despite the fact that literally the structure is organized around Adam's physical journey, the metaphorical implications of that journey and the pervasive presence of that more static form, the meditation, are so manipulated that it is almost as if Adam remains stationary, deep in his intellectual and spiritual problem, while the world, in detached and self-sufficient segments, passes in representative panels behind him. Structurally the tale resembles the minor nineteenth-century sketch called the procession. Like "Fancy's Show Box" and other similar pieces of Hawthorne, the local texture of *Wilderness* is thick with symbolic, em-blematic, even allegorical objects: the special boot, the snow-capped Zelzsteinberg, Zellert's hogpen. Out of fifteen chapters, in only two—four and fifteen—is Adam engaged actively, dramatically, in the life that swirls about him.

Because *Wilderness* has most frequently been judged by the canons of ordinary realistic fiction, its very constituent parts—"portentous" symbols, "cramped" style, "didactic" manipulations of character and action, "abstract" and "metaphysical" musings on human nature, circum-stance, and fate—have been judged as significant flaws.[40] But, wheth-er we like them or not, these *are Wilderness*. Even the feeling that Adam Rosenzweig is finally a colorless and largely uninteresting pro-tagonist stems from the parablelike form of the work. He is representa-tive man, aboriginally imperfect, undergoing his trials in a contingent world, itself bereft of perfection. Behind Adam are cultural heroes from Hebrew, Christian, and Greek literature, whose dilemmas come down to us not as psychological case studies but as archetypal repre-sentatives. Everyman, Bunyan's Christian, Oedipus, Job, even Adam east of Eden lurk behind the conception of Warren's figure.[41]

If Adam Rosenzweig is more passive than some of these archetypal heroes, the passivity is largely a condition of his obsessive drive to meditate on what he sees, to make philosophical sense of experience that seems so inimical to those ideal patterns he believes experience *should* reveal. The processional sequences provide him with the varied faces of a contingent reality with which he must eventually come to terms, and in these sequences the most memorable moments emerge not from Adam but from subordinate characters, not from spiritual searching but from physical experiencing.[42] One critic's observation that the life of *Wilderness* picks up noticeably after Chapter 5 is perceptive, for those who find the protagonist dimensionless can at least enjoy the gusto with which Warren renders his supporting characters.[43] These vignettelike sequences begin in Chapter 5, with Adam's temptation by riches; and while it is finally an overdone and talky episode given over almost entirely to monologues by Aaron Blaustein, who in his forty years has gone from basket-peddler to financier, Warren does manage to invigorate a conventional American success story with sporadic life.

From this point on, the work is carried by separate episodes that serve to deepen the shock and chagrin that Adam shows when the human condition is dramatized. In Chapter 7 Adam helps a young woman with farm chores as her husband, a veteran of Chancellorsville, lies dying of his wounds. Chapter 8 is an episode at Gettysburg soon after the battle, dominated by a bloated, oratorical doctor-preacher who, with his two jug-sharing companions, hopes to get an army commission for a "business of perambulatory embalming." Chapters 9, 10, and 11 are devoted to the winter encampment, the boredom of which is relieved by a "shindig" in which a drunken war hero taunts and abuses Negroes and an Irish washerwoman receives "ten on the bare doup." Throughout the winter encampment Adam observes with despair the careful, orchestrated spying of Hawksworth and his Negro assistant that results in the sutler's murder. This segment is the most conventionally novelistic part of *Wilderness* because character relationships are dramatized and merged with significant moments of external action. The processionlike movement resumes after this segment with an episode involving a bushwhacker and his wife, frontierlike characters who recall figures out of *World Enough and Time* and "The Ballad of Billie Potts" and look forward to the central episode of *Audubon*.

Despite its time and setting, the Virginia campaigns of May, 1864, *Wilderness* is an "inside narrative" in the Melvillean sense. There is significantly no sense of a panoramic engagement between armies of men; and even as backdrop to Adam's inner drama, the Civil War only at its edges is significant to the protagonist's spiritual career. The sutler's wagons arrive at Gettysburg *after* the battle; the novel ends just *before* the Battle of the Wilderness. The most dramatic actual involvement we see is that of Adam caught in the civilian anticonscription riots in New York City, an event itself treated by most historians as a kind of footnote to the war.

Warren carefully restricts Adam's movements to the boundaries controlled by the North and people whose sympathies are officially northern. It is this society—the "right side"—that sorely tries Adam's idealism, forcing an adjustment to the pragmatism and outright cynicism of those who oversee, control, or participate in this just war. Adam's recurring response to acts and words is to probe for what he believes must be secret motives—motives that are in fact noble but that must be masked by an accommodating cynicism or indifference. Although eager to ferret out what he believes will be confirmation of his idealism, he is never fully satisfied that he has found such secret motives. Adam, for example, can ask Mose, "Why did you save my life in New York?" and Mose can answer, " 'If'n you tried to climb up—if'n you got to clawen and couldn't make it—and maken a racket—then all them folks might of tried to climb up thar . . . . An that shelf, hit warn't room fer but two. Two at mostest. Did'n aim to have to fight 'em all off.' " (W, 221).

If in the bare statement this act of generosity is reduced to practical considerations of self-interest, the actual process of motive and act that emerges in the dramatic relationship of Mose and Adam is at least ambiguous. There is for Adam's edification not a single act, public heroism or private generosity, that is not tinged with ambiguous motives or ambivalent responses. A succession of such incidents bleakly confirms for Adam his uncle's parting prediction, "You would enter a world where virtue is not possible." The generous act is consistently undercut by the words of the doer himself. Every time he probes into motives for an act rightly performed, and he probes obsessively, Adam is rebuffed. Hawksworth, his silent superior, refuses to accept Adam's commendation for moral courage displayed many years earlier. Mose refuses to make more out of his rescue of Adam than practicality. Both the bushwhacker and his wife, in the midst of their sordid intrigues, extend consideration to Adam, but he is unable to get them to admit their generosity beyond the refrain of resignation, "A man gits tahrd."

In Warren's scheme, however, generosity denied is still generosity and even the selfish motive may still be redeemed by the altruistic. A seaman's advice, for example, *does* get Adam ashore; the cowardly frontier opportunist justifies his checkered career by quoting "the sage of Concord," but he *has* saved a man's life; a radical passivist turned killer does *not* kill Adam; the German mercenaries at Chancellorsville may have displayed too little courage needed for victory, but Meyerhof *is* dying of wounds received in that battle. But these are perspectives unavailable to Adam until the end of the story. His quiet but crusading self-righteousness demands clarity of virtues before they can even be ratified as virtues. His most characteristic cry is, "Was no man, in his simply humanity, more to any other man than a stir or voice, a sloshing in the dark?" The answer is yes, but not because his humanity is simple. The heroic demand for unsullied virtue is an ideologue's dream reminiscent of Warren's Jefferson, and only when Adam admits his own complexity and that of other men, high and low, can he shed his role as ideologue and accept that of the true pilgrim.

Warren states that the most interesting portion of Melville's "The Armies of the Wilderness" deals with "the period of waiting in the winter of 1863–64," when Federal and Confederate troops faced each other along the Rapidan River in Spotsylvania County, Virginia (HM, 368). Significantly, this "period of waiting" occupies three chapters in *Wilderness,* the most crucial for Adam's pilgrimage. In the midst of deprivation, makeshift quarters, boredom, and internecine tensions, Adam undergoes his most pressing trials. Although he still does not know why, it is during this period that he ineradicably assumes the "old taut stoicism," the gestures and the visible sufferings of the Jewish stall vendor. In this winter loneliness he meets his greatest temptations: hatred for the animalistic Simms Purdew, a hero of Antietam; sex with Mollie the Mutton, the Irish washerwoman; ambivalent paternalism toward Mose, the free Negro whom he is teaching to read; alienation from his employer, Jed Hawksworth. Adam cannot deny his feelings of hatred of the men who watch with wet lips and glittering eyes the public lashing of Mollie or the "sweet rush" of exhilaration as he finally utters the words to Mose which link him to the commonality of men: "you black son-of-a-bitch."

In the breaking up of winter camp and the crowded march out, Adam stands unpersoned, devalued, watching those whose "stare of uninterest had bleached him into nothingness," except for one old man who spits at him. "Whatever the old man and the others had done . . . whatever their reasons, or compulsions, for doing it, there was, somehow, a justice in the act. The act corresponded to something in himself" (W, 236–37). Warren explores the peripheries of hate and self-hate as they impinge upon Adam's dream of selfless dedication, without minimizing the weakness of natural man and without any strong confidence that permanent redemption is possible. By the end of the novel Adam has killed a man, not in self-defense but in defense of another man nameless to him. Robbed of his own boots, he has taken those of the dead Confederate, which in turn had been taken from yet another Yankee's feet: "He could try, he thought, to be worthy of their namelessness, and of what they, as men and in their error, had endured."

But that insight is a long time coming to the stiff-necked Adam. Pride in one's differences from other men often afflicts Warren's characters, especially those, like Beaumont, whose intellectual pride separates him from his fellows, and those, like Adam, whose spiritual pride serves much the same function. Adam's pride is thrown into relief in his relationship with Hawksworth and Mose during the winter encampment when all relationships are turned inward. There is a chilly correctness in his attitudes toward both the sutler and the Negro, and in both cases it is based more on ideological than human considerations. Hawksworth remains a silent man, deeply divided in his loyalties, and Adam's own divided loyalties are just as troubling. He is trapped into gratitude to Mose for saving his life, but he comes to detest the "giggle, the secretly hugged joke," and the mutual spying of Hawksworth and Mose arouses in Adam an ambivalence toward the Negro that he recognizes as hovering close to outright rejection.

His hearty tone in praise of Mose's crude lettering betrays what he really feels—"the hopelessness, the aimlessness, and, in his very guts, the revulsion." Even the rescue he comes to view as merely a fortunate stroke in a "blind lottery." Adam muses that while he was being saved, others were being lost to the waiting mob outside. The inevitable result is that Hawksworth also becomes a stand-in for Adam. Both the sutler and his assistant have uttered the phrase of contempt to the Negro, but it is the sutler—Ole Him, Ole Bukra—who dies; as the survivor, Adam muses on the "sly, sad game of spying that must have gone on, month by month . . . each for the other's shame." It is this muted three-way drama, enacted almost backstage, that is meaningful in Adam's search. It is no surprise that he can look about him, at the end of the long, tedious winter when the vast forces are again gearing up for battle, at what Warren terms "the irrelevant vision of armies moving." *Peripheral* and *central* take on something of each other's meaning.

If *Wilderness* skirts the obvious events of the war that seemingly lie ready-made for the enterprising novelist, its focus is in a moral sense central to the significance of the drama as we have come to understand it in its transmission through oral historians, theologians, philosophers, and poets. Behind and beneath the heroic scrims of the great battles, the grand disposition of men and their commitments and arms, Warren suggests the mingled and ambiguous underdrama that played concurrently, act for act, scene for scene, with the major event. Indeed, there is about *Wilderness* the purposive air not of an antidrama but of a counterdrama—a kind of moralist's alternate service in which the central action is assumed to be not in error but incomplete. If that central action in our history resembles an almost classic engagement of opposing sides of high-minded idealists, Warren's tale resembles a procession of rag-tag pragmatists for whom flesh takes precedence over word.

The much-maligned "thinness" of this book is finally an imperceptive complaint. It is not that Warren forsakes the hard local detail characteristic of his best fictional prose. The fictive specificity that any realistic-oriented work embodies is readily apparent throughout *Wilderness*, though that kind of specificity is not Warren's paramount concern. Individually, almost every page carries the force of concisely imagined circumstantiality: the frozen mud thaws *gummily*; ice fragments slide through the river like *sputum*; Duncan's *banged coccyx* is a perverse parallel to Adam's deformed foot; a barking dog in the distance resembles a *cunning little Bavarian toy*; a woman utters a *sustained whinnying sound* as she plunges a knife into a man's thigh; Hawksworth's lips are heavy *with a piece of chewed straw hanging out one side of the mouth*; winter military quarters are log cabins with doorways requiring the men *to crouch to get through* and with roofs of *tenting laid over boards from hardtack boxes*. Such specificity, however, is rigorously subordinated to Warren's larger purpose—to write a narrative informed by the characteristics of the sketch, the parable, the apologue, the procession, the exemplum.[44] The general style is spare and stylized; the sentences tend to be short; the movement, more meditative than narrative, proceeds chiefly through repetition of such phrases as *if only* and *he thought*. Metaphysical questions more than dramatic interractions of personality constitute the heart of the book.

The flatness of *Wilderness* owes something to the deemphasis on time in this work. As Warren himself has observed, time is the very medium of existence for the ordinary novel, and the essence of the novelist's art is his control of the "densities, lapses, and involutions" of time (TD, 72–78). That control is at once brilliantly and conventionally demonstrated in *All the King's Men*. But in *Wilderness* the shaping medium is space; even the structure of the journey, that most primitive of spatial processes, deemphasizes the growth in time of the protagonist, that most elementary requirement of quest narratives, by converting the protagonist into a virtual abstraction. The effect is similar to that old device of theatrical business: to create the illusion of movement on the stage, roll the scenic backdrop. The most vital elements in *Wilderness* are those scenic panels, and the most conventionally memorable action involves the self-contained dramas enacted by supporting players in front of them. *Everyman* is the model drama and Dante's *Commedia* the model poem behind all modern versions of the spiritual journey, including the greatest, *The Waste Land*; the very nature of their forms requires that subordinate characters and situations, examples and temptations, be dramatically more interesting than the quester himself. So it is with *Wilderness*. Warren's great gift for the creation of eccentrics merges with formal demands to make the part-time characters, those who enact miniature dramas before their respective scenic panels, considerably more interesting than the protagonist whose central story it is. Aaron Blaustein, Maran Goetz Meyerhof, Dr. Sulgrave, Simms Purdew, Monmorancy Pugh: although they exist as dialectical counters to Adam Rosenzweig, the very clarity and strength of their outlines give them a vitality denied the more abstract quester.

In all these vignettes—"scenes hieratically conceived," as one critic has put it[45]—action, such as it is, is almost self-contained; and each one is a challenge to Adam, who sees in them opportunism, brutality, victimization, betrayal, and cynicism. America, 1864, is a fallen world, a fact that Adam is reluctant to accept as all: he sees, and deliciously relishes, similar human flaws in himself, but he still seeks for traces of the virtues he once believed had flourished in America. And Warren is careful to give Adam those traces; there are occasions for honor, courage, love to which Adam responds quickly. But he must seek also the articulated motive, the public admission of the urge toward idealistic behavior even in characters who can barely articulate anything more complex than epithets and curses.

By the time the "eight maniacal scarecrows" burst upon Adam in his seclusion in the woods, he has journeyed through himself as much as he has from Bavaria to Virginia. The tangled human complexity he has resisted for so long, in himself as in others, coalesces in his own crucial act. When the Confederates come upon him, he can feel a "sweet sadness fill his heart," even after they assault him needlessly, because they are only foraging troops. But "moral repugnance" replaces "sweet sadness" when one of them is on the verge of killing one of the northern soldiers who has overtaken them. Adam fires a weapon and, for the first time in his life, kills. His idealism is not totally shattered, but it is tempered necessarily by recognition of the merely human. If the final chapter brings this proud idealist to acknowledge a hard-earned lesson ("He did not know what he would have to do now, or with what heart. He knew, however, that he would have to try to know what a man must know to be a man."), the long journey is thematically anticipated on the opening page of the first chapter. As he stands beneath the white mountain after his father's funeral, Adam muses, "If the mountain had not gleamed so white," a clause that is succeeded

by a series of five other similarly structured conditional clauses. Together, the formal subjunctive mood of Adam's musings and the
heavy iteration of color images suggesting innocence and idealism
(*white, whipped cream, puff of cloud, washed glitter of blue*) are
premonitory signals for the protagonist's character and quest: an obsessive commitment whose very formulation contains its own questioning
of value. If both the grammatical precision and the lexical choices contribute to that quality of *Wilderness* that many readers consider an
approximation closer to lyric than to narrative, that feeling is confirmed
two pages later when Adam murmurs the opening lines of his father's
poem, which encapsulates the political idealism the son will eventually
extrapolate into his own moral idealism:

> "If I could only be worthy of that mountain I love,
> If I could only be worthy of sun-glitter on snow,
> If man could only be worthy of what he loves."   (W, 5)

The easy progression from *I* to *man* is the contaminating clue to Adam's
proud idealism, and it is a far different sort of equation from Blaustein's
remark to Adam on his first evening in America: "But listen, everything is part of everything else." From *we should all be worthy* Adam
must eventually turn to *I must learn to know what a man must know
to be a man.* The shift in effect makes *Wilderness* a tale of counterconversion. Adam begins his journey, despite the content of his belief, with
all the attitudes of the religious hero.[46] The provisional nature of experience is something this religious hero cannot comprehend, much less
accept; when Adam at long last does understand it, he embraces it,
and thereby sheds the absolutism with which he holds his truth. The
humble acceptance of the values of other sinful men who endure
despite their nature is, as one critic points out, an integral part of
Adam's spiritual rebirth.[47]

Adam belatedly comes to terms with Blaustein's insistence upon
human connectedness, and in his admission he becomes part of all those
mingled acts of goodness and evil, linked not only to the sutler and his
free Negro but also to Mordacai Sulgrave, Simms Purdew, Monmorancy
Pugh, and all the scattered others both despised and honored. Wearing
another man's boots means sacrificing his own intricately designed left
boot, which has betrayed him into self-indulgent suffering and which
has been a visual reminder of his separation from other men. By
putting on an ordinary pair of boots worn by both Union and Confederate soldiers, Adam signifies that the chain of complicity is also a
chain of hope.[48] Adam enters into the world's agonies as a naïf, but he

is a naïf with remarkably unresilient standards that he would apply to all those he meets. With such a sensibility, the world and the men in it can only disappoint and punish.

The human temptation, once that disappointment and punishment come, is to swing to the opposing extreme, to conclude that man is nothing but the twitch of nerve and heave of blood, to brood like Jefferson:

> we were only ourselves,
> Packed with our own lusts and languors, lost,
> Each man lost, in some blind lobby, hall, enclave,
> Crank cul-de-sac, couloir, or corridor of Time.
> Of Time. Or self. . . . (BD, 7)

For Adam the impulse to liberate is self-righteous and ends only in self-entrapment; like Amantha Starr, he breaks through into a recognition of that self-entrapment, a recognition that can liberate. Although *"a man's deepest dream is all he is"* may be his hopeful belief in man's nobility, Adam must also "walk in the world" as that other alien, Audubon, learns. What the great naturalist writes, after his struggle with a world that ignores, insults, and disappoints him for so long, can as well apply to Adam Rosenzweig at the end of his spiritual journey: "a world which though wicked enough in all conscience is *perhaps* as good as worlds unknown" (SP, 98).

In a curious way, *The Legacy of the Civil War* is as novelistic as *Wilderness*. Its texture comprises the characteristic density of local detail, vignettes of precisely rendered acts stemming from a generous recognition of complex motives and a comprehensive accounting of the ongoing cultural consequences of human deeds of one historical moment. The snarled metaphysical ruminations of Adam Rosenzweig replace the rich vitality of novelistic action, and the spare episodic experiences of peripheral characters in the wings replace the grand major action of the conflict itself on the central stage. Both works show Warren's diverse skills as historian, novelist, poet—and moralist.

If in his meditations on the Civil War Centennial Warren constructs a persuasive argument for the complexity of that great conflict, in *Wilderness* he creates a fictional character who perceives the war in the most simplistic ways. To insist, with Adam, upon applying the pure ideal of human liberty to what was inevitably a human situation, and therefore a most impure social and moral context, is to fall victim to the aggressive righteousness of what Warren describes as the Treasury of Virtue—that penchant of the North both during and after the Civil War. Adam becomes Warren's fictional example of the religious zeal that actually endangered the practical business of carrying on the war. Standing almost alone among the shakers and movers as a compassionate pragmatist, the great man of the time was of course Lincoln, who epitomized (in Warren's view) the tragedy of commitment as well as its resolution, the dilemmas, the moral entrapments and ethical risks. Adam Rosenzweig is, unhappily, no little man with a Lincolnesque vision, but an imaged embodiment of all those idealists who badgered Lincoln because he was less the Holy Warrior than they. Like the New England moralists, Adam impatiently reduces ambiguity to a trifling; although he is forced to see it everywhere and in every situation, he wants desperately to see it as a temporary balking of the Good, a kind of nagging malevolence that blindly resists the enshrining of idealism as the necessary principle.

As both *The Legacy of the Civil War* and *Wilderness* make clear, and as Warren's other historical works underscore, the resisting world is all there is, and we deny it in favor of imagined perfections only at our own risk. The alibis and evasions that Adam finds so ideologically alien in his sojourn in wartime America cannot be banished because they are as much the badge of humanness as the rage for ideal constructions. Both books are muted celebrations of the Civil War Centennial. Both are structured in representative panels, reflecting the great issues of that conflict in galleries of human images.

An Art of Transparency

Some of Warren's persistent critics have never adjusted to the spectacle of a writer who is simultaneously the talky philosophical novelist and the raunchy purveyor of drugstore gothic.[1] Charges of bad taste and tactlessness aside, the critics who find that a bosomy romance marketed for female book-club members is an inappropriate vehicle for smuggling in notions about existentialism are really addressing themselves to generic questions of what a novel must be or do in order to qualify as a novel in the first place. Such prescriptions have never gone begging, but in Warren's case, as in most others, they are finally irrelevant to the novel as practiced. Except for *Night Rider*, Warren's career as short-story writer and novelist is the record of unwell-made fictions. They are often baggy and capacious (*World Enough and Time* and *Flood*); their structures often imitate the meandering associationism of the narrators (*All the King's Men* and *Band of Angels*); characters strike us as excessively compulsive or eccentric, acting out typal situations rather than functioning as people living out individual lives (*Band of Angels* and *Meet Me in the Green Glen*); the fictions are often cheerful mixes of conventional modes and styles (*At Heaven's Gate*, *The Circus in the Attic*, and *The Cave*); and, most significantly, they juxtapose equally intense urgencies toward philosophical speculation and naturalistic observation.

From the beginning his uniqueness as a writer of fiction has been the curious way in which Warren is driven both to propound abstract philosophical problems and to explore the concrete actualities of time and place. If the first impulse eventuates into narratives heavily larded by characters who are psychologically divided between opposing needs and an authorial presence who delights in complicating issues of moral will with polarities and dichotomies, the second shows up in narratives almost overburdened by brisk, often violent action and by an authorial presence who delights in painting the world in primary colors, documenting its facts and detailing the most crucial of human activities with extravagant precision. Both tendencies are often seen in the same novel.

For Warren, finding the technical means to accommodate his penchant for both philosophy and literary realism has been a struggle for and with appropriate forms. Like Faulkner, but in less obvious ways, Warren has never rested in the security of a single realized form: each novel, whatever its thematic connections with all others, has its own formal integrity arising from the inner demands of each narrative. Some efforts have of course finally fallen short of their conception. Warren's experimentation with the sentimental tradition in *Band of Angels* is perhaps no more successful than Melville's in *Pierre*, but the articulation of Warren's novel proceeds at least from a fully conscious scheme and it develops logically from its own aesthetic premises, as Melville's does not.

One characteristic device that emerges out of Warren's search for appropriate forms is what has been called "rhythmic proportioning," the technical distribution of voices and events among major and minor characters, stylistic juxtapositions, narrative variations and parallelism.[2] Despite the technical success of the first-person narrative in *All the King's Men*, Warren has more commonly indulged an instinct for alternative insights that tend to deepen or extend the fable as it is dramatized in a single consciousness; the intensity and economy even of that novel—a result of Jack Burden's fully explored consciousness —are counterbalanced not only by the Cass Mastern inset story but also by the educative stages in Burden himself. *Band of Angels* fails because its narrator's consciousness, while just as fully explored, is not very interesting, and Amantha Starr's lack of complexity necessarily means fewer educative stages to mark the moral growth.

The later fiction is an art of transparency because the primacy of philosophical and moral speculation is undisguised. Ordinary narrative contexts no longer are required for characters to speculate on their own reality or to agonize over apparent insights that, upon reflection, fail to answer urgent needs. This development, most clearly seen in *Wilderness* and *Meet Me in the Green Glen*, does not mean that Warren dispenses with social notation—the contours of the fictive worlds of Civil War America and a TVA-shaped South are drawn from the same store of precisely imagined details to which he has always turned to depict character and place—but he uses his gift for realistic observation in different measures and for different purposes. Mimetic representation of a chosen world ceases to be the *donnée*. It becomes merely another ingredient, like setting and characterization narrowly conceived, and like those other conventions of realistic fiction is rigorously subordinated to a rhetoric of intellection, to dialectical play and nakedly abstract musing.

The hard, clear detail in this later fiction occurs frequently but not in the tumbling, clotted profusion we see so often in *All the King's Men* and *World Enough and Time.* Some moments of observation are captured with enough effectiveness to be memorable as images of recall: a crewcut engineer, with his round freckled face and peeling red nose, amiably cracking his knuckles; a carcass of a pink, scraped hog, its entrails drawn and purged, hanging head down from a slaughter beam beside a steaming black pot; an old gossip of quality, her baby-pink wattles shaking, exuding an odor of orris root and peppermint; little girls in mauve fairy costumes tap-dancing on a politician's campaign truck to an apathetic crowd. These are images, however, that bear no special weight in the disposition of narrative. The sharply defined images we get in Jack Burden's smart garrulousness, observed either solemnly or cynically, always bear relevance to the narrator's dilemma. With the dispersion of point of view in some of the later fiction, the images are free-floating observations fashioned in an idiom—like Standard Received Intellectual Discourse—unattached to personal qualities of individual characters. What is often lost by this technique is the feeling of an actual world, as if Warren, with some of the more radical postmodernist innovators, is saying that fictive illusion is nothing more than a placebo for the serious reader and can be summarily handled, if not dismissed.

But the realistic details in the later fiction are not merely scarcer than in the earlier; when such specifics of observed reality do occur, their very specificity tends to be strung out, sorted, analyzed, sometimes with microscopic concern. When Brad Tolliver in *Flood* remembers his wife across a candlelit table it is with total recall; it begins with the memory of "a small scale of lipstick sticking up minutely from the now somewhat lax lower lip, like the beginning of a fever blister, a little to the left side," and it ends with preternatural vividness:

> He saw her lift the upper lip slightly and draw it back; bring the even row of upper teeth out to cover the lower lip, exposing the canines, one of which, he noticed for the first time, was a little discolored as though from a dead nerve; and draw the lower lip slowly out, against what seemed to be the painful pressure of the upper teeth. When the lower lip was released, he saw that the little flake, or scab, was gone. The lip had been raked smooth by the sharp even

pressure of those upper teeth, and now in its provocative laxness, gleamed bright with saliva.   (F, 66)

The portentous specificity suggests that this is a crucial scene between Brad and Lettice, but it is not. He is in love with this woman, and the lingering, clinical memory is a visceral reminder of that love—what he calls the "nakedness of knowing her." For Brad these small remembered gestures signify love, mutability, immersion in the moment. For Warren, they mean these things too, but in addition they are promises of regeneration that are embodied in human flesh; the recognition of one's humanness must precede more aspiring resolutions of the spirit.

When similar scenes occur in *At Heaven's Gate* or *All the King's Men*—the anger-laced badinage and lovemaking of Jerry Calhoun and Sue Murdock, and the "Jackie-Boy" scenes of Jack Burden and Anne Stanton—they involve the most ordinary gestures observable to the recording eye, but they attain significance because they are part of a rich context of other gestures, other acts. The speakeasy scene in *Flood* is abstractly important, and Warren's rhetorical expatiation draws attention to it in a kind of homiletic diagram.

When Angelo Passetto explores the upstairs of the Spottwood house for the first time in *Meet Me in the Green Glen*, we follow him for three fully documented pages of itemized objects ("carpeting . . . frayed to the wood"), movements ("three paces that led to the door"), perspectives ("the light on the face in the mirror flickered"), and directions ("on the inner wall to the left"). The scene is further realized by details of sensory perception: the sound of rain on the roof, the feel of "dry rodent droppings" under the thin soles of patent-leather shoes, the smell of dust and damp. The elaboration of the scene, however, is not intended to supply the kind of mimetic actuality that we expect in the realistic novel: its function is to underscore Angelo's shadowy self, and the contrasting grittiness of actuality, through the climactic moment when this character sees his image in the mirror of an armoire. The confrontation with the shadowy self becomes the justification for the minutely conceived and ponderously paced scene. The philosophical query that animates *Meet Me in the Green Glen*, which becomes the *raison d'être* for plot, character, setting, and action, is *what is real? which is the dream?* The abstract power of dialectic subsumes the more modest contexts of mimetic fiction.

This technical development in the later fiction raises inevitable questions of effectiveness because, if for no other reason, Warren himself has written on the writer's necessity for conveying theme not through abstraction, in "the poverty of statement," but in animating images validated by circumstance and experience (SE, 155). But he has also addressed himself to the potential strength of a rhetoric of intellection that he finds in some of Dreiser's work: in the Cowperwood trilogy especially he argues that "the power of the dialectic significantly compensates for certain bleaknesses in realization" (TD, 86–87). For many readers nourished by either the realistic or symbolic traditions of fiction, such arguments are not persuasive. Certain scenes in *Meet Me in the Green Glen* are indeed bleak in their realization, and a dialectic that insists upon its own self-conscious play, which is obtrusive to a fault even in a fiction of "statement," hardly compensates for a missing sense of felt life. As Warren goes on to argue, the "threshold of realization" in any given scene cannot be scientifically determined, and each reader must judge for himself whether "the current of life, the sense of action as form," manifests itself in the rendered scene (TD, 88). This sense comes through effectively in certain moments even in the later fiction: Brad Tolliver's scenes with Jingle Bells, his tryst with Leontine Purtle; Angelo's tenacious struggle to keep busy, repairing the John Deere tractor and the bathroom plumbing. But if these later novels are judged by such rubrics, themselves a legacy of traditional fiction, most of them since the mid-1950s inevitably suffer. The most successful are *A Place to Come To*, which follows the form of spiritual autobiography devised in *All the King's Men*, and those works that are clearly experimental (*The Cave*) or that frankly return to older and more directly moral narrative forms (*Wilderness*).

The bluntness of the moral drama in *Wilderness*, dominating as it does every conventional ingredient of the novel form, occasioned Leonard Casper's observation several years ago that the entire fiction reads like one of the inset stories that Warren once used to reinforce situations and themes of his major narratives, except that *Wilderness* seems stripped of that larger context which documents the world; what is left is the configuration of a spiritual journey that comprises the very process by which tentativeness, inquiry, trial and error emerge into philosophical resolution.[3] If *Wilderness* is the first of Warren's fictions in which the narrative of social notation is firmly subordinated to moral apologue or parallel parable, the first explicit, and still his most interesting experiment is *The Cave*.

In this novel Warren lavishes his customary energies upon a created world that is almost a parody of his earlier, realistically delineated world of politicians, cranks, fathers and children, agrarian exploiters and reformers, commercial wizards and failures. However harmonious the novel becomes on its own terms, we are forced to accept *The Cave* as an artifact finally richer in statement than in drama; furthermore, that statement is emphasized by the use of such naked devices as stereotype and caricature, parody and ironic fable, and bemused omniscience —all bestowed generously upon figures who are bundles of attributes more than they are characters. Time sequences in *The Cave* are more complex than in earlier novels. Unlike the solid blocks of flashbacks that mark the structure of *All the King's Men*, this novel (as well as the fictions which follow it) is structured around flashbacks in brief, fragmented chunks of memory attuned to momentary moods and vagaries of thought of the several characters. The richness of interpolated stories and the alternating idioms of diverse characters are converted in *The Cave* to "participatory narration," in which multiple points of view are the technical equivalents of the theme—the mutuality of redemptive needs sparked by a disaster affecting an entire community.[4]

Stylization emerges as a hallmark of Warren's fiction beginning with *The Cave*. The novelistic adaptations in this novel suggest more the occasional practice of Camus, John Updike, and William Golding than that of the earlier Warren or that general tradition of gamy southern naturalism into which many readers are still content to place him. Although he has always been fascinated by certain kinds of stylization (the double perspective of "Billie Potts" and the conceptual exploitation of the sentimental heroine in *Band of Angels* are two examples), in *The Cave* Warren makes that principle of organization the norm: it guides characters and shapes their actions, and it knits together both theme and structure into what is finally a cohesive and impressive work.

In the first chapter of *The Cave* a persona hovers over the scene at the cave like an indulgent Keats. The speculative, irony-tinged overview begins with the boots, then shifts successively to a picture of their owner (at this point he is only "the man") polishing them with care in some suspended past; the surrounding glade (described in Arcadian extravagance); the guitar; its owner several miles away; and back to the beech-shade of the glade again. The boots and guitar are not realistic objects providing scenic context for the actions of characters; they are human objects that emblematically direct our attention to them in their separateness, visually investing them with a significance still withheld. The device is not scene-painting in the way we think of it in conventional narrative: to accommodate human figures. The boots and guitar are spatially arranged to assume, momentarily, the landscape itself, enlarged and lighted in the manner of a still life. When the persona does introduce appropriate figures for such a garden spot, it is almost as if he is calling "the boy and the girl" from a transcendent reality to people a miniature garden world out of some Appalachian Watteau. The time is June; the glade is caught in a "breathless hush," the limestone outcropping, beneath the "down-swooped boughs" of "the biggest beech of all," has an opening where the air is cool and the overhang is laced with fern. The entire tolling forth of the young couple is a conscious invocation of Keats's fair youth and his maiden beneath trees whose "happy, happy boughs" cannot shed their leaves.

But this picture is not so much a frieze as a slow-motion picture: the youth and his girl are not frozen in stances of becoming but they are moving, even if slowly, towards being. Furthermore, human imperfection—the "breathing human passion" that leaves the heart "high-sorrowful and cloy'd," a feverish brow, and a "parching tongue"—reflects the natural imperfection inherent in this deceptive glade. Despite romantic scene-painting, this garden world exists by the grace of mutability itself. Loss is inherent in the empty boots; the sun is caught just past its meridian; the locust penetrates the silence with a "grinding metallic" whir that sounds like a "remorseful" buzz saw "working fiendishly away at the medulla oblongata"; the "dizzying heat-dazzle" makes the human vision "shake"; cancer-ridden Jack Harrick intrudes violently upon the scene with his suspicion that he has already begun to smell; the jaybird, whose light could be pinched out "with no trouble at all," perches on the neck of the guitar and then darts away as the thin note "vibrates spookily" and "dies fastidiously into the sky." For whatever variety of ideality—human or natural—is perceivable in this garden, the Mercutio element is there too, to temper any suggestion of the pure and the perfect.

The Cave is not the kind of fiction Willa Cather described in "The Novel Démeublé."[5] Its setting is precise, full, and furnished; but the precision and fullness are less important than the emblematic weight of scene. Moreover, as with objects and landscapes, so with the human figures who arrange themselves about and in them: the later fiction presents characters as mobile representations invested with significance, as opposed to those characters of the realistic novel who, with notions of their own, often seem bent on competing with their creators' plans for them. The widely ranged voices we hear in *At Heaven's Gate* and *All the King's Men* come in the later fiction to be absorbed by a presiding consciousness, a persona that can surmount what Andrew Lytle has called the "reportorial prolixities of omniscience."[6] Especially in *The Cave* this presiding consciousness parcels out speeches and thoughts to figural characters in sound-alike idioms. Even those distinctive acts usually compelled by the logic of narrative and the nature of the individual characters are calculatingly set aside, isolated momentarily from their context, and rhetorically infused with meaning determined by that governing consciousness. Sequential acts tend to fuse with symbolic action, the effect of which is a thinning out of the kind of textural density that marks Warren's earlier fictive worlds. The result is a prose that is less narrative than it is meditative, philosophical, lyrical.

The plethora of acts, deeds, conversation, and tics that function chiefly as contributions to the felt life of the world in which they occur is one of the legacies of realistic fiction. If William Dean Howells is not the admired model for Warren, he is nevertheless the great inescapable example that is implicitly acknowledged in both the fully rendered contemporary scene of *At Heaven's Gate* and *All the King's Men* and the cluttered, precisely re-created milieux of *World Enough and Time* and *Band of Angels.* In our literature Hawthorne, Poe, and Melville are the great symbolic fictionists for whom such acts, deeds, conversations, and tics are stylized more than rendered, not as material indexes to life as it is lived but as spiritual markers to the subterranean drama of the self. These models are those to which Warren has frequently returned, often at the expense of his equally gifted talent for circumstantial notation, partly because his imagination works consistently if not always compellingly on a moral rather than a social level.

As the epigraph from Book VII of *The Republic* announces clearly, *The Cave* posits man's difficulty in separating shadow and substance but ominously suggests that even the removes from reality are the reality too. Warren's aesthetic decisions are appropriate. They include the choice of characters that almost seem drawn from a ragbag of caricatures and types; language that, in juxtaposing cadences of ceremony and the hokey folk idioms of popularized regionalism, ends up as stylized artifice unifying a vision of man that is itself stylized; and a mood created by mannered prose richly studded with the metaphors of reality-shadow (*image, shadow, dream, ritual, fantasy, impromptu drama, the fusion . . . of the dream and the actuality*). There are caves literal and caves symbolic, and quasi caves like cool glens and green back rooms of houses and banks where competing identities are met and sometimes clarified.

Flood, Meet Me in the Green Glen, and *A Place to Come To* all continue Warren's exploration of spiritual passages. Two of their protagonists (Brad Tolliver and Jed Tewksbury) are lineal descendants of Jack Burden: educated, successful, worldly wise, and psychologically ailing. Their stories are enacted in a familiar Warren environment of sons alienated from fathers and home, learning to live with, yet reluctant to be accommodated to, their replacement by surrogates. Dissatisfaction is the emotional norm; and the action consists of the compulsive return, psychologically and physically, to the source. Anticipated and worried over in several poems and novels, that compulsive return of man, with its natural link in the cyclic action of salmon, goose, and bee, is its most definitive in the alternate idioms of "Billie Potts":

> Therefore you tried to remember when you had last had
> Whatever it was you had lost,
> And you decided to retrace your steps from that point,
> But it was a long way back.
> It was, nevertheless, absolutely essential to make the effort,
> And since you had never been a man to be deterred by difficult circumstances,
> You came back.
> For there is no place like home.   (SP, 279)

The difficulty of retracing steps in *Flood* and *Meet Me in the Green Glen* is literally more intensive because it must be conducted in a landscape destined for physical obliteration by floodwaters, a narrative fact that is reinforced by metaphorical equivalences suggested by the kind and quality of action Warren recounts. Retardation—action slowed by submarine images of submersion and (in *Flood*) cinematic images of "bleeding," transitions, montage, and slow motion—not merely the kind of aesthetic stylization that calls attention to itself, but as in many American films celebrating violence, the technique simultaneously italicizes the visceral rawness of the narrative action and disinfects the melodrama that is the surface of every Warren narrative.

Because of Warren's own variation of the "flashforward," the town of Fiddlersburg and the valley of the green glen are in effect already buried in water, narrative facts that extend the submarine imagery so favored by Warren at least as early as "Bearded Oaks."[7] This technique comprises a cluster of related devices, used variously to render the Great Sleep of Jack Burden, his fanciful reconstruction of the self as foetus, and his drowning in the ooze of history in a hotel room in California; it recalls the merging of a willed consciousness and a will-less nature that Jeremiah Beaumont experiences first as pleasure in the river and then as protection in the swampy empire of Ole Big Hump. Though Brad Tolliver's father had come "boiling out of the swamp" to make his way in Fiddlersburg, he had periodically made his return to the swamp and the kind of innocence associated with conscienceless beasts; so his son, who returns to seek out Frog-Eye, one of those beasts. Even in the empty house that survives the flooding, Brad Tolliver feels like a diver entering "a chamber long submerged": "He felt how it was, how the house, the town, maybe the world, had been flooded long back, and here he was, in that gear out of nightmare, moving in painful, lead-footed retardation into that room" (F, 358). The violence of "that room" and that of Cassie Spottwood's house in the green glen are in effect drained of melodrama by such images, so that the violence is translated into moral equations, abstract ingredients for philosophical resolution. Cassie's face is often seen glimmering through window glass; darkness comes "flooding" upon her, "pouring in, filling up the room"; Angelo's attic explorations proceed somnambulistically, as in dream, in which the literal movement is less important than its symbolic motivation. Because of its blatant aesthetic effects, *Meet Me in the Green Glen*, even more than *Flood*, seems to aspire to the kind of narrative-lyric suites that Warren constructs by interpolating physical action (in panels of frozen gesture or slowly accreting movement) with mental glosses, interjections, and interpretive, often acerbic, disquisitions: "The Day Dr. Knox Did It," "Old Nigger on One-Mule Cart," "Rattlesnake Country."

In their various ways all the recent novels exhibit rhetorical or structural devices that give them this special quality of translucence. The light of authorial purpose does not illuminate plot and characterization as mimetic conventions with an inspired life of their own; it irradiates these novelistic ingredients with an aim almost homiletic. In *Flood*, the younger writer's first success comes with a book of stories called *I Want to Tell You Something*. In a sense each of the novels beginning with *The Cave* carries the title of Brad Tolliver's book as its secret title; whatever the quality of the vehicle, the thematic freight is the important thing.

In Warren's later fiction, the desire to know, the obsession to understand relationships, is transformed into an aesthetic device so that vehicle and its burden come close to being fused into a single element. If this aesthetic development shows anything about his persistent themes, it attests to the fact that there is no ease in Zion. The search for the true self must be made over and over again and through aesthetic maneuvers progressively indifferent to conventions we associate with Howellsian realism. If the rhetoric of Jack Burden is an important clue to our understanding of his difficult progress to self-knowledge, that of Jed Tewksbury is even more so. *A Place to Come To* is spiritual autobiography whose very rhetoric *is* the subject. Gone is the kind of displacement that allows Burden to be a newspaperman and a history student; Tewksbury is a professor—a Dante specialist—who is also an exiled southerner. The transparency of this novel is such that motive, resolution, commitment, and vision are configured as both structure and texture; the problem that the novel both asserts and tentatively solves is how can a man pierce through his own feints and stratagems to his true self? The moral progress that we follow is the action of the later fiction generally, itself an act articulated by Warren's obsessive use of italics. Physical movement and phenomenal detail, though they are not replaced, are suffused by rhetorical constructs whose very prominence announces their author's direct engagement with issues he considers most important. The author's voice in these fictions becomes almost as transparent as the vulnerable, searching "I" of Warren's later poetry.

XIV.   The Cave: *Ceremonies of Effort*

In his essay on *Nostromo*, Warren observes that Conrad was more interested in the kind of experienced humanism typified by Emilia than he was in the more flamboyant "radical skepticism" of Decoud or Monygham. Such a humanism, he concludes, emerges only out of character-in-action, when the human will meets the hard, sometimes intractable facts of other human wills in particular situations. From the clash, the recoil and clash again, comes that reward of the active consciousness: an understanding of "the cost of awareness and the difficulty of virtue" (SE, 48–49). The observation is useful for our reading of *Nostromo*, of course, but the double fascination is perhaps more Warren's than it is Conrad's.[8]

In most of his novels, Warren sends his protagonist out of an intensely private world, where commitment has been either ill-defined or too easily pledged, into a public world where, if he is strong, his experience will enrich and validate that personal vision of self. The search for self-knowledge is a response to two contradictory desires: the searcher's need for a definition of his private being that will isolate him from the mass and celebrate his uniqueness, and his need for immersion in the group, the cause, the spirit of community. If in the search for self-knowledge he arrives at the clearing, the needs of identity and community will have been harmonized. The protagonist may succeed or, more often, fail, but in each case he will come away from his experience with an appreciation of the high cost of awareness. From *Night Rider* onward, the protagonist resembles a Decoud or a Monygham more than he does an Emilia, a circumstance that sheds a particular light on how, in Warren, the strenuousness of human effort often outstrips its rewards. Perse Munn, Jerry Calhoun, Jack Burden, Jeremiah Beaumont, Amantha Starr, Adam Rosenzweig, Bradwell Tolliver—all achieve self-knowledge, but only after the most painful, prolonged, and costly exertion, which is to say that Warren, like Conrad, goes "naked into the pit, again and again, to make the same old struggle for his truth" (SE, 58).

None of Warren's novels demonstrates the strenuousness of human effort, the defining of self through community, quite so insistently as does *The Cave*. Here, failure after great struggle is still seen as a dismal fact of man's lot, but a viable, even impressive success is dominant for the first time in a Warren novel. Because it is the only one of Warren's novels which lacks a true protagonist, the structure of *The Cave* suggests that all characters, however different they may be, are equally illustrative of the theme.⁹ By exploring them from multiple angles, Warren emphasizes both the strenuousness and the reward of human effort. Reward commensurate with that effort comes to no fewer than seven characters (Jo-Lea, Monty, Jack and Celia Harrick, Brother Sumpter, Nick, Bingham). Two minor characters (Nick's wife and Dorothy Cutlick) achieve less, but their efforts are also less intense. One minor character (Mrs. Bingham) and one major (Isaac) make "wrong" peaces, but they are exactly the right peaces inasmuch as these characters inevitably fulfill their separate natures.

Narrative action, because it is severely selective, ceases to be mimetic in *The Cave*. Stripped of any action that is not purely functional, this novel consists of intense, highly charged moments conceived and dramatized almost wholly to advance theme: the difficult struggle of not just one but several characters to strike through illusion—the masks they wear and the social roles they play—to their essential identities.¹⁰

For articulating this process, Warren relies on a device, at once technical and thematic, which for want of a more precise term may be called *gesture*. Absorbing its functions from two traditions—realistic fiction with its dependence upon literal action, and the symbolic novel (such as *To the Lighthouse*) with its dependence upon action so rigorously compressed that its invested larger meanings dominate its original literalness—gesture is both physical and symbolic. The expression of the personal and the particular, this device becomes a kind of fictive shorthand, simple signs denoting complex structures. Gestures become the varied responses to given situations shaped in meaningful patterns by reiteration, incremental repetition, and parallelism. Although it is Warren's most effective means for delineating external character in *The Cave*, gesture is also his most economical device for manifesting the indirect, the internal, the oblique. In this story of illusion and reality, gesture shadows forth the total reality of the gesturer. Warren's later art of transparency is nowhere else so successfully consistent; *The Cave* is his most severely stylized fiction.

One of the more remarkable aspects of stylization in *The Cave* is the structural, metaphorical, thematic figure of Jasper Harrick, a noncharacter almost in the same sense that James's Mrs. Newsome of *The Ambassadors* is a noncharacter. His compulsion as a separate identity we know only at secondhand; yet we see the pervasive power of that compulsion informing the acts of everyone who is a character. His experience is the paradigm of self-definition. He is metaphorical, archetypal, mythical, bigger-than-life, even stereotypical; and it is against him that "real" people test the validity of their own more fragmented searches for self-definition. Jasper Harrick, it should be noted, never appears except in the flashbacks of other characters; he says very few things, even by report, and only one statement is noteworthy: his mother remembers his explanation for being a compulsive caver—"in the ground at least a fellow has a chance of knowing who he is" (C, 241).

This motive of self-definition becomes the impulse of all the other principals; in Jasper's fatal act, his own entombment, the motive suddenly is manifested in a physical, tangible way, which in turn supplies the others with both motive and act. Around the cave mouth Warren assembles his congeries of searchers, who are as much watchers and waiters as they are grievers. Their very disposition resembles ceremonially filled space. By virtue of that spatial placement, their almost choreographed interaction, the way their inner, private needs are displaced by the plight of the man trapped inside, the scene becomes a visual elegy—that is, a form that makes serious theater out of raw grief but at the same time ratifies the disparate needs of the individual grievers by submitting them to the artificialities of convention. A measured formalism not only elevates appetitive man into aesthetic man; it paradoxically also releases a new understanding of himself as indivisible, of himself as a vital part of community. The ceremonies at the cave mouth are the intricate means by which the celebrants attain full humanity. They are the clearest illustration in all of Warren of one of the social implications of certain New Critical beliefs. "The object of a proper society," says John Crowe Ransom, "is to instruct its members how to transform instinctive experience into aesthetic experience."[11] In their varied responses, these characters assembled at the cave mouth receive not necessarily what they want, but what they need. Those who enter the cave in search of Jasper do so frankly in hope of redefining their own identities; but even those whose quest takes them no farther than the cave mouth are searchers as well.

These searches, moreover, are underpinned by earlier and less grand gestures, which not only reveal motives of the acts and speeches of each individual searcher, but also supply a texture of motif that anticipates, corroborates, and intensifies the structural climax at the cave.[12] The who-am-I theme is imaged in characters who realize, however dimly, that their present identity must be validated both verbally and physically.

In Warren's fictional world, speech accomplishes what it has always done for man in the actual world: it makes subjective emotions external and objective facts internal. In answering the double needs of a Warren protagonist—his impulses toward identity and community—the verbal gesture possesses the double function of marking individual boundaries and erasing them. It not only defines the gesturer, but also suggests something of his dilemma in establishing intercourse between his private world and the public world in which he seeks to justify himself.

Those Warren characters who are blessed (or cursed) with the gift of vision, imagination, intelligence, or simply the mysterious compulsion to do right by a standard equally mysterious, are those who place the most value on saying, as if the words themselves may somehow act as agents for completing an experience still in the future. This largely unconscious use of verbal magic is an attempt not only to communicate wishes and desires but also to establish the word as a coextension of the reality it names, to underscore the belief that by saying certain things in certain agreed-on ways, the sayer can shape his future and force events to turn out the way he wants them to. "Words," says Warren elsewhere, "are not only a threshold, a set of signs, but a fundamental aspect of meaning, absorbed into everything else."[13]

In *The Cave*, Jasper's entombment provides not only the orienting scene, but also the chief orienting symbol by which an individual's sense of his own identity is tested. The entombment, for example, is the occasion for the restaurant owner to assert his identity, to deny that *Nick Pappy*, even though it is "what Johntown had decided was a good enough name for Nicholas Papadoupalous" (C, 41), is either proper or adequate. He asks Mrs. Harrick to pronounce his name, since no one in Johntown had ever done that. His argument is as poignant as it is simple: " 'they got things they call you. Like Nick Pappy. But if it is not your right name, it looks like sometime you don't know who you are, maybe' " (C, 304). It is Celia who remembers the shrug and the strange look of her son as he had explained his need for proper identity. It is Celia who sympathizes with, even though she cannot understand, the central problem so massively symbolized by her son's gesture. So even though she is "not handy with Greek," she tries three times to pronounce *Papadoupalous*, and Nick is satisfied.

For Monty Harrick, the problem of identity is even greater than it is for Jasper. He must not only live in the shadows of a legendary father and a well-known older brother; he must also resist two versions of the public consensus: to the town generally that he is not even a chip like Jasper, and to the Binghams, old blocks and chips notwithstanding, that he is still a hillbilly. Monty's maneuver is to seize upon the epithet *hillbilly* and force Jo-Lea to repeat it, as if an aggressive, willed iteration will somehow substantiate his reality and transform an epithet of alienation into one of acceptance and union.

Monty's search for an identity that will satisfy both his private and public needs is paralleled by Jo-Lea's insistence that she and her father are separate identities. She can use the phrase "I'm me" with repeated firmness and act upon it, whereas Monty qualifies the phrase for himself with "I don't know who I am." He remembers Jasper's assurance (rather, he interprets it)—"that trick of being himself so completely"—and then falls into the self-pitying depression of a younger brother because he "couldn't even be himself, whatever that was" (C, 19).

Jo-Lea's success and Monty's momentary failure in "naming" an identity are similar to Goldie Goldstein's success and Isaac Sumpter's failure. Goldie can say firmly to Isaac, " 'I want you because you are you' " (C, 113), but Isaac, who carries the burden of ill-defined identity, can respond only with indecision. Like Monty to Jo-Lea, he confesses to Goldie that he does not even have a sure identity to give her. And of all the characters in *The Cave*, Isaac is the one who is most concerned about his name. Even before his embarrassment at being taken for a Jew in college (Goldie is the first to call him "Ikey"), his concern is more deepseated. He has an obsessive fear that he was named Isaac to be sacrificed. "Personally, I don't think you'd be up to it," he taunts his father. "Assuming that you really heard the voice of God putting the bee on you, would you really cut my throat?" (C, 96–97). All his moments of regret, however, when he wishes he were someone else, are offset by his dreams of glory, of seeing his by-line over a sensational story that he partly creates. He becomes, finally, shoddily, what he fears—the stereotyped Jew. His exploratory gestures before the mirror are a psychological rehearsal for his role as media entrepreneur, the man in charge of production of his commercial show, The Search for Jasper Harrick:

> Isaac Sumpter drew himself up to his height, which was five feet, nine inches, straightened his good shoulders, curled his lip with the sardonic incisiveness, and with a tone that seemed to say that now he had, indeed, discovered all, said: "Isaac Sumpter."
> Then added, in a conniving whisper, with the pitying smile into the glass: "Ikey—Little Ikey."

> He shrugged, dropped his hands, palms outward, in a parody of
> the classic gesture of the Jew's resignation and irony and repeated,
> in the accent of the stage Jew: "Ikey—Little Ikey." (C, 99–100)

The opportunity at the cave gone, Isaac flees to New York, fulfilling
himself at last not in other individuals (an obviously inadequate formula in itself) and not even in a stereotype, but in his particular image
of a stereotype. He breathes life into a copy of a copy of his identity.
The vision of himself in the mirror is transferred to his mind as the
defining name and epithet by which he will complete his search for
identity. In a chillingly appropriate way, Isaac's search is successful.[14]

Monty's success in establishing a clear identity is of a different order.
The words of Jasper should provide the principal impulse toward self-
identity for the other characters, but since his few speeches are reported
from at least two removes—and deliberately faked as well—their importance is diluted by charges, countercharges, and recriminations. Warren's scheme, using an almost noncharacter—long on symbolic ramifi-
cations and short on realistic life—is a bold and imaginative one in the
contextual drama of *The Cave*; but it is also troublesome. The figure
of Jasper, in his absence and thinned-out abstractness, becomes less
convincing for the reader, perhaps, than for the other characters, whose
full-bodied response may strike us as slightly disproportionate to Jasper
as stimulus. Credibility—and thus dramatic force—is strained, replaced
by a symbolic figure of impressive dimensions, a mythic, though perhaps tawdry, hero capable of legend.

The task of verbally creating the symbol of transformation finally
falls to Monty, who in his improvised ballad sings both for and about
Jasper. Chapter VI is essentially Monty's; here, for the first time, the
guitar becomes the explicit vehicle for the gift of song, the talisman
of creativity. Standing in new boots that are catalogue duplicates of
Jasper's, Monty takes the initiative by stationing himself at the cave
mouth; soon encouragement comes flowing from the bystanders, some
of whom had previously been friendly, some hostile or indifferent, some
merely curious. As he dignifies his brother in song, he simultaneously
forges his own identity, an independent one that harmonizes both his
separateness from and his continuity with Jasper's. The conclusion of
this chapter is a kind of premature Orphean triumph in which the entire assembly rises to sing the stanzas that Monty has just created.

Names and epithets, then, enriching or diluting one's sense of self,
become significant indexes for several of these searchers. For many of
them, identity resides only tentatively, even uncomfortably, in the name.
The restaurant owner must be satisfied to be identified more by his

yellow Cadillac than by his name; his wife must answer to many ersatz identities required by both herself and Nick (*plain* Sarah Pumfret, *artiste* Giselle Fontaine, *fantasy* Jean Harlow, *tubercular* Mrs. Pappy); Dorothy Cutlick can assign no more meaning to her own name than she can to the Latin declensions which she repeats silently during her dutiful sexual sessions with Nick ("a person's name is not a good enough name for the ache a person is"); Jasper Harrick, vital as he is, struggles to retrieve an identity from the community's fiat that declares him the shadow of his father ("a chip off the old block"); and even the old blacksmith himself remembers the uncertain reality of the tribute paid to him in Johntown's legends for the identity he prizes ("old heller of high coves and hoot-owl hollows") since to Celia he is not Jack Harrick but John T., and since he himself doubts "who Jack Harrick was, or if Jack Harrick had ever existed."

Words, whether used to cloak or to reveal, place their users in the position of declaring themselves; and when motives are made manifest, they stand as a defining trait of the characters who manifest them. The insistence on exploring names or epithets (most dramatically in the cases of Monty and Isaac) is the verbal gesture that particularizes the individual search for identity: the public correlative of a private need. But more: in Warren's dramas of confrontation, when the self seeks to focus more sharply its own blurred identity, words are not the only vehicle for this special communication. There is also the language of hands, the physical acknowledgment of the human need to know and to be known. The touch of a hand—or even the perfunctory hand-shake—possesses a certain residual value as a timeless symbol for human communion. In Warren's novels, such a touch functions literally— as physical gestures must in any novel. But Warren extends the literal gesture to its traditional symbolic function and then rings his own changes on that: the human touch may herald the visible need for that communion, the fear of it, or the doubt that communion is even possible. Its function is simultaneously literal and symbolic.

If entrapment in *The Cave* is the central metaphor for the difficulties of establishing personal identity, the human touch becomes the central metaphor for exploring the struggle to release, enrich, or redefine that identity. It can particularize a universal feeling of what might be called secular sacramentalism, the notion (more instinctive than rational) that not only one's health but also one's salvation depends on a right relationship with his fellows. It can also be used to pervert that notion and serve selfish purposes; even then, however, it reminds its user of what he should know at all times: that communion is possible but difficult. Touch symbolizes the greatest corporate virtue—human communion—but the rich, diverse, and complicated motives for touch dramatize the difficulty of that virtue.

Of all the characters who place importance on touch, Celia Harrick is consistently defined by that gesture. She sees the touch of the hand as necessary for herself, to complete herself within the entire spectrum of humanity. She must declare herself a part of the weakness of being human, and she offers her own weakness as a test for others who would share their strengths. She knows that touch is contaminating, but she senses that it is also regenerative.

The love and devotion she feels for her husband are accompanied and undercut by a sympathy for his weakness, a flaw magnified by disease. Since Jack Harrick's image of himself—as hillbilly rouster—has never included the intimation of weakness, he is the type (so Celia reasons) who "does not know that he has a cracking point." She prays that she may be the one to hold his hand when he does uncover that human flaw in himself. But her reiterated whisper, "I want to hold his hand," is something more than spiritual prayer. Verging also on the memory of sexual desire, it reminds her of her own weakness, her own "breaking point" in succumbing to the sensuality of Jack Harrick; and the memory at one time causes her to bite the flesh on her arm and at another to press closer in the arms of Nick Papadoupalous.

In moments of accusation, she blames Jack Harrick not so much for the blatant vulgarity of his heller role as for establishing the standards whereby Jasper, fulfilling expectations, becomes successively a favorite of the Johntown women, a hero in Korea, and an obsessive caver. She condemns the social pressure from the town which has forced Jasper to respond appropriately to the nudgings and chuckles over "old Jack's boy." And she remembers the touching: "They would put their hands on him—that awful old drunk Mr. Duckett, he put his hands on him" (C, 297). Celia assigns this leering, winking, joking relationship as the reason for Jasper's caving—"To get away from the hands on him." At the same time she feels that she has failed Jasper precisely because she did not reach out her hand and touch him: "If only she had touched him. If only she had been able to reach out and touch him, then everything might have been different" (C, 241).

The difference here is not merely the difference between the reactions of the wife and the mother. There is a kind of maternal protectiveness about Celia, to be sure, but her desire to touch Jasper is essentially the same as her desire to hold old Jack's hand; it comes from a simultaneous perception of weakness—justifiable or not—and an impulse to ally her own weakness with what Nick observes as "the humanness" of these situations. In an early chapter, when the blacksmith suddenly drops to his knees with a near-incoherent proposal, the "heller of high coves" succumbs to the stereotyped humble lover in need of encouragement from his lady. When the war hero and carbon-copy heller suddenly turns serious, when his pinched and quiet face looks as if he might cry out in anguish, he communicates the need for touch even without words. In the first case, Celia responds with a hand in the lover's hair. In the second, she is unable to put out her hand to touch her son. This at least is Celia's point of view. The failure of the gesture toward her son accounts in part for the intensity with which she repeats that gesture toward her helpless husband in his wheelchair. As they sit waiting in front of the cave, she crouches beside Jack Harrick's wheelchair, "one hand on the old man's right knee, supporting herself, comforting him, in that contact defining their oneness in the moment of sad expectancy and tremulous hope" (C, 208). Touch, then, goes out not only in response to human weakness, but also as the manifestation of human weakness itself. The need is to be comforted as well as to comfort another: *This is my life, the woman was thinking. I can live it if he puts his hand on my head.* He laid his hand on her head. She had been staring toward the cave mouth and that touch on her head was a complete surprise. The tears were suddenly swimming in her eyes" (C, 208).

The aura about Celia extends to others. And as she becomes the focus for a kind of sacramental impulse, the touchstone that reveals human need in all its manifestations, so Warren tactically transforms the gesture of touch into a metaphor that extends radially throughout the narrative. *The Cave* is laced with hands that touch or fail to touch. As a technique, this gesture functions both literally and symbolically; and, diffused as it is among many characters and episodes, it is most successful in establishing coherence of theme. Warren begins with a commonplace, the most obvious physical act in the social world, and ends with an aesthetic device that, through parallels, repetitions, and variations, makes a profound statement on man in a chaotic world of competing realities.

It is finally only Jack Harrick who can achieve a satisfactory reciprocity with Celia, and this can come only with his regeneration. Significantly enough, the closing scenes are sustained by a series of gestures of touching, where ambiguity is resolved in mutual recognition of human inadequacies. Old Jack Harrick reminds Jo-Lea that Monty, in the cave, "will hold his Big Brother's hand, and tell him good-bye."

He asks her to spend the night at his house with Celia "and hold her hand." Since Jo-Lea is pregnant with Monty's child, this invitation marks the strengthening of a family relationship that has been strained for many years. Finally, once alone, Jack sings as he strums the guitar:

> "He is lying under the land,
> But I know he'll understand.
> He is lying under the stone,
> But he will not lie alone—
> I'm coming, son, I'm coming, take your Pappy's hand."   (C, 402)

And when Celia comes to him, he lays "his hand on her head, not the weight of it, just lightly." The respect for mutual weakness engenders its own strength: the strength of acceptance without despair.

"The cost of awareness and the difficulty of virtue": in acting out the truth of that rubric, the Harricks achieve more satisfactory identities at the end of their ordeal than those they have at the beginning. If Celia, Jack, Monty, and Jo-Lea show some success after great struggle, the resolution of the Sumpters' dilemma is more bracing. Bereft at last of his own moral compromises, Brother Sumpter achieves a grim stoic dignity; his son hurtles toward his own fulfillment with expedient single-mindedness. From old Sumpter's point of view, the entire struggle to save Harrick's son is merely an elaborate drama, divinely ordained and staged, to save *his* son Isaac. It is not clear whether Sumpter believes he is acting out a figural Abraham role or not, but Isaac accuses him of it even before the incident occurs, and Sumpter says to himself: "*He is my son, and he is beautiful, and God will give him back to me*" (C, 190). And, in an almost stuporlike voice, he says to Celia and Jack Harrick: "It is my son who will be saved" (C, 206). But to whatever degree he is conscious of his role, the drama does offer a testing of both father and son. Isaac has accused his father of not having the courage to kill him as a sacrifice in response to God's command and has speculated, half-seriously, that "Little Ikey is the one better pray hard" for a substitute sacrifice. He taunts his father with the possibility that there "might be a snafu in the celestial bureaucracy and somebody might not deliver that miraculous ram in time to save bloody little miraculous Isaac's little neck" (C, 97). Isaac gets his chance for salvation when Jasper in the cave becomes the substitute sacrificial ram. But if this is a miracle, Isaac never recognizes it. In manipulating the occasion for his own material advantage, he further alienates himself from the human communion.

Isaac's failure compels his father to go into the cave, to act not out of, but against, his own faith and morality to save Isaac: he lies and rearranges the evidence in the cave to substantiate Isaac's lie. After his father emerges from the cave with the report that Jasper is dead, Isaac reaches out his hand to touch his father's arm: "The old man looked down at the demanding hand. Then, effortlessly, he reached his own free hand around, lifted his son's touch from him, meeting no resistance, and without a word . . . rose into the open air beyond" (C, 334). There is more than a reversal of roles here. The old man does not sacrifice himself for his son. Out of an overwhelming love for Isaac, he sins against the very God in whose name he preaches; he chooses human loyalty over divine loyalty, and in that act tastes the bitterness of human weakness more strongly than ever before. In the horror of his own act, however, he cannot yet show his solidarity with human weakness, and he shrinks from the touch of it, even when it comes from his own flesh. The love of his son cannot free him from the guilt he feels. Isaac's sin is less than his own, and Old Sumpter feels that all other people, even with their imperfections, are superior to himself. When Nick tries to support him at the cave mouth, he jerks away, yelling, "Don't touch me! . . . I am not worthy . . . of your touch!" (C, 349). And in the moment when he confronts old Jack, he asks him not to shake his hand but to spit on him.

That confession to Jack Harrick in turn stimulates old Jack's confession that he actually wanted to love his son. And that confrontation paves the way for the regeneration of both men. Paradoxically, through his perception of weakness, when he recognizes his involvement in the human condition, Sumpter is better able to purge himself of spiritual pride and to attain a strength previously unknown to him. His sympathy for weakness can now gain for him a strength that will lead to his salvation. That sympathy, on the other hand, has only confirmed Isaac's scorn for weakness, including his own, and fostered an attitude that will lead him to refine the means for using human weakness and to remove himself further from any hopes of salvation.

Warren attempts to solve a built-in narrative problem in *The Cave*— the dispersion of dramatic force—by a conceptual shorthand. Sacrificing a dominating protagonist for the first time, he relies on multiple protagonists and a host of minor characters, a technical choice more crucial than it first appears to be. Because dramatic power is diminished, "rich meaning" is forced to take up the slack. All of the characters share in varying degrees the common search for self-identity; thus, the proliferating of both verbal and physical gestures: they serve to externalize individual dilemmas in accommodating private and public needs.

In this sense gesture is not a new device in *The Cave*. As a novelist whose gifts have included both a keen sense of the concrete detail and a philosophical urge toward the universal statement, Warren has always experimented with techniques that will reconcile both. His customary tactic has been to give circumstantial fullness to the individual character who, however much he shares in the strengths and weaknesses of the human community, emerges as an independent creature worthy of having a story told about him; such a character, while a part of the realistic-naturalistic machinery of the narrative, can also assume certain typical postures of his species. He can, in short, be a reasonable imitation of a man and still come to serve as a viable symbol of Man.

In none of his other novels does Warren rely so heavily or so consistently on naked artifice to objectify personal response to moral challenges brought about by man's constant nature working itself out within necessary human contexts. On this matter and in this manner, Warren lavishes most of his talents, and though his particular interests do not give this novel the anchored-down circumstantiality usually found in his fictive world, they do go far in making *The Cave* a durable novel with its own impressive scaffolding. His given requires and receives from the reader not natural identification with the things and peoples of a "natural" place, but an astonished and compassionate confirmation that psychic truths still coil and recoil in a natural world that has been imaginatively shattered and reassembled as obvious artifice.

The familiar search for the true self continues, but in *The Cave* Warren is even more insistent that the true self lies in a mysterious but real concern for the nonself. Fathers must come to terms with sons and sons with fathers; women with their men's adulteries and men with their women's compromises; brothers with their brothers' achievements and failures. In the shared commonality of weakness and imperfection lie strength and perhaps even regeneration.

XV. *Buried Lives and Acts of Recovery*
Flood *and* Meet Me in the Green Glen

1.

We know from Jack Burden's chronicle that the making of choices is necessary if one is to wrest control of a life devoid of purpose. And we know too that a long and agonized progress toward regeneration is possible because Jack Burden is a man who at least plays out a role until he recognizes its inadequacy, at which time he finds another. Making choices is a more difficult task for Brad Tolliver of *Flood* because he has *no* real role to play. Our introduction to him, in the frustrated gamesmanship he plays with Jingle Bells, establishes a dominant image of fakery, ersatz identities, and the use of stage properties for carrying the burden of the self.

Indeed, the opening of *Flood* not only introduces this central dilemma to which subsequent event, character, and image will return; in its disposition of characters, its sense of local scenic detail magnified as in a still life, its heavily condensed and symbolic action, and its manipulation of rhetoric and personae by a master consciousness, it also illustrates one kind of translucence that marks Warren's later fiction. Less mannered and more conventionally narrational than the opening of *The Cave*, the first chapter of *Flood* nevertheless shows a conscious and delicate adjustment of the ordinary properties of mimetic fiction to the rhetorical demands of fable and apologue.

On the road to Nashville, familiar from his past, Brad Tolliver approaches a limestone bluff crowned by cedars. This literal space bears a talismanic significance, though the meaning itself is withheld. The spot is still recognizable, even though some of the natural features have disappeared in the intervening years. What is more troubling to him, however, is what has been added: decorative cement objects advertising a nearby motel. The creek now flows in its channel through man-made banks of stones mortised in earth, and the water flows around cement water lilies, cement frogs, and a cement dwarf perched on a boulder fishing with a real line: "Bradwell Tolliver wished that the water did not look real. What worried you was to find something real in the middle of all the faking. It worried you, because if everything is fake then nothing matters" (F, 4). The narrative voice goes on to lay out a virtual anatomy of fakery: the sleaziness of the Seven Dwarfs Motel is matched by the ostentation of the protagonist's white Jaguar; the synthetic fairytale world of Happy Dell is momentarily invaded by the return of a native who no longer can be sure of his flashy success in an automobile whose very name has come to stand more for the power of the huckster than that of the world of natural force from which it is appropriated. The fake setting, which almost obscures the real creek, is spatially dominated by fake characters whose external appurtenances almost obscure their identities.

At the gasoline pump, the Negro who mutters "Yassuh" and "Boss" and wears a jester's outfit is really a sophisticated black student from Chicago who parodies the Southern Darky (that older image which was itself one guise for accommodating the true self). In their brief meeting here, both Tolliver and Jingle Bells enact a little ritual of non-communication—mock ingenuousness and expediency on the one side and condescension and guilt on the other. The bumbling emotions of Tolliver are not clarified by his dollar tip to Jingle Bells, who grins as the Jaguar speeds away: "He wondered what had made Mac lay on that fake Southern accent. Hell, the Jag even had California plates. Who did Mac think he was kidding, try to be so God-damned Confederate?" Paradoxically, Jingle Bells's very misapprehension, his blurred misreading of the physical evidence, is the carrier of truth, the author's first important emblematic statement about this Hollywooden Tennessean whose central problem of identity, while unknown to the gas attendant, has already been framed in a translucent episode.

What is pointed about this narrative opening is not its specifically symbolic function or the use of foreshadowing as a technique, but the baldness with which the scene is presented, the frank directness of the author's own interests, and the near lack of concern for the mediation of certain conventional requirements of realistic fiction, especially mimetic credibility of character. In his earlier work, Warren depicts uncommon spiritual debility through common fictive techniques. We follow Slim Sarrett's story, demonstrating the psychic perversions of the modern alienated intellectual, with a certain expectant familiarity derived from the entire literature of modernism, and Isaac Sumpter's story, displaying those same perversions actively willed, with the fascinated horror we once reserved for gothic fiction. Warren's techniques for rendering Brad Tolliver are neither fully realistic nor fully stylized. We follow his story, incorporating elements of mid-passage crisis drawn freely from both the spiritual autobiography and the secular case study, with a sense of poignance especially suited for "A Romance of Our Time."

Tolliver is more complex than either of these earlier characters. Awash in a drift simultaneously moral, psychological, and professional, he is intellectual enough to evaluate his condition and articulate enough to use his considerable talents (screenwriter, raconteur, worldly sophisticate) to stave off the kind of definitive acts to which the logic of despair might otherwise lead. He looks fitfully for something better than the succession of ragtag roles that never quite satisfy his sense of self. If Fledgling Artist was his one true achievement, the easy corruption of consciousness has long since routed it. What is left is an embarrassing past clogged with unfinished missions and failed relationships: playing Committed Soldier in Spain, Living Well to revenge such models as the Gerald Murphys and the Scott Fitzgeralds, becoming Master Screenwriter. Fiddlersburg turns out to be world enough and Yasha Jones's project proves time enough for Tolliver to reassess that past. His compulsive reliving of anguished moments shows that though he is afflicted by a corrupted consciousness, nothing from that past has been lost; and his task is to show himself what is left, what demonstrations of error, what fragments of truth, can be retrieved to shape a coherent and morally meaningful life.

As Warren's narrative shows, that task is just as difficult for Brad Tolliver as it is for Jack Burden or Jeremiah Beaumont or Amantha Starr. If these earlier protagonists find momentary surcease in historical determinism or romantic idealism, Tolliver finds his in surreptitious dreams of radical freedom, a state that would deny a misspent past, those messy reminders of commitments unmade, deeds undone, and wrong roads taken that constantly threaten to engulf his present. His recourse from such pressures is to recapitulate that regressive gesture which earlier defined his father: flight back to the swamp, a return to the innocence of pure creaturehood.

The figure who represents this primitive state is Frog-Eye, a swamp-rat who could be one of the descendants of La Grand' Bosse but who represents for Tolliver rare human freedom, the incarnation of Independent Man. Intellectually he minimizes such a construction of both Frog-Eye and his father, who had come "boiling out" of the swamp, by the flourishes of his customary irony; emotionally, however, he is prey to those urges, some of them romantically primitivistic, some merely escapist. His acts, if not his words, testify to a temperament that associates the swamp with freedom. With his knowledge of both the American character and the American past, Warren knows better than his protagonist of the dangers lying at the heart of such sentimentality. Tolliver's escapes to the swamp recall the postlude of *World Enough and Time*, another "romantic novel" in which Warren decisively explodes the nineteenth-century belief in the benevolence of nature and the temptation to equate frontier wilderness with human innocence.

Like almost everybody else for the past half-century, Warren sees the painful irony implicit in the way our most exemplary fictional creation, Huck Finn, has come to be symbolic of American innocence. Mark Twain's gloss on the genesis of *Adventures of Huckleberry Finn* contributes as much to this association as our reading of the novel itself. The dominant trait of Tom Blankenship, the son of the town drunkard and model for Huck, was, as Mark Twain remembered, his nearly perfect freedom: "His liberties were totally unrestricted. He was the only really independent person—boy or man—in the community, and by consequence he was tranquilly and continually happy, and was envied by all the rest of us."[15] Tom Blankenship was a boy; but Tolliver is a man. When his protagonist envies the freedom of Frog-Eye, Warren makes it clear that mindlessness, quiet rapacity, and animalistic indolence are not virtues but are themselves the consequences of "natural" man whose liberties are "totally unrestricted." To envy them is to make human freedom meaningless. Discouraged by the thought that "you are you in Fiddlersburg," Tolliver yearns to be "any nigger," with "the simplicity of purpose, the integrity of life, the purity of heart, even if that purity was the purity of hate." Frog-Eye is not "any nigger," but Tolliver's escape to the swamp to join him in "freedom" is a psychological dodge to keep him away from the complexities of the self. To sink into "the blank cup of nature," as Beaumont does in *World Enough and Time*, is to close out the difficult but necessary choices which being adult entails.

As Warren uses those moments in the narrative, the image of the flight to the swamp suggests both the despair of an inadequate selfhood (Brad) and the suffocation of the self by the community through which it is defined (Brad's father). If the world was too much with his father, the self is too much for Brad; taken together, these dilemmas constitute the arena in which choices other than escapist must be made if individual regeneration is to come. Just as Tolliver's life, though shopworn, is still capable of a satisfying restoration, so is the town he scorns.

The reality of this place is not so much a pastoral image of a soon-to-be-lost world, in which man and nature once existed in harmonious relationship, as it is a representational image of community. The people of Fiddlersburg are in large what Brad Tolliver is in small—not notably better adjusted to either nature or each other than people individually and collectively elsewhere. In one of the last scenes Tolliver muses on his old mentor, Izzie Goldfarb, and imagines him in his unmarked plot in the graveyard "waiting for the waters that would come over him and over all the nameless ones who had lived in this place and done good and done evil." Of all the citizens about him, in fact, it is only Goldfarb who is authorially awarded the assurance of having lived an unburied life. He is an outsider imposing a perspective on Fiddlersburg that allows him to be both a part of the community and separate from it, to view his responsibility to history in the light of present need. He is untrapped by time or place, and Tolliver comes finally to understand what Goldfarb always knew: that history is necessarily an unclear mixture of good and evil because human beings are constituted of both. With that realization—a simplistic one, given Tolliver's intellect—comes also the realization that he no longer needs to exhume the old Jew's body and that he no longer needs to think of himself as a displaced person. The historical Fiddlersburg is not boundaried in geographical space: *"There is no country but the heart."*

What Warren as presiding consciousness achieves in the last chapter of *Flood*, however, an abstract truth that resolves the parryings of moral issues on a transcendent level, is not quite achieved by Tolliver, whose sensibility is not only slightly distanced from the narrating voice but also stubbornly resistant to its instinctive gestures toward narrational resolution. Tolliver is only tentatively poised to enter into that regenerating state that, like that of Brother Potts, can pronounce all things blessed.[16] His psychological lacerations will require longer to heal than the bullet wound from Calvin Fiddler's gun. Because they are accretions of a lifetime, his self-inflicted injuries cannot suddenly vanish in a single self-sacrificing act; indeed, the sneaking tendency to contemplate that act as heroic becomes for him, like all his other deeds both good and bad, "the grimace and tic and pose and gesture" of a crazy man who wants to call them "something else." One significant clue to the extraordinary slowness with which Tolliver is brought into line with the transcendent insight of the narrating voice lies in the conceptual links between Goldfarb and Fiddler.

Tolliver only dimly perceives the connection between his nagging drive to locate old Goldfarb's grave and his decision, finally overcoming a long resistance, to visit Cal Fiddler in prison. The use of both is synecdochic in Warren's development of the theme of regeneration and reclamation.[17] As formalized space, graveyard and penitentiary are places of incarceration necessary for and sanctioned by a human society; specifically they are cultural institutions that coalesce the range and variety of both past and present and incorporate the ineradicable nature of human experience: love, jealousy, crime, guilt, punishment, penitence. Both graveyard and prison are repositories of buried lives, but both Izzie Goldfarb and Cal Fiddler demonstrate, the first instinctively and the second through experienced grief, some of the ways that the commonness of ordinary life can be irradiated. Goldfarb's disinterested love and Fiddler's scientific charity are two instances of how all Fiddlersburg, tawdry and forgettable, is yet redeemable.

Although he willingly assigns the old Jew a unique role in the life of the town—a wisdom figure, necessarily alone, who preserves his integrity of self—Tolliver wants to use him egoistically; to find the grave and to relocate the body in the new town would be to find and relocate himself without the stain of a past which he is unable to reassemble in any coherent way. But the price of resurrection is death —coming to terms with that past, acknowledging responsibility for its shame as eagerly as taking credit for its glory—which is to say the death of the old self, after which reclamation is possible. If as model Goldfarb is now mute, Cal Fiddler is finally garrulous in spelling out to an ambivalent visitor just what kinds of reclamation are possible for one who has settled for "the grimace and tic and pose and gesture" as substitutes for the self. Like Tolliver, Fiddler for most of his racked life is profoundly and desolately alienated, and his own spiritual state calls forth some of the same escapist responses to make the alienation bearable. In the end, however, Dr. Calvin Fiddler through choice and by dint of resolution after great agony finds himself just as capable of disinterested love as Izzie Goldfarb with his seeming effortlessness; the distinction Tolliver makes in his summary of Goldfarb—he was alone but he was never lonesome—is applicable to Fiddler too after his reclamation.

After their first visit to the penitentiary, Tolliver remarks to Yasha Jones: "The only reason everybody in Fiddlersburg does not get himself in the pen out of lonesomeness is because Fiddlersburg is a kind of pen already, and everybody knows already he is with folks who are as lonesome as he is." Although this little disquisition on the Fiddlersburg lonesomeness is a cultural indictment which primarily reflects a personal malady, Tolliver's characterization is generally persuasive because it is supported by what we superficially know of the varied lives of Blanding Cottshill, Leontine Purtle, Maggie, Mother Fiddler, even Brother Potts. Spurred on by his inventive wit and relishing his own heavy irony, Tolliver continues:

> "Hell, the whole South is lonesome. . . . Hell, the South is the country where a man gets drunk just so he can feel even lonesomer and then comes to town and picks a fight for companionship. The Confederate States were founded on lonesomeness. They were all so lonesome they built a pen around themselves so they could be lonesome together. The only reason the Confederate army held together as long as it did against overwhelming odds was that everybody felt that it would just be too damned lonesome to go home and be lonesome by yourself." (F, 165–66)

This waggish dilation is merely one of several passages in *Flood* that skillfully dramatize the daylight sensibility of Tolliver—bemused and wryly contemptuous—but it also provides an implicitly larger context for extending the logic of Warren's characterization. If a village, even a region, suffers from some common limitation, it should be clear to a man of Tolliver's gifts that the single-minded concern for one's own dilemma is finally self-defeating; even the Confederate soldiers did go home, and if they were destined to be lonesome by themselves, they also were able to gather up the pieces of their broken lives and assume their places in familial and social relationships. If, as Tolliver says, "you are you in Fiddlersburg," then many other townspeople could make the same despairing cry—and some, in their varied ways, do just that.

Maggie admits that events involving her are terrible not because of rape and violence per se but because they modify her sense of who she is: "you don't know any center of *you* any more, you don't feel *you* any more, and you are sick because everything is sliding out of focus, out of equilibrium, as when those canals go wrong in your ears." With that impairment goes the difficulty of resuming ordinary activities, for how, she reasons, "can you live if there is no *you* to do the living?" What Lettice tells Maggie is what both Maggie and her brother must eventually learn: "you have to make your *you* out of all that sliding and brokenness of things." The ideal forms of the self are simply not available in a world which is itself imperfect. Out of only what is called variously "the crazy tied-togetherness of things," "the tangle of things," "some spooky interpenetration of things," can a self emerge. And in their final interview, Cal Fiddler tells Tolliver of a similar insight that comes at last to him, "that there is no *you* except in relation to all that unthinkableness that the world is."

Although there are moments when Tolliver senses the potential health-giving aspects of the "tangle of things," not until the very end of his troubled search does he make the leap into an appreciation of what this general wail must mean: that only love detached from its purely selfish object can provide true spiritual relocation. Maggie and Yasha Jones's harmonious union is one way; Brother Potts's and Lettice's commitment to the service of others is another. Tolliver's ambivalent return to Fiddlersburg signifies a need for restoration. Trying to capture the uniqueness of his hometown after many years, to forge some artifact available to all who would see Yasha Jones's film, may satisfy the artist in him, but the more compelling motive is personal, to purge his fear that his self, like most of his art, is fake. The mere return to Fiddlersburg does not release him from his egoistic self-burial: "*I can make,*" he says, "*no connection between what I was and what I am.*" He despairs, for even though he works conscientiously, "nothing connects." His work, like his life, resembles his file folders on Fiddlersburg: notes, observations, fragments. Even when he shifts his working schedule as a scriptwriter, to return unconsciously to "the old Darthurst schedule" that produced his only art he can take seriously, such tattered attempts still fail to cohere because his spiritual state remains unfocused.

As Yasha Jones knows, the uniqueness of Fiddlersburg paradoxically lies in the commonness of its human needs and deeds, but for the floundering writer that averageness seems only paltry and pathetic, a succession of lives already buried and imaginations already drowned. The professional need to reacquaint himself with the life of Fiddlersburg, ostensibly to catch what the director calls the "depth and shimmer" of the doomed town, immerses Tolliver instead in replays of his own past in which, despite bright, even lurid surfaces, the depths are too murky for the light that would show him its meaning. Armed with a formidable irony, he can see only the shoddy and the meretricious in Fiddlersburg or its people—a perspective that insures the inappropriateness of a melodramatic and cliché-ridden script as a guide for the "beautiful motion picture" that Yasha Jones wants to make;

the very document is the "evidence" by which Fiddlersburg "will be convicted of the crime of having existed. When soon oblivion's deepening veil hides Baptist Church, poolroom, and the You'll Never Regret It Café, my little dossiers will insure conviction" (F, 101). This unacceptable script will also condemn the writer to another term of moral drift that constitutes his existence.

In the midst of friends and kin who manage their reclamation with great effort, Tolliver and Cottshill stand apart as, in the lawyer's words, "stateless persons" and "DPs for eternity and thence forward." Indicative of Tolliver's slow crawl to awareness is the almost prurient fascination he shows for the Seven Dwarfs Motel throughout his stay in Fiddlersburg and the evasions he practices and the aversions he betrays for the prison. But though he resists the connection, his creator does not.

The shabby motel clinging to the mortised creek banks anticipates that more visible symbol of human frailty, the prison, presiding over the obliterating waters. This looming scenic symbol, the place of penitence, houses Cal Fiddler, literally incarcerated there, performing the deeds and thinking the thoughts necessary for personal reclamation. Both insider Maggie, in her familial function of caring for Mother Fiddler, and outsider Yasha Jones, in his efforts to document his vision according to a perception of sympathy for the human fallibility he shares with Maggie, enact their own revival in the shadow of the penitentiary. And though her penitence is worked out far beyond the boundaries of Fiddlersburg, Lettice Poindexter, "goosed by God" into becoming a self-sacrificing nun, has not been untouched by the shadow of the prison. That institution, defining the very landscape, is a symbol in precisely the way Warren has described the characteristics of the symbol: "focal, massive, and not arbitrary" (SE, 220). It is a looming architectural fact in the geography and history of one town in Tennessee—an institution accepted in all its factuality by the citizens of the town, but since it also holds a hometown Fiddler within its walls it also looms as a visible reminder of crime, guilt, and retribution. Thus what is a literal and moral reality for the people of Fiddlersburg becomes both an aesthetic and moral symbol in the gradual unfolding of the narrative. Baptismal redemption, the figurative death by drowning, may offer the chance of a new life on a new basis, but the prison still dominates the buried land. Both the "moderne" Happy Dell and the massive prison throughout *Flood* are artifacts proclaiming man's continuing frailty. It is revealing that Tolliver in his vulgarized screenplay can connect the survival of the motel, but not the prison, to the flooding of the town: "I can see it now," he tells Yasha Jones, "As Fiddlersburg, with its wealth of Southern tradition, unassuming charm, homely virtue, and pellagra, sinks forevermore beneath the wave, the Seven Dwarfs Motel will rise in spray, glimmering like a dream" (F, 38). It is easier for him to assume the persistence of human frailty than the necessity of punishment and penitence. What substantially counters Tolliver's ironic fantasy is the reality of the perdurable prison, not glimmering dreamlike in spray, but clinging stubbornly, defying extravagant hopes that the flood can be all-redeeming without its office.

The promise of rebirth is strong at the conclusion of *Flood*. The soon-to-be-buried town and its human past, selectively translated to a new level, are literally ushered into a future with renewed possibilities of growth through communal ceremonies. Not just the dying Brother Potts, the presiding priest of these ceremonies, but all the celebrants join in affirming new life rather than lamenting the passing of the old. For Brad Tolliver, that means giving up the literal search for the grave of Izzie Goldfarb, for finding it would be an act of empty piety, of a piece with his other misuses of the past.[18] Although he has not repudiated that past as he has so often been tempted to do, his slavish immersion in it, a cynical and aggressive assertiveness of it, has been just as crippling. As Warren puts it elsewhere, "a true understanding of the past involves both an acceptance and a transcendence of the acceptance" (JGW, 58). The flooding of Fiddlersburg is beneficent, and if the townspeople accept that fact earlier than the returned native, it is merely Warren's way of suggesting that the alienated intellectual's effort to come to terms with such truths is more agonizing and prolonged than it is for those less gifted.

2.

To be valid at all, the hyperbolic charge of one reviewer whose primary interest is literature of the theater—that "nothing happens, dramatically" in *Meet Me in the Green Glen*—must be set against the account of another whose primary interest is Romantic poetry: This novel subordinates "narration to representation of evolving states" of consciousness in order to deal with "what it is to come into being *now*."[19] Warren is not what has been confusingly called one of the "post-contemporary" novelists whose articles of aesthetic faith include the destruction of characterization, setting, linear narration, coherent point of view, and consistent structures of images. Like most of his fiction, *Meet Me in the Green Glen* is placed squarely in events that

are inherently violent, even melodramatic: its conclusion, in fact, re-
volves around two of the staples of popular culture, a courtroom murder trial and the eleventh-hour effort to seek clemency from the governor; and an epilogue, bristling with facts and figures, recounts the
eventual fortunes of the main characters. The figures in this novel
experience love, envy, hate, and revenge as in countless other fictions.
Its structure is built upon basic third-person omniscience, and its texture
is spun out from a handful of images related to the oldest of literary
themes—illusion and reality. These conventional ingredients, however,
are not ends in themselves; they mark the point at which Warren begins.

More radically economical than either *The Cave* or *Flood*, *Meet Me
in the Green Glen* is not merely a reprise of the buried life that thematically informs those novels. Into the life of Cassie Killigrew Spottwood, whose dutiful but unloving care of her paralyzed husband has
made her spiritually comatose, comes Angelo Passetto, a Sicilian immigrant fleeing both the world that seeks to punish him and a self that
he is still struggling to define. As Cassie has buried her life in service
to her husband, so by a strenuous exercise of will Angelo buries his
in ritualistic work schedules which he intersperses with fantasized versions of a reality he fears. Although their gradually evolving love, passing through the phases of mere lust and novelty, transforms both their
lives, the price of that transformation is an act of murder.

Earlier figures of priapic energy, old Harrick and old Tolliver, tend
to function at least sporadically as reminders of lives lived viscerally
if not wisely. The inadequacy and poignancy of their unexamined lives,
visually explicit in the images of the disease-wracked Harrick confined
to his wheelchair and the drunk-lonesome Tolliver weeping in the
swamp mud, are in *Meet Me in the Green Glen* elevated to a central
status in the bedridden figure of Sunderland Spottwood. Hate-filled and
helpless, with only the fierce eyes a reminder of his former vitality,
this inert consciousness is a constant frame of reference for others
whose lives are similarly disabled and, paradoxically, the chief activating
source of their action.

Spottwood's very presence supplies the energy by which the other
buried lives may be reclaimed or reinterred. The disintegrating house
with its green glen setting, and the farm sinking slowly back into
vegetative nature, which itself is destined to be claimed by water, constitute another of Warren's submerged worlds in which lovers, "Twin
atolls on a shelf of shade," go through their passion beneath "the layered light." Spottwood is like a mythic deity into whose presence the

alien intruder hesitates to enter and whose being still commands fealty in service and gold. Indeed, Cassie's responsibility for feeding, cleaning, and shaving him continues to have prior claims even after she enters into a liaison with Angelo in the next room; and Murray Guilfort carries his monthly tribute year after year, living all the while "under that amiable contempt" he still sees in the stricken face. When Guilfort sees Spottwood, he sees not a fifty-four-year-old invalid, but "young Sunder—booted, spurred, young, whooping as he rose in the stirrups," galloping down a road in "the sunshine of nearly forty years ago" (MM, 30). Big-footed, big-handed, a man of insolent blue eyes and arrogant masculinity, Sunder is more a legend than a man, a summarizing image of reproach, even after his literal death, draining Guilfort of the fragile new identity he gradually assumes.

Successful and mobile, Guilfort can make only the smallest gestures of vengeance in the presence of Spottwood: rage defused into vague, metaphorical violence—"rapt in the dream of the future and his mystic transformation, his muscles would go tense and strong, his breath would come fast, and there was a deep image and enactment of striking and striking and striking again, in darkness." Sunderland Spottwood lies a ravaged, helpless man. No matter: Guilfort wishes him dead so that nobody can remember an earlier self whom he now seeks "to forget, expunge, bury, or absorb into the man who was now called Murray Guilfort, and to whom people bowed respectfully on the street," but the imagined act cannot finally eliminate the self-contempt: "Then, as distinctly as a voice, the thought was in him: *There are beggars and buyers and stealers and pickers of remnants, and you are among them.* Then: *There are seizers and takers, and you are not among them*" (MM, 146). Ironically, it is only through association with Spottwood, through his courtroom defense of their friendship ("if a man's attempt to be faithful to a friend is a cause for shame and provocation for the obscene leer, then—") that Guilfort seals his new identity—public servant, patron of the town's architectural heritage, Supreme Court justice, cocksman. He is able to garner both public esteem and private envy, the respectful nod and the obscene leer.

If the now-supine Spottwood can still energize the career of Murray Guilfort, his exacting brutality lives on to influence the lovers beneath his roof. For Cassie, what significantly passes from the time of Sunderland's paralytic stroke to his murder is not the dutiful attention to the helpless man for whom she has always extended a rote devotion but her awakening to a love that proves stronger than lust. Unwelcome but unremitting, its power cuts through two buried lives, transcending mere circumstances of marriage and a deadened domesticity to create a passionate, self-sufficient world in the very province of the old. When that created world is threatened, the very center of the old buried world reasserts itself for the last time. If in the dominating presence of Spottwood envy can drive Murray Guilfort to an imagined enactment of murder, frustration over the loss of love drives Cassie to its literal enactment.

The nature of the love between Cassie and her Sicilian partner insures against its being any kind of norm, but its very extremity serves as an enlivening touchstone for the failure of love in three marriages: Murray Guilfort's, Leroy Lancaster's, and Cy Grinder's. Although it is incomplete and ultimately self-destructive, that love stands also for sacrifice and redemption, powerful and self-ratifying values unavailable to those incapable of any kind of creative love. Guilfort comes to his recognition too late as a result of his experience with Angelo and Cassie's tragic passion; to both Lancaster and Grinder come at least understanding of and compassion for their unloved wives as a result of their experience. The most extensively detailed of the radiating influence of Angelo and Cassie's love is negative.

The masking of his envy of Sunderland Spottwood and his love of Cassie by seemingly faithful acts of charity serves as an effective analogue to Murray Guilfort's more general fraudulence: he is never able to perceive the shabby conventionality of his old friend's masculine energy, and the imaginative energy he pours into his love of Cassie prevents his ever recognizing the love his wife feels for him. As much as Cassie's before Angelo's arrival, his life is buried; as much as Sunderland's after his stroke, his vitality has atrophied. A picker of remnants, Murray Guilfort fashions his vicarious life from the scraps available in the green glen, scraps of a love that is more than a little bogus and a friendship that has long ago passed into fear and hate.

Only on his final day the nature of his surrogate life is revealed to him in two successive waves of discovery; both bring anguish. Although it comes too late for any substantial regeneration, that discovery hinges on his ambivalent relationship to both Cassie and Sunderland. In the first wave Murray becomes aware, almost preternaturally, of an alternate kind of energy to that which his stricken friend still represents to him: the joy of ordinary lives being lived in the full present. Driving away from having seen Cassie in the green glen for the last time, angered because she laughs off his confession of love, he notes with special clarity the world of the ordinary, people whose lives are nondescript but whose identities are firm: a woman giving suck to her baby smiles at him, children hanging on a wire fence wave to him, two boys fishing from a bridge lift up faces "pale and pure," an old Negro resting on his hoe grins at him. All these anonymous people living out their lives in apparent fullness of purpose are a reproach to his emptiness, and the experience triggers in him a reassessment of those closer to him—Cassie and her love for Angelo, Bessie and her love for him—whose acceptance of their destinies, based though it may have been on delusion, offers an even more painful reproach. Despite his despair, after taking a fatal number of sleeping capsules, Guilfort realizes the consequences of his act, "and in that instant, like waking to a blaze of light, he knew that he must undo it, he must go back and walk in the world, for that would be enough, that would be bliss, merely to be in a world where people, each walking in his dream, looked at you from within the individual glow, and smiled at you, perhaps waved" (MM, 371).

No one in this novel is exempted from a sense, sometimes fugitive, sometimes reiterant, of living as if in a dream, but Guilfort's is particularly damaging because it not only scorns those "lies" and "fool dreams" of others but also masks its own dreamlike existence with the illusion that only Murray Guilfort knows how the world is hung. Too late he realizes: *"The dream is a lie, but the dreaming is truth"*—which is to say that despite the implicit pathos of shaping the otherwise intractable materials of the world into a construct that answers to one's own private needs, the force of love, the shaping impulse if not the thing shaped, is the glory as well as the despair of the human animal.[20] Bereft of this ability, Guilfort's pathos is greater than that of any other character.

The second wave of his discovery is that Bessie had really loved him: he was beloved and never realized it. His frustrated insight into the stunning power of love available not only to Angelo and Cassie but also to his late wife is an anguished discovery because it has never been available to him. It leads him into a vision of "all the people moving over the land, moving in streets, standing in doorways, lying in the darkness of houses, all in their monstrous delusion." Despite the comprehensive "delusion," the terms are unmistakably those of value, of joy *in being*.

As with Murray Guilfort and Bessie, so it is with Cy Grinder and Gladys: both men, trapped in their old love for Cassie, joined to the aging flesh of unloved wives. But there is a difference. *Meet Me in the Green Glen* ends not with Guilfort's suicide but with Grinder's anguish, an anguish born of reawakened compassion that comes to him in images of light. Grinder is struck by the fact that he had never noticed that the sleeping face of the "heavy and slow-footed" woman who lies beside him is "very much like the face of the little girl who lay in the next room." But both are illuminated by moonlight leaking into the house, and, outside, so is he. For the first time he begins "to wonder" what the woman thinks, how she feels, and his wondering is "mysterious to him." His suffering is a moment of no little significance—for himself and, because of its placement in the novel, for the burden of Warren's theme.[21]

The narrative begins in "splotchy, sliding-down grayness, as though everything, the sky and the world, was being washed away with old dishwater"; it ends with a transfiguring moment: "There was the moon, with the sky, and the whole world, in its light." It is not that the first is reality and that the second is dream. The lethargy of Cassie Spottwood's world is not that different from the busyness of Cy Grinder's: both are purged by love. If the thrust of the narrative shows how the unidentifiable self, afloat in dullness, loneliness, paralysis, can be shaped by an active love, it does not promise that an awakening to full humanity exempts one from the anguish that, along with the joy, is necessarily required "to walk in the world." What Warren elsewhere calls "a new self" is shaped in part by a sense of separation from others, from a world that, though it seems alien, is "there" in all its presentness; and through "continual and intimate interpenetration" of the self and others in "an inevitable osmosis of being" man discovers his "new self."[22]

3.

If for Warren historical moments readily generate object lessons, he is just as alert to the modern instance that will serve the same purpose. The impulse that finds morally instructive raw materials in Beast Butler's New Orleans and in an émigré in New York during the draft riots of 1863 is related to the personal observation that can transform contemporary commonplaces into fully wrought fictions. "At a certain level an idea takes hold," Warren says of his compositional habits. "Now it doesn't necessarily come with a form; it comes as an idea or an impulse" (*Talking*, 258). With our available evidence of how he develops stories, it is not difficult to imagine that the account of how Yasha Jones of Hollywood decides to make a movie about doomed Fiddlersburg is but a slightly transposed version of how Robert Penn Warren of Connecticut comes to write a novel about a little southern town doomed by time and recoverable only through a reclaiming memory and an incarnational imagination. Jones remembers the instant when, over his egg cup, "he had seen the paragraph in a newspaper saying that a little town in Tennessee, dating from pioneer times, would be inundated for a great new dam. He remembered the moment, the excitement, the little skip of the heart, the fleeting sense of disorientation, all so seemingly unrelated to the drab little paragraph" (F, 101).

But Yasha Jones is an outsider, and when he comes to Fiddlersburg he comes with no memories of people there and the patterns of their lives—and, in fact, with few preconceptions. Robert Penn Warren is a benign exile, and when he returns to the South he resees it, reexperiencing the cultural givens of his own land. "I can't be anything else" other than a southern writer, he says. "You are what you are. I was born and grew up in Kentucky, and I think your early images survive" (Talking, 237). Flood and Meet Me in the Green Glen are both written by a southerner whose imagination is instinctively alive to what separates those "early images" and those that assault the returnee, the was becoming is. As he himself remembers their origins, memento mori shapes both works.

The gestation of Flood began as early as 1931 when Warren passed through southwest Tennessee seeing Grant's headquarters near Shiloh and flooded-out areas caused by the building of dams. The germ of Meet Me in the Green Glen came to him while on a hunting trip with his brother in Tennessee, during which they drove up a stream bed in a game preserve in what had once been a prosperous farming valley. "We saw the ruins of a nice house in there, and this sense of a lost world in that valley" suggested the novel.[23] What threatens the significance of the return is, of course, sentimentality, the melancholy sense of inevitable change that reminds the observer of his own. Heavy-handed irony prevents Brad Tolliver from falling into that trap, but it also prevents, until almost too late, his ability to make "connections," to see the meaningful relationship between what he was and what he is. Warren rejects, along with his protagonist, any easy reenactment of "a piece of the past" (Talking, 103); the past may be claimed by memory, even hallowed, but it must also be seen and measured against present needs of not merely the self but all those lives making up the nonself. Brad's last thought is "There is no country but the heart." Warren's comment on Flood both echoes and extends his character's insight: "Ultimately home is not a place, it's a state of spirit, it's a state of feeling, a state of mind, a proper relationship to a world" (Talking, 102).

The once-familiar world, reseen, reexperienced, is capable of supplying Warren "the sense of an image that makes that thing available to you indefinitely, so you can go back to it, can always find that peephole on the other world . . . that moment of contact with . . . reality."[24] The Floyd Collins entrapment of 1925, not far from Nashville when Warren was still a student at Vanderbilt, supplies that "sense of an image" in a fiction written more than thirty years later. Like *The Cave*, *Flood* and *Meet Me in the Green Glen* begin with an image, an idea, grounded in contemporary observation. Behind these novels are sociological facts that for millions of southerners had psychological and cultural consequences; in Warren's hands those facts embody aesthetic and moral significance. Floyd Collins, flooded-out areas, game preserves: these become the peepholes on another world. The drama of the submerged self in these novels has literal reinforcement; and this familiar theme, enacted in the looped and intricate narratives, then metaphorizes the literal through the imagery of caves, depths, caverns, labyrinths, flooding.

If Warren has minimized the difference between his historical and contemporary fictions, one reason is that both are generated by the same urgency; if something from the past is to be useful, it must have "the image of an issue," a "simplified and distant framed image" of an "immediate and contemporary issue, a sort of interplay between that image and the contemporary world" (*Talking*, 129). Except for the specific metaphorical patterns of *World Enough and Time*, Jeremiah Beaumont's story could just as well be called *The Man Below*—the original title of *The Cave*. The submerged self always entails a journey of excavation.

XVI. A Place to Come To: *Notes on a Life to Be Lived*

If most of Warren's earlier fiction assumes the shape of an old, even mythic, fable—the young idealist's fall from a dream of his own ahistorical transcendence into the push and tug of history—most of his later assumes the shape of a gloss on that fable.[25] Why is the dream, Warren asks, not self-sufficient? What does its sour diminishment say about the dreamer? about the disabusing world? The ideal, though not wholly a timeless construct designed to flatter the dreamer's ego, can finally be justified only by submitting it both to Time, which jerks along in splendid indifference to man's most cherished plans, and to that world of human necessity, the context in which man strives, needs, hopes, suffers—and dreams. A weary resignation to destiny, *the way things are*, only intensifies the bitterness left by the shattered ideal and deepens the despair at the discovery that the self is alone. The regeneration of the self is not possible until the acknowledgment of that essential reality of indifferent Time is matched by the perception that the self must be shared, that it must enter into a communion of human need, which is to say a recognition of the common reality of all men.

All of Warren's fiction, as well as much of his other work, seems intended, as it were, to counter Thomas Jefferson's extravagant vision of America as a people "not chosen to fulfill history but a people freed from history."[26] The stormy progress of his protagonists begins when their ideal version of the self and the world they have fashioned fails to be fulfilled in Time. Although she is not the most persuasive, Amantha Starr is perhaps the most programmatic instance of Warren's reiterated narrative: the anguished and unsuccessful attempt to free oneself from history. The truth that finally sets this protagonist free and insures her regeneration is her recognition that *she*, while not fulfilling history, is a part of it. Amantha Starr is not Warren's first protagonist to survive her long agony, but her story is the first to end in joy. The epiphanies of recovery experienced by later characters—Adam Rosenzweig, Brad Tolliver, Cy Grinder—are described in more reserved and tentative terms, but in each case regeneration requires sympathetic identification of the self with the Other.

The bleak prospects of the wandering self are nowhere bleaker than in *A Place to Come To*, the confessional memoir of a university professor whose half-hearted commitment to his profession, perfunctory enough to prevent his story from becoming another academic novel, serves as an index to his tenuous human relationships generally. A successful Dante scholar, Jed Tewksbury is haunted by a past and a place that, though they progressively seem unreal, recur as unpurged memories: of a poor-white, friendless childhood in northern Alabama, of a mother who works in a cannery and who urges him to "git and stay gone," of a father who dies, "still hanging on to his dong," in a drunken fall while "standing up in front of his wagon to piss on the hindquarters" of his mules. Warren's return to a first-person narrative, a congenial point of view that forestalls some of the structural problems in such novels as *The Cave* and *Flood,* is also a nominal return to the form of spiritual autobiography most explicitly explored in *All the King's Men, World Enough and Time,* and *Band of Angels.*[27]

Warren's depiction of the self's cold exile in the world is punctuated by subsidiary and interlocking themes: of the prodigal father and a paternal legacy seen by the son as destructive; of the surrogate father who betrays the son; of the temporary stabilizing of lacerating tensions through marriage, substitutionary bouts of sexual affairs, and the adoption of naturalistic and deterministic philosophies. Jed Tewksbury's sense of exile stems not only from his separation from his old home but also from his failure to find another home, a social matrix in which the self can be nourished. Like that of so many of Warren's characters, Jed's peremptory need is not merely to create a nourishing present but to accept a spotted past as its prerequisite; only through this most difficult process can he be assured of "the blessedness of knowing that men were real, and brothers in their reality." The Other must serve as referent for the separated I. His drama is thus a larger drama of spiritual exile: the American's great obsession is not the much-touted sense of place, but the stumbling search for place.

As Warren has indicated, Jed Tewksbury may be his first major character possessed by a passionate hatred for the South, who is haunted by his southern home. But those kinds of tensions—guilt, shame, residual loyalty, nostalgia—that so prolong Jed's self-definition are some of the same ones that drive Slim Sarrett and Isaac Sumpter to their spiritual doom and that set up discordant urgencies in Jeremiah Beaumont, Hamish Bond, Jasper Harrick, Brad Tolliver, and Cy Grinder. All the images that mean anything in a person's life, says Warren, are formed very early, and images "mean a lot of things besides pictures"—attitudes, for example, that may not (and do not, in Warren's work) conform to the idyllic Agrarian vision of southern man in harmonious unity with his environment.[28] Warren long ago complained that T. S. Stribling, the Tennessee novelist, had never been much interested in "the dramatic possibilities of a superior Southern white man brought into conflict with his native environment."[29] One is reminded, in reading *A Place to Come To*, that these possibilities have always been of interest to Warren. The pattern of return, both literal and imagined, is the most frequent structural device for the protagonist as exile, and that struggle with one's physical home— its values, its lingering capacity to reward and punish, its ability to assert its own numinous identity—is often an aesthetic analogue for that greater struggle for self-definition on which one's very psychic health depends.[30]

1.

A Place to Come To is a virtual anatomy of alienation viewed as the characteristic state of modern man. Most of the characters who affect the life of the narrator, Jediah Tewksbury, are victims of deracination, the spiritual plague of the twentieth century. His Chicago mentor, Dr. Heinrich Stahlmann, a product of "German mission" and *Kultur*, escapes Hitler's regime with his psychically damaged and dying Jewish wife, but guilt for not having returned to Germany—"to claim my patrimony of honor," to offer "the public testimony of my curse upon what my land had become" (PCT, 71)—turns to bitterness; the day he celebrates his new American citizenship is also the day he commits suicide, Jed's physicist friend Stephan Mostoski is a Polish Jew who can proclaim: "I have no country that I recognize as my own, and I am trying to be happy in that condition." Mrs. Jones-Talbot is a restless southerner who for twenty years escapes Nashville for London (and a titled husband) and London for the battle-torn villages of Italy (and an idealistic lover) and finally returns with little sentimentality for the southerner's famous sense of place; thus briskly liberated, she and Jed discuss during one of their Dante sessions the Italian piety for *la terra* against their own implicit lack. They agree that *"patria,"* "earth, soil, place, home, father-land" are all inadequate equivalents to describe the "things that made you what you are and that must be lived by because you are you." Mrs. Jones-Talbot's Italian lover, Jed's wartime compatriots, and Jed's Nazi prisoner, a former classical scholar whom he kills, all are reproaches to these two exiles' own lack of any deep commitment to *la terra.*

A much closer reproach to Jed, as a part of what he calls the "matter of Nashville," is the completeness of life-as-lived, the easy and ful-filling adjustment of self to place, which Jed sees in the Cudworths, friends whose "painful reality of their joy" he cannot face. "The joy sprang from their willed and full embracement of the process of their life in time," he observes, "and I, God help me, was in flight from Time."

Jed flees instinctively to Rozelle, that other exile from Dugton, Alabama, not so much because she is from his hometown but because she shares his own sense of rootlessness, the faith that identities can be made irrelevantly, even in spite of, one's past. Both time and place—Claxford County, Alabama, of their youth—disappear in their sexual alliance, a "steely encapsulating present" that, though they are only vaguely aware of it, is nevertheless forged because of the bruising dis-appointments of that past. In this phase Jed can advance his argument for being, *debatuo ergo sum,* with a naturalistic certainty that the "pressures and slidings of flesh" are the only reality. He takes som-nambulistic pleasure in that reality, a curtain-drawn bedroom world in which Rozelle draws him "unresisting, into the deep, rich slime of being." Likening it to the black hole of the physicists, Jed can recognize the affair as "a devouring negativity into which all the nags and positives of life" momentarily disappear, and in the intensity of this relationship, his professional duties on the campus and his social life in the Carrington set are increasingly performed as "shadowy routine." Jed and Rozelle are more rackingly, if not more profoundly, alienated than all the other exiles in the novel and their fates more poignant because of the reality of the place from which they both come: "Dugton," Jed tells her, "is the rock from which we—you and me both—were riven."

We're just what we are: that simple acceptance that they both utter at various times and in varied ways turns out to be more agonizing and prolonged than the stoic serenity that the words suggest. The Rozelle whom Jed meets in Rome many years after the Nashville ex-perience is a brittle, aging, but still sensual woman whose anger and emptiness culminate in a final, appropriate marriage—to the "Hindu swami" who once read poetry aloud to admiring females at Nashville parties. Now a successful dealer on the international drug market, her husband is really a southern black, not an Indian, whose own alienation consists of playing his own private jokes on southern whites (including marriage to a socialite's widow) and in mastering the use of masks and identities for dealing with the duplicity of the world. Rozelle comes full circle—from a first tycoon husband trying desperately to expunge his shanty Irish origins by surrounding himself with the people and appurtenances of wealth, to a southern patrician slowly disintegrating because a settled life of easy privilege dilutes his sculptor's talent, to a drug entrepreneur whose relishing of deception and adjustment to his own deracination only sporadically require a surreptitious return to nigger-talk and soul food.

Dr. Stahlmann, Motoski, Mrs. Jones-Talbot, Rozelle and two of her three husbands: all work out their own adjustments to the existential fact of exile. If as Jed's scientist friend asserts, solitude is culturally, not personally, generic—"We are merely feeling the first pangs of modernity . . . the death of the self which has become placeless"— Stephan Motoski's advantage, as Jed observes, is his professional discipline: "Physics itself is a study of the vastness of solitude—infinite motion in infinite solitude. While I suffered the disadvantage that sometimes my professional subject matter, however much I and other scholars might bleach it, treated of moments of human communion, however delusive, and of human community, however imperfect" (PCT, 348). Jed Tewksbury never achieves Motoski's cool intellectual distancing from the implications of deracinated man, and his role as international scholar is played against a persistent undertow of bitterness at his state and of fear that no identity at all lies beneath the role. His "disadvantage" saves him, however, even though he enters into his participation in the human communion and human community very late and with more self-discipline than with instinctive joy.

The want of energy and decisiveness that we sense throughout Jed's account—signified by his bemused speculation on "the way things turn out" and his recurrent brooding on "some deep fatality in things"— stems not from some rigorous belief in destiny but from a sense of self so fluid that it tends to take the conformations of each successive world that accommodates him. Jed refers to the trauma of his father's death, notably the circumstances of that locally notorious event, as his "unfended weakness in the face of the way the world was"; but the real trauma extends itself in replication far beyond boyhood—with all the taunting re-creations in the schoolyard—and beyond young adulthood— with all the nourished anger at his poverty and loneliness—into his life beyond Dugton. While they are painful endorsements of that early discovery of "the way the world was," his experience of cruelty, poverty, and class consciousness and his sense of being used surrogately and egoistically are never purged but are stoically buried. The result is that the world itself becomes unreal, illusory. As his mother bleaches all reality from Dugton, "a valley of humiliation and delusive vanities, through which I was to pass on my way to revelation," Jed discovers another world through a process of primitive magic: he comes to Latin because "if you found the names for all the things of a world, you could create a world that was real and different."

Except for his Latin classes, his years at an undistinguished private college pass dreamlike, his fellow students passing him along the gravel paths in scenes "almost as spookily unreal" as the childhood scenes he now calls "unreal." Only in Chicago does he momentarily arrive at what he calls the "discovery of freedom" in his state of "placelessness, timelessness, of ultimate loneliness." The ailing receptivity of his "nausea of blankness" is first filled visually by his sight of the Castle of Otranto, Dr. Stahlmann's house, with its clutter of books, furniture, pictures, carvings, and bibelots; and the visual crowdedness of that first impression leads to a conceptual transformation: "I had at last, effortlessly, pierced that forbidden wall through which, by this little chink or that, I had been striving to catch a glimpse of the bright reality beyond." This sanctum, then, becomes the "blessed actuality," while all the world reels away in its unreality. With only "blind need: blind, without idea, without image," Jed can only guess that his surroundings are "generous with mysterious meaning," and after thirty months in this great house, the mentor's words *imperium intellectus*, ratify the promise of this "bright reality."

It is a brief and bittersweet revelation, however, for it is followed by the old scholar's confession of heavy disillusionment. Even as he listens to Stahlmann discoursing on the *imperium intellectus* ("all the slow, sad blunderings of my past existence . . . were being redeemed into a perfected meaning of life"), he also hears his mentor contemptuously summarize the failure of any such world "timeless and placeless" at the hands of a reality more grindingly real, the energy of a tangible and base world "of the nations."

The shock of Stahlmann's suicide and its motive on the narrator can be measured not in what Jed says—the reporting is almost laconic— but in his subsequent mental acts of evasion. Once deprived of the only "bright reality" he finds palatable, he characteristically sets about abstracting the "unreal" world into constructs of a reality more purely visceral and naturalistic than the wolfish great world itself. Three such constructs are sorted out of his experience: in Italy as a liaison captain among "desperadoes," back in Chicago as graduate student and husband of Agnes Andresen, and in Nashville as professor and lover of Rozelle. Jed's involvement in each depends upon a perception of individual destiny as the sum of drift and circumstance, of power without detectable meaning or purpose. Armed with a bemused detachment, Jed enters into human relationships determined primarily by the interest, curiosity, and passion of others. He has no heart for making such self-sufficient worlds meaningful, but he discovers that, though they can be fashioned mechanically through rote-like labor in his professional life and through immersion in alcohol and sex in his personal life, they can be endured. In each case the successive worlds, shaped only cursorily by his own efforts, are tried out unconsciously as places for the self to come to. There is little balm in any of them.

If during the war alongside his Italian comrades Jed can say that "this quite unphilosophical and totally unwashed crew was my *patria*," after the war "they all had some place to go"; he, however, returns to Chicago, to the place he later describes as that "benign and *fourmillante* hive of de-selfedness." He reads the *Divina Commedia* not only as an antidote for those war experiences but also as a source of potential meaning for a chaotic present: Dante's "vision of all-embracing meaningfulness," he notes with vague hope, itself emerges out of violence and perfidy. In this sense Dante as model remains only potential. In the immediacy of his war experiences, his despair far outweighs any meaningfulness, confirming in fact the disillusion he suffers at the Castle of Otranto.

His enthusiasm blunted, he resumes his studies with workmanlike skill and ego-stroking political savvy; completing his dissertation now becomes a "parlor trick." In this kind of mechanical stoicism he enters into marriage with Agnes, reporting of himself in the third person, "He asked her to marry him . . . because she loved him." Their apartment turns into what Jed calls "our little floating island, cut off from the world." What little meaning that relationship provides—and it fails to deliver up to him an identity that is less formless than that at any earlier stage in his life—comes, predictably, in a tension created by his clinical dutifulness to a young wife dying of cancer and the intellectual fervor suddenly generated by that dying. The result is his essay on *Dante and the Metaphysics of Death*. "I gathered what data I could on the process by which death was defining the relation, past and present, between Agnes Andresen and Jediah Tewksbury. In my studies

I undertook to analyze the idea that for Dante death defines the meaning of life, that, indeed, the core drama of the *Divina Commedia* depends upon this idea" (PCT, 106). What comes from this tension is a promising professional future at what he guiltily assumes to be the expense of a life. Only after her death does he realize that he loved her, and with it he also realizes that his success would have been impossible "except for the protracted agony and lingering death" of a woman who had loved him disinterestedly, without motives. It was, he says, as though the brilliant essay had assumed the function of a death warrant: If his wife had lived, he reasons, "I would never have loved her—would, in fact, have killed what love she had for me. Her death had been the birth of love and her life would have been its death."

To the disillusionment represented by his expulsion from the Castle of Otranto, abetted by the impersonal wartime cruelty and violence among the partisans, has now been added a radical and more personal guilt, an overlay of despair that contributes much to his self-contempt and nothing to his self-definition. By the time Jed enters his Nashville phase he is secretly scornful of his professional success, watchful and wary in his personal relationships, especially with those whose inner selves seem to be perfectly accommodated to their nourishing environment. The sense of being alone, of having no identity in relation to place, is not annealed by his return to the South. Nashville, while it gives cultural and psychological definition to most of the selves he meets, is not, he proclaims, "sacred and revivifying earth to Old Broke-Nose."

In this period of self-loathing both his professional and social lives he regards as distasteful unreality. His lectures are "idiocies, lies, and irrelevancies," and his reaction to the Carringtons and their friends swings from a boozy passivity to flashes of disgust: "What falsity, what self-deception, what lies." It is a period in which Jed is only half-aware of his oscillations between apathy and restlessness, of a self waiting for a fate. Events, rather than people, from his past assume haunting shapes, "existences" with eyes and foreknowledge of his destiny that they are unwilling to divulge. All events seem to blur with everything else. "After a dance, the next day, I would find it still going on somewhere in the back of my head." Such words as *blankness, hypnosis, dream* all signal the "waiting" that Jed senses is preliminary to his fate. Social activities *swirl*, in the metaphorical meaning of that word borrowed from the typewriter of a society editor, suggesting the "gossamer of illusion, delicious and fraudulent," the "enchantress" who binds him in "mystic intimacy," and the flood of music that envelopes him in sensual communion, "powerless in the flow of time." Out of this atmosphere of "unspecifiable sensuality" Rozelle assumes a specifiable shape, and Jed enters into their adultery with the clinical curiosity of a detached naturalist observing the coupling habits of woodchucks.

Jed welcomes the liaison with Rozelle not only for its reductive pleasure—what he terms "the clutch, struggle, and spasm," the "barren simplicity" of biological nature—but also for its decisiveness in closing off the prolonged waiting, his passive slow-motion drift into becoming a part of a communal pattern. The shadowy afternoons, he writes, "were lived with the undertone of angry self-contempt and of sardonic relief that now I did not even have to play with the pretense or the self-delusion of joining Nashville, or any other goddamned place, of being Southern, or any other goddamned thing. . . . Now I was free to be only what I was in the moment in which I was." The sardonic relief is clear enough. With Maria McInnis' flight from Nashville, Jed need no longer worry that their social pairing might lead to a more domestic kind, which in turn would assume a pattern when, as Maria and Jed, they would enter "that present communal dream inhabited by Cudworth and all the rest." An angry self-contempt, however, must accompany that relief because the coupling is merely technically proficient, satisfying in a purely naturalistic sense. The biological act in its egoistic purity is also the paradoxical moment in which the self is purged, translated out of itself. Both the act and his partner in the act, however, exist for Jed not for themselves, not even as triumphant simple lust, but as vehicles for a need even more profoundly urgent than lust—to "abolish the self that had once stood under the chinaberry tree in Claxford County, Alabama."

In recurrent memory that trauma becomes more ontological than personal: the discovery of the way the world is. If the Carrington world he passively and ambivalently waits to enter is not *the* world at all but a "dream in which these people around him, in Nashville, Tennessee, seemed to live," Jed is also perceptive enough to understand that his sexual afternoons with Rozelle constitute a dream too. The lovers occupy their own "closed orbit." Jed wants to hear nothing that might "fracture the thin shell of the enclosed world of the timeless" in which he plunges into "the contextless darkness of passion."

2.

Nashville is an interim in the career of Jed Tewksbury, but its significance goes far beyond the single year he actually spends there.

Book Two, devoted to the "matter of Nashville," has in this novel of three books a predictable structural centrality—and its 194 pages make it the longest of the three—but the quality of the re-created events in the narrative is so compulsively slowed down that this year of Jed's life resembles a *redreamt* dream, lingered over, detailed, dissected, as if its meaning can somehow be grasped only through the dreamer's retrospective agony. This segment of his life contains no traumas such as those that mark Book One, and it is ultimately eventless, unlike Book Three, in which we get a brisk tattoo of ostensibly important moments: a second marriage, the birth of a son, divorce, academic honors, a knifing by a street punk, a visit to North Dakota to visit the grave of his first wife on the twenty-fifth anniversary of her death, and a visit to Italy to see his wartime comrades thirty-four years later.

It is not that Book Two is a well-defined dark night of the soul through which the narrator must pass in order to claim an achieved and clarified self; that state is destined to come, with little fanfare, long after Nashville. When Jed returns to Chicago he enjoys a severe kind of happiness that he attributes to survival of the old self, not the breakthrough into a new. He can unprovisionally assert, with the cocksureness of a Jack Burden, that selfhood "is the moment of perception between pastlessness and futurelessness," but this premature declaration simply ignores a past, including his Nashville year, that still retains a claim on him and a future that will come whether he wills it or not.

Upon his return to Dugton, Jed can finally feel that even inanimate objects of his past assert an "indestructible and absolute identity, the fullness of being and possibility," a "numinousness" that empowers them to draw him forth from what he calls "the long drowse of my being." Book Two—long before that moment of resolution—is the most exhaustively recalled instance of that long drowse. While they retain their identity, objects, people, and events of the Nashville year surrealistically merge, supplying not numinousness but a narcotic that draws Jed more deeply into that long drowse. Book Two is essentially a meditation on a state of mind, a verifiably objective moment that is nevertheless presented as, simultaneously, a dream and its interpretation. What for Jed is clearly tantalizing about this period is the effortless way it provides him physical and spiritual drift. A place, companions, a society are all ready-made, calling for no enterprise of his own. Professional duties are barely part of Jed's consciousness of this time—as "spookily unreal" as his remembered scenes from undergraduate days. We see more, hear more, understand more about the professional temperament of this man in his Friday afternoon sessions of Dante appreciation with two Nashville matrons than in any formal classroom.

Even specific social gatherings, though located and categorized according to season or occasion, tend in his recollection to assume a general atmosphere characterized by such words as *drowsy, boozy, shadowy, blur, desultory, confusion and interfusion*, and *swirl*; the settings are dominated by the great entertainment room of the Carrington barn, with its jungle-like profusion of plants, its long board table, fireplace, pictures and sculpture, and calibrated "sourceless" light. A self-conscious Jed can describe a party whose singular purpose is to promote formally what an entire way of life celebrates informally: "strangers here did not seem strangers in this world of unself-conscious gaiety and willingness to live in the innocent flow of experience in which to ask for nothing was to receive all." Even as he senses a kind of low-keyed group will to see him paired with Maria, Jed understands their own unspoken conspiracy to keep the relationship casual: "So I could float, contentedly, bodilessly, in the vacuum of my nondesiring and of her non-expectation."

In a sense the narrative pace of Book Two, the very leisureliness of its recital, allows the re-creation of a time of dreams to become also an anatomy of the dreamer. Jed at one time can say, "Maybe I— whatever the *I* was—was nothing but a dream the body was having"; but, despite the hospitable medium that encourages and nourishes the dreaming, the dream itself is substantial, incorporating, as all dreams do, transposed images and anxieties that constitute the past, and thus the present, physical reality of the dreamer. The man of no intimate connections who remembers a boyhood of no close friendships can only be stunned into a renewed sense of his emptiness when confronted by the memorable but painful image of two happy faces "alive in the candlelight, but shining, too, with an inward incandescence communally shared." The anger and betrayed innocence of the poor white, though generally dissipated by the enticements and placations of privilege and the warming protection of the social group that willingly opens its doors to him, erupt occasionally in suppressed rage at the fakery, shoddiness, and self-deception of the world that has adopted him. A wealthy couple drives, "as God predictably willed, a bright-red new Cadillac coupe." The Carrington place, Mrs. Jones-Talbot's "architectural whimsy," the Butler mansion in Florida: emotionally Jed faces each one the first time, "as though I'd never been in any house where rich people lived."

The early deprivation of Jed Tewksbury, though superficially economic, is another of Warren's perceptive instances of how material poverty wreaks spiritual havoc. Unlike the occasional sentimentality of his fellow Agrarians, Warren's vision of the poor white, both the "cropper" and the small-farm owner, has never been projected as pastoral, a mode, at least in the hands of Stark Young, Donald Davidson, and occasionally John Crowe Ransom, in which suffering and resentment recede into the safety of aesthetic form. The perceptive linking of poverty and spiritual dislocation, though it runs counter to that fond notion that man and nature exist in harmonious unity, has from the beginning made Warren different from most of his friends of *I'll Take My Stand.*

Ashby Wyndham, who leaves the farm of his father, attains a certain dignity in his theological absorption, but the heavy price is psychic distortion; Jerry Calhoun's father, who stays on the farm, is an admirable figure of fortitude and love, but Warren's depiction of his life has none of the agrarian idealizing that we see in Andrew Lytle's "The Hind Tit" and Ransom's "Reconstructed But Unregenerate." The hard-scrabble rise from below-the-ranks sears the spirit of old Tolliver long before his son is stricken by a later, more fashionable malaise. It is inconceivable to think of any of Warren's friends setting about to write a poem in which a poor white murders his family with an icepick or a short story in which a poor white hangs himself on a new gate. If Cy Grinder is a partial portrait of the poor white who makes peace with his shame of a family past and with the social snobberies that damn his ambitions, Jed Tewksbury is a complete one. Although he sees his past bereft of dignity, he is nevertheless shaped by that past, and his mother and stepfather finally converge into an image of steadfastness, contentment, and love, qualities that reproach his own emptiness. Although his education allows him to surmount the social snobberies of Nashville, the process is not smooth, and the cynically amiable exterior conceals the wary suspicions of the social outsider.

The decline of the comfortable Lawford Carrington, for example, occurs less from the demand of narrative logic than from the requirements of psychic revenge in the protagonist, as if the ruin had been willed by Jed-as-dreamer. Significantly, Carrington's coldness, frustration, and cruelty are never dramatized but are reported. The degeneration into eventual suicide has the inevitability of magic, charms, spells. Jed's very rhetoric dooms his patrician rival. What Jed does not consciously see—but which his images reveal—during his affair with Rozelle Hardcastle (never Rose Carrington) is that his cruel demotion of Lawford Carrington to the status of "non-person," an "appurtenance of the expensive machine of the Carrington household," is not merely the bemused contempt of the seducer for the cuckold; it is also the result of the peasant's tongue-biting resentment of the lord, the poor white's muffled rage at the patrician's luck in an already determined world that inequitably parcels out fortune and talent.

In its precision of grievances, Jed's catalog of scorn for Carrington might at first suggest the insight of an incisive but tolerant Nick Carraway seeing Jay Gatsby for the first time:

> The graceful manners, the engaging modesty, the whitetoothed smile, the careful attention to the opinions, tastes, comforts, and vanities of guests, the elegant bohemianism of huaraches, espadrilles, and Turkish slippers, of red silk shirts open low to exhibit the not-too-proletarian hair on his chest, of denim and suede jackets, of white duck pants and turquoise-encrusted belts, of commanding grace in the saddle and powerful strokes in the Olympic-size pool, of well-modulated anecdotes, of the schooled finish of his sculpture—all, I suddenly decided that night, as we whipped past the lights of approaching cars, were nothing but a façade, a mirage, a *trompe d'oeil*. There was no Lawford Carrington.   (PCT, 212)

The descriptive items selected to characterize the man are not neutral; what betrays the rhetoric is a kind of curled lip, felt if not seen, issuing words normally considered hortatory (*graceful, engaging*) that slip almost imperceptibly into a diction that is more ambiguous (*elegant bohemianism, not-too-proletarian hair*) so that the accretive technique and the conspicuous juxtaposition of learned skills (riding, swimming, storytelling) and faddish indulgences (huaraches, Turkish slippers) serve finally to damn the man who is the referent of all these items. In its stripped revelation, it is not a Gatsby we see through the eyes of a Carraway; "Mr. Nashville Himself" is a Tom Buchanan felt and surmised by the deprivation of a George Wilson. The secret referent of this controlled indictment is not the *have* of Lawford Carrington but the *have-not* of Jediah Tewksbury. To proclaim that there "was no Lawford Carrington" is itself delusive, of a piece with Jed's instinct that the hurtful diminishment of poverty is the exclusive index to the world's reality. The complacent luxury of the Carrington society may be a world of "dream" to Jed, but for its moment in time it does exist, just as Jed's world of Dugton, which now seems "unreal," once existed.

At the beginning of Book Three, a spiritually battered Jed flees Nashville, just as a year earlier he had fled Chicago, bearing the scars of one more difficult period in his life. Although he fails to make the connection, his summary of the life he had been living during the Nashville interim—"the intensities, lies, self-divisions, dubieties, duplicities, and blind and variously devised plummetings into timeless sexuality"—describes as well, except perhaps for the sexuality, his postwar years in

Chicago. In terms of spiritual autobiography there is no conspicuous turning point here: leaving Nashville is simply flight, generated by nothing more profound than discomfort and frustration occasioned by his affair with Rozelle. Jed himself recognizes the absence of any meaningful peripeteia in the meandering drama of his life. Leaving Nashville, however, is "an escape into time, into its routines and nags, which make life possible after all."

Book Three, in its curiously flattened-out effects, is a matter-of-fact record of a solitary who nevertheless marries, fathers a son, divorces, and resumes a career with acceptable energy if not enthusiasm—presumably the "routines and nags" of most lives. Making peace with disappointment, the sobering acceptance of the gap separating expectation and fulfillment, is one aspect of the moral realism we see throughout Warren's fiction as grudging discoveries of protagonists, spurred on, sometimes subliminally, by the hard-bitten insights of peripheral folk characters. In *A Place to Come To*, Perk Simms's generalization on the nature of man sounds familiar: "Ain't worth powder and lead to perish. Ain't nothing but spindle bones stuck in a pair of pants." But, unlike that of Ashby Wyndham or Anse Gillum, Simms's life is blessed by mutual love. It is an achieved state, forged under difficult circumstances with Jed's mother and influenced by the shaping memory of previous spouses, and it is a state that eludes Jediah Tewksbury whose protective sensibility and wary emotional commitments block him from "knowing that men were real, and brothers in their reality." Instead of a poverty-haunted house irradiated by love, domestic habit, and mutual understanding, Jed inhabits the attic of the scholarly recluse, venturing out occasionally from his "vast number of cards that measured three by five inches" to seek the company of another *isolato* and even less often to share the companionship of his grown son.

In his modest accommodation to actuality, Jed discovers in his sentimental return to Italy no new truth but a confirmation of an old one that he has reluctantly accepted: "every man has to lead his own life and has little chance of knowing what it means, anyway." Musing on *the way things turn out* refers specifically to the spectacle of the tangled and unexpected logic in the later lives of his partisan comrades; but the confirmation that comes to this man, feeling now "rather blank of heart and head," anticipates also the experience of his final meeting with Rozelle. His return to Dugton is even more elegiac than the trip to Italy, for it means visiting the graves of his mother and father, renewing his buried memories of again-familiar objects in the little shotgun bungalow, until each of them—the pathetic china bulldog, crocheted chair cover, and stereopticon viewer—glows "with a special assertion of its being—of my being, too, as though only now, after all the years, I was returning to my final self, long lost." This retrospective visit, however, does something more than bring an "elegiac dampness" to his eye; returning to his lost self means also the birth, belated as it is, of concern and responsibility for needs that are less grand or petty than they are merely human. What Jed learns from old Simms is respect for the integrity of a man whose full humanness is not diminished by the circumstances of his particular place. While one's birthplace has no mystical virtue, says Warren, "I do attach a significance to the way a man deals with the place God drops him in. His reasons for going or staying. And his piety or impiety" (*Talking*, 271). In an extension of human sympathy never before made, Jed enters willingly into the hurts and frail heroisms of his stepfather, a stranger, going so far as joining with him in a pact to arrange for the old man's funeral. In humble recognition of his own needs, Jed writes to his former wife, asking for her "company," because "it is what I feel myself most deeply craving."

Jed's spiritual restoration is the least extravagant, the most minimal, of that of any of Warren's protagonists, not because it comes only in the last dozen pages of his story—Amantha Starr's and Adam Rosenzweig's come even later—but because it remains so muted. Dayprings of joy and bursts of sudden insight are frequent signs of regeneration in Warren's work, but for Jed Tewksbury the stoicism engendered by having to live with one's own ineradicable nature continues into the final pages of his story.

CONCLUSION

For nothing we had,
Nothing we were,
Is lost. All is redeemed,
In knowledge.

         —Brother to Dragons (1979)

    . . . but what is knowledge
Without the intrinsic mediation of the heart?

         —Brother to Dragons (1979)

Conclusion

In the course of his travels prior to writing *Segregation*, a chance remark during an interview triggered in Warren a remembered exchange from a further past:

> I remembered a Yankee friend saying to me: "Southerners and Jews, you're exactly alike, you're so damned special."
> "Yes," I said, "we're both persecuted minorities."
> I had said it for a joke.
> But had I? (S, 27)

Warren is too serious a man to be solemn during friendly badinage, but in his rage for self-criticism and the stern standard by which he measures all men equally, Warren writes from the perspective of the Man Outside. The repetitive chords of psychological bondage, glorious failure, nagging guilt, and poverty both material and spiritual are not the common ones we hear generally in historical evaluations of the American, but they are frequent ones in those of the southerner.[1]

Being "so damned special" carries great risks, not the least of which is the brand of whining defensiveness that occasionally mars the essays in *I'll Take My Stand*. But that tone is rare in Warren, just as it is rare in Faulkner. "In separateness only does love learn definition," says Warren in one of his early poems. The title of one of his essays is "Love and Separateness in Eudora Welty." The complexities of any emotion or event are those that in Warren's scheme require the clarity of definition no less than the man who experiences it. Warren's Audubon, like that earlier Audubon in Welty's "A Still Moment," is the outsider, too, whose characteristic tones are celebratory; though sometimes stoically bemused, he is never defensive. He and old Goldfarb of *Flood* possess what is most valuable for the outsider: perspective. That gift is a realism not always possible for the insider. To know the fragmented world as it is and not as it is fondly imaged is no less important than to know the self that must learn to walk in it; Audubon learns that his life was

> what it was, as he was,
> In the end, himself and not what
> He had known he ought to be.

The particularly fulfilling image for the scientist who was also a naturalist and who killed birds in order to know them (and in knowing them, preserved them) is finally a moral perspective:

> To wake in some dawn and see,
> As though down a rifle barrel, lined up
> Like sights, the self that was, the self that is, and there,
> Far off but in range, completing that alignment, your fate.   (SP, 94)

As has been aptly observed, Warren is, in a sense, his own best example of postlapsarian man: "the outsider returning with knowledge as communion."[2] If he indeed thinks of himself as part of one of the "persecuted minorities," he has made the most of it with his recurring stress on the need for corrective vision. Perhaps the Jew is his own objective correlative as the "damned special" outsider: Adam Rosenzweig, the Bavarian Jew in the American Civil War, and Goldfarb, whose very presence in the midst of Fiddlersburg complacencies is a token of potentially regenerative wisdom.

The writers of the Southern Renascence were literary amphibians, at home in their natural medium, a tradition that was theirs by the accidents of time and place, and making a home for themselves by breathing the exhilarating air of modernism. The works of most of them bear the ambiguous scars of transition—the very creation of *both* Temple Drake and Dilsey by the greatest of these artists is witness to the difficulties, and the earned victory, of finding moral and aesthetic equivalents for their experience of living in two worlds. As insiders, these writers accepted the principles, events, and figures of a heroic past as their birthright; as outsiders, they could see this birthright huckstered away in defensive postures which left them naked to their enemies. As one distinguished critic long ago observed, the circumstances of this generation were happy not only because they could believe in the values of their tradition but also because they could *disbelieve* in them.[3] The best work of Faulkner, Ransom, Tate, Davidson, Porter, Caldwell, Gordon, Welty, and Wolfe stems from their amphibious double vision; their worst results from a too-urgent, simplistic drive to take their stand for either an inherited tradition or an emerging modernism.

But if the South has always been more homogeneous than any other comparable region in America, it has also been marked by spirited disagreement (and even mutual ignorance) among its representative artists. Ellen Glasgow regarded Faulkner simply as a sordid exploiter of southern deficiencies; she could even be offended by the irreverence of her Richmond friend, James Branch Cabell. The Fugitives of Nashville stood in terror of being associated with such institutionalized groups as the Poetry Society of South Carolina; and Thomas Wolfe, though he might hate the New South compulsion for progress implied by the Chapel Hill social planners, looked with even greater scorn on the "Neo-Confederates" of *The Fugitive* and *I'll Take My Stand*. In its social composition, its economic base, its politics, and its literature, the South is not monolithic and never has been—as we have been reminded most notably over the years by C. Hugh Holman.[4]

In the case of Robert Penn Warren, the assumptions of a usable past have been more corrosively tested from the outsider's perspective than for most of his contemporaries; the double vision accounts for literary artifacts whose tensions reflect the cultural environment of a South far different from that which we see in Faulkner, Welty, and Porter. And while Warren shares Kentucky and Tennessee as native region with Tate, Ransom, Davidson, and Lytle, he has been more intellectually than imaginatively engaged by either the heroics or the foolishness of the Deep South that these other upper southerners have concerned themselves with—its failure to have a homogeneous, theological religion; its self-cultivated image of gentility, courtesy, and honor; its self-conscious preserving and conserving habits that insured the survival of a culture based on class and race. As a Kentuckian, Warren could be as conscious as his fellow writers in Mississippi on the deep rifts in principles and customs occasioned by a fratricidal war and the economic devastation of its aftermath. His boyhood was as filled with stirring legends, history lessons, and oral tales passed on by grizzled survivors as was Faulkner's, but for Warren it is *not* forever "not yet two o'clock on that July afternoon in 1863" as it is for "every Southern boy fourteen years old."[5] As a border-state southerner growing up in the early 1920s, he would be as prepared as his fellow Agrarians to flinch from the commercial spirit of progress, of boosterism, of aggressive entrepreneuring of New South dogma, but he would never quite find alternatives to it in a refashioned image of an arcadian South.

322 THE ACHIEVEMENT OF ROBERT PENN WARREN

During the Fugitives' Reunion in 1956, Warren was noticeably un-enthusiastic about the connotations of *aristocratic*, a word tossed around rather more easily by the other participants to describe their common enterprise a quarter of a century earlier: "I thought," he said, "we were trying to find—in so far as we were being political—a rational basis for a democracy."[6] Simply as factual occurrences, Warren's work has more poor-white characters than blacks, and he is temperamentally more attuned to their great griefs and privations, their small victories and frail virtues, than to the same characteristics in the lives of southern blacks.

Warren is enough of a border-state realist to know that such reputed virtues as independence, self-sufficiency, and stoicism—often attributed as regional traits of the generality of southerners—may, when applied to hillmen, countrymen, plain folk, and poor whites, have little to do with conscious and willed character. They may be last-ditch, inescapable responses to poverty both economic and cultural and, as such, may be seen as irrelevant virtues or even as questionable attributes. Yet Warren is incensed by what he interprets as authorial snobberies and "hick-baiting" in the novels of T. S. Stribling, who might as well be saying: "No decency of spirit is possible in a house without modern plumbing."[7] And it is no accident that a far greater number of "wisdom characters" in his own work are drawn from the hard-scrabble classes than from the patrician or middle classes. Even when he pays homage to Civil War participants there is a conspicuous absence of the gen-eralized heroism that we, along with the speaker, admire in Tate's "Ode to the Confederate Dead": Warren tends rather to recall them in images of tobacco-chewing victims caught up in the same ambiguities of loyalty and values and hostage to the same mortality the realists de-pict in the twentieth-century war novel. If Warren's conception of these nineteenth-century "ancestors" occasionally echoes Mr. Compson's notion that the southern personages of the Civil War generation were "victims of a different circumstance, simpler and therefore, integer for integer, larger, more heroic" than his own, it does so not because these figures represent Confederate principles or regional pieties, but because they represent the Father, whose achievements in knowing the self and ac-cepting one's fate emerged from struggle no less strenuous and com-plexly human than the Son's.[8]

The eyes of the Father may stare from the portraits with such "severe reprehension" that the Son can never guess the pain behind them; but the achievements of "Founding Fathers, Nineteenth-Century Style,

Southeast U.S.A."—not just Houston, Bowie, and Clay, but the name-less and forgotten grandpas as well—represent nevertheless an image of human struggle that, says Warren, is always a rebuke to the present: "It's a better rebuke than any dream of the future. It's a better rebuke because you can see what some of the costs were, what frail virtues were achieved in the past by frail men. And it's there, and you can see it, and see what it cost them, and how they had to go at it. . . . The drama of the past that corrects us is the drama of our struggles to be human, or our struggles to define the values of our forbears in the face of their difficulties."⁹ Even in the defensive exposure of John Brown in his first book Warren attempts to understand the complexities of one man's struggle to be human; the conclusion that John Brown was mad, sug-gests Warren, not only trivializes his role and his initiating acts but also capitulates to the tendency of social scientists to render human behavior mechanistic—and therefore inhuman.

Just as more poor whites than blacks populate Warren's world, so are there more middling men of integrity than those revered gentle-men who capture the imagination of Warren's friends; we see fewer Major Buchans, General Archbalds, Aleck Maurys, and Cousin Luciuses signifying traditional values than those more modest men who wrestle the angel, fight stomp-and-gouge, take falls by the corn-crib, and, even when they prosper, never forget the owl call or the "smell of burnt bear fat on dusk-air." The Warren figure that most approximates those characters out of Tate, Ellen Glasgow, Caroline Gordon, and John Donald Wade is Aaron Pendleton Starr of *Band of Angels*, and that approximation is slight. The most notable gentleman of quality and self-assurance is Colonel Fort of *World Enough and Time*, and his strengths—generosity, sympathy, and political realism—must be tested against the violence, shifting alliances, and moral indeterminacy of a frontier society.

In a fine conversation recorded between Warren and Cleanth Brooks, one divergence in the two friends' interest and emphasis is small but telling. Brooks, who was a scholar of southern culture before he was a critic, summarizes the contrasting mythic impulses that founded New England and the South and that provided vital continuities in the re-spective histories of these regions. The controlling myth of the north-east, says Brooks, was millennialist that, however secularized, stimulated the "quest for the perfect society"; the southern myth was arcadian, the urge to re-create, "on a new and more bountiful soil," the Roman republic. Warren, however, suggests that many of the special qualities of the South "are really qualities that simply belong to old America, qualities that can still be observed in backcountry New England" as well as in backcountry South.[10]

There is point to Virginia Rock's modest observation, "Warren is a Southern writer, but his work is infused rather than dominated by his Southernness."[11] I would add that his work is more specifically informed by his *border* southernness, a piedmont sensibility that responds less to the quaint honor and romantic clannishness of extended kinships than to their strain, hardships, distanced respect, and ambivalent nourishments; a temperament that takes as imaginative resource the animating moralities of pietistic, fundamentalist, nontheological religion—those very traits of southern life that Ransom, Tate, and Stark Young deplored.

Warren's particular place in southern writing may be illuminated by a brief comparison between the Kentuckian and Richard Marius, a Tennessee novelist almost exactly a generation younger. As a south-central Kentuckian living practically on the Tennessee state line, Warren inherited codes, mores, customs, speech patterns, cultural interests, and political and religious attitudes from a border environment, one that is strongly balanced between North and South. As an East Tennessean, Marius grew up in a family of divided loyalties, not between Yankee and Confederate sympathies but between fiercely evangelical Methodists on his mother's side and a fallen-away Greek Catholicism on his father's. Both Warren and Marius grew up reading and being read to in isolated rural areas; both absorbed the religious awe occasioned by social and natural events; both still regard physical nature as embodying "meaning"—an immanence even if precise articulation of its meaning cannot be made; both in their childhood heard stories of fierce substance and ritualistic form; and both write fiction that can stand as ethical critiques of the fanciful and embossed traditions associated with the Old South. Marius says, "I bristle when anyone calls me a 'southern' writer. I am a novelist of the border."[12] Warren does not bristle at that attribution, but his work qualitatively and texturally reflects the border.[13] In temperament both Warren and Marius have affinities closer to Mark Twain, the Southwest humorists, Thomas Wolfe, and Erskine Caldwell than they do to William Gilmore Simms, Faulkner, Eudora Welty, and the southern local colorists.

There is no question that Warren's Kentucky years comprise one of the richest sources of his art. Like Yeats, the

> toil of growing up;
> The ignominy of boyhood; the distress

> Of boyhood changing into man;
> The unfinished man and his pain
> Brought face to face with his own clumsiness . . .[14]

are for Warren not merely inert phases of a past which he is patronizingly content "to live over" again in the manner of postbellum romancers or which, as in Faulkner, "isnt even over yet." The past for Warren must be understood primarily in order for him to know himself. The re-created landscapes in poem after poem—usually antiphonally balanced between both actual and imagined present—are not of a land of heart's desire in the manner of newspaper poets and James Whitcomb Riley, since the mature man's compulsive return to the years between nine and fourteen is not to assuage the corrosions of a racking maturity but to reexamine situations, episodes, images that were corrosive even then.

The confluence of political and religious attitudes in the border South, and Warren's own sense of separation from many of those in whom such attitudes were absorbed and articulated naturally, results in recurring aesthetic postures of emotional intensity and desperation. The fall from innocence is a substantial part of the fable in every novel and a generative loss in many poems, but the almost visceral struggle to regain innocence in some form is also part of the fable and the source of its energy. What the self discovers in its fitful journey toward knowledge is that the "so damned special" must be completed by the common; the integrity and uniqueness must join in communion, the acknowledgment of continuities in what it means to be human. Since it is ultimately intractable, human nature is a mystery that will be solved in some atemporal glory to come; in the meantime, it must be respected for its complexity. This is the moral realism that southern writers in general seem to understand, but it is a characteristic that appears in great gallumping examples in Warren, who is less quiet about the varieties and degrees of tension to which man finds himself susceptible. He is as skillful as Eudora Welty in isolating the small detail that bespeaks a larger tumult, but his preference seems to be the larger tumult itself, rendered in patterns called moral drama by his admirers and melodrama by his detractors.

When he was a student at Vanderbilt, Warren was immediately enamoured of Ransom's *Poems About God* because, as he remembers it, he was fascinated by the "double connection" in his teacher's volume. He detected the relationship between the sense of technique, "the structure of a thing as related to the life of the poem," and the physical life which lay behind the poem, "landscapes and people."[15] It is precisely this "double connection" that distinguishes Warren's own performance as a poet—and that can often raise an otherwise perfunctory fiction into an enlivening personal document. The novels are by their very nature more recessive and less personal than the poems, and we need not become biographical heretics to observe the importance of transposed events, images, "landscapes and people" from Warren's boyhood projected into the textures of *World Enough and Time*, "Blackberry Winter," "When the Light Gets Green," "The Patented Gate and the Mean Hamburger," and *A Place to Come To*. Such transpositions are not the anagrammatical kind we are familiar with in *Look Homeward, Angel* (Chapel Hill/Pulpit Hill, Bus Woody/Gus Moody); they partake of dream and nightmare and surreal intimations of experience, twicetold tales sifted for another telling, not to exploit local history and geography but to delineate the subterranean territory of the self.

For Warren there has always been a sense of profound linkage between the local and the mythic: rudeness to a mother causes reverberations in second-century Rome; a trapped caver recalls not merely Floyd Collins but Plato; the human uses of political power suggest Dante, Machiavelli, and William James as well as Huey P. Long; a town flooded out by the waters of a TVA dam participates in the ancient rituals of baptismal drowning and regeneration. The shaping fable of the self lies behind every work, and Warren is the preeminent example of the artist who sees that fable glimmering in the pedestrian lives of poor whites and nondescript ancestors as well as politicians, romantic dreamers, and Thomas Jefferson. The resonance of *self* as a working concept goes back at least to the figure of Oedipus, uttering grandly through the hieratic mask and exhibiting the "struggles of a self trapped in the anguish of its fate" (DP, xiv). But for Warren it goes back even further: to the figure of his father, who "set out to be a lawyer and writer and actually published some poetry in his youth," trapped in the freely chosen domestic responsibilities of family and home (*Talking*, 240).

It may be superfluous to speak of the "personal" motive in the writing of a poem or a novel, inasmuch as any serious work cannot but be its maker's image; but early and late, Warren's creative achievement constitutes a personal statement, an internal commitment, a vision fleshed public by words. And it is also true that in the vast coherence of this modern man of letters the explicitly public modes of his career—his essays on other writers, his historical and biographical writing, his journalism, his lectures—are, in spite of their occasional or topical genesis, part of that great achievement. All his works constitute, to borrow Warren's own metaphor, a "seamless web." His concern for the generic accuracy of some of these public forms—or even the choice of some of his subtitles—is evidence enough that Warren himself considers them, no less than his aesthetic forms, to be the products of a unitary self: in their several manifestations, all his "made" things are shaped by the urgencies, compulsions, and nagging struggles of a single self.

For all its resemblance to sociological case studies, his *Segregation*, emphasizing the "Inner Conflict in the South," is really about "self-division," that split "within the individual man" that we also see analyzed in the cases of Jack Burden, Jeremiah Beaumont, and Jed Tewksbury. Despite its political breadth and scrupulous methodology and its reliance upon technological aids, *Who Speaks for the Negro?* is thematically and structurally informed by one private sensibility— the author's. The anthology of Melville's poems is called "A Reader's Edition," not in the sense of regularized or popularized texts that bibliographers once distinguished from the accurate transcriptions for scholarly use, but in the sense that the selection and interpretation of the poems are made, as Warren puts it, by "myself." Warren's contribution to the Civil War Centennial is called "Meditations," and his revised version of the Jefferson Lectures of 1974 "may be better taken," he says, as meditations than as essays. Both *meditation* and *essay*, in all their tentativeness and proneness to distortion, still carry a heavy impress of individual response, but whatever *Democracy and Poetry* may be called, it represents, "in some degree, an utterance of a rather personal sort, a personal exploration, if you will" (DP, xvi).

Partly because of his informing concern for moral imperatives, the need for finding one's truth despite all the conscious and rationalizing urgencies to frustrate it, Warren has always tended to revel in his depiction of the physical world in and through which the self must define itself. If the great drama is religious and philosophical, the stage on which the soul undergoes its painful progress is relentlessly physical and concrete. The centripetal moral forces are always countered, resisted, and sometimes defeated by centrifugal forces—the "inwardness of self" operating both against and within "the outwardness of the world."

That world is of course not always the literal Kentucky and Tennessee of Warren's youth, but his discovery that Ransom was "making poetry out of a world I knew" (*Talking*, 225) led Warren unerringly to that world, landscapes and people, which would prove to be his imaginative place to come to. Despite the agony that his poor harried protagonists undergo in their sojourn in its "outwardness," the world is never too much with Warren himself, whose keen relish for the crowded densities of actuality coincides with his exceptional skill in observing detail in what would usually be, for other moralists, a generalized backdrop for the inner struggles being enacted before it. Local objects glow into significance by virtue of their isolating specificity: the "power of isolating common things" that Warren sees as Katherine Anne Porter's genius is his own. Workclothes, farming implements, the books and furniture of a gentleman's study or a graduate student's apartment, the food of blacks and poor whites: they are never itemized as general categories but broken into their resonant specificities: overalls drying after the workday; rusted plowheads weighting rickety garden gates; the cheese-smelling leatherbound books among the framed Piranesis; the roach- and ant-infested kitchen; the chitlings, collards, and sorghum.

No other writer, not even the explorers of American Studies or material folklore, has made so much out of our cultural artifacts: portraits of Signers, rifles, electric chairs, campaign trucks, hunting shirts and broadcloth coats, country graveyards, WPA murals, big houses and shotgun bungalows, letters and broadsides. If there has always been a particular verve in Warren's explicit exploration of the human past—what Jack Burden calls "the ash pile, the midden, the sublunary dung heap"—that verve is not noticeably lessened in the depiction of the human present. In both the past and present, warts and wens always seem to be plumper and brighter than those seen by other writers; expectorated phlegm is always more glittering, pus is yellower and more concentrated, mental defectives slobber more profusely.

It is perhaps unfair for a writer to allow a succession of egoists, idealists, solipsists, and absolutists to march forth in such a world, indifferent to its indifference to them or determined to shape its recalcitrant imperfections into a more perfect place. The all-consuming, single-directed energies which we see in such seekers as Percy Munn, Amantha Starr, and Adam Rosenzweig, confront a world which exercises its own powers and perquisites. What Warren once referred to as the "jags and injustices of human relationships" are part of that world. In their ordinary human affairs, the merely day-to-day accommodations as well as the ideological demands for freedom, or truth or justice, Warren's people must contend with and exist in a context of human error, contingency, and inconsistency.

For all his bad luck and self-delusion in a world he often misreads, the dreamer still enjoys Warren's sympathy, and it could not be otherwise for a dualistic temperament much influenced by John Crowe Ransom. The drama of the self is consistently played out in primary oppositions variously expressed, in one critic's catalog, as "ideal and real, or idea and fact; man and external nature; innocence and guilt; end and means; science and religion or art; heritage and revolt, or father and son; history and the individual life."[16] To *be*, man must dream; he must imagine, even create, an image of himself as a man of worth, unique and special, separate from all others. To *survive*, he must submit that private image to public experience, the dream to fact, to what Jeremiah Beaumont calls "the jostle and pudder of things."

If Warren's friend Andrew Lytle can assert that the turn of the twentieth century marked "the last moment of equilibrium," the last time man, "without having to think, could say what was right and what was wrong," Warren casts doubts on the notion that there ever was such a moment of equilibrium.[17] What he sees in the literature of Hawthorne, Melville, Mark Twain, and Dreiser reinforces the agony which constitutes the narrative lives of most of his protagonists. And although the personae in the mature poems can never be sure of right and wrong, they yet struggle with the question that is severely moral: how shall a man live?

It is a question informing many works that we regard as characteristically American. In some—*The Scarlet Letter, Huckleberry Finn, North of Boston, The Sun Also Rises*—the question is asked in the interstices and peripheries of the formal artifact; in others it generates the artifact itself, not obliquely but frontally: "The American Scholar," *Walden, Leaves of Grass, Paterson, An American Dream*. Whatever we may say about the diverse struggles for style and form that these works represent, their common link is the moral urgency with which their authors ask the question: how shall a man live? And if the answers range from the conventionally homiletic to the radically hortatory, they all follow from the same implied declaration: I want to tell you something. In none of these works is the answer pulpit-easy; the characteristic method assumes resistance by contraries, ideological polarization, confrontation and debate.

Warren has admitted his abiding interest in that grandest American dialectic, the moral and psychological tension between what is roughly identified as "Puritan dichotomies" and "Transcendentalism." Calling himself a "little footnote" in the long history of this intellectual tension, he suggests that the recurring theme of father and son in his own work expresses his urge to fuse the two halves of the dialectic— "the fact and idea," "the Emersonian and the Hawthornian."[18] But to assume that Emerson and Hawthorne represent only the poles of the dialectic—that they are not sufficiently engaged by the ongoing interplay between those poles—is clearly an inadequate reading of both writers. As for Emerson, Warren is convinced, at least publicly, that the transcendental path is too assertively sunny, that the benign Concord woods hold no enticements, threats, or satanic rituals that darken the imagination of his neighbor Hawthorne—although, as Warren makes clear in his first book, Emerson's benignity led to its own kind of darkness: naïveté, self-righteousness, hypocrisy. The uneven poetic suite "Homage to Emerson" is less a tribute than a challenge to its subject from a latter-day skeptic, who systematically summons up domesticated, even homely, images—spider, boyhood masturbation, warts —to suggest metaphysical imperfection and human frailty, a larger Evil that Emerson presumably could never confront; even the rarefied air of the stratosphere and the artificial light above the airplane seat as the appropriate medium for a reader of *Essays* become a sly rebuke.

Although Warren suggests that his urge is to fuse the two halves of "the Emersonian and the Hawthornian," the life of his own poems and novels requires that the fusion remain potential only; the dialectic itself, rather than its resolution into monistic harmony, reflects the actuality of man's existence—is, in fact, the true image of man's fate. Jack Burden, Jeremiah Beaumont, Adam Rosenzweig, Amantha Starr, Thomas Jefferson, Audubon: all struggle to reconcile dream and fact, a state of being most devoutly wished for and a problem most unceremoniously foisted upon their unprepared selves. In the terms of Warren's cultural milieux—both the Protestant family heritage of Kentucky and Tennessee and the intellectual and artistic communities with which he has been congenially linked for all his career—that dilemma may be seen as the battle between the consolations of progressivist philosophy and science and the bracing reminders of Christian orthodoxy.

The sturdy doctrine of human fallibility is most notably exemplified in Willie Stark's mission to Jack Burden, which is to send his man poking around in Judge Irwin's past: "There is always something." The incriminating traces of the Littlepaugh connection thus ratify not only the Boss's belief in universal imperfection but also his confidence that man's evil cannot remain hidden. "So I had it after all the months," Jack ruefully concludes from his evidence. "For nothing is lost, nothing is ever lost." But if Willie Stark is one kind of mentor for Jack Burden, Cass Mastern is another. While this more benign moralist endorses a doctrine of general human corruption not far different from Willie Stark's, he also believes in the ultimate effectuality of human character, which might serve as a counterforce to human depravity. If he feels unworthy to "preach Abolition," he says to his cynical brother, "meanwhile there is my example. If it is good, it is not lost. Nothing is ever lost." Through both its negative and positive functions in *All the King's Men*, this motif prepares for the kind of later discovery associated with the rubric, "We're all one flesh at last." If the early fiction and poetry affirm a naturalistic vision (or, from another perspective, orthodox Christian truths about human nature), the later work repeatedly asserts the possibilities of regeneration through a humbling acknowledgment of a human commonality through sympathy and love. But possibility is not achievement, and Warren's reiterated cry of *joy* and *delight* is never a final and finished note. The sobering effects of man's evil and the deterministic tinge of a world in which man must learn to walk are not banished by the momentary affirmations we find in much of the later work.

For all his suspicion that the voice he hears at 35,000 feet affirms an unearned joy and delight, Warren betrays in his two major modes since the mid-1950s, in both substance and method, remarkable affinities with the mature Emerson. In "Experience" Emerson begins by soberly answering his own question, "Where do we find ourselves? In a series of which we do not know the extremes, and believe that it has none." Thus as early as 1844 the apostle of human primacy and vision meditates on the temperamental barriers to perception. Self-confidence must be accommodated to the limitations of the private self: "It is very unhappy, but too late to be helped," he says, "the discovery we have made, that we exist. That discovery is called the Fall of Man."[19] The struggle to find joy and delight in limitation is the real matter in Emerson's mature work, and it is no less halting and provisional than Warren's. The dialectical movement in the great essay "Fate" (1860) is the clash between limitation and liberty, destiny and will. The opening sentence of the last paragraph of "Fate"—"Let us build altars to the Beautiful Necessity"—sums up the characteristic position of the untranscendental Emerson.[20] That position has been perceptively summed up by Emerson's most distinguished commentator as "agnostic optimism"; with a slight shift in emphasis—perhaps "optimistic agnosticism"—the same revealing terms sum up, I think, the moral and philosophical coherence of Warren's career.[21]

If self-knowledge is the adhesive rubric which we have all come to attach to Warren's work, we cannot fail to consider the bracing implications of that struggle. A difficult acceptance, one uniquely possible for man, is the fact that the self, with or without knowledge, is not enough. The paradox is a centrally Christian one: we lose a self to gain it. The lesson says that potential peace lies not in the self's willful accretion but in a freely offered diminution. The submission of private to public, self to community, and the adjustment of motive and act to the general welfare: in this recognition man finds himself "humanly acceptable." It is a recipe more easily given than followed, of course, and Warren shuns such doctrinal assertions. In his most revealing statement of personal belief, Warren says: "I am a creature of this world, but I am also a yearner, I suppose. I would call this temperament rather than theology—I haven't got any gospel" (*Talking*, 234).[22] In work after work he investigates the crucial area somewhere between alienation and ideology, mapping its disputed boundaries, finding the clearing where his creatures, if they are lucky, can claim both individuality and brotherhood.

Notes

Introduction

1. W. H. Auden, "Nature, History and Poetry," *Thought*, XXV (September, 1950), 420–22.

2. Robert Penn Warren, "Knowledge and the Image of Man," in John Lewis Longley (ed.), *Robert Penn Warren: A Collection of Critical Essays* (New York: New York University Press, 1965), 237.

3. George Core, "In the Heart's Ambiguity: Robert Penn Warren as Poet," *Mississippi Quarterly*, XXII (Fall, 1969), 318.

4. "Fate," in *The Complete Works of Ralph Waldo Emerson*, ed. Edward Waldo Emerson, Centenary Edition (Boston: Houghton Mifflin, 1903–1904), VI, 22–23.

5. John Crowe Ransom, "The Inklings of 'Original Sin,' " *Saturday Review of Literature*, May 20, 1944, pp. 10–11. For a sampling of early opinion of Warren's work see Neil Nakadate, *Robert Penn Warren: A Reference Guide* (Boston: G. K. Hall, 1977), 8–23. The best corrective for the still-prevalent notion that violence in Warren's works is gratuitous and sensationalistic is Louise Y. Gossett's *Violence in Recent Southern Fiction* (Durham, N.C.: Duke University Press, 1965), Chap. 1, which persuasively links violence to the various characters' struggle for identity in a pattern of rejection, flight, and return. See also "Robert Penn Warren and the Uses of the Past" (*Review of English Literature*, IV [October, 1963], 93–102), in which John R. Strugnell argues that despite the mingled motives behind the violence in Warren's works, the central impulse is "always the individual's attempt to avoid being engulfed by the tide of history and to lose his identity" (100). Warren himself has discussed violence as "a component of ourselves" in "Violence in Literature," a symposium with William Styron, Robert Coles, and Theodore Solotaroff in *American Scholar*, XXXVII (Summer, 1968), 490.

6. One of the Studies in Naturalism is omitted in subsequent *Selected Poems*.

7. "Bearers of Bad Tidings: Writers and the American Dream," *New York Review of Books*, March 20, 1975, p. 17.

8. In reference to Dreiser's embrace of both idealism and cynicism ("Woe be to him who places his faith in illusion—the only reality—and woe to him who does not"), Warren links "naturalistic insight" and "Christian charity" (TD, 86).

9. Cleanth Brooks, *A Shaping Joy: Studies in the Writer's Craft* (London: Methuen, 1971), 7.

ONE. Repudiations and Reconciliations: A Cycle of Themes

1. "Genealogy," *Thirty-Six Poems* (New York: Alcestis Press, 1935), 28.
2. The mythic parallels have been noted by Victor H. Strandberg in *A Colder Fire: The Poetry of Robert Penn Warren* (Lexington: University of Kentucky Press, 1965), 115.
3. Frederick P. W. McDowell, "Psychology and Theme in *Brother to Dragons*," *PMLA*, LXX (September, 1955), 572; Strandberg, *A Colder Fire*, 149.
4. Dennis M. Dooley, "The Persona RPW in Warren's *Brother to Dragons*," *Mississippi Quarterly*, XXV (Winter, 1972), 19–30.
5. Marshall Walker, "Robert Penn Warren: An Interview," *Journal of American Studies*, VIII (August, 1974), 236. This interview is reprinted, with notes, in Walker's *Robert Penn Warren: A Vision Earned* (New York: Barnes and Noble, 1979), 241–63. Subsequent references to this interview are keyed to the book version.
6. The "extraordinary innocence" in this respect is Warren's, not Emerson's. The entanglements of political liberals with the radical abolitionists in the 1850s are considerably more complex than Warren in 1929 was willing to recognize. Not merely Emerson but Hawthorne, the good party-man Democrat, was caught up in the dilemma.
7. Walker, *Robert Penn Warren: A Vision Earned*, 248.
8. "Formula for a Poem," *Saturday Review*, March 22, 1958, p. 23.
9. Newton P. Stallknecht first noted the philosophical parallels and relevance of Coleridge's Mariner to *All the King's Men* in a symposium on Warren's novel in *Folio*, XV (May, 1950), 19–20. John Edward Hardy, in "Robert Penn Warren's Double-Hero" (*Virginia Quarterly Review*, XXXVI [Autumn, 1960], 583–97), has pointed out the nautical metaphors and other local effects to reinforce the basic story of quest: Burden "is always on the road, always reliving the journey. He is the Ancient Mariner" (593).
10. Friedemann K. Bartsch, "The Redemptive Vision: Robert Penn Warren and Spiritual Autobiography" (Ph.D. dissertation, Indiana University, 1977), 7 *passim*. The formal characteristics are analyzed in J. Paul Hunter, *The Reluctant Pilgrim: Defoe's Emblematic Method and Quest for Form in "Robinson Crusoe"* (Baltimore: Johns Hopkins University Press, 1966), 89.
11. In *Brother to Dragons: A Tale in Verse and Voices, A New Version* (New York: Random House, 1979), Warren's line reads: "Is he whose hand was *fatally* elected to give the stroke" (87, emphasis added). For a summary of other differences between the 1953 and 1979 versions, see my note 9 herein, Part Two, "Making Peace with Mercutio: Warren the Poet."
12. The quasi-sociological study of "victimology" posits the theory that certain victims of assault and murder help condition, provoke, and shape the crime. Although some are masochistic or otherwise disturbed, many victims merely project personality traits which "offend the offender" and unconsciously invite retaliation. There is some indication that Warren is attracted to this behavioral theory not only because of its seeming psychological truth but also because it is yet another instance of an operable dialectic, the ethical source of so much aesthetic vitality in his work. Even in the serenity of a "Lullaby," dialectic shows up as paradox: "Throats are soft to invite the blade, / Truth invites the journal-

ist's lie. / Love bestowed mourns its own infidelity" (*You, Emperors, and Others: Poems 1957–1960* [New York: Random House, 1960], 5).

13. See Victor H. Strandberg, *The Poetic Vision of Robert Penn Warren* (Lexington: University Press of Kentucky, 1977), Chap. 3, for a perceptive treatment of the theme of the "undiscovered self."

14. "Lullaby: Exercise in Human Charity and Self-Knowledge," one of the poems in the "Garland for You" sequence in *You, Emperors, and Others*, 5–6, was omitted from subsequent *Selected Poems*.

15. The most cogent statement on the "conservative imagination" is Chapter 5 of Chester E. Eisinger's *Fiction of the Forties* (Chicago: University of Chicago Press, 1963).

TWO. Making Peace With Mercutio: Warren the Poet

1. "*All the King's Men:* A Symposium," *Folio*, XV (May, 1950), 3.

2. Marshall Walker, Robert Penn Warren: An Interview," in *Robert Penn Warren: A Vision Earned* (New York: Barnes and Noble, 1979), 255.

3. For a more detailed account of Warren's aesthetic ties to Ransom see Warren's own "Notes on the Poetry of John Crowe Ransom at His Eightieth Birthday," *Kenyon Review*, XXX (Summer, 1968), 319–49, and my "A Note on John Crowe Ransom and Robert Penn Warren," *American Literature*, XLI (November, 1969), 425–30. The influence of Eliot on Warren's early poetry is best treated by Victor H. Strandberg in *A Colder Fire: The Poetry of Robert Penn Warren* (Lexington: University of Kentucky Press, 1965), 9–23. Warren's first published poem, "Prophecy"—the product of a summer stint at Fort Knox in the Citizens' Military Training Camp in 1922—owes little or nothing to either Ransom or Eliot. The recently discovered poem is reprinted in Don Kington, "Pulitzer Prize Winner Robert Penn Warren and His Fort Knox 'Nugget,'" [Louisville] *Courier-Journal Magazine*, June 3, 1979, pp. 20, 22–23.

4. *Selected Poems: New and Old, 1923–1966* (New York: Random House, 1966), 297. First gathered in *Fugitives: An Anthology of Verse* (New York: Harcourt, Brace, 1928) and reprinted in *Thirty-Six Poems* (New York: Alcestis Press, 1935) and the first two *Selected Poems* (1944, 1966), "Letter of a Mother" was omitted in *Selected Poems, 1923–1975* (New York: Random House, 1976).

5. I am not speaking here of the kind of stylistic juxtapositions favored by Eliot and Pound that are frequent in Warren's early verse, but of the counterpointing of stylistic levels that Leonard Casper has called "rhythmic proportioning" —an appropriate aesthetic response to the necessary play of dialectic threading of Warren's work: "a counter-pulse of folk idiom beating against a sophisticated talk, exemplum against ordinary chronicle, chorus against citizen of the streets, reverberant voices one against the other." See "Ark, *Flood*, and Negotiated Covenant," *Four Quarters*, XXI (May, 1972), 110. William Bedford Clark's terms for the two styles of "Billie Potts" are *narrative* and *reflective* ("A Meditation on Folk-History: The Dramatic Structure of Robert Penn Warren's *The Ballad of Billie Potts*," *American Literature*, XLIX [January, 1978], 637).

6. The revised version of the original poem is shorter by more than thirty lines, and the revisions include the dropping of some of the more colloquial expressions. The longer "Billie Potts," published in 1944 in the *Kenyon Review*

and reprinted the same year in *Selected Poems: 1923–1943*, has been replaced by the more economical version, which I have used, in the succeeding editions of *Selected Poems*.

7. Floyd C. Watkins, "A Dialogue with Robert Penn Warren on *Brother to Dragons*," *Southern Review*, XVI (January, 1980), 4; Ralph Ellison and Eugene Walter, "The Art of Fiction XVIII: Robert Penn Warren," in John Lewis Longley, Jr. (ed.), *Robert Penn Warren: A Collection of Critical Essays* (New York: New York University Press, 1965), 29, 37; Peter Stitt, "An Interview with Robert Penn Warren," *Sewanee Review*, LXXXV (Summer, 1977), 471, 475. Also from this same period came eventually *Audubon*.

8. Leslie A. Fiedler, "Seneca in the Meat-House," *Partisan Review*, XXI (March–April 1954), 208–12; Warren, "The Way It Was Written," *New York Times Book Review*, August 23, 1953, pp. 6, 25.

9. The pivotal place of this work in Warren's career is confirmed by the appearance of "A New Version" of *Brother to Dragons* in 1979. In his Foreword Warren argues for its being, "in some important senses, a new work." Although he read and found "fascinating" Boynton Merrill, Jr.'s *Jefferson's Nephews: A Frontier Tragedy* (Princeton, N.J.: Princeton University Press, 1976), he denies any relationship between certain historical revisions and Merrill's book (Watkins, "A Dialogue with Robert Penn Warren on *Brother to Dragons*," 4–5). He follows Merrill's spellings of *Lilburne* and *Letitia* (changed from *Lilburn* and *Laetitia* in the 1953 version) and adjusts Charles Lewis' title from the more speculative "Dr." to one more appropriate for a planter, "Colonel," but he retains his original imaginative simplification of the historical record, omitting, for example, Lilburne's first wife and several young children and placing the grave of Lucy Lewis, not that of the first wife, at Rocky Hill. As C. Hugh Holman remarked in a paper at the 1979 MLA session on *Brother to Dragons*, Warren's most decisive "declaration to Clio . . . of 'Non Serviam' " is the change of the young slave's name: from *George* (the historically correct name which is used in the 1953 version) to *John*.

The most interesting changes in the new version, however, stem from narrative and poetic impulses. Thomas Jefferson is no longer so naïve in his rigid innocence and R.P.W. is less the hectoring cynic. Meriwether Lewis appears earlier and is given more lines to make his parallel with Lilburne more pronounced. There is a sharp reduction in the sometimes simpering effects of the use of diminutives, especially Letitia's references to herself as "little Tishy" and Isham's reference to Lilburne as "Bubber." Warren heightens motivation by making the crucial broken pitcher of Lucy Lewis a gift from Jefferson himself. Structurally the poem is divided in the new version into sections (I through VII—resembling the shape of the poetic suites favored by Warren in the 1960s and 1970s) which generally follow natural breaks in the narrative action of this ghostly congress as it is presided over by R.P.W. Metrically Warren tends to follow his most recent poetic practice by shortening the longer, more stately lines of a manner characteristic of his poetry of the 1950s, to reduce sharply set rhetorical passages, and in general to tighten and condense the poetic sentence.

Because of a "significant change of rhythm" and the heightening of certain "dramatic effects," the new *Brother to Dragons* shows, as Warren notes, "an important difference in the total feel" of the work. It now has, as Warren says, a "more fluid and natural verse movement" (Watkins, "A Dialogue with Robert Penn Warren on *Brother to Dragons*," 3). Although I am convinced that the 1979 version is superior to the original as a work of art, I have chosen to base my observations on the original version because of its centrality as a document in the evolution of Warren as poet. Unless otherwise noted, my references are to the 1953 version.

10. Richard G. Law, in *"Brother to Dragons:* The Fact of Violence vs. the Possibility of Love," *American Literature,* XLIX (January, 1978), 560–79, argues persuasively that Warren's remarriage during the period of the composition is of biographical and aesthetic importance—the discovery "in a new relationship of the nature of love" becomes in one sense "the source and the subject of the poem" (p. 562). The biographical importance of this work is also stressed in George P. Garrett, "The Recent Poetry of Robert Penn Warren," in Longley (ed.), *Robert Penn Warren: A Collection of Critical Essays,* 223–36; Monroe K. Spears, *Dionysus and the City: Modernism in Twentieth-Century Poetry* (New York: Oxford University Press, 1970), 177–96; and Robert H. Chambers, "Robert Penn Warren: His Growth as a Writer" (Ph.D. dissertation, Brown University, 1969), 21–23. Whatever the biographical sources, however, Neil Nakadate accurately assesses the importance of R.P.W. when he says, "At the end the poem is more Warren's than Jefferson's, a matter of reconciliation of man in the present rather than re-creation of men in the past" ("Voices of Community: The Function of Colloquy in Robert Penn Warren's *Brother to Dragons,*" *Tennessee Studies in Literature,* XXI [1976], 121).

11. The relevance of this passage to the two styles of "Billie Potts" has been discussed by William Bedford Clark, "A Meditation on Folk-History," 639–40, and Floyd C. Watkins, "Billie Potts at the Fall of Time," *Mississippi Quarterly,* XI (Winter, 1958), 19–28. The inadequacy of received forms to comprehend and encompass the moral import of content is a sentiment expressed again in a 1975 poem, "Old Nigger on One-Mule Cart Encountered Late at Night When Driving Home From Party in the Back Country." The raw episode, which dates back to the early 1930s, resists aesthetic transformation at the time; years later Warren remembers:

> only the couplet of what
> Had aimed to be—Jesus Christ—a sonnet:
> One of those who gather junk and wire to use
> For purposes that we cannot peruse.
> As I said, Jesus Christ.   (SP, 15–16)

12. Warren's work may also owe something to Louis MacNeice's radio plays. The stylized and parable-like *Christopher Columbus* (1942) emphasizes the quest theme as interior corollary to the physical voyage across the Atlantic; and *Enter Caesar* and *The Dark Tower* (both 1946) are modern morality plays which experiment with all the technical means available to radio as a medium. See Louis MacNeice, *Varieties of Parable: The 1963 Clark Lectures* (Cambridge: Cambridge University Press, 1965), 129–30. Coincidentally, *Brother to Dragons* appeared the same year as Dylan Thomas' radio play, *Under Milk Wood;* both works are marked by symbolic conflicts between man's public and private lives

and a development spatial and experimental rather than linear and conventional.

13. Kenneth Keniston, "Alienation and the Decline of Utopia," *American Scholar*, XXIX (Spring, 1960), 186.

14. Walker, "Robert Penn Warren: An Interview," 255.

15. "Dragon-Tree," *Selected Poems: New and Old, 1923–1966*, 12. This poem was omitted in *Selected Poems, 1923–1975*.

16. Richard Slotkin explains the significance of ritual cannibalism in American frontier lore in *Regeneration Through Violence: The Mythology of the American Frontier, 1600–1860* (Middletown, Conn.: Wesleyan University Press, 1973), 125.

17. Victor H. Strandberg, "Robert Penn Warren: The Poetry of the Sixties," *Four Quarters*, XXI (May, 1972), 33. See also A. L. Clements, "Sacramental Vision: The Poetry of Robert Penn Warren," *South Atlantic Bulletin*, XLIII (November, 1978), 60–61.

18. Sister M. Bernetta Quinn has discussed the several manifestations of Warren's "painter's eye": the transformation of external geography into interior landscape, the role of landscape as "actor," the use of Time as landscape, and all as transfiguring aspects of Canaan as Promised Land. See "Robert Penn Warren's Promised Land," *Southern Review*, VIII (Spring, 1972), 329–58.

19. E. M. Gombrich, *Art and Illusion* (New York: Pantheon, 1960), 60.

20. "The Enclave," *Incarnations: Poems 1966–1968* (New York: Random House, 1968), 59. This poem and "The Faring," which constitute a segment titled "The True Nature of Time," are omitted in *Selected Poems, 1923–1975*.

21. Technically the whole of *Audubon* is rhetorically imbricated with past and present moments, fluid and shifting speakers, and floating pronouns; the vision-like movement which such devices encourage is one more example of Warren's insistence since *Promises* upon involvement of subject and author, author and reader, reader and subject. See Guy Rotella, "Evil, Goodness, and Grace in Warren's *Audubon: A Vision*," *Notre Dame English Journal*, XI (October, 1978), 15–32.

22. Much of the biographical information in the following pages is drawn from Alexander B. Adams, *John James Audubon: A Biography* (New York: G. P. Putnam's 1966).

23. *Audubon, By Himself: A Profile of John James Audubon, From Writings Selected, Arranged and Edited* by Alice Ford (Garden City, N.Y.: Natural History Press, 1969), 4, 73, 85.

24. *Letters of John James Audubon: 1826–1840*, ed. Howard Corning (2 vols.; Boston: Club of Odd Volumes, 1930; rpt., New York: Kraus, 1969), I, 74–75, 91, 160.

25. *Ibid.*, II, 71–72, 5.

26. Louis L. Martz, "Recent Poetry: Established Idiom," *Yale Review*, LIX (June, 1970), 565–66.

27. All the intercalated general articles from Audubon's *Ornithological Biography* (1831–1839) are reprinted in *Delineations of American Scenery and Character by John James Audubon*, ed. Francis H. Herrick (New York: G. A. Baker, 1926).

28. Francis H. Herrick, *Audubon the Naturalist: A History of His Life and Time* (New York: Appleton, 1917), I, 273–74, 284.

29. Corning (ed.), Letters of *John James Audubon*, I, 74–75.

30. C. W. Webber, "The Viviparous Quadrupeds of North America," *South-*

ern Quarterly Review, XII (1847), 273–75, quoted in Dickson D. Bruce, Jr., "Hunting: Dimensions of Antebellum Southern Culture," *Mississippi Quarterly* XXX (Spring, 1977), 259–81.

31. The trilogy: *Or Else—Poem/Poems 1968–1974* (New York: Random House, 1974), reprinted (except for "News Photo") in the *Selected Poems* of 1976; *Now and Then: Poems 1976–1978* (New York: Random House, 1978); *Being Here: Poetry 1977–1980* (New York: Random House, 1980). Ten poems constitute "Can I See Arcturus from Where I Stand? Poems 1975," which, though not published as a separate volume, open the *Selected Poems* of 1976. Conceptually and technically these poems are coextensive with the poems of the trilogy.

32. Warren, *Jefferson Davis Gets His Citizenship Back* (Lexington: University Press of Kentucky, 1980), 1.

33. For a detailed account of the "psychodrama" of voices that governs the later poetry see Victor Strandberg, "Warren's Poetic Vision: A Reading of *Now and Then*," *Southern Review,* XVI (January, 1980), 18–45.

34. The "Afterthought" appears on pp. 107–108.

35. Peter Stitt, "Robert Penn Warren: Life's Instancy and the Astrolabe of Joy," *Georgia Review,* XXXIV (Winter, 1980), 715–16.

36. In only about a dozen poems in the volume are the central points made without recourse to questions, often in series; the titles of two poems are questions; "Lesson in History" manages to include thirteen questions in only eleven couplets.

37. Warren's formal loosening of his poems since the 1950s follows the general development of poetry after World War II, in which the lengthened line of variable feet becomes more visible. After *Promises* Warren's volumes share the pervasive discontent among younger poets, most notably the so-called "Confessionals" whose dissatisfaction with the Eliotic and Poundian personae led to the often compulsive need to speak in one's own voice, giving shape to naked urgencies in direct, stripped-down images. Warren's own "I" is never so naked, never so ravaged a consciousness as Anne Sexton's or Robert Lowell's, partly because of resurgent counterchecks of discipline and manipulative irony welling up from his earlier practice. Victor H. Strandberg believes that the effects of the Projectivist principles and practices can be seen in Warren's poetry beginning in the 1950s, especially in the emphasis on content, the breaking up of conventional syntax, and perhaps the increasingly elliptical grammar (*The Poetic Vision of Robert Penn Warren* [Lexington: University Press of Kentucky, 1977], 261–63). These common characteristics may well mean direct influence, but I suspect it is more accurate to say that Warren participates in the general deformalizing effects of the various schools after 1945, including the Beats, the Confessionals, the Projectivists, and perhaps even the Deep Imagists.

38. Karl Kroeber, *Romantic Narrative Art* (Madison: University of Wisconsin Press, 1960), 76–77.

39. Spears, *Dionysus and the City,* 187.

40. Kroeber, *Romantic Narrative Art,* 69.

41. The phrases are Stanley Plumly's in "Warren Selected: An American Poetry, 1923–1975," *Ohio Review,* XVIII (Winter, 1977), 38.

42. A. L. Clements tends to see the thematic progression of Warren's poetry more cleanly and undeviatingly than I believe is warranted. That poetry, as he

describes it, "begins in pain, makes its progress through darkness to death, and then, perfectly aware of the often inexplicable violence and suffering that human flesh is heir to, through its earned and integrated vision ends in rebirth, truth, selfhood, even joy" ("Sacramental Vision," 65). That is indeed the general movement, but there are jags and detours aplenty in which the speakers continue to struggle, without success, to answer their most urgent drives to know, to understand, and to make sense of their world and the self in it. This very tentativeness I take to be a strength, Warren's refusal to settle for easy assent while still retaining a firm belief in the rich potentiality of "joy."

THREE. Discourse as Art: Warren's Nonfiction Prose

1. Warren acknowledges the classroom too as a generator of his criticism (Talking, 287).

2. This is not the place for a defense of the kind of criticism called New Critical except to point out that the general level of more recent discourse among those critics hostile to "close reading" of literary texts is noticeably lower than that of the earlier opponents such as the Neo-Aristotelians of Chicago, whose arguments could be taken seriously. Lexical barbarism and substantive thinness accompany the single cohesive principle of that parti-colored criticism based on linguistic theories and cultural phenomena in vogue since the early 1970s; ignoring the text, "liberating" the reader from the text. This emphasis isolates the text as the offending barrier to human ingenuity, a shrewd insight that, even in reacting against it, testifies to the pervasive influence and stubborn integrity of the basic article of faith promoted by the New Criticism.

3. Robert B. Heilman remembers the gentlemanly accommodation by which Brooks and Warren persuaded others of their pedagogical and aesthetic convictions: "Baton Rouge and LSU Forty Years After," Sewanee Review, LXXXVIII (January–March 1980), 130.

4. Selected Essays, 273. In his note to Selected Poems: New and Old, 1923–1966, Warren uses the same language to describe the principle of selection in the choice of poems "which seem to lie on the main line of my impulse."

5. John Hicks, "Exploration of Values: Warren's Criticism," South Atlantic Quarterly LXII (Autumn, 1963), 508–509.

6. "Wyatt's 'They Flee From Me,'" Sewanee Review, LXVII (January–March 1959), 28.

7. The subjects of this critical exercise are sometimes surprising. Warren's own sympathy for literary naturalism is justification enough to write a small book and a long poem to commemorate the centennial of Dreiser's birth, but only a New Critic's perceptive response to the effective dimensions of Dreiser's style can account for the appreciative tone of Warren's essay on An American Tragedy (Yale Review, LII [October 1962, 1–15]). To write admiringly about Dreiser's way with words is to flout academic pieties that have been operating steadily since H. L. Mencken's time. Indeed, Warren challenges the general conventional notions of the canon of American literature, and only a remarkable gift of intelligence and taste, coupled with a sense of confident authority, could dispute the prevailing judgments of a generation ago that Melville wrote wretched poetry and that Snow-Bound is a static genre-piece.

8. C. Vann Woodward, *The Burden of Southern History* (Baton Rouge: Louisiana State University Press, 1960), 87.

9. Robert Drake (ed.), *The Writer and His Tradition* (Knoxville: University of Tennessee Press, 1969), 21.

10. Louis D. Rubin, Jr., Introduction to the Torchbook Edition of *I'll Take My Stand: The South and the Agrarian Tradition* (New York: Harper, 1962), vi. Subsequent references to this edition are incorporated in the text. The book was the focus of a 1979 MLA session, "*I'll Take My Stand*: Fifty Years Later."

11. Paul M. Gaston, *The New South Creed: A Study in Southern Mythmaking* (New York: Knopf, 1970), 100.

12. Walter Hines Page, "The Rebuilding of Old Commonwealths," *Atlantic Monthly*, LXXXIX (May, 1902), 654.

13. As Louis D. Rubin, Jr., rightly observes, the "Statement of Principles"— as well as the individual essays—was frankly concerned with "delineating the evils of industrialism," not with proposing economic programs to remove them. See *The Wary Fugitives: Four Poets and the South* (Baton Rouge: Louisiana State University Press, 1978), 201—the best of this splendid critic's many books on southern subjects. Two earlier studies of the Nashville group are still indispensable: Louise A. Cowan's *The Fugitive Group: A Literary History* (Baton Rouge: Louisiana State University Press, 1959) and John M. Bradbury's *The Fugitives: A Critical Account* (Chapel Hill: University of North Carolina Press, 1959). See also Virginia J. Rock's "They Took Their Stand: The Emergence of the Southern Agrarians," *Prospects*, I (1975), 205–95.

14. In retrospect, Donald Davidson judged that the joint effort was not primarily economics, theoretical or practical, but a common "feeling of intense disgust with the spiritual order of modern life." His 1935 essay, "*I'll Take My Stand*: A History," is collected in M. Thomas Inge (ed.), *Agrarianism in American Literature* (New York: Odyssey Press, 1969), 190–202.

15. Rubin discusses the inconsistencies in aim and orientation among the contributors in *The Wary Fugitives*, 207–28.

16. W. J. Cash, *The Mind of the South* (New York: Knopf, 1941), Chap. 1. While the Agrarians' public stand advanced the cause of southern identity, its "difference" that Progress was attempting to erase, the Twelve Southerners were never able to eradicate the "feudal fantasy" endemic to the Old South myth, especially "the old dualism of individualism and paternalism, of the plantation system and the liberty of property." See Thomas Lawrence Connelly, "The Vanderbilt Agrarians: Time and Place in Southern Tradition," *Tennessee Historical Quarterly*, XXII (March, 1963), 22–37. Rubin's formulation of this point is even more pertinent: by using "agrarian *versus* industrial" as their crucial focus, the Twelve Southerners "finessed the problem of the low-country-up-country, Populist-aristocrat schism, since an Agrarian could be anyone who lived on the land, whether dirt farmer or plantation grandee" (*The Wary Fugitives*, 214–15).

17. Rubin, *I'll Take My Stand*, xiv–xv.

18. *Ibid.*, xiv.

19. "The Briar Patch," in *I'll Take My Stand*, 259.

20. Davidson to Tate, July 21, 1930, in John Tyree Fain and Thomas Daniel Young (eds.), *The Literary Correspondence of Donald Davidson and Allen Tate* (Athens: University of Georgia Press, 1974), 251.

21. It is unlikely that any group of southern intellectuals of the early 1930s could have been less evasive then the Twelve Southerners about the ineradicable presence of the black in southern society. It is arguable, certainly, that the Chapel Hill progressives earned better marks in this regard. Certain historical revisionists of the revisionists might set the record straight, but the imaginative cultivation of the image in poetry and fiction of the antebellum South generally posited the agrarian myth of the South as Garden, with the Negro as little more than benign decoration. Except for (in passing) Tate's sharp-eyed evaluation in his 1936 essay, "The Profession of Letters in the South," the relationship of slavery and southern literature had to wait forty years for its full exploration—in Lewis P. Simpson's *The Dispossessed Garden: Pastoral and History in Southern Literature* (Athens: University of Georgia Press, 1975).

22. The Agrarians' notion of southern antebellum society as continuous with European, especially marked in contributions of Ransom ("Reconstructed But Unregenerate") and Tate ("Remarks on the Southern Religion"), is echoed later by Richard M. Weaver in George Core and M. E. Bradford (eds.), *The Southern Tradition at Bay: A History of Postbellum Thought* (New Rochelle, N.Y.: Arlington House, 1968).

23. "Literature as a Symptom," in Herbert Agar and Allen Tate (eds.), *Who Owns America?: A New Declaration of Independence* (Boston: Houghton Mifflin, 1936), 264–79.

24. *I'll Take My Stand*, 10, 53, 70, 142, 165, 214–15, 350.

25. As a human documentary, *Who Speaks for the Negro?* ranks favorably with Wilma Dykeman and James Stokely's fine *Neither Black Nor White* (New York: Holt, Rinehart and Winston, 1957), which still stands after more than two decades as the most compelling and authentic study of the contemporary South. Both books are imaginative examples of the personal uses of public fact and opinion, and both are analyses illuminated by historical perspectives and discriminating intelligence.

26. The tone and the frank indulgence with which Warren as "narrator" engages in introspection are themselves elements in the sense of reliability that the book communicates. According to one critic, it is "as if Jack Burden . . . had finally gone back into the newspaper business." See Albert Murray, "Asking Questions, Searching Souls," *New Leader*, June 21, 1965, p. 25.

FOUR. *The Lying Imagination: Warren the Novelist*

Politics and Morals

1. Irving Howe, *Politics and the Novel* (New York: Horizon Press, 1957), 162; Joseph Blotner, *The Modern American Political Novel: 1900–1960* (Austin: University of Texas Press, 1966), 361.

2. Neil Edward Nakadate, "The Narrative Stances of Robert Penn Warren" (Ph.D. dissertation, Indiana University, 1972), 28.

3. Leonard Casper, *Robert Penn Warren: The Dark and Bloody Ground* (Seattle: University of Washington Press, 1960), 102; Charles H. Bohner, *Robert Penn Warren* (New York: Twayne, 1964), 65–66.

4. John M. Bradbury, *The Fugitives: A Critical Account* (Chapel Hill: University of North Carolina Press, 1958), 204–205.

5. John L. Stewart, *The Burden of Time: The Fugitives and Agrarians* (Princeton, N.J.: Princeton University Press, 1965), 472.

6. Caroline Gordon, *How to Read a Novel* (New York: Viking, 1957), Chap. 6.

7. Leonard Casper, "Trial by Wilderness: Warren's Exemplum," *Wisconsin Studies in Contemporary Literature*, III (Fall, 1962), 53.

8. Percy Lubbock, *The Craft of Fiction* (London, 1921; rpt. New York: Viking, 1957), 271.

9. Eric Bentley, "The Meaning of Robert Penn Warren's Novels," *Kenyon Review*, X (Summer, 1948), 409.

10. Two critics have pointed out the parallels of the historical events with contemporary politics at the beginning of World War II: Angus Wilson, "The Fires of Violence," *Encounter*, IV (May, 1955), 75–78; Warren French, *The Social Novel at the End of an Era* (Carbondale: Southern Illinois University Press, 1966), 190–92.

11. In addition to their valuable observations about this novel, two critics also accurately insist upon the distinction between the philosophical impasse of the protagonist and his creator's larger view, which becomes a critique of Munn. See Alvan S. Ryan, "Robert Penn Warren's *Night Rider*: The Nihilism of the Isolated Temperament," *Modern Fiction Studies*, VII (Winter, 1961), 338–46; and Richard Law, "Warren's *Night Rider* and the Issue of Naturalism: The 'Nightmare' of Our Age," *Southern Literary Journal*, VIII (Spring, 1976), 41–61.

12. John L. Longley, Jr., "Self-Knowledge, the Pearl of Pus, and the Seventh Circle: The Major Themes in *At Heaven's Gate*," in John L. Longley, Jr. (ed.), *Robert Penn Warren: A Collection of Critical Essays* (New York: New York University Press, 1965), 60.

13. Ralph Ellison and Eugene Walter, "The Art of Fiction XVIII: Robert Penn Warren," in Longley (ed.), *Robert Penn Warren: A Collection of Critical Essays*, 31; John Baker, "Robert Penn Warren," in *Conversations with Writers I* (Detroit: Gale Research, 1977), 291.

14. John M. Bradbury, *The Fugitives*, 206.

15. The land in *At Heaven's Gate* suffers from both defection and incursion. Private Porsum, Ashby Wyndham, and Jerry Calhoun leave it for the corruption of the city, and Murdock draws it into his net of financial exploitation. This work is not a city novel in the sense that *Studs Lonigan* or *Manhattan Transfer* is a city novel; nor is it an agrarian novel in the manners of either *My Ántonia* or *God's Little Acre*. Warren's relationship to the realistic tradition in fiction has always been substantial but oblique—much like that of Frank Norris and Stephen Crane to the theory and practice of W. D. Howells. Hauntingly evocative passages in the James Agee manner are set against the toughly sentimental descriptions out of Raymond Chandler and James M. Cain; the depiction of neither the city (the actual setting) nor the country (the implied moral standard) functions as an integral element in *At Heaven's Gate* as it would do in realistic fiction. Even more than *Night Rider*, Warren's second novel uses scenic description, palpable as it is, as metaphor. Sparsely economic, its source nevertheless lies closer to Hardy and Dreiser, much as its moral elaboration and poetic refinement come out of Warren's love of Dante and a New Critical predilection for contextual reinforcement and coherence.

16. The most subtle use of agrarianism is Warren's identification of the exploiters with the party of science and the geologists with the party of religion, categories frequently invoked by Warren's Vanderbilt contemporaries. Variant terms, coming from John Crowe Ransom, intensify the distinction: "The pleasures of use are self-regarding, intense, and destructive of the object, while the pleasures of enjoyment are unselfish, expansive, and respectful or conservative of the object" (*God Without Thunder: An Orthodox Defense of Orthodoxy* [New York: Harcourt, Brace, 1930], 137). In this scheme, Murdock belongs to the party of use and Jerry's professor to the party of enjoyment.

17. Benjamin DeMott, "Talk with Robert Penn Warren," *New York Times Book Review*, January 9, 1977, p. 22. *Ibid.* In another interview (*Talking*, 79–80) Warren describes the writer's material as a story "that somehow catches hold of him, like a cockleburr in his hair. . . . An observation or an event snags on to an issue in your own mind, feelings, life—some probably unformulated concern that makes the exploration of the connection between that thing and the issue rewarding."

18. Warren's deemphasis occurs in many interviews, but see particularly his own essays, "*All the King's Men*: The Matrix of Experience," *Yale Review*, LIII (Winter, 1964), 163–64; and "A Note to *All the King's Men*," *Sewanee Review*, LXI (Summer, 1953), 476–80. The best of several studies of the relationship of Willie Stark and Huey P. Long is Ladell Payne's "Willie Stark and Huey Long: Atmosphere, Myth, or Suggestion?" *American Quarterly*, XX (Fall, 1968), 580–95.

19. Quoted in T. Harry Williams, *Huey Long* (New York: Knopf, 1969), 749.

20. Arthur H. Scouten believes that it was the general political and economic problems in the South, and the "planter / sharecropper dichotomy" in particular, that made Huey Long relevant for Warren: "Warren, Huey Long, and *All the King's Men*," *Four Quarters*, XXI (May, 1972), 25.

21. Warren, "A Note to *All the King's Men*," 478.

22. *Ibid.*, 477–80.

23. The theory behind *Proud Flesh*, Warren has said, was that the man of power "is powerful only because he fulfills the blanknesses and needs of people around him. His power is an index to the weaknesses of others." See Marshall Walker, "Robert Penn Warren: An Interview," in *Robert Penn Warren: A Vision Earned* (New York: Barnes and Noble, 1979), 246. The political implications of both the play and the subsequent novel are reminiscent of Archibald MacLeish's famous antifascist radio play, *The Fall of the City* (1937), which asserts that people invent their own oppressors.

24. Warren, *All the King's Men: A Play* (New York: Random House, 1960). The most thorough treatments of the various versions of the play are William M. Schutte, "The Dramatic Versions of the Willie Stark Story," in "*All the King's Men*": *A Symposium* (Pittsburgh: Carnegie Press, 1957), 75–90; and Leonard Casper, *Robert Penn Warren*, 116–20, 134–36.

25. Charles Kaplan, "Jack Burden: Modern Ishmael," *College English*, XXII (October, 1960), 19–24; Ted N. Weissbuch, "Jack Burden: Call Me Carraway," *College English*, XXII (February, 1961), 361. Roy R. Male sees Hawthorne's Coverdale as the fictive ancestor of Eliot's Prufrock and Warren's Burden in *Hawthorne's Tragic Vision* (Austin: University of Texas Press, 1957), 151–55.

See my "Hawthorne's Coverdale: Character and Art in *The Blithedale Romance*," *American Literature*, XLVII (March, 1975), 21-36, for some of the formal and psychological configurations of this narrating device.

26. Warren, "A Note to *All the King's Men*," 478.

27. Norton R. Girault, "The Narrator's Mind as Symbol: An Analysis of *All the King's Men*," *Accent*, VII (Summer, 1947), 220-34.

28. Henry James, Preface to *The Ambassadors* in *The Novels and Tales of Henry James*, New York Edition (New York: Charles Scribner's Sons, 1909), XXI, xiii.

29. The most resonant doubling in the novel is implicit in Burden's two excursions into the past, his struggle as a fledgling historian with the Cass Mastern papers and as a political operative with the Case of the Upright Judge. Mastern and Judge Irwin share a similar pattern of taint: both cuckold their best friends; the actions of both men drive another man to suicide and bring suffering upon an innocent woman; and both admit and accept responsibility for their actions. Since both Mastern and Irwin are his "kinsmen," Burden in effect explores the continuities of guilt as it descends to him.

30. Burden may be the quintessential twentieth-century man in his cool reverence for Machiavelli, but one of his Machiavellian adages—"The pocketbook is where it hurts. A man may forget the death of the father, but never the loss of the patrimony"—is not in fact predictive of his own case. Burden sacrifices without difficulty Irwin's inheritance. The epigraph from the *Purgatorio* offers a more accurate guide to the metaphysical design of this novel, in which, as one critic gracefully puts it, "the cynicism of one Florentine is redeemed by the optimism of another." See Friedemann K. Bartsch, "The Redemptive Vision: Robert Penn Warren and Spiritual Autobiography" (Ph.D. dissertation, Indiana University, 1977), 129.

31. Joseph Blotner observes that the epigraph, with its suggestion of redemption, counters the title, with its connotations of "the fall" (*The Modern American Political Novel*, 222).

32. My interpretation of the protagonist's growth obviously runs counter to those critics who see no development in the "smug" and "priggish" Jack Burden. For two contrary views see Roger Sale, "Having It Both Ways in *All the King's Men*," *Hudson Review*, XIV (Spring, 1961), 68-76; and Saul Maloff, "Reconsideration: *All the King's Men*," *New Republic*, CLXVIII (March 3, 1973), 28-30.

33. See, for example, Robert B. Heilman, "Melpomene as Wallflower: or, The Reading of Tragedy," *Sewanee Review* LV (January–March, 1947), 154-66; and Eric Bentley, "The Meaning of Robert Penn Warren's Novels," 407-24.

34. Glen M. Johnson, "The Pastness of *All the King's Men*," *American Literature*, LI (January, 1980), 555. Johnson's study of Warren's manipulations of the chronology of Huey Long's career is a valuable confirmation of the novelist's aesthetic and moral purposiveness.

35. "In Memory of W. B. Yeats," *W. H. Auden: Collected Poems*, ed. Edward Mendelson (London: Faber and Faber, 1976), 198.

Romance and History

1. Ralph Ellison and Eugene Walter, "The Art of Fiction XVIII: Robert Penn Warren," in John L. Longley, Jr. (ed.), *Robert Penn Warren: A Collection of*

Critical Essays (New York: New York University Press, 1965), 30. Of his own fiction Warren has said: "I don't think they're historical novels. What I'm trying to find is what happened, something that has the distance of the past but has the image of an issue . . . a sort of interplay between that image and the contemporary world" (*Talking*, 128–29). As early as the 1930s Warren was linking historical fiction with local color as quaint exploitation of manners, costumes, and decor ("Not Local Color," *Virginia Quarterly Review*, VIII [January, 1932], 154). Generally, however, the requirements for the "historical novel" are minimal: that it mingle historical events or persons in the writer's invented narrative and that the writer's imaginative latitude does not include tampering with verified or major historical events and persons.

2. W. J. Cash, *The Mind of the South* (New York: Knopf, 1941), 124.

3. Even the most resolutely historical of Faulkner's fictions, *Absalom, Absalom!* (1936), did not get its full critical due until the early 1960s—though the neglect doubtless stemmed from reasons other than its status as historical novel.

4. Warren has always minimized the extent of his historical research. "I never research a book, except if I get in a pinch on some detail, then I will look that up," he told Peter Stitt in 1977. But when he was thinking about writing *World Enough and Time*, he began to "soak" himself in "Americana of the early nineteenth century, histories of Kentucky and Tennessee—that sort of thing" (*Talking*, 234). Even *Night Rider*, according to one critic, is not wholly a work deriving from family stories and legends of the tobacco wars. J. Létargeez, in "Robert Penn Warren's Views of History" (*Revue des Langues Vivantes* XXII [1956], 533–43), has argued for Warren's probable use of the authoritative history of those wars, James O. Nall's *The Tobacco Night Riders of Kentucky and Tennessee* (Louisville: Standard Press, 1939), for both narrative events and their real-life participants.

5. Although John L. Stewart sees John Brown as the prototypical figure in Warren's fiction, the recurring "lonely egotist" finally demonstrates to him that Warren is a repetitious and narrow writer. See "Robert Penn Warren and the Knot of History," *Journal of English Literary History*, XXVI (March, 1959), 102–36, and the revised version in Chapters 3 and 9 of *The Burden of Time*, especially pp. 141–42, 447–48. In *Robert Penn Warren and History: "The Big Myth We Live"* (The Hague: Mouton, 1970), 22–23, L. Hugh Moore sees Warren both as a philosophical novelist (whose chief risk is allowing abstract ideas to remain dramatically unassimilated in the narrative) and as a historical novelist (whose chief danger is a too-generous reliance upon melodrama and sex). William C. Havard sees Warren as both and neither: "He is not a historical novelist who is also a philosophical novelist; he is rather a novelist who accepts historical experience as fundamental to philosophical understanding as that understanding is unfolded through the creative imagination." See "The Burden of the Literary Mind: Some Meditations on Robert Penn Warren as Historian," *South Atlantic Quarterly*, LXII (Autumn, 1963), 518.

6. *The Letters of Herman Melville*, ed. Merrell R. Davis and William H. Gilman (New Haven: Yale University Press, 1960), 70; Preface, in Harrison Hayford *et al.* (eds.), *Mardi: and A Voyage Thither* (Evanston and Chicago: Northwestern University Press and the Newberry Library, 1970), xvii; *The Letters of Herman Melville*, ed. Davis and Gilman, 70. See also Nina Baym, "Melville's Quarrel with Fiction," *PMLA*, XCIV (October, 1979), 912; Sir Walter Scott,

Essays on Chivalry, Romance, and the Drama [1834] (Freeport, N.Y.: Books for Libraries Press, 1972), 129.

7. Floyd C. Watkins, "*Gone With the Wind* as Vulgar Literature," *Southern Literary Journal*, II (Spring, 1970), 87.

8. Walter Sullivan, "The Historical Novelist and the Existential Peril: Robert Penn Warren's *Band of Angels*," *Southern Literary Journal* II (Spring, 1970), 110.

9. C. Vann Woodward, *The Burden of Southern History* (Rev. ed.; Baton Rouge: Louisiana State University Press, 1968), 33.

10. The formula applies first to *John Brown*, which Warren himself recognizes as the kind of narrative he was to follow thereafter in his fiction (*Talking*, 128). In his study of Flannery O'Connor, Gilbert H. Muller in passing refers to Warren's "underrated" *World Enough and Time* as "an historical novel of the absurd which is replete with murder, rape, and decapitation." The sensationalism, he implies, dramatizes a vision of a "dark and incongruous" world shaken by "continual spiritual warfare." Muller's assumption is that a writer's view of his world determines the texture of any of his created worlds whether set in the present (like O'Connor's) or in the past (like *World Enough and Time* and *Band of Angels*). See *Nightmares and Visions: Flannery O'Connor and the Catholic Grotesque* (Athens: University of Georgia Press, 1972), 78.

11. Eudora Welty, "Place in Fiction," in *The Eye of the Story: Selected Essays and Reviews* (New York: Random House, 1978), 117.

12. At one point in his discussion of Dreiser, Warren contrasts the method of factual reconstruction used in *The Financier* and *The Titan* with that used by historical novelists: "the historicity of the ordinary historical novel lies in situation and decor into which the actors, with their 'perennial humanity,' are introduced" (*Homage to Theodore Dreiser, on the Centennial of His Birth* [New York: Random House, 1971], 74). Against the dismissive tone can be placed an admission: "I have a romantic kind of interest in the objects of American history: saddles, shoes, figures of speech, rifles, and so on. They're worth a lot. Helps you focus. There *is* a kind of extraordinary romance about American history. That's the only word for it . . . a kind of self-sufficiency" (Ellison and Walter, "The Art of Fiction XVIII: Robert Penn Warren," 31).

13. *American Literature: The Makers and the Making* (New York: St. Martin's Press, 1973).

14. Karl Kroeber, *Romantic Narrative Art* (Madison: University of Wisconsin Press, 1966), 181.

15. *World Enough and Time* is based on a locally famous case in Kentucky in 1825–1826. The documents of the case are reprinted in Loren J. Kallsen (ed.), *The Kentucky Tragedy: A Problem in Romantic Attitudes* (Indianapolis, Ind.: Bobbs-Merrill, 1963); and samples of some of the literary uses of this material are included in Jules Zanger (ed.), *The Beauchamp Tragedy* (Philadelphia: Lippincott, 1963). In "Warren's *World Enough and Time* and Beauchamp's *Confession*," *American Literature*, XXXIII (January, 1962), 500–11, I have noted both Warren's fidelity to the case and his significant departures from the historical record. Elsewhere Warren himself shows his wide-ranging familiarity with the Kentucky Tragedy (*Talking*, 71–73, 252).

16. That the meshing of Word and Flesh, Idea and World, is doomed to remain only potential is foreshadowed when as a child Beaumont reads Bunyan's

Pilgrim's Progess and Franklin's *Autobiography*. If the first is our definitive statement for rejecting the world, the second is, for Americans at least, the definitive statement for embracing the world. Warren's interest in symbolic reading matter is made even more explicit in his discussion of *The Arabian Nights* and *Robinson Crusoe*, the two books that Dreiser's Clyde reads in his last days (*Homage to Theodore Dreiser*, 125–26).

17. Beaumont is an alienated man in two related ways. He is, in the old Russian sense, a superfluous man—superfluous, that is, to the order and on going of society. His only contribution is to inject moral crisis into that larger world. But he is also an unwilling picaro, capable of disrupting the social order because he is never fully, organically, a member of that society. This mingling of two kinds of alienation brings on the characteristic moral distortion that swings wildly between the extremes of craftiness and ineptitude.

18. William James, *The Varieties of Religious Experience: A Study in Human Nature* (London: Longmans, Green, 1916), 87.

19. T. S. Eliot, "Short Sketch of Rousseau's Life," Lecture I of "Modern French Literature" (Oxford lecture series, 1915), syllabus in Houghton Library, Harvard University.

20. Gilbert Imlay's edition of Filson's *Kentucke* (1784) appeared in New York in 1793, coupled with his own interpretation of the West, *Topographical Description of the Western Territory*, which painted Kentucky, in the words of Richard Slotkin, "as a Godwinian utopia of liberty, pastoral economy, and rampant freedom for the development and pursuit of Romantic love" (*Regeneration Through Violence: The Mythology of the American Frontier, 1600–1860* [Middleton, Conn.: Wesleyan University Press, 1973], 398). Imlay's edition was used as a source for Humphrey Marshall's *History of Kentucky*, published in Frankfort in 1812.

21. In the "massive stupor and dark twitches of the wild land," the heavy ironies of the title and the epigraph are clear. If the Spenserian "blossome of faire vertue" seems a bit wilted even in the "antique world" of Beaumont's Frankfort, the self-contained world of Old Big Hump is both more ancient and more debased.

22. Ellison and Walter, "The Art of Fiction XVIII: Robert Penn Warren," p. 30.

23. See also Warren's distinctions between the arts of the historian and the novelist (*Talking*, 92–93).

24. Warren's fascination with dialectical tension as technique is seen as early as "The Ballad of Billie Potts," with its alternating folk idiom and learned commentary. The somewhat undramatized, receded, and reported relationship between Jack Burden and the Cass Mastern papers suggests the enlargement of the technique in later works, pointing to the use of R.P.W. as interlocutor and counterpoint to Jefferson in *Brother to Dragons*.

25. Joseph Frank, in "Romanticism and Reality in Robert Penn Warren," *Hudson Review*, IV (Summer, 1951), 248–58, believes that the intervening sensibility is too much inclined toward sympathy—that there are too much admiration and too little irony in his point of view. Frederick P. W. McDowell, however, thinks this voice relies too much on "travesty and irony" in the definition of Beaumont's character: "The Romantic Tragedy of Self in *World Enough and Time*," *Critique*, I (Summer, 1957), 34–48.

26. Technically the narrator functions as the *histor* as Robert Scholes and Robert Kellogg describe the device: "the narrator as inquirer, constructing a narrative on the basis of such evidence as he has been able to accumulate." Neither a character nor the author, he is a persona, "a projection of the author's empirical virtues." This authority is entitled to present facts and explain them, to use them even for "moral instruction of the reader." See *The Nature of Narrative* (New York: Oxford University Press, 1966), 265–66.

27. Ellison and Walter, "The Art of Fiction XVIII: Robert Penn Warren," 20–21; Bradbury, *The Fugitives*, 216.

28. Although *World Enough and Time* is "about the romantic temperament," Warren adds that he has "a modern man telling it and commenting on it as a modern man" who claims to have the documents "as I had some documents— and sees them in the modern way" (*Talking*, 252). In emphasizing the interplay between the modern sensibility and historical figures, Warren says that "Jack Burden and Cass Mastern have the same relationship as the 'I' narrator and the Jereboam Beauchamp-Beaumont fellow in *World Enough and Time*" (*Talking*, 119).

29. Scott, *Essays on Chivalry, Romance, and the Drama*, 148.

30. Austin Warren, Introduction, *The Scarlet Letter*, by Nathaniel Hawthorne (New York: Rinehart, 1947), v.

31. Amantha's idiom, for better or worse, is permanently preserved in the nineteenth-century tradition of sentimental fiction of which *Gone With the Wind* is a culmination. Amantha's young-lady postures are no more saccharine than Melanie Hamilton's of Mitchell's novel, and her young-bitch postures are as gutsy as Scarlett O'Hara's.

32. Walter Sullivan doubts that many people of whatever age in antebellum Kentucky ever really "troubled themselves much about the problem of identity" ("The Historical Novelist and the Existential Peril," 110).

33. For all his ingenuity in trying to make his narrator more interesting, Warren admits the omission of "enough richness and depth" in her experience—"at least it isn't brought out." See Walker, *Robert Penn Warren: A Vision Earned*, 254.

34. Stewart, *The Burden of Time*, 488–91.

35. Amantha, as C. Hugh Holman succinctly puts it, "must learn for all of us that no man is free except in the act of surrendering freedom" ("The Southerner as American Writer," in *The Roots of Southern Writing: Essays on the Literature of the American South* [Athens: University of Georgia Press, 1972], 12).

36. Amantha Starr is not the first American heroine who frankly cultivates her sexuality as a weapon of considerable power. Edith Wharton's Undine Spragg in *The Custom of the Country* is perhaps our best portrait of the type, which also includes James's Kate Croy in *The Wings of the Dove* and the impressive Jane Hastings of *The Conflict*, one of muckraker David Graham Phillips' few notable novels. But Warren's heroine is perhaps closer to the emotional parasitism of Howells' Marcia Hubbard of *A Modern Instance* than to any of these: both work their will through a quiet selfishness and a calculated passivity that exhaust the good will of her paramours and the patience of the reader.

37. Amantha seems to be a more histrionic version of the passive dreamer that Warren finds at the center of Dreiser's creation of Clyde Griffiths: self-absorption paradoxically prevents the discovery of the deepest meaning of

self, and the longing to enter the great world unimpeded is to court a "dream-self, a self-to-be-created, a role to play in the rich and thrilling world—a *role*, we may say, to take the place of a self" (*Homage to Theodore Dreiser*, 128). In addition, Amantha's expedient manipulation of that imagined self bears strong resemblance to Clyde's use of his own sexual attraction: "a device," says Warren, "of blackmail, by which, somehow, his weakness feeds on the kindly or guilty weakness of others" (134).

38. The process by which Amantha pursues her identity through her relationships with others is perceptively detailed by Terence Martin in "*Band of Angels*: The Definition of Self-Definition," *Folio*, XXI (Winter, 1956), 31–37.

39. The growth in Warren's appreciation of Melville's poetry can be traced from "Melville the Poet," written in 1945 (SE, 184–98), to "Melville's Poems" (*Southern Review*, III [Autumn, 1967], 799–855) to the expanded introduction to *Selected Poems of Herman Melville: A Reader's Edition* (1970).

40. For representative abstracts of contemporary reviews of *Wilderness* see Neil Nakadate, *Robert Penn Warren: A Reference Guide* (Boston: G. K. Hall, 1977), 170–85.

41. L. Hugh Moore, "Robert Penn Warren, William Styron, and the Use of Greek Myth," *Critique*, VIII (Winter, 1965), 75–87.

42. Warren has commented on this curious disproportion. Originally intended as a 30,000-word novella, *Wilderness* grew to about 65,000 words, largely because Warren became more and more fascinated with the world outside Adam. The development of the central character did not keep pace with that of the "incidental characters," which began to be more important, and the "ratio" of interest between Adam and the other characters "shifted" in the process of writing (*Talking*, 105); see also Walker, *Robert Penn Warren: A Vision Earned*, 254.

43. Allen Shepherd, "Robert Penn Warren as Allegorist: The Example of *Wilderness*," *Rendezvous*, VI (Spring, 1971), 13–21.

44. The most impatient critic of Warren's use of nonrealistic modes is Charles Thomas Samuels, "In the Wilderness," *Critique*, V (Fall, 1962), 46–57. "Lacking any mimetic variety," says Samuels, the novel "resembles nothing so much as a medieval exemplum" (53).

45. Leonard Casper, "Trial by Wilderness: Warren's Exemplum," *Wisconsin Studies in Contemporary Literature*, III (Fall, 1962), 45.

46. W. H. Auden has discussed the nature of the religious hero in *The Enchafed Flood; or, The Romantic Iconography of the Sea* (New York: Random House, 1950), 97. Specifically, Adam Rosenzweig resembles the compulsions we associate with seventeenth-century Puritans more than nineteenth-century Bavarian Jews. As Richard Slotkin has put it, the "hero of the Puritan quest is not the captain of conquering soldiers but a figure fleeing in solitude from sin-begotten humanity" (*Regeneration Through Violence*, 39).

47. Flo Witte, "Adam's Rebirth in Robert Penn Warren's *Wilderness*," *Southern Quarterly*, XII (July, 1974), 376.

48. Bartsch, "The Redemptive Vision: Robert Penn Warren and Spiritual Autobiography," 244.

An Art of Transparency

1. Oscar Cargill, Wallace W. Douglas, Roger Sale, Alfred Kazin, and most

of the British critics. For specific references consult Nakadate, *Robert Penn Warren: A Reference Guide.*

2. Leonard Casper, "Ark, *Flood*, and Negotiated Covenant," *Four Quarters*, XII (May, 1972), 110.

3. Casper, "Trial by Wilderness: Warren's Exemplum," *Wisconsin Studies in Contemporary Literature*, III (Fall, 1962), 52–53.

4. Casper, "Ark, *Flood*, and Negotiated Covenant," 110.

5. Willa Cather, *On Writing: Critical Studies on Writing as an Art* (New York: Knopf, 1962), 33–43.

6. Andrew Lytle, *The Hero with the Private Parts* (Baton Rouge: Louisiana State University Press, 1966), 44.

7. Warren's use of aqueous imagery is discussed in Barnett Guttenberg, *Web of Being: The Novels of Robert Penn Warren* (Nashville, Tenn.: Vanderbilt University Press, 1975), 30–31, 119–20, 148–49.

8. I agree with Monroe K. Spears that "the best single essay about Warren is Warren's essay on *Nostromo.*" See *Dionysus in the City: Modernism in Twentieth-Century Poetry* (New York: Oxford University Press, 1970), 180.

9. Leonard Casper, "Journey to the Interior: *The Cave*," *Modern Fiction Studies*, VI (Spring, 1960), 66.

10. The shift in technique in *The Cave* is also crucial to Warren's vision of human possibilities. In the novels after 1959 the same pattern emerges: the gray fact of existence resists man's control or even his understanding, but the dedicated human effort, in the midst of failure, can provide tentative success in the protagonist's overwhelming concern for psychic wholeness. Philosophically, Warren sees this success just as difficult to attain as that in earlier novels; however, in its dramatic working out, the success is easier: the hurdles come down against the reiterated onslaught of rhetoric and assertion.

11. Ransom's discussion of the educative effects of such aesthetic forms as rituals, pageants, and artistic conventions upon "appetitive" man occurs in "Forms and Citizens." The relationship between Milton's individual talent and the received form of the elegy is the subject of "A Poem Nearly Anonymous." Both essays appear in *The World's Body* (New York: Charles Scribner's Sons, 1938).

12. See "Robert Penn Warren's 'Dialectical Configuration' and *The Cave*," *CLA Journal*, X (June, 1967), 349–57, in which Richard Allan Davison discusses the interrelationship of key images; and Guttenberg's *Web of Being*, 97–103, for the relationship of water and womb imagery to the existential theme of the void and the Platonic theme of "the dream of the ideal."

13. Warren, "*An American Tragedy*," *Yale Review*, LII (Autumn, 1962), 9. A shorter version of this essay became the introduction to the Meridian edition of Dreiser's novel (Cleveland: World Publishing, 1962).

14. Mistaken frequently for a Jew, Isaac flees the land of his birth to make his fortune, like a real Jew, in New York City. The ironies are several-layered: like the alienated Jew, he is decisively cut loose from a homeland that is traditionally more homogeneous than many other regions, and like his biblical namesake, he traffics in fraudulent advice and trickery involving his very identity; but unlike the modern Jew he is taken for, Isaac refuses to recognize his guilt or to accept responsibility.

15. *Mark Twain's Autobiography*, ed. Albert B. Paine (New York: Harper, 1924), II, 174.

16. John L. Longley, Jr., has called Brad Tolliver "the most dramatic failure of fulfillment and redemption" among the "ensemble" characters of the novel, but he also suggests Tolliver's dim awareness of which steps he must take toward moral recovery at the end of the book. See "When All Is Said and Done: Warren's *Flood*" in his edited volume, *Robert Penn Warren: A Collection of Critical Essays*, 171, 177; and the expanded version, "Robert Penn Warren: The Deeper Rub," *Southern Review*, I (Autumn, 1965), 968–80.

17. John T. Hiers, in "Buried Graveyards: Warren's *Flood* and Jones's *A Buried Land*," *Essays in Literature*, II (Spring, 1975), 99, calls the graveyard and the prison the "structural polarities" of the novel by which Goldfarb and Calvin Fiddler are contrasted.

18. In Casper's words, "pious concern for the body has become less important than the resurgence of Goldfarb's spirit" ("Ark, *Flood*, and Negotiated Covenant," 113).

19. Gerald Weales, "Fiction Chronicle," *Hudson Review*, XXIV (Winter, 1971), 722; Michael Cooke, "Recent Fiction," *Yale Review*, LXI (June, 1972), 601.

20. "Loving is redemptive, whether or not returned," observes Guttenberg (*Web of Being*, 155).

21. Guttenberg perceptively links the beneficent function of moonlight at the end of *Meet Me in the Green Glen* to the Coleridgean "reversal" of this symbol that Warren finds in *The Rime of the Ancient Mariner* (*Web of Being*, 153).

22. Warren, "Knowledge and the Image of Man," in Longley (ed.), *Robert Penn Warren: A Collection of Critical Essays*, 241.

23. *Talking*, 103; Walker, *Robert Penn Warren: A Vision Earned*, 256.

24. *Fugitives' Reunion: Conversations at Vanderbilt, May 3–5, 1956*, ed. Rob Roy Purdy (Nashville, Tenn.: Vanderbilt University Press, 1959), 143–44.

25. Guttenberg finds the source for this pattern in Coleridge and an "affinity" with Heidegger. One "falls from the harmony of childhood into the chaos of the world. His redemption begins with the realization that the chaos is an extension of himself. From that realization comes a sense of involvement and responsibility, of freedom and direction, all of which define the reintegrated will and make possible a new world." (*Web of Being*, 162–63).

26. Lewis P. Simpson, *The Man of Letters in New England and the South: Essays on the History of the Literary Vocation in America* (Baton Rouge: Louisiana State University Press, 1973), 211.

27. I obviously disagree with Guttenberg, who argues briefly that the novels using a single character as focus tend to be "less successful than the novels which split their focus . . . several ways" (*Web of Being*, 165).

28. *Talking*, 237; Warren's purpose is not to save Jed Tewksbury's soul but to give him a soul that might be saved, and it is similar to Faulkner's purpose with Temple Drake in *Requiem for a Nun*. See Lewis P. Simpson, "Isaac McCaslin and Temple Drake: The Fall of New World Man," in Donald E. Stanford (ed.), *Nine Essays in Modern Literature* (Baton Rouge: Louisiana State University Press, 1965), 88–106.

29. "T. S. Stribling: A Paragraph in the History of Critical Realism," *American Review*, II (February, 1934), 474. The germ for *A Place to Come To* is an incident, dating back to Warren's Vanderbilt days, involving a freshman who dropped out to make his way in the North (*Talking*, 270–71).

30. "Interview with Eleanor Clark and Robert Penn Warren," 55, 62.

Conclusion

1. These contrasts have been summarized most effectively in C. Vann Woodward, *The Burden of Southern History* (rev. ed.; Baton Rouge: Louisiana State University Press, 1968), Chap. 1.

2. Neil Edward Nakadate, "The Narrative Stances of Robert Penn Warren" (Ph.D. dissertation, Indiana University, 1972), 8.

3. Louis D. Rubin, Jr., "Southern Literature: The Historical Image," in Louis D. Rubin, Jr., and Robert D. Jacobs (eds.), *South: Modern Southern Literature in its Cultural Setting* (Garden City, N.Y.: Doubleday, 1961), 37.

4. C. Hugh Holman, *Three Modes of Southern Fiction* (Athens: University of Georgia Press, 1966); "Her Rue with a Difference: Flannery O'Connor and the Southern Literary Tradition," in Melvin J. Friedman and Lewis A. Lawson (eds.), *The Added Dimension: The Art and Mind of Flannery O'Connor* (New York: Fordham University Press, 1966), 73–87; "The View from the Regency Hyatt," in George Core (ed.), *Southern Fiction Today: Renascence and Beyond* (Athens: University of Georgia Press, 1969), 16–32.

5. William Faulkner, *Intruder in the Dust* (New York: Random House, 1948), 194.

6. Rob Roy Purdy (ed.), *Fugitives' Reunion: Conversations at Vanderbilt, May 3–5, 1956* (Nashville, Tenn.: Vanderbilt University Press, 1959), 213.

7. "T. S. Stribling: A Paragraph in the History of Critical Realism," *American Review*, II (February, 1934), 469.

8. William Faulkner, *Absalom, Absalom!* (New York: Random House, 1936), 89.

9. *Fugitives' Reunion*, 210.

10. Lewis P. Simpson (ed.), *The Possibilities of Order: Cleanth Brooks and His Work* (Baton Rouge: Louisiana State University Press, 1976), 109–11.

11. Virginia Rock, "The Twelve Southerners: Biographical Essays," in *I'll Take My Stand* (New York: Harper, 1962, Harper Torchbook), 383.

12. Richard Marius, "The Middle of the Journey," *Sewanee Review*, LXXXV (Summer, 1977), 463. Marius is the author of *The Coming of Rain* (1969) and *Bound for the Promised Land* (1976).

13. In another connection Warren contrasts the cultural and political ways of life of the Border South and the Deep South: "Jefferson Davis, like many Southerners of the early era, had been a somewhat unself-conscious Southerner. . . . Besides, the South he had been born in [Kentucky] lay far to the north of Mississippi. Now, however, Davis, the wanderer, was becoming a Mississippian. He was being 'Southernized' not only by association and study but by occupation: he was a planter and a slavemaster." See *Jefferson Davis Gets His Citizenship Back* (Lexington: University Press of Kentucky, 1980), 40.

14. "A Dialogue of Self and Soul," *The Variorum Edition of the Poems of W. B. Yeats*, ed. Peter Allt and Russell K. Alspach (New York: Macmillan, 1973), 478–79.

15. Simpson (ed.), *The Possibilities of Order*, 4.

16. John M. Bradbury, *The Fugitives: A Critical Account* (Chapel Hill: University of North Carolina Press, 1958), 214.

17. Andrew Lytle, *The Hero with the Private Parts* (Baton Rouge: Louisiana State University Press, 1966), 173.

18. Marshall Walker, "Robert Penn Warren: An Interview," in *Robert Penn*

Warren: A Vision Earned (New York: Barnes and Noble, 1979), 250.

19. *The Complete Works of Ralph Waldo Emerson*, Centenary Ed., ed. Edward Waldo Emerson (Boston: Houghton Mifflin, 1903-1904), III, 75.

20. Emerson, *Works*, VI, 22-23.

21. Stephen E. Whicher, *Freedom and Fate: An Inner Life of Ralph Waldo Emerson* (Philadelphia: University of Pennsylvania Press, 1953), 172.

22. See also Simpson (ed.), *The Possibilities of Order*, 103: "I simply take what I have taken from the Christian tradition, but see that 'something' only in humanistic, naturalistic terms," says Warren. His interest, he tells Brooks, is to try to find Christian values "in terms of humanistic action," and orthodoxy as a "governing metaphor which speaks the deepest about human experience."

Index

Marvell, Andrew, 50
Mastern, Cass (AKM), 29, 36, 43,
    163, 190, 195, 197, 200, 202, 232,
    263, 329
"Masts at Dawn," 84
Mather, Cotton (*Magnalia Christi
    Americana*), 234
Mazzini, Giuseppe, 251
Meet Me in the Green Glen, 12, 262,
    263, 265–66, 269, 270, 271, 294–
    99, 300–301
Melville, Herman, 44, 120, 126, 131,
    143, 153, 210, 213, 214, 235, 249,
    251, 253, 255, 263, 269, 327; "The
    Armies of the Wilderness," 255;
    "Bartleby," 153; *Battle-Pieces*, 126,
    249; *Billy Budd*, 251; *Clarel*, 126;
    "In a Bye-Canal," 133; "Malvern
    Hill," 133; "The March into Vir-
    ginia," 133; *Mardi*, 210; *Moby-
    Dick*, 153, 210, 249; *Omoo*, 210;
    "On the Slain Collegians," 133;
    Pierre, 126, 210, 263
"Melville the Poet" (1945), 133;
    "Melville's Poems" (1967), 116,
    126; "Melville's Poetry" (1970),
    124, 126, 133
Messina, Joe, 193
Metaphysical poetry, 50, 111
"Mexico Is a Foreign Country: Five
    Studies in Naturalism," 4, 9, 53, 96,
    111
Milton, John, 50
"Mission, The," 103
Mitchell, Margaret, 207; *Gone With
    the Wind*, 207, 208, 212
"Monologue at Midnight," 53, 55
"Moonlight's Dream, The," 108
"Mortmain," 19, 70, 76, 80, 81, 88
Muirhead, John, 122
Munn, Percy (NR), 15, 26–27, 28,
    39, 43, 64, 149, 160, 161, 165–78,
    273, 326
Murdock, Bogan (AHG), 12, 28, 161,
    179, 180–81, 185–91
Murdock, Sue (AHG), 15, 27, 43,
    180, 184–90, 265
Murphy, Sara and Gerald, 287

"Natural History," 13–14, 84

New Criticism, the, 50, 117–19, 121,
    123, 126–27, 275
"News Photo," 97
Night Rider, 15, 25, 26–27, 32, 43,
    152, 160, 162, 165–78, 179, 180,
    191, 192, 208, 232, 262, 273
"Night Walking," 105
"No Bird Does Call," 105
Norris, Frank, 180*n*; *Epic of the
    Wheat*, 7
"Notes on a Life to Be Lived," 76
Now and Then, 97, 100–103, 112

O'Connor, Flannery, 2
"October Picnic Long Ago," 106–107,
    108
Oedipus, 252, 324
"Old Flame," 100
"Old Nigger on One-Mule Cart," 271
"On Into the Night," 105, 108
Or Else, 97–100, 101, 102, 104, 112
"Original Sin: A Short Story," 1, 4, 7,
    39, 53–54, 135
Ovid, 91
Owsley, Frank, 132, 142, 143

Page, Walter Hines, 137
"Passers-By on Snowy Night," 107
Pasetto, Angelo (MM), 265–66, 271,
    295–98
"Patented Gate and the Mean Ham-
    burger, The," 324
"Penological Study: Southern Ex-
    posure," 86
"Picnic Remembered," 2, 53
Place to Come To, A, 12, 33, 37, 43,
    266, 269, 302–16, 324
Plato, 216, 234, 324; *The Republic*,
    269
Poe, Edgar Allan, 132, 269
"Poem of Pure Imagination, A," 25,
    37, 42, 46, 57, 121–23, 126, 129,
    213
"Pondy Woods," 53, 57, 59
Porter, Katherine Anne, 128, 129,
    319, 326; *The Cracked Looking-
    Glass*, 128; *Old Mortality*, 128
Pound, Ezra, 4, 50, 51, 52; *Hugh
    Selwyn Mauberley*, 52
Powell, Adam Clayton, 146, 147, 151

124, 129, 131, 143; "Among the Hills," 75; "Letter from a Missionary of the Methodist Episcopal Church South," 121; *Snow-Bound*, 130–31
Who Speaks for the Negro? 6, 116, 141, 144–55, 213, 325
Wilderness, 23, 33, 43, 141, 162, 209, 249–61, 263, 266
Wilkins, Roy, 146, 148
Williams, Raymond, 135
Williams, T. Harry, 193, 204
Williams, William Carlos (*Paterson*), 327
Wilson, Edmund, 130, 132
Windsor, Kathleen, 207; *Forever Amber*, 208
Winthrop, John, 234
Wolfe, Thomas, 128, 319, 322–23; *Look Homeward, Angel*, 324; *Of Time and the River*, 128
Woodward, C. Vann, 133
Woolf, Virginia (*To the Lighthouse*), 274

Wordsworth, William, 108, 122
World Enough and Time, 1, 17, 23, 29–31, 32, 39, 59, 87, 91, 133, 135, 143, 162, 209, 213, 214, 215–35, 236, 253, 262, 264, 269, 288, 303, 321, 324
"World Is a Parable," 85–86
Wyatt, Sir Thomas ("They Flee From Me"), 132
Wyndham, Ashby (AHG), 5, 27, 29, 30, 31, 60, 162, 181, 188–90, 313, 315

Yeats, William Butler, 323
Yerby, Frank, 207
You, Emperors, and Others, 19, 48, 70, 76, 111
Young, Stark, 141, 143, 207, 313, 322; *So Red the Rose*, 207
Young, Whitney, 147, 151

Zola, Emile, 33